# Praise for *The Forgotten Iron King of the Great Lakes*

"This is a book that Great Lakes history has long needed. Eber Brock Ward was a major figure in the development of the Midwest region and a pioneer in the fields of transportation and industry. Michael Nagle's finely researched and written book plugs a large gap in the history of the inland seas."

—Theodore J. Karamanski, professor of history, Loyola University Chicago, and author of *Mastering the Inland Seas: How Lighthouses, Navigational Aids, and Harbors Transformed the Great Lakes and America*

"Michael Nagle graces us with an illuminating biography of Eber Brock Ward, a business titan of Michigan's nineteenth century. Nagle brings complexity and nuance to the life of this influential and, some would say, nefarious public figure who lived an equally intriguing private life."

—Alan Gallay, Texas Christian University

"In writing this biography, Michael Nagle leveraged the ambitious life of industrialist Eber Brock Ward to craft a comprehensive bridge between antebellum America and the roots of the Gilded Age. Nagle weaves the compelling threads of E. B. Ward's story together for the first time in this finely researched Great Lakes saga."

—Joel Stone, curator emeritus, Detroit Historical Society

"All who complete graduate work in the study of history and aspire to write published works know the expectation that the author exhaust the sources of the topic. Professor Mike Nagle is tireless in his quest for knowing and exemplifies this ultimate standard. It is surprising that no other historian has been aware of and motivated to write a biography of Eber Brock Ward, a major manufacturing leader in Michigan's history. Mike Nagle is adept at telling this intriguing and revealing story of an interesting character."

—William M. Anderson, former director, Michigan Department of History, Arts & Libraries

"One would think that these outlandish tales would make Eber Brock Ward and his role in pushing Michigan from an extractive economy into the Industrial Age unforgettable. But that's not how it went. Author Michael W. Nagle shows how Ward fell into oblivion despite scandals and exploits that would make him Twitter-famous today. One bizarre tale follows another as he hops from shipping to mining to manufacturing to becoming Michigan's richest man. As this bad-boy Horatio Alger raised his personal fortune, he also raised eyebrows and hackles. Ward may not have been remembered, but people who read Nagle's book will never forget him."

—Joe Grimm, author of *The Faygo Book* (Wayne State University Press, 2008) and coauthor of *Coney Detroit* (Wayne State University Press, 2012)

# The Forgotten Iron King
## of the Great Lakes

*Great Lakes Books*

A complete listing of the books in this series can be found online at
wsupress.wayne.edu.

*Editor*

Thomas Klug
Sterling Heights, Michigan

# THE
# Forgotten Iron King
## OF THE
# Great Lakes

---

## EBER BROCK WARD, 1811–1875

---

# Michael W. Nagle

Wayne State University Press

Detroit

ISBN 978-0-8143-4993-9 (hardback)
ISBN 978-0-8143-4994-6 (e-book)

Library of Congress Control Number: 2022939287

Cover image courtesy Detroit Historical Society. Cover design by Will Brown.

Wayne State University Press rests on Waawiyaataanong, also referred to as Detroit, the ancestral and contemporary homeland of the Three Fires Confederacy. These sovereign lands were granted by the Ojibwe, Odawa, Potawatomi, and Wyandot Nations, in 1807, through the Treaty of Detroit. Wayne State University Press affirms Indigenous sovereignty and honors all tribes with a connection to Detroit. With our Native neighbors, the press works to advance educational equity and promote a better future for the earth and all people.

Wayne State University Press
Leonard N. Simons Building
4809 Woodward Avenue
Detroit, Michigan 48201-1309

Visit us online at wsupress.wayne.edu.

*For Buffy,*
*my wife and best friend*

# Contents

# Preface and Acknowledgments

It's not every day a person has the opportunity to meet a real-life princess. In the fall of 2018, my wife and I traveled to Belgium to visit Chimay Castle as part of the research for this book. It was quite an adventure. After completing our tour through the castle, we had the chance to speak with Princess Élisabeth de Chimay, who was ninety-two years old at the time of our visit. Meeting a princess is unnerving, but she was very welcoming and immediately put us at ease. She took the time to chat with us personally and answer a series of questions about Eber Ward's daughter, Clara, who was married to a previous prince of Chimay. Clara Ward led a scandalous life, and her marriage to the prince of Chimay ended in divorce. When I asked Princess Élisabeth about Clara, she declared, "We don't talk about her," adding, "The family did not appreciate the way she behaved." Clara "was very pretty," she admitted, but "she was fast." Princess Élisabeth confirmed the rumors of Clara's infidelity. Her comments encouraged me to discover more about Eber's disreputable daughter.

A second adventure took place on Bois Blanc Island, where Eber lived for two years while his father served as the lighthouse keeper. We visited the island in June. Rain accompanied us as we boarded the ferry and started on our journey; the sun greeted us as we arrived. We were mesmerized driving on the island's gravel roads and exploring the interior. I had heard about the new lighthouse and wanted to find it, but I also understood it was quite isolated and in private hands. We drove to Lake Mary, then traveled on our mountain bikes from there. We happened across Mr. Babcock, whose great-grandmother had served as a keeper of the lighthouse. He warned us the two-track to the

Chimay Castle, Chimay, Belgium. (Author's collection)

lighthouse was very primitive, but we were determined to make the trip, so he gave us directions. The trail proved to be as rough as he predicted, and we stopped twice because we weren't sure if we were going the right way. After nearly an hour of riding, and shortly before we were ready to give up and turn around, we saw an opening and a sign indicating the lighthouse was just ahead. It was quite a trek, but well worth the effort. We walked the beach, reveling in the rustic beauty of the island and its deep history. We could only imagine how isolating it would have been to maintain the original lighthouse day after day, for several years. The experience was humbling.

It was following a series of conversations with my good friend Rick Plummer that I became determined to research the life and write a biography of Eber Brock Ward. In 2015, we attended the Michigan History Conference, sponsored by the Historical Society of Michigan. Each of us was given a random copy of the *Michigan Historical Review* in our bag of goodies when we registered. As luck would have it, one of us was given a copy of the Fall 2013 edition, which included an excellent article by Justin Wargo about the controversy concerning

Eber Ward's will and subsequent trial. I was familiar with the article and encouraged Rick to read it. I mentioned that I had thought about researching Ward for my next project, but was leaning toward another subject. After reading the article, Rick became fascinated with Ward's life and family. We spent much of that weekend talking about Ward's personality, accomplishments, and shortcomings. He argued that I should pursue Eber Ward and tell the complete story of his life. Luckily, I followed his sage advice.

Any serious study of Eber Ward must begin at the Detroit Public Library's Burton Historical Collection. The Burton contains an excellent collection of Ward's correspondence and other related materials. Fortunately, I discovered that some of Ward's transcribed correspondence is available at the Clarke Historical Library, located at Central Michigan University. Bowling Green State University's Historical Collection of the Great Lakes contains many key resources addressing Ward's activities in the maritime industry and other aspects of his business interests. The Milwaukee County Historical Society has resources covering Ward's activities in Milwaukee's Bay View community, particularly his involvement in the iron and steel industry. Numerous historical societies in Michigan offer specialized collections of Ward materials, including the Mason County Historical Society in Ludington; the Community Pride and Heritage Museum in Marine City; the Leelanau Historical Society in Leland; and the Wyandotte Museum in Wyandotte. The Detroit Historical Society houses many interesting artifacts, including the wonderful, and incredibly large, portrait depicting Ward at the apex of his power described in the epilogue. The William L. Clements Library on the campus of the University of Michigan in Ann Arbor contains a daguerreotype of Eber Ward and his wife Polly (possibly the oldest such image produced in the state of Michigan), as well as a painting that includes a young Emily Ward by John Mix Stanley titled *Moonlight Adventure on the St. Clair River: Going for Strawberries*. The event that inspired this painting of Emily is discussed in chapter 1.

Numerous individuals offered a range of assistance with this project. Among others, I am particularly grateful to the West Shore Community College Board of Trustees and President Scott Ward, who supported my research with a sabbatical award for the fall semester of 2018. Bill Anderson, Seán Henne, and Rick Plummer each read early drafts of the manuscript very closely, and their comments and suggestions were a tremendous help. Others who read portions of the manuscript and offered their comments include Alan Gallay and the late Donald W. Whisenhunt. The staff at Wayne State University has been great to work with. I would like to recognize Marie Sweetman, Kristin Harpster, Carrie Downes Teefey, Annie Martin, the anonymous reviewers, and the Great Lakes Books series editor, Thomas Klug, for all of their work to transform this manuscript into a published book. A special thanks is due to Robin DuBlanc, who served as copyeditor. Her careful reading of the text and thoughtful suggestions have significantly improved this work.

Many individuals at a number of institutions facilitated the research process. Numerous staff at the Burton helped greatly, but I would like to particularly thank Dawn Eurich and Sean Marshall. Others who offered aid at their various institutions include Frank Boles and Bryan Whitledge from Central Michigan University's Clarke Historical Library; Sarah Jordan, Jesse Rose, and Audrey Wicklander from the Wyandotte Museum; Elizabeth Desmarais from the City of Marine City and Gary Beals from Marine City's Community Pride and Heritage Museum; Jeremy Dimick and Joel Stone from the Detroit Historical Society; Janet Curtiss from the St. Clair County Library in Port Huron; Kim Kelderhouse and Elizabeth Adams from the Leelanau Historical Society; Dennis Northcott from the Missouri Historical Society Library and Research Center; and Rebecca Berringer and Michelle DeKuiper from the Mason County Historical Society. Special recognition is due to Ned Nordine, who researched Eber Ward and Princess Chimay in the local Ludington newspapers housed at the Mason County Historical Society. Christina A. Reynen conducted helpful research dealing with Ward's concerns in Chicago. A special thank-you to Joëlle Dauwe, who acted as a gracious host on our visit to Belgium and made the trip to the castle possible. Joëlle Dauwe met my wife and me at the Brussels airport and drove us to Chimay Castle. I don't know what we would have done without her assistance. After our time at the castle, she and her husband Laurent Grenier treated us to a spectacular dinner. Our Ludington friends Marina and Zane Knoer helped us connect with Joëlle. Doug, Diane, and Leslie Seitz provided a trove of information about Ward, including valuable letters and images that contributed greatly to this work. My friend Paul Anders allowed me to stay at his apartment so I could continue research in Detroit.

Many of my colleagues at West Shore Community College deserve thanks for answering my many questions or for just putting up with random facts I shared about Eber Ward over the last several years. These include David Cutler, Paul Drelles, Eden Foley, Jessica Houser, Darby Johnsen, Terry Johnson, Natalie Ruth Joynton, Geoff Kramer, Jennifer Lundberg Anders, Brooke Portmann, Matt Sanderson, Connie Schwass, Erwin Selimos, Sonja Siewert, Renee Snodgrass, and Katie Stewart.

My daughters, Maggie and Elizabeth, deserve a special thank-you for putting up with numerous vacations that also *just happened* to involve trips to historical locations or archives. This book is dedicated to my wife Buffy. Without her support, this work never would have been attempted, much less completed.

While I have learned that collaboration is a key component of any successful writing project, any mistakes in fact or interpretation are mine alone.

# Introduction

*Ward's narrative is unique in how quickly his*
*legacy diminished and disappeared.*
—Justin Wargo, 2013

The life and achievements of Eber Brock Ward are unfamiliar to most people today, but he was a pathfinder of industry who shaped the economies of Michigan, the Great Lakes, and even the nation, as the United States expanded its industrial might in the nineteenth century. Born in 1811, Ward rose from modest beginnings to become the richest man in Michigan at the time of his death in 1875. Eber's big break came when he began working for his uncle Samuel Ward. He started out as a cabin boy on sailing vessels, but eventually became his uncle's partner. The two developed a large, possibly the largest, fleet of passenger steamers on the Great Lakes. By 1856, "Captain Eber" was labeled the "acknowledged master of the Lakes" by the *Daily Cleveland Herald*. But Ward did not stop there. He eventually founded iron and steel operations in Wyandotte, located just outside of Detroit, as well as in Chicago and Milwaukee. Another contemporary newspaper, the *Chicago Tribune*, estimated that Ward's facilities employed about three thousand men, whose wages supported a collective population of fifteen thousand. The Chicago paper ultimately crowned him "iron king of the West" in 1873.[1]

Other nineteenth-century business moguls chose to dominate and control a single industry. John D. Rockefeller famously monopolized the oil industry; Andrew Carnegie built Carnegie Steel. Cornelius Vanderbilt's activities revolutionized the transportation industry, first with steamboats and then with railroads. Ward chose a different path. His business empire focused on diversification and he invested in a range of different industries. Ward recognized that railroads would soon compete with his steamboats, so he took over the Flint & Pere Marquette Railway in 1860 and served as its president until his death. He engaged in the lumber industry: he owned valuable timbered property along the Pere Marquette River in Western Michigan and built two enormous sawmills along the Lake Michigan shoreline in Ludington. He also possessed a large sawmill and shipbuilding operation in Northwestern Ohio's Black Swamp. Ward invested in several mining operations, most notably Silver Islet, located in the waters of Lake Superior. When he recognized in the 1870s that Americans were dependent upon plate glass imported from Europe, Ward founded the American Plate Glass Company outside of St. Louis.

E. B. Ward was able to build a diverse business empire by adopting progressive business practices. Throughout his career, he consistently reinvested profits back into his business operations. Furthermore, Ward developed efficiencies by employing vertical integration to cut costs and ensure he could secure

Eber Ward conducted business throughout the Great Lakes. (Courtesy of Rebecca J. Mott)

maximum profit. Ward's foresight in linking control over transportation with heavy industrial manufacturing shows he was a trailblazing industrialist whose actions predated those of Carnegie and Rockefeller by decades. His iron and steel factories demonstrated this most effectively. Ward invested in properties where iron ore was mined. He also built and owned the ships to transport the ore. His mills produced iron rails, which then were purchased by his railroads. Ward also consistently adopted the latest and most effective technologies, and in 1865, he became the first in the United States to produce steel using the more efficient Bessemer method. At the pinnacle of this business empire was Ward himself. Although he consistently sought qualified individuals to run the day-to-day operations of his independent businesses, everyone recognized that Eber Ward was in charge. He was an absolute ruler who sought progress reports concerning his companies' operations and issued detailed instructions when he believed it necessary.

What motivated Ward to create his vast empire? He was driven by an intense competitiveness to build and create his own kingdom while exhibiting a willingness to crush anyone in his path. When dealing with rival businesses he adopted the mantra "It is much safer to be feared than to be loved," made famous by Niccolò Machiavelli in *The Prince*. Whether Ward adopted this strategy after reading Machiavelli's work is lost to history. Nevertheless, numerous business adversaries succumbed to his iron will—while Ward remained unmoved by criticism. Of course, as he built his diverse empire, he couldn't be everywhere at once; Ward needed people he could trust. Often, his answer was to recruit and empower members of his extended family to manage his complex operations. Relatives such as Gleason Lewis helped with financial matters. Ward's brother-in-law, Stephen Clement, oversaw his Chicago rolling mill while simultaneously serving as president of the Milwaukee Iron Company. His cousin, Beulah Brinton, helped immigrants working in Milwaukee adapt to life in the United States. Her husband Warren eventually served as mill superintendent.[2]

Ward's reliance on family to serve in key positions did not always prevail. With his attention continually focused on business affairs, conditions in his immediate family suffered greatly. Ward attempted to create a dynasty by having his sons take over key parts of his empire, yet these efforts ended in failure as his sons proved more adept at spending their father's money than in contributing to the family business. It is likely Eber's absence during his children's formative years contributed to their failures—he never prepared them with the background necessary to be successful. Furthermore, his intense focus on business interests over immediate family undoubtedly contributed to the failure of his first marriage, which ended in divorce.

Like many of his contemporary business barons, Ward also was adamantly opposed to the unionization of his labor force. Conditions for workers often were difficult and dangerous. He also took steps to control aspects of his employees' lives. This led to conflict with laborers and more than one strike at his facilities. Furthermore, although he criticized Washington, DC, as a center of lobbying and corruption, this did not stop his own lobbying efforts in the nation's capital when he actively sought to limit the number of lifeboats on his vessels. These actions may have contributed to a greater loss of life on the Great Lakes.

William Downie, a Detroit resident and admirer of Eber Ward, commented on Ward's personality and his quirks. Eber carried himself with an intensity that could be intimidating to those around him. Downie observed that Ward was a man of "agreeable manners, quick to action, open hearted and generous." However, if Ward believed himself to be in the right, he would "brook no opposition" and could become "viscously high tempered" as he passionately argued his case. When it came to his business operations, his arguments most often carried the day. While in deep thought, Ward "continually squinted with each eye alternatively" while peering intently into the eyes of those with whom he was conversing, which could have an unnerving effect. He habitually "poured silver change from one palm to the other" and pulled a "chainless, openfaced watch" out of his pocket to check the time. Ward "did not chew, smoke, drink, or gamble, being exceptionally temperate" and "very philanthropic."[3]

Ward's lifetime coincided with a unique era in the development of the American West, particularly the Great Lakes and Michigan. The steady growth of power and influence Ward gained over time mirrored that of Michigan, which entered the Union as the twenty-sixth state in 1837. His formative years saw the migration of many easterners to the states and territories of the Midwest. Wagon trails played an important role in American expansion westward, but numerous migrants traveled west via steamboats for at least a portion of their journey. Ward was intimately involved in this movement, first as a young boy running errands on sailing vessels and ultimately as the owner of a large armada of steamboats. Thousands of travelers each year made the trip west on his railroads, which rode on the iron and steel rails produced at his mills. Ward even recognized the potential benefits of establishing a gateway to the waters of Lake Superior and played an important role in the creation of the Soo Locks in the 1850s. He also helped to shape the nation's economy in the years following the Civil War. Ward called for the expansion of manufacturing, particularly in the Midwest, and described this as the nation's new Manifest Destiny, which would lead to economic expansion and stability into the future.

During the Civil War, he was a staunch supporter of the Union and Abraham Lincoln. When some of his fellow industrialists complained about the adoption of an income tax, he issued a public letter declaring he would "cheerfully . . . continue to pay my income tax" because he believed it was his patriotic duty to do so during the national crisis. Ward emerged as a vocal opponent of slavery and contributed financially to causes designed to limit slavery's expansion. He even directed his steamboat captains to aid runaway slaves seeking freedom, although there were limits to his support for African Americans. While he regularly hired black laborers to work on his steamboats, they were relegated to subservient positions, and African Americans were employed at his iron and steel mills only rarely.[4]

Eber Ward's many achievements have been overlooked due to a range of factors. During his lifetime, Ward's competitiveness earned him a number of enemies. He adopted aggressive tactics to defeat rival steamboat lines and even had one opponent thrown in jail to pressure him to sell property Ward coveted. Following his death, members of Ward's family fought to control his estate. The resulting trial, which captured national headlines, mistakenly painted a portrait of Ward as a man who was not of sound mind and was under the influence of spiritualists. Furthermore, his legacy was overshadowed by the actions of his daughter Clara, who earned her own newspaper headlines after marrying a Belgian prince and leading a scandalous life.

# Historiography and Organization of the Book

Only a handful of historians have studied Ward's contributions in detail. A 1942 dissertation chronicled Ward's life and accomplishments, but it remains unpublished. A 1952 master's thesis recounted many of Ward's activities, but it, too, remains unpublished. Both works offer helpful insight into Ward's life and character, but each is dated. Interest in Eber Ward's daughter, Clara, has generated interest among some popular writers. They often mention Ward, but their focus is on the actions of Clara. Justin Wargo has undertaken the most scholarly study of Ward's endeavors in recent years, producing two excellent articles on specific topics dealing with Ward's life. However, a full-length biography is warranted to recognize Ward's significance. This work is an attempt to fill that void in the historiography of the Great Lakes.[5]

The book begins with a prologue identifying the events surrounding Ward's death on January 2, 1875. Chapter 1 addresses Ward's early life and family background. Eber's mother Sally died when he was only six years old. This brought Eber closer to his sister Emily, who became his life-long confidant. Although Eber's father was often absent during his formative years, when he was named the lighthouse keeper on Bois Blanc Island, father and son lived together for two years. Under his father's tutelage Eber learned the value of hard work and developed an intense opposition to slavery.

Chapters 2 and 3 focus on Eber's relationship with his uncle Samuel Ward. Eber began as his uncle's protégé, and then became his partner as the two developed a huge fleet of passenger steamers on the Great Lakes. Eber's 1837 marriage to Polly McQueen, his uncle's ward and niece, brought the partners closer together.*

When Samuel died in 1854, Eber inherited his fortune and business. Chapter 4 outlines Eber's entrance into the production of iron and steel. In 1853, he founded the Eureka Iron Company (also known as the Eureka Iron Works) in Wyandotte. Although Eber had moved to Detroit and his sister Emily lived in

---

* Polly McQueen was Samuel's niece by marriage. Samuel's wife was Elizabeth (Lamberson) Ward. Polly was the daughter of Elizabeth's sister, Catherine (Lamberson) McQueen. Eber and Polly were related, but not related by blood.

Newport, the two remained close; Eber financed the costs of operating an academy run by Emily.

Chapter 5 covers Ward's involvement in Republican Party politics. As an active opponent of slavery, he emerged as a figure who influenced national events. At one time, he was considered a possible candidate to serve as treasury secretary. Chapters 6 and 7 outline Ward's steps to expand his business empire and offer his vision for manufacturing to serve as the new Manifest Destiny for the Midwest economy. The establishment of iron and steel facilities in Chicago and Milwaukee are detailed, as well as Ward's activities in the lumber, mining, and plate glass industries. As his empire grew, so did the stresses that accompanied its growth, which were compounded by the chaos in his family life, particularly following his second marriage, to Catherine Lyon, and the Panic of 1873. The Panic was a major nationwide economic depression. These events took a collective toll on Ward's health and he suffered a stroke and died in 1875.

Chapter 8 describes the fight over Ward's estate, valued at $5.3 million at the time of his death. The subsequent "Ward Will Case" captured national attention. In the end, Ward's second wife Catherine received the estate's most valuable assets while the children of Ward's first marriage received very little. The chapter also highlights the exploits of Eber's daughter Clara, who was only two years old when her father died. When she reached the age of sixteen, Clara married a prince from Belgium, but the marriage ended in divorce when Clara left her husband for a Hungarian violinist. Clara's exploits continued until her premature death in 1916—but not until she had married two more times, earning international headlines all the while. This work ends with an epilogue that chronicles Ward's major accomplishments and offers an evaluation of his actions and importance.

# Goal

Eber Brock Ward was a major figure who shaped the history of the era in which he lived. He was a pioneer whose practices foreshadowed those of other Gilded Age business tycoons who would lead the United States into the industrial age. Shortly after his death, the *Detroit Free Press*, a newspaper that was often highly critical of Ward, chronicled his lifetime of achievements. The paper highlighted his triumphs not only as a business leader but also as a philanthropist and a man of honor who never touched alcohol or tobacco. The article finished by declaring, "To reiterate that his death is a great public calamity is to record a truth which thousands will sorrowfully attest." Perhaps an additional calamity involving his life is that so few people today are familiar with his vast set of achievements. The goal of this work is to rectify this misfortune and to highlight Eber Ward's legacy as one of the important industrialists of the Gilded Age.[6]

# Prologue

## January 2, 1875

*Dropped Dead. It was the Great Millionaire and Manufacturer,*
*Eber B. Ward. It happened on Griswold Street, This Morning.*
—*Detroit News* headline, January 2, 1875

It was cold and he had a job to do. Eber Brock Ward put on his overshoes, coat, and muffler and left his office to complete some business at Detroit's Superior Court. Although it was a Saturday, he had been working for nearly an hour since leaving home that morning. The light snow that had fallen overnight still covered the streets, but this was of no consequence to him. As he walked toward his destination, he had things to consider. The last two years had been difficult. His intricate set of business holdings had been struck by the financial crisis, which devastated much of the nation's economy beginning in 1873. He was most concerned about maintaining production at his iron and steel mills in Chicago, Milwaukee, and Wyandotte. He had been able to keep them afloat only with proceeds from the sale of lumber from his sawmills in Ludington, Michigan. Additionally, Ward hoped that soon he would be able to pay his employees in cash, rather than the scrip he had been forced to issue for the last several months. Luckily, his reputation and credit were still strong enough to allow him to issue scrip, but he could not pay his employees this way for much longer. If only he could secure an additional line of credit, he would have the cash necessary to move forward. He had successfully weathered similar financial storms in the past. This too he could overcome. He just needed some cash and a little more time.[1]

In years past, when he was a young man, a contemporary had described him as average, yet quite fit, in appearance. He carried himself with the swagger of a sailor who had "a cold blue eye, a ruddy face, and . . . an 'iron jaw' betokening a firmness of purpose that characterized his life." Now, on that cold January morning, with a thick head of white hair that once was dark, he was more stout than fit. Yet, he still carried himself with a vigor and firm step despite his advancing age.[2]

The previous week actually had been pleasant. On Christmas Day, Eber had celebrated his sixty-third birthday, and his health had been relatively good the last year. He seemed to be fully recovered from a bout with apoplexy, which had left him bedridden for several weeks, but that was over five years ago. The energy and strength that had been missing during his illness had returned. Just yesterday, Ward had suspended all business activities in the morning to celebrate the New Year, even opening his home to receive several visitors for their traditional New Year's Day calls. These days, he felt good. He was just under a lot of pressure and could not sleep well at night.[3]

As usual, Ward walked briskly while he made his way along Griswold Street. But then, he came to a sudden stop, threw up his arms, and collapsed to the ground. He had fallen just outside of E. K. Robert's banking office. Several bystanders rushed to see if he was hurt. Eber was only semi-conscious, and his face appeared dark and swollen. He was carried inside the office and a doctor was summoned. His breathing became labored. Mr. King, one of the men who took him to the office, cried out, "He is dying."[4]

What might have been going through Eber Ward's mind as he fought for his life? It is unlikely he was thinking of his children, in whom he was greatly disappointed. It is possible an image of his first wife, Polly, came to him, although the two had divorced, so his concern might have turned to Catherine, his second wife. She was much younger than Ward and the two had been married for the past six years. As he drew his last breaths, Eber more likely thought of his father, who taught him the value of hard work and an intense hatred of slavery; his uncle Samuel Ward, who served as his mentor and business partner; and Emily Ward, his sister and confidante with whom he had his closest, life-long relationship. Did he have any regrets? Only Eber could answer that question, yet he could not speak.

Three doctors were now at the scene. Each endeavored to administer to Ward. Observing an occasional involuntary movement of his muscles, they were prepared to attempt a blood-letting. But when they looked closely at him, they noticed his face had lost all color and his jaw had slackened. Nothing they could do would save him now. Eber Brock Ward was dead. A crowd soon formed outside the office as news of Ward's death spread quickly through the streets of Detroit. A police officer kept the growing number of spectators from crowding around the body. The coroner arrived and impaneled a group of men in the office to serve as jurors in a hastily organized inquest. After hearing testimony from one of the doctors and a witness, a verdict was rendered. Once again, Mr. Ward had been struck with apoplexy; this time, it had killed him.

Eber Ward had lived a true rags to riches life story. Yet, as much as he had accomplished, he was a mere mortal and not even his vast wealth could prevent him from death on that cold January morning.

# 1

## Modest Beginnings

*In the autumn of 1818 I started with my family from Vermont to go to Kentucky. When we reached Waterford, PA, my wife was taken sick and in twenty-four hours was a corpse, leaving me grief stricken among strangers with four little children to care for.*
—Eber Ward Sr., 1852

Several events and individuals shaped the early life of Eber Brock Ward. The Ward family was relocating to Kentucky when their fortunes changed in an instant—shortly after his sixth birthday, E. B. Ward's mother died suddenly. Rather than settling in the South, E. B. Ward moved to Ohio with his father and sisters to live among family and friends. It would be the Midwest and Great Lakes, not the South, where he later would make his fortune. Following the death of his mother, a bond was forged between E.B. and his siblings; particularly with Emily, his oldest sister. This became stronger as their father was absent for extended stretches of time during their childhood years. When they became adults, Emily served as E.B.'s most trusted confidante. Another individual who shaped E. B. Ward's future was his uncle Samuel Ward. At the age of eleven, E.B. served as a cabin boy on one of his uncle's ships, which exposed him to life on the Great Lakes and laid a foundation for a future partnership between the two. Finally, beginning in his teens, E.B. began to spend more time with his father, and the two became close. Their relationship deepened when

Mr. Ward became the lighthouse keeper on Bois Blanc Island, and for about two years, E.B. would be his assistant.

## Early Life and Family

In the tiny village of New Hamborough, near the city of Toronto, Ontario, Eber Brock Ward was born on December 25, 1811. His arrival must have served as quite a Christmas present for his parents, Eber Sr. and Sally Ward. (To differentiate between father and son, as they both have the same name, Eber Brock Ward's father will be referred to as Eber Sr., Eber Ward Sr., or Mr. Ward in this narrative.) The household into which Eber Brock was born was bleak and transient. Over the course of the previous several months, his family had bounced from one community to another. His father, although hard working, was restless. In an era when farming was the dominant occupation, Mr. Ward had little interest in agriculture. This left him with neither a clear path in life nor a steady income to support his family. Unfortunately, young E.B. was unhealthy during part of his infancy. His sister Emily recalled her parents' concern. "For a long time they didn't think he'd live, and that if he did live he would be a sickly child, and would never amount to anything. They were all mistaken."[1]

E. B. Ward's parents came from families with deep New England roots. Both Eber Sr. and Sally (Potter) Ward were born in Wells, Vermont. Eber Sr. was born in 1782 and could trace his ancestors back to the Great Puritan Migration of the 1630s, when Andrew and Esther Ward arrived in Salem, Plymouth Colony. They had traveled, along with many other Puritans, to Plymouth in hopes of freely practicing their faith. Subsequent family members moved to the valleys of Vermont and settled in Rutland County, where they established self-sufficient farms. Eber Brock Ward's grandfather, David Ward, served as a Baptist minister and owned a small farm. Eber Ward Sr. was one of ten children born to the Reverend Ward and his wife Abigail (Pray) Ward. Eber Ward Sr. was the oldest boy; his closest sibling in age—and outlook—was Samuel.[2]

Sally Potter, E.B.'s mother, was born in 1788. Her father, William Potter, hailed from New London, Connecticut. He traveled to the town of Pawlet, Vermont, in the 1760s and then settled for good in the nearby community of Wells; both were located in Rutland County. The communities were small. Pawlet boasted only nine families in 1770, but by the end of the American Revolution, many veterans began to settle in the county, drawn by the region's rich, abundant soil and the prospect of establishing their own farms. Sally's mother was Phebe Woodward. She and William Potter married about 1771 and had seven boys and four girls; Sally was the oldest daughter. Since Sally and Eber were from the same small community, their paths likely crossed at school, church, and other social gatherings. The two eventually were married in Wells on May 17, 1807.[3]

Following their wedding, Sally and Eber Ward Sr. lived on a farm owned by his father, but they did not remain long, as Eber Sr. loathed farming. Mr. Ward moved around a great deal; as his daughter Emily later declared, her father "was a rover." In the fall of 1807 the Wards considered moving to Kentucky, where Eber Sr. could work as a laborer or even teach school; they considered it a "land of promise." Instead, two years later, in 1809, the couple moved to Salina, New York, near Syracuse, where Eber Sr. worked in the salt industry. Syracuse already was recognized as "the Salt City" due to the prevalence of salt production in the area. While living in Salina, the family's first child, Emily, was born. Soon thereafter, they moved to Manlius, New York, where Mr. Ward continued in the salt industry. The family's second child, Sally, was born in Manlius. In each of these locations, Eber Sr. was joined by his younger brother Samuel, who likewise had little interest in farming. The brothers were not as successful as they had hoped in the salt industry, so Eber Sr. and his family relocated to Ontario while Samuel traveled west to Ohio.[4]

When E. B. Ward was born on Christmas Day in 1811, the Wards had little time to rejoice, as tension was brewing between the United States and Great Britain, soon to culminate in the War of 1812. The conflict involved trading rights on the open seas, impressment of American sailors into the Royal Navy, and British support of Native Americans who resisted American settlement in what was then known as the Northwest (today's states of Ohio, Indiana, Illinois, Michigan, and Wisconsin). In June 1812, the United States declared war. Americans were no longer welcome in Canada, so the Wards returned to Vermont to live with the Reverend David Ward, Eber Sr.'s father. In early 1813, Abba, a fourth child, was born. This meant that between 1809 and 1813, Sally Ward had given birth to four children, none of whom had been born in the same city. Relocating so often in an era without automobiles, or even trains, must have taken quite a toll on the young family.[5]

Mr. Ward's fortunes soon changed, particularly following a partnership with his brother Samuel. The brothers had always been close, and each had a sense of adventure and a gnawing desire to challenge the expectations others had of them. As a boy, Samuel refused to attend school and proved ungovernable, but he had an excellent business sense. When he reached adulthood, a longtime friend described him as "about six feet in height, rather spare in form and angular in feature, with a gleaming, but kindly gray eye and alert, but pleasant expression and manners."[6]

When the fighting raged in earnest between the Americans and the British in the War of 1812, Samuel realized American naval forces stationed near Lake Ontario would need supplies. He and Eber purchased food and other provisions from family and neighbors in Vermont and transported them to western New York. From there they hoped to deliver the much-needed goods by boat to American forces. This appeared to be an excellent strategy; they could thwart the invading British and help the fledgling U.S. Navy while earning a profit. Samuel built a small boat and headquarters near the American naval station at Sackett's Harbor, located near the entrance of the St. Lawrence River into Lake Ontario. Once their headquarters was established, Eber Sr. was responsible for conducting business at Sackett's Harbor. Samuel sailed the boat filled with foodstuffs and other goods from Vermont and other locales. Their efforts proved lucrative, albeit short-lived. On May 29, 1813, British forces attacked Sackett's Harbor. Eber and Samuel joined the battle to defend the American naval base. The attackers were successfully repulsed, but the British burned some of the storehouses and ships in the harbor. Among the losses was Samuel's ship, which had been docked at the time of the British assault. The brothers' supply of the navy ended, but not before Samuel had reportedly earned $3,000 (the equivalent of $40,735.59 in 2020 dollars).[7]

Eber Ward Sr. found financial success over the next few years, but it left Sally Ward and her four young children increasingly isolated as Mr. Ward's business ventures required him to be away for long stretches of time. For the remainder of 1813 and into 1815, Mr. Ward spent his time trafficking salt, fish, fishing supplies, and other provisions on Lake Erie between ports in Buffalo, Erie, Salem (now known as Conneaut), Toledo, and Maumee, Ohio. Meanwhile, his wife and children lived in Vermont on a farm near Sally's family. Her husband's presence surely was missed, but one incident in particular reinforced the family's isolation. One night, after the children had gone to bed, a strange man pounded on the door of their home. Sally answered the door only to discover a large, burly man who wore what appeared to be a soldier's uniform. He barged into the house and demanded to stay the night. Sally refused and ordered him to leave. Just when the intruder appeared ready to strike her, Sally's brother Joshua tackled the man, beat him mercilessly, and sent him away. Fortunately, the altercation ended without any family members getting hurt, but the absence of Mr. Ward must have taken a toll on Sally and the children. On the other hand, the family had obtained financial stability. The same model of separation from family while making one's fortune would be true for E. B. Ward, who experienced extended separations from his wife and children while tending to his business interests.[8]

## Tragedy Strikes

In the years following the war, Mr. Ward traveled throughout the Great Lakes working a range of jobs and transporting goods to customers at different ports. He also bought and sold fish, which held the potential for significant profits. In 1816, Eber acquired one hundred barrels of fish in April and then traveled to Pittsburgh, where he sold them at a small profit. He spent the following winter away from his family in Maumee, Ohio. In the spring of 1817, he assembled two hundred barrels of fish and headed to Erie, Pennsylvania. From there, he bought a boat to carry his cargo and traveled as far as Livingston, Kentucky, about sixty miles south of Lexington. While in Kentucky, he bartered his fish for tobacco, which he planned to sell at settlements in the Great Lakes. He finally returned to his family in Vermont in October 1817 after a separation of nearly two years.[9]

The months Mr. Ward spent in Kentucky were a financial success, but they also made a large impression upon him. After all, years earlier he and his wife had identified it as the "land of promise." He described the country surrounding Lexington as "fertile and handsome beyond description," where the "inhabitants were polite to strangers, of gentile appearance, and appear to live in affluence and plenty. Indeed, four hours labor in each day will support a man comfortably in this country." However, not all was paradise in the

Commonwealth. Eber Sr. abhorred the institution of slavery and condemned Kentucky's slaveholders: "These people are surrounded with slaves who have not only to perform all the drudgery but even chase away flies who have the impudence to enter their sacred abodes." He questioned the religious values of Kentucky slaveholders. He labeled them blasphemers and hypocrites because they considered themselves pious supporters of liberty, asking, "Is there a God in Heaven who has power to crush with His finger those vile blasphemers of His name? Can a merciful Jehovah sit on His throne and view the sufferings, the tears, the prayers of those desponding slaves . . . ? If I am in a dream I hope to wake and rectify my mistake." As the son of a Baptist minister, Mr. Ward took his own faith very seriously. He praised the "Quakers, Newlighters, and generally the Methodists [who] emancipated their slaves, a sure proof of the sincerity of their profession."[10]

Significantly, Mr. Ward's anti-slavery views emerged prior to the publication of William Lloyd Garrison's abolitionist newspaper the *Liberator* in 1831. When Mr. Ward made the trip to Kentucky in 1817, the largest anti-slavery organization in the country was the American Colonization Society, which had the limited goal of gradual emancipation and transportation of former slaves to Africa. E. B. Ward would hold anti-slavery views similar to his father's when he grew into adulthood. As will be discussed later, he contributed financially to anti-slavery organizations and became a strong advocate of the Union cause. It is likely E. B. Ward's opposition to slavery was kindled by many conversations with his father, based upon the latter's firsthand observations, and condemnations, of slavery.[11]

While the presence of slavery stained Mr. Ward's visit to Kentucky, it did not lessen his desire to relocate to the Blue Grass State. After he returned to his family in Vermont following his two-year absence, plans were made to move the entire family to Kentucky during the winter of 1817–18. The children must have felt a combination of apprehension and excitement as they prepared to move. Emily, the oldest, was just shy of nine years of age. Sally, next in the birth order, was seven. E. B. Ward turned six on Christmas Day in 1817, while Abba was the youngest at three. They planned to travel west through the Mohawk Valley and rest for a short time with family outside of Rochester, New York. From there, they would turn south until they reached the Allegheny River, where they would hire a boat and travel through Pittsburgh to the Ohio

River. They would continue to Cincinnati, and then on to Lexington, Kentucky. If completed as planned, this trip—involving two adults, four children under the age of ten, and all the family's belongings—would cover an estimated 850 miles, all during the middle of winter.[12]

Shortly after Christmas in 1817, the Wards said their last good-byes to relatives in Vermont and set off with their belongings in a covered sleigh drawn by two strong horses. Three long chests, packed with linens, clothing, family heirlooms, and other household goods, were used as seats. These sat atop feather beds, covered with cloth, providing a spot for the children to sit, sleep, or play. Emily remembered, "As long as father and mother were with us, we had plenty to eat and were warm and cozy in the sleigh." Around noon each day they would eat lunch, "and father would have cider heated for us to drink, to warm us up. At night we would stop at some log tavern, where we would sleep, and eat a hot supper and breakfast in a big room that was both kitchen and dining-room." They traveled every day but Sunday. In mid-February, after six weeks of hard travel, they reached the town of Willink, New York, and Eber's sister, Keziah (Ward) Lewis. Unfortunately, by the time of their arrival, Mr. Ward was sick with pleurisy, a potentially fatal lung ailment.[13]

For several days, Sally Ward remained at her husband's side; initially, it was unclear if he would survive. But after six weeks' convalescence at his sister's home, Mr. Ward was nursed back to health. The family's journey continued in early March. The children became excited at the prospect of a long boat ride. Young Eber, in particular, was fascinated by the water; he always seemed to be playing with a boat of some kind. Regrettably, the children never took the boat ride. Near Waterford, Pennsylvania, in the western part of the state, they were forced to stop their journey. This time, Sally Ward had become ill. It is possible that she, too, suffered from some sort of a lung condition. Her health deteriorated rapidly. Within three days, on March 16, 1818, the date of Emily's ninth birthday, tragedy struck: Sally Ward died. Mr. Ward and his four young children were left grief-stricken. It was a devastating blow for the youngsters, as they found themselves alone with a father they barely knew. He had simply been away from home for too long. It was still winter when young Eber watched in shock as his father built a large fire under a great oak tree. When the ground thawed, Eber Sr. dug a grave, laid his wife to rest, and placed a simple cross in the ground to signify the spot. Years later, after he became a successful businessman, E. B. Ward attempted to return to the site of his mother's grave so he could bring her body to the family burial plot in Detroit, but it had been so long he was unable to find its location. Following Sally's sudden death, Mr. Ward abandoned his dream of relocating the family to Kentucky. Instead, he decided the children needed to be with family, so he made plans to join his brother Samuel, who was living in Salem, Ohio.[14]

The sudden death of his mother, particularly when E.B. was so young, was devastating; a major turning point in his life. If she had survived the journey, the Wards would have settled in Kentucky and most likely have remained there, or another region of the South, for many years. Instead, E. B. Ward spent his formative years living in the Midwest and Great Lakes region. As an adult, he would show tremendous business foresight and strove to diversify the economy in the region where he lived. Rather than influencing Kentucky and the South, E. B. Ward would shape the future of the Great Lakes and Midwest. Sally Ward's death also brought the children closer to one another. Over the next few years the motherless children spent time with relatives, many of whom they had not seen on a regular basis in the past. Meanwhile, Mr. Ward worked a range of jobs that took him to locations throughout the Great Lakes. The children became increasingly dependent upon one other for support; this was particularly true for Emily and Eber. Although she was only three years older than Eber, Emily replaced his mother as the individual he relied upon.

## Samuel Ward

Following the end of the War of 1812, Eber's uncle Samuel Ward married Elizabeth Lamberson and relocated to Salem (Conneaut), Ohio. His successful trading during the war had made him a wealthy man, so he chose to continue in this business. Salem was a logical place to establish his base of operations with its convenient, natural harbor and proximity to isolated settlements in need of supplies. He built the *Salem Packet* in 1816, a small, twenty-seven-ton schooner, and used it to transport goods to small villages between Buffalo and Green Bay. For its first few years, the *Salem Packet* was one of only a handful of vessels conducting business in the upper lakes. Samuel's floating bazaar must have been a welcome sight when it arrived at the isolated hamlets along the

Samuel Ward was Eber Brock Ward's uncle and mentor. The two eventually became partners. (Courtesy of the Community Pride and Heritage Museum, Marine City)

shores of the Great Lakes. At any given time his cargo might include wine and whisky; powder and shot; tea and sugar; fishhooks and line; along with spices, calico, and a range of other general merchandise. In April 1818 Samuel Ward used the *Salem Packet* to pick up his brother Eber, together with the four motherless children, and transport them to his home.[15]

For the next four years young Eber and his siblings lived with family or friends in Salem, but Eber Ward Sr. still had to earn a living to support his family, so he often was absent. Upon occasion, he worked for his brother Samuel, taking charge of the *Salem Packet* and making trading trips in the summertime. He also helped to establish a store for Samuel in Mackinaw City. The children were left in the care of Elizabeth Ward, Samuel's wife, or friends of the family. Being separated from their father, particularly after having lost their mother so recently, left them lonely and desolate. When her father left in the spring of

1820 for several months of work, Emily remembered, "Abba and Sally could not restrain their tears." As his own correspondence shows, the separations were difficult for Mr. Ward as well. In the fall of 1820 he traveled to Green Bay and wrote to his children, who were staying with friends, to let them know he had arrived safely. He planned to remain there for the winter. He expressed regret that he would be unable to hear their voices: "My heart is pained," he declared, and he felt "anxiety for your welfare which a parent alone can feel." Yet, he also was comforted by the fact the children were in the hands of those who would "treat you with kindness" and that "there is a God to protect us." In her father's absence, Emily took charge of the younger children, serving as both sister and mother for her siblings. Caring for others in need became a role she assumed for the remainder of her life.[16]

The War of 1812 had been a turning point for Native Americans in Michigan because it resulted in a major defeat, with the balance of power having shifted in the favor of the Americans. In the aftermath of the war, in 1818, the public lands in Michigan Territory were opened for sale to white setters. At the time, most Americans considered much of Michigan to be an unsettled wilderness. In reality, Native Americans had been living in, and shaping, the region's landscape for centuries. Samuel Ward was one pioneer who became interested in purchasing property in this new territory as he saw an opportunity to expand his shipping business. With a tremendous amount of new land available, Samuel, like his nephew E.B. in later years, took a gamble. He believed that settlement would increase, and if that happened, his business would grow. Accordingly, he purchased two sections of property between the Belle and St. Clair Rivers in Newport (today known as Marine City). Samuel was familiar with the region, located midway between Lake Erie and Lake Huron, because he had sailed through it on many voyages as he passed to and from Detroit. The area was not perfect; it was flat and swampy. In the summer, water could become stagnant, leading some residents to experience symptoms similar to malaria until they became acclimated to their new environment. It would take time to drain the swamps. Nevertheless, Samuel viewed the location as ideal. His goal was to establish a shipping empire. The land was strategically located along a major shipping line and there was plenty of water, including numerous creeks and rivers that could serve as canals where dry docks could be built. He envisioned a future site where ships could be constructed and then easily launched.[17]

Samuel Ward moved to Newport with his wife and son Jacob in 1819, building a home that same year; he would reside in this community for the remainder of his life. The Wards initially lived in a typical pioneer home. An early visitor described it as "like that of all the early settlers of round logs, roofed with 'shakes,' a chimney piled cob-house fashion, of shakes and clay and the whole finished off . . . with daubing and chinking." Samuel also built a warehouse, much larger than his home, that he slowly filled with commodities that pioneers desired.[18]

Two years after Samuel relocated to Newport, there were still only about a hundred families living in St. Clair County. Captain Ward (as Samuel came to be known) quickly became one of community's leading citizens. As one longtime resident described him, "Capt. Sam was the king of this community, arbitrator of all disputes" and while he was a competitive and shrewd business-man, "he was socially very agreeable, and always made friends." The majority of the county's residents earned their living farming and fishing; some engaged in lumbering. Cash was scarce, so much commerce was conducted through barter. The tax roll for 1821 indicates that Samuel owned two horses, three oxen, four cows, four young cattle, sixteen hogs, and household items valued at $80. Only two other individuals in the county were recognized as hav-ing more value in household items. In 1822 territorial governor Lewis Cass appointed Samuel to serve as an associate justice of the county court, a position he held for five years. The next year he partnered with William Gallagher to construct a sawmill and gristmill in nearby China Township. In 1831, when the first post office was established, he was appointed the first postmaster. At one point Samuel Ward owned a tavern located on the Belle River, on land pur-chased from a French family that originally had farmed the property. Captain Ward also established a brickyard. Some of those bricks may have been used to build a new "commodious" brick Greek Revival–style home about 1832. The home was quite impressive and could be seen by all travelers passing by Newport on the St. Clair River.[19]

By the fall of 1822 Eber Ward Sr. had followed his brother Samuel to New-port. Emily and young Eber joined him, but Sally and Abba remained in Salem with friends. The voyage from Salem to Newport was one that E.B. would not soon forget. Their trip would not be taken on his uncle's schooner. Instead, they traveled aboard the *Walk-in-the-Water*, the first steamship to operate on the

Great Lakes. Built in Buffalo in 1818, the steamer was 135 feet in length and accommodated more than a hundred passengers. It was faster and more reliable than Captain Ward's *Salem Packet*, and it represented his keenest competition. Uncle Samuel agreed to accompany his brother's family as they traveled to Newport so he could observe how the *Walk-in-the-Water* operated. Young E.B. enjoyed the three-day voyage and became excited as the ship reached its top speed of ten miles per hour, a rate considered incredible at the time. Emily noticed her brother "talking with the sailors, asking them all sorts of questions about the sails, the management of the ropes, and everything he could think of in regard to the ship." Before they reached their new home, "he could steer the boat pretty well, knew all the nautical terms, could help furl and reef and set the sails." None of the passengers could know that this young boy would one day own and operate one of the largest fleets of steamships in the Great Lakes.[20]

Upon arrival at Newport, Mr. Ward and his family initially moved in with Samuel Ward's wife and son. Before long, however, another log cabin, similar to Samuel Ward's, was constructed. Eber Ward's family lived in this two-room home. One room included a living area with a large fireplace where the cooking was done. Emily, who at thirteen presided as housekeeper, slept in this room; young Eber and his father slept in the other, which also was used for storage.

The next summer, when Mr. Ward made a contract to deliver a hundred cords of hemlock bark, commonly used in the tanning process, to Detroit, E.B. accompanied his father. Eber and his father worked together, chopping down the hemlock trees and stripping off the bark, which then was sent to Detroit. While the two worked, Mr. Ward insisted that young Eber keep on task. His father valued a full day's work, and it was during this time that Eber developed the strong work ethic that remained with him into adulthood.[21]

Several weeks later, the two were employed to help build a sawmill twelve miles south of Fort Gratiot. Mr. Ward described their time that summer: they traveled "in a small open boat with food, bedding, a jug of whisky, and a mat made of bulrushes for a roof to my shanty. . . . We had plenty of food and would have been very comfortable, but for the gnats; they were intolerable." E.B. Ward would never touch whisky his entire life, and while his father criticized those who drank to excess, he must have consumed alcohol in moderation. E.B. performed well, working alongside his father, until late that summer. When the hot weather came, he became sick with malaria and his father worried he might die. Mr. Ward hired some Native Americans with whom he had been working to return E.B. to Newport so could be nursed back to health, while he continued his work on the sawmill. Young Eber eventually made it back home and recovered, but not before he spent several miserable days and nights tossing and turning with a dangerously high fever.[22]

Following his recovery, E.B. spent time with friends in and around the rivers and lakes of Newport fishing, hunting, and doing a range of chores. Like many boys of his age, he strove to make money of his own. When he was young, he trapped muskrats and other animals to sell for pocket money. Then, in 1823, when he was only eleven years old, E.B. spent the summer working for Captain Samuel Ward. This provided him with his first opportunity to work on his uncle's ships. He spent the sailing season running errands for the captain and other officers on a lake schooner. He took to his position easily and was quick to learn, just as he had been when he took the trip aboard his first steamer the previous year.[23]

Samuel Ward built the schooner *St. Clair* in 1824. This was the first of many ships he built in Newport. The *St. Clair* was "a schooner of twenty-eight tons burden . . . modeled like a canal boat, having full ends, her rudder hanging over the stern." It is likely that E. B. Ward was involved with the construction of his uncle's ship in some manner. Samuel Ward's wife Elizabeth also contributed to its construction; she spun and wove the material used for the ship's sails. Captain Ward had a unique mission in mind for the *St. Clair*. It would be the first Great Lakes–built vessel to make its way through the soon-to-be-completed Erie Canal.[24]

The Erie Canal was the brainchild of New York politician DeWitt Clinton. He envisioned that New York City would become "the greatest commercial emporium in the world" if it could be connected to the West via canal. Critics labeled his pet project "Clinton's Big Ditch," charging that construction would take years to complete and would be far too costly. Clinton was elected governor of New York in 1817. On July 4, only three days after he was sworn into office, construction began on the enormous project, which would be financed and owned by the State of New York. Numerous natural obstacles challenged the state's engineers. According to historian Ronald E. Shaw, "Although no adequate engineering training was available in the United States, the canal became a school of engineering in itself." After eight years, the project was completed in October 1825—two years ahead of schedule. The canal stretched 363 miles and was forty feet wide; its depth was four feet. A system of eighty-three stone locks enabled passengers and cargo to travel between Albany and Buffalo. Completion of the colossal project set off a series of celebrations. Numerous dignitaries, including Governor Clinton, traveled through the canal on the *Seneca Chief* beginning in Buffalo on October 26. Ten days later they arrived in New York to one of the greatest celebrations in the city's history. Clinton symbolically demonstrated the "wedding of the waters" by taking two casks of water from Lake Erie and dumping them into the ocean. A great procession of seven thousand marchers then paraded through the streets of Manhattan. Private homes and public buildings were illuminated as the marchers passed by. Over 1,500 wax candles and 750 oil lamps lit up city hall. The celebration culminated with a fireworks display at 10:00 p.m.[25]

Captain Samuel Ward realized the significance of the Erie Canal's completion and was prepared to take advantage of this new route to eastern markets. In hopes of receiving a large payday, he sailed to Green Bay, accompanied by his cabin boy nephew, and traded for a range of cargo. An article in the *Michigan Herald* in July 1826 relates the start of the journey to the canal. "The *St. Clair*—Captain Samuel Ward—cleared from this port last Thursday for New York, with a cargo of potash, fish, beeswax, furs, peltries, etc. chiefly products from this territory. This is the first attempt of a lake vessel to pass through the Erie Canal." Samuel then sailed the *St. Clair* to Buffalo, where the ship reached the canal. At this point, the ship's masts and riggings were taken down and two horses, which Samuel had brought with him, were positioned upon the towpath. From there, the horses towed the *St. Clair*, along with her cargo and passengers, the entire length of the newly completed canal. The journey took eight or nine days. Just ten years later, when David Ward (E. B. Ward's cousin) traveled westward through the canal, he described it as potentially hazardous if passengers weren't paying attention. "Across the canal were many bridges which would not allow a person to stand upright on the deck of a canal boat and pass under safely, so that when the passengers were on deck a constant watch had to be kept to warn them of 'bridge ahead.' Even then occasionally passengers were knocked down and sometimes severely hurt by passing under these bridges." Thankfully, the *St. Clair* completed its journey through the canal without incident, becoming the first ship from the Great Lakes to travel all the way through the canal with a shipment of trade goods. A new era had been born.[26]

Once they reached Albany, the masts were returned to the ship and the *St. Clair* sailed triumphantly down the Hudson River to New York City. If Samuel Ward had expected his ship to be met with the kind of excited celebrations the *Seneca Chief* had prompted when the canal was completed, he was disappointed. Instead, he was required to pay a toll. This was the same fee others were required to pay, but since he had piloted the first ship to complete the historic journey, he believed he would be greeted with a gun salute or maybe even a bounty. Though he was disappointed at the lack of celebration of his achievement, the voyage was not a total loss. He sold his cargo at New York at a considerable profit. He then took on new merchandise in New York and the masts and riggings were once again taken down. He then traveled north on the Hudson, then westward to Buffalo, and then back home. According to one of his contemporaries, Captain Ward's efforts "netted him the handsome sum of $6,000" ($139,177.26 in 2020 dollars). This was a substantial profit, but he never made a return voyage through the Erie Canal.[27]

It is unclear why Samuel never repeated the trip. It is possible that he felt slighted by the toll charge and lack of recognition for his achievement, although a more reasonable explanation might be that it was a time-consuming hassle to take the mast down to pass through the canal only to raise it again to complete the journey. Samuel also discovered he could continue to make a steady profit transporting people and goods from Buffalo to regions west; the rate he charged was $15 per passenger and $5 per barrel of bulk freight. Passenger traffic was increasing because of the Erie Canal, and by the late 1820s, Captain Ward was all too happy to accommodate a growing number of customers. He could transport goods and people throughout all of the lower Great Lakes on the *St. Clair* and other ships he subsequently had built. One can only imagine the response he faced when his floating marketplace arrived to bring much-needed supplies, as well as news, to the growing settlements throughout the region. E. B. Ward worked intermittently for his uncle in the 1820s. This provided quite an education for the young man. He learned about shipping, commerce, and the geography of the West. This was his first apprenticeship in the field of business.[28]

The timing of young Eber's connection with Samuel Ward is significant. The completion of the Erie Canal ushered in a new era for the Great Lakes region. Waterways had been the key to the nation's transportation system going back to the era of the Revolution, but the country's great rivers flowed north to south. The Erie Canal allowed for the movement of goods and people east to west, increasing the flow of commerce to and from communities in the Great Lakes. This led to the growth of cities such as Buffalo and Cleveland on Lake Erie, and Chicago and Milwaukee on Lake Michigan. Detroit, which due to its central location had been the most important commercial hub for the region's Native peoples in their trade with the French in the eighteenth century, expanded its role as a traditional transportation hub to become one of the leading commercial centers of the late nineteenth-century United States. The Midwest emerged as a breadbasket for the nation as wheat and additional farm products could be easily and inexpensively shipped to eastern markets. Later, E. B. Ward became a leading advocate for the states of the Great Lakes and Midwest to diversify their economies by including a manufacturing base.[29]

## Michigan Territory Grows and Emily Has an Adventure

When Emily and E. B. Ward moved to Newport to live with their father in 1822, Michigan was a sparsely populated territory. Michigan was not admitted into the Union as a state until 1837. Census data from 1820 indicates the population of Michigan Territory was a mere 8,927; by 1830, it had more than tripled to 31,639. This population growth was preceded, and made reality, by the actions of the federal government as it first conquered and then took steps to remove Native Americans from their ancestral lands. The government's ability to seize the territory, whether by treaty or by force, opened the region for white settlement, although to the detriment of the indigenous population. Federal action, combined with their own hard work and ambition, meant that many white pioneering families like the Wards prospered following their arrival in Michigan Territory.[30]

As the population grew, the Michigan Territorial legislature called for the establishment of public schools. In 1827, legislation required that "every township containing fifty families or householders should be provided with a good schoolmaster of good morals, to teach children to read and write and instruct them in the English or French language, as well as in arithmetic, orthography and decent behavior for six months in each year." Some private schools existed before that date; Newport's first school, located in a log-cabin schoolhouse, began holding classes in 1822. The region's first teacher was Jacob G. Streit. Emily Ward probably attended classes taught by Mr. Streit, but it is doubtful that E.B. received much formal education. When he did attend, it was likely only in winter. His father provided as much instruction as his busy schedule would allow, but E. B. Ward's principal education was hands-on and practical. It came with the work he conducted with his father and, most important, his apprenticeship under his uncle Samuel on the Great Lakes.[31]

By 1825, and possibly earlier, Emily began teaching school. Either that year or in 1826, Sally Ward joined her siblings and father in Newport, while Abba remained in Ohio with friends. Emily was sixteen years old in 1825 and already had demonstrated a strong personality and ability to persevere on her own. Ever since the death of her mother when she was nine, she had been a surrogate mother to her siblings. She also managed the household in Newport. When Sally arrived, Emily's "rule in the household was firm, but administered with the kindliness of heart." Her sister and E.B. respected her authority. Emily worked hard and led by example, never asking her siblings to do anything she was unwilling to do.[32]

Her leadership and quick thinking were shown in more than one incident while the family lived in Newport. One June afternoon, Emily led a group of three others on a trip to pick wild strawberries on the Canadian side of the St. Clair River at Sombra. She was accompanied by her sister Sally, Samuel Ward's five-year-old son Jacob, and a girl named Margaret. They crossed the river in a rowboat, then pulled it high up on the shore so it could not be reached by the waves. The quartet had a fun time picking berries; then, with their baskets full, they made their way back to the shore, only to find their boat gone—young Jacob had pushed it into the water and it had floated away in the current. Neither Emily nor the others could swim. The children cried as they faced the possibility of spending the night in the woods. Emily knew of a small island downstream, near the Canadian shoreline, where she believed the boat was likely to become stranded, but she had to find a way to get there safely. Noticing some driftwood logs and other discarded wood along the beach, she hatched a plan. Using their sunbonnets, aprons, and skirts as rope, the children bound the logs together into a raft. It was quite frail, particularly for the swiftly moving St. Clair. Sally and Jacob remained behind because the raft was only large enough for two people. Emily later recalled, "It required a brave heart either to go or stay; for in the distance we could hear the occasional howl of a wolf, and on the water was a little raft that looked as if it might fall to pieces at a moment's notice."[33]

Emily knew a group of Native Americans had established a temporary hunting and fishing camp not far downstream. She hoped they might be able to help them secure the raft, pick up the others, and return home. It had taken more than two hours to assemble the raft. By the time they began drifting downstream, the moon had risen—luckily a full moon. It provided just enough light to see where they were heading. As they neared the Indian encampment the residents "screamed and shouted with laughter" at their "crazy craft." But, Emily related, "The Indians were very kind to us: the men went and got the boat and untied the raft, and the women wrung out the clothes and took us to a wigwam" where they were warmed by the fire and their clothes were dried. The Indians also helped them return to Jacob and Sally, whom they found huddled together and crying. Speaking of the event later in life, Emily declared, "I have never yet seen an Indian treated with kindness but what he returned

*Moonlight Adventure on the St. Clair River.* This John Mix Stanley painting depicts Emily Ward's harrowing experience on a makeshift raft after her rowboat was lost in the current of the St. Clair River. (Courtesy of the William L. Clements Library, University of Michigan)

it by equal kindness, and he never forgets a favor, as I know from experience." Throughout her life Emily was a resourceful leader who took charge of her destiny.[34]

With the Wards' home strategically placed along the St. Clair River, there were often visitors Emily entertained, some American traders or settlers and others Indians. While Emily's relations with Native Americans were generally positive, one incident reflected the frustration held by many throughout Indian country. Despite their lessening political and economic power in the aftermath of the War of 1812, Indians continued to hold onto some tracts of land. White settlers considered them a barrier to American expansion and pressured Native Americans to accept treaties that forced them to cede land and live on smaller reservations in return for cash payments, goods and, in many cases, the ability to hunt and fish in traditional locations. This was true for the Saginaw Indians, whose leaders agreed to a treaty with the U.S. government in 1819. Many settlers, however, trespassed on land strictly reserved for the Saginaw, who reacted by harassing settlers.[35]

One summer day in 1826, a large number of Saginaw in full war paint arrived unannounced at the Ward family home. At the time, only Sally and Emily were there. Mr. Ward and E.B. were gone for a "training day," when all adult men and older boys trained for military movements. As Emily described it, the Indians, ignoring her, wandered into the house and "went to the cupboard, and took the bread and cake and everything eatable. They drank some vinegar there was in a barrel in the corner, and then began looking around after something in particular, but which they didn't find; finally, one old fellow looked at me and said 'Whiskey?'" There was some whisky in a storeroom, but Emily refused to hand it over. The Indians threatened Emily and she shouted for Sally to fetch the men. This prompted the Indians to leave quickly, but not before teasing and then whipping Sally. The entire experience was very frightening and not soon forgotten.[36]

## Apprenticeships for Eber and Emily in New York

Following the confrontation with the Saginaw, Mr. Ward reconsidered the isolation his children faced living in Newport. Moreover, as a small frontier village, it offered limited access to education. He arranged for the children to leave the area. Abba remained in Ohio, living with family friends and attending school. Sally went to Wells, Vermont, to live with members of her deceased mother's family; she also went to school. E.B. and Emily traveled to Rochester, New York, where each would explore an apprenticeship; Emily was trained in millinery and E.B. eventually clerked in an office and library. Even Mr. Ward explored new options. For much of the remainder of the decade, he continued to work for Samuel Ward or on his own, earning money cutting wood, catching fish, making potash, and transporting these and other products throughout the Great Lakes. He also lobbied to become the lighthouse keeper on the island of Bois Blanc, located along a key shipping channel in the Straits of Mackinac. He received this appointment in 1829.[37]

It was unsurprising that Mr. Ward would make arrangements for Emily to apprentice in the field of millinery, as women in this profession played an important role in the female economy of nineteenth-century America. Milliners designed and made hats for women. They were skilled workers who "transformed a variety of raw materials—straw, buckram, wire, and silk—into an equally varied number of hat and bonnet shapes." Dressmaking and millinery were a pair of the rare occupations available to women that offered prestige and good pay; they might earn twice as much per week as a seamstress. Just as male artisans served apprenticeships, it was likely that Emily was bound to a mistress craftswoman for a period as long as three years. She would earn no wages while learning her craft. Instead, her father likely paid a significant sum for her to receive training. Emily initially would have learned how to construct the body of a hat. Over time, she was taught to decorate the hat according to the most popular fashions. An advertisement for a millinery shop in the *Detroit City Directory* boasted that it maintained an inventory of hats including "the latest fashion, of dress and plain Bonnets, consisting of Velvet, Satin, and Satin-Beaver," along with French, English, Tuscan, Florence, and Oriental styles in a range of colors. In addition to learning the proper construction and ornamentation of hats, milliners received training in reading, writing, and bookkeeping. Later in life Emily Ward displayed a keen business sense. She often advised and even partnered with her brother E.B. in some of his business ventures. Her business savviness could be traced back to her training in this era.[38]

When E. B. Ward first moved to Rochester, New York, with Emily, he studied the trade of varnishing and furthered his education. In a letter to his father from 1828, he described his situation: "I stay with Mr. Scott and am going to school about one month. I have an excellent opportunity for books and improve my time to the best advantage. I did very little varnishing after you left here, but I intend to do considerably at it in the spring as it is the best season of the year for that business." However, he abandoned the trade later in the year, for reasons unknown, and by January 1829 he had found full-time work as a clerk in an office and library. E.B. quickly took to office work and made a positive impression on prominent men in the community. Emily observed, Eber "is a clerk for a Mr. Scott and has gained the good will of two or three of the first men of the place by his strict attention to business and integrity." His ability to connect easily with others facilitated his business activities throughout his career. The decision to clerk for Mr. Scott also demonstrated a glimpse of his growing ambition. He strove to become more than a skilled laborer; his future lay in the world of business and finance.[39]

Emily and E.B. enjoyed their time in Rochester. Although separated from family, they appreciated their independence. By the end of 1828, Emily was nineteen years old and E.B. turned seventeen. For the first time, they resided with neither relatives nor close family friends. In Rochester, the siblings did not live together, but they provided support for one another. In a letter to her sister Sally, Emily related, "Eber and I enjoy ourselves as well as could be expected . . . we are poor, but we intend to be honest, industrious, and frugal. We go to church every Sabbath or we could say we stayed home almost the whole time." Their father was glad to know they were doing well. He offered advice as to how they should conduct themselves and the people they interacted with "Next to industry and uprightness of character . . . is your company; better keep little or no company than associate freely with the low or vicious; in their company you can neither be long industrious, upright or respected, but—I hope I have not need to caution you on these subjects."[40]

Independence could also be nerve-wracking, particularly if there was a delay in mail delivery. After their father visited in the fall of 1828, E.B. wrote his aunt Kezia Lewis expressing anxiety about his father's safety. "I feel very much concerned about our father who left here about three weeks ago and promised that he would write certainly as often as once a week." Mr. Ward was traveling with his brother David and E.B. feared "some dreadful accident has happened not only to him but to Uncle David. . . . I think he has been murdered." He closed his letter, "I remain your affectionate, but afflicted nephew." Even after they learned of their father's safety, Emily expressed her previous concern in the next letter she wrote to her father. "We received yours of the 1st November last evening . . . we had looked in vain for letters from you since we left Buffalo. We entertained serious apprehensions respecting you. We were afraid some unforeseen accident had happened." Their anxiety owed to problems with the postal service; it had taken seven weeks for their father's letters to reach them.[41]

By the summer of 1829, conditions for members of the Ward family again transformed when Mr. Ward began work as the lighthouse keeper on Bois Blanc Island. This was considered a "plum position." The U.S. secretary of the treasury had the power to make the appointment, but the secretary often relied on the recommendation of local customs collectors. Mr. Ward probably had lobbied for the position as soon as Congress appropriated $5,000 to build a lighthouse on the island in May 1828. His correspondence shows that he was in communication with Duncan Stewart, the customs collector at Michilimackinac, in early 1829, possibly earlier. Undoubtedly, the fact that his brother was Samuel Ward, one of the region's most important ship captains, helped his cause. Mr. Ward likely knew Stewart from his own frequent travels through the Great Lakes. While the lighthouse would not be completed until the start of the 1830 shipping season, the appointment began in August 1829 so he could prepare for his new job. All the members of the Ward family had to make preparations as well. E.B. left New York and joined his father as his assistant on Bois Blanc Island. Emily and Sally would relocate and join their sister in Salem, Ohio.[42]

## Bois Blanc Island

The position of lighthouse keeper may have been considered a "plum" assignment, but according to historian Charles K. Hyde, life as a keeper in the Great Lakes was "isolated, lonely, routinized, boring, and occasionally dangerous." Bois Blanc Island was particularly isolated. When Mr. Ward first moved to the island, he described it as "desolate," his closest neighbors "on an island about eight miles off, but they could only be reached by water." To make matters worse, E.B. was accidentally left on the mainland when his father initially moved to the island. This allowed young Eber a final opportunity to enjoy himself without much responsibility, although it forced Mr. Ward to work alone for the first two weeks. Once E.B. arrived, Mr. Ward described conditions on the island as the pair settled into a routine. "Eber and I live tolerably contentedly. We have plenty to eat, good health and plenty employ. We are so busy at work that we can hardly get time to write and seldom read. Our business is making nets and preparing for fishing, tending Lighthouse, raising a few vegetables, and catching fish. About three weeks hence we shall do nothing but fish and tend lights till winter." For the next two years, E.B. lived on the island with his father, leaving only occasionally. It was during this time that the two finally developed a close relationship.[43]

Written instructions from Stephen Pleasanton, the superintendent of lighthouses for the United States, help to identify Mr. Ward's responsibilities as the lighthouse keeper on Bois Blanc Island. "You are to light the lamps every evening at sun-setting, and keep them continually burning bright and clear till sun-rising. You are to be careful that the lamps, reflectors, and lanterns are constantly kept clean and in order." Additionally, "wicks are to be trimmed every four hours, taking care that they are exactly even on the top." For the first two weeks, while he lived on Bois Blanc alone, Mr. Ward had to wake up each night every four hours to complete this task, similar to a parent feeding a newborn. Once E.B. joined his father on the island, they could take turns with their many tasks. It was mandatory that keepers be able to read and write because they had to "keep an exact account of the quantity of oil received from time to time; the number of gallons, quarts, gills [a measurement equal to four ounces], &c. consumed each night" and submit a copy of these records to the superintendent. Each of these tasks had to be completed every day—several times each day during the shipping season—regardless of the weather. They were prohibited from selling "any spirituous liquors on the premises of the United States," and they were required to treat any visitors with "civility and attention" as long as their visitors conducted themselves in an "orderly manner." Finally, they were not allowed to leave the lighthouse "at any time without first obtaining the consent of the superintendent," except in an emergency. Mr. Ward lived rent-free at the lighthouse and earned the modest salary of $350 per year ($8,619.74 in 2020 dollars).[44]

Eber Ward Sr. was named the lighthouse keeper at Bois Blanc Island in 1829. For two years Eber Brock and his father lived together on the island. (Author's collection)

Much of the work E.B. and his father completed during their first summer and fall on the island, in 1830, was to prepare for the upcoming winter. Mr. Ward's correspondence included requests for items to be shipped to them. Plenty of supplies were available on the mainland at Mackinaw City, but prices there were exorbitantly high. It was much cheaper for his daughters to transport required materials purchased at their home in Salem. He asked his daughters to sew clothing for him and his son, even if it did not fit exactly. The most important pieces included "a roundabout jacket for Eber lined with flannel and made pretty long, two pair of pantaloons and one vest; for me two pair of pantaloons, one vest and a coat. . . . These clothes are intended for hard service, not ornament. The pantaloons should be made long [so] they can easily be cut off if too long. Some pieces for patching these clothes should accompany them." He also requested "three or four pairs of thick woolen mittens lined on the outside with woolen cloth." Mr. Ward also boasted in his letters that he and E.B. "have now fifty chickens all doing well," and they had planted a small garden: "We have a little salad, a few onions and peas and expect a tolerable supply of beans, squashes, and cucumbers; our potatoes look well." Because they could not raise everything they needed on the island, he hoped his daughters could send dried peaches, butter, flour, pork, and pickles. In a request the following year, he declared, "Flour, pork, and whiskey are indispensable articles; we must have them." Those too, had to be imported.[45]

As long as the lighthouse keeper ably performed his regular duties, he was allowed to earn extra money by engaging in other work. Mr. Ward and E.B. caught, preserved, and sold fish to supplement their income. E.B. did much of the fishing, proudly declaring to his sisters that he had caught nearly thirty-five barrels of "large Trout here, no doubt the largest lot ever caught in this country in one season. . . . We have taken more than all the people at Mackinac, although there have been 20 or 30 people engaged in it." Mr. Ward was responsible for salting the fish properly. In an era without refrigeration, fish was shipped in barrels and mixed with brine so they could be properly cured and preserved. The elder Ward took great pride in the quality of fish he sold, learning over time the proper recipe to use for his brine, depending upon the season: fish caught in the summer required more salt than fish caught during other times of the year. He told Emily, "I was not as well prepared as I shall be and have learned something more about curing fish, and for the future I intend no fish shall vie with mine either in appearance or flavor." Unfortunately, the issue of transporting the barrels of fish to distant markets like Detroit, Toledo, and Buffalo, where they could be sold at a profit, proved complicated. Often passing ship captains took the fish and sold them on commission. At other times, Mr. Ward paid for their transport to market. This arrangement worked well if the captain was honest, but in 1831 Ward learned that Captain Holmes, a man he once trusted, had cheated him out of a great deal of money. He was stunned and declared his surprise "at the ingratitude as well as dishonesty of Captain Holmes. . . . It is hard to believe him such a villain."[46]

The incident with Captain Holmes made an impression on young Eber. In the short run, following the theft, his father shipped much of his fish with his brother Samuel or had E.B. accompany the fish to ensure proper delivery. But Eber never forgot the incident. When he owned his own businesses, he always worked to control as many aspects of his operations as possible. In the future, he would own mines where iron ore was dug from the ground. He also owned the ships that transported the iron ore to rolling mills that he owned, where it was transformed into steel. Railroads under his control then purchased the steel his companies produced. In many ways, Eber would implement the principles of vertical integration before many of his contemporaries.

E.B. recalled, "About a hundred barrels of fish were caught each year" during the two years he spent with his father on Bois Blanc Island. A barrel of fish generally sold for between $6 and $8. Although Mr. Ward acquired a large debt as a result of his initial investment in fishing supplies (netting, a boat, barrels, and so on), over time he saw a profit. Mr. Ward's correspondence is littered with references to the number of barrels of fish sent to a range of people. Often individual barrels were earmarked and sent to specific creditors to pay off his debts; others were sent directly to family members. Once E.B. sent his sisters the "largest and fattest trout we have ever taken." He encouraged them to "divide it to suit yourselves, as it will be a rare dish." Because of his fishing endeavors, E.B. became even more familiar with sailing on the Great Lakes. His father described one of his fishing expeditions in a letter to his daughters. "Eber will start in a day or two from here to Thunder Bay Island, where a lighthouse is building. He is to explore the island and examine some fishing grounds thirty miles this side of the island. He will probably go to that fishing ground to fish in the fall." The fishing that fall was disappointing, but E.B. came to know that region of Lake Huron quite well. He also earned money working as part of the crew building the lighthouse that year.[47]

As long as E.B. and Mr. Ward remained on Bois Blanc Island, they were physically separated from Emily, Sally, and Abba, although they communicated through letters. Following some failed deliveries in the first few months after their arrival at Bois Blanc, mail delivery for most of the year was regular, but it came and went only once per month. Mr. Ward's correspondence often included fatherly advice on a range of issues, particularly his daughters' interaction with young men. He advised them, "By no means allow your house to be a rendezvous for young men on whatever pretense, particularly in the evening; young women of character admit the visits of their most honorable suitors only in daylight." He warned them against the advances of some specific young men in their community. "Some gentlemen, Flag, Knapp, Dart &c you may receive compliments from, but never be courted by them." He reminded them to "attend church when you can" and to "read the Bible." He also warned his daughters to avoid men who drank too much. "Drunkenness destroys all domestic enjoyments, and women with drunken husbands are sufferers above all others. . . . Fifty thousand dollars soon disappears when handled by a drunkard, while the temperate man yearly adds something to his estate." Mr. Ward's criticism of excessive drinking likely shaped E.B.'s views of alcohol. In later years, E.B. refused to hire employees who drank alcohol.[48]

By 1831, Abba was considering marriage. Emily, inclined to support the match, wrote to her father, but Mr. Ward was hesitant because he had only a "trifling acquaintance" with the young man. He told Emily, "Your opinion is probably as good as that of your sex in general, but in no other thing are females so liable to judge amiss as the characters of men." This condescension likely frustrated Emily—or maybe not, because it was typical of males in this era. He was probably concerned that his daughter might end up in a failed marriage like his sister Kezia Lewis. In the late 1820s, Kezia wrote her brother, "I am driven from my home, separated from my children" by her husband. She outlined the "disadvantages a woman labours under in managing business, particularly of such a nature" as caring for her children after she had been mistreated and abandoned by her husband. Kezia retained the services of a young attorney named Millard Fillmore who was practicing in New York. Fillmore later served as the thirteenth president of the United States. Kezia eventually moved to Newport, lived with Samuel Ward, and taught school.[49]

Mr. Ward took steps to help his daughters in the millinery trade. By 1831 Sally and Abba had joined Emily as producers of women's hats. Mr. Ward purchased his daughters a subscription to *Godey's Lady's Book*. This popular magazine, which included descriptions of the latest fashions, was read by women who produced hats and dresses as well as by consumers. He also gave them extra money to travel to larger cities so they could see the most popular styles firsthand in order to reproduce them for local customers. Although Emily and her sisters were involved with the millinery business for a time, none remained in it for long. The sisters, once married, did not carry on in the profession.

Emily's true interest centered around educating children, so she eventually obtained a teaching position.[50]

The correspondence between Mr. Ward, Emily, and E.B. reflected an intimacy that developed among the three concerning personal and financial matters. Shortly after assuming his post at the lighthouse, Mr. Ward confided in Emily "that I expect to receive money soon" from the government, but asked her "not [to] let any know." It is unclear why he wanted this kept secret, but he did owe money to several individuals when he sent the letter. The following year he lamented the fact that he owed "three hundred and fifty dollars, or a year's salary" to his brother Samuel and Oliver Newberry, a businessman from Detroit. E.B. must have been concerned about his father's debt when he wrote to Emily, "Mention nothing to father respecting this letter. Our debts are at this time probably upwards of $400."[51]

At one point, Mr. Ward considered a transfer to the lighthouse at Thunder Bay and E.B. traveled there to inspect conditions. Mr. Ward requested that Emily "not let the object of Eber's visit to Thunder Bay be known." Following the failure to catch many fish in Thunder Bay, and concerned by the mounting debts, E.B. confessed to Emily, "Disappointment appears to be our eternal companion." Mr. Ward also seemed to acknowledge his loneliness one spring while E.B. was gone for six weeks fishing and making sugar: "I have seldom seen a human face for forty days." Mr. Ward may have been absent during his children's formative years, but a bond developed as his children reached adulthood.[52]

The two years E.B. and his father spent together on Bois Blanc Island involved constant work. They had to maintain the lighthouse, haul wood, shovel snow, fish, repair nets, tend gardens, preserve and prepare food, and perform countless other tasks. Despite these responsibilities, Mr. Ward described their conditions in a positive light. He professed, "This is a desirable spot. . . . We have no bickering, strife or treachery." His great regrets were that his wife was no longer alive and that he lived far from his daughters. Mr. Ward and E.B. enjoyed receiving correspondence from family and friends. They particularly relished receiving newspapers from different cities. Once Emily secreted a letter within a newspaper that had been folded "with real masonic intricacy and design," much to the delight of her father. E.B. appeared to flourish with his additional responsibilities as he worked beside his father as "a noble fisherman as well as the material tender of the lights."[53]

Mr. Ward said proudly that over time, E.B. "has grown famously on whitefish." Yet he also expressed concerns about his son. E.B. had always had a voracious appetite for knowledge, and he worried his son might "soon turn savage" if he remained isolated on Bois Blanc Island for too long. E.B. himself complained to his sisters, "I have read but very little" because he was working so much. Mr. Ward realized his son was growing physically, but after two years on the island, he understood his son needed to grow his business opportunities as well. So in the fall of 1832, E.B. left the island and began a new apprenticeship working for Captain Samuel Ward. This time, E.B. would not serve as a cabin boy. Instead, he captained his own ships and eventually became his uncle's business partner.[54]

## Conclusion

E. B. Ward received little formal education, but his life experiences and his relationships with others enabled him to successfully grow and mature. Following his mother's death, he learned to survive with only one parent, and the close bond he formed with his sister Emily remained intact for the rest of his life. Although his father was absent at times during his childhood, the two years the pair spent on Bois Blanc Island created a strong connection between them. Life on the island was isolated and while each had to work hard, one can imagine long conversations between them that enhanced young Eber's education and provided valuable life lessons that shaped his worldview. As a boy, E.B. spent only a short time under the tutelage of his uncle Captain Samuel Ward. However, that time was significant. When E.B. left Bois Blanc Island, presented with the chance to partner with Samuel on the eve of his twenty-first birthday, a new chapter in his life opened. He seized this opportunity with authority.

# 2

# From Protégé to Partner

*When I first saw him [Eber B. Ward] he was about 22 years of age, of*
*rather unprepossessing appearance, hardly of the average stature, with a*
*cold blue eye, a ruddy face, and what is known as an "iron jaw," betokening*
*a firmness of purpose that characterized his life. . . . I esteemed him as*
*altogether more fit than his uncle to "go down [to] the sea in ships."*
—William L. Bancroft, 1894

Eber Brock Ward was destined to become the wealthiest man in all of Michigan. Several factors enabled his success, but none was more important than the partnership with his uncle Samuel Ward. E.B. came to work full-time for his uncle in 1832, on the eve of his twenty-first birthday. It was a fortuitous era to be in Michigan. The territory experienced a tremendous population increase in the early 1830s and, as a result, joined the Union as the twenty-sixth state prior to the end of the decade. Samuel Ward, assisted by his protégé Eber, transported a growing surge of migrants and their goods to locales throughout the Great Lakes and profited greatly. Both Samuel and Eber took risks and worked tirelessly to establish their business operations in Michigan, yet their prosperity was facilitated by actions of the federal government to defeat and remove Native Americans from the land, thereby opening the region to white settlement. Over time, E.B. showed he was up to any challenge put to him by his uncle and eventually was given command of the *General Harrison*, Samuel's most important ship. Eber also slowly began to take over many of the day-to-day operations of the business and gradually became more of a partner with his uncle, as opposed to his assistant. Eber was described by some as ruthless in later years; as his partnership grew with his uncle, some of his business tactics began to demonstrate the more cunning—or ruthless—tactics he would employ. While Eber's partnership with his uncle Samuel laid the foundation of his future wealth, his relationship with his father and sister Emily continued to be close, at times proving stronger than his relations with Samuel.

## Population Growth in Michigan Territory

Initially, settlement in Michigan Territory had been slow, even following the displacement of Native Americans from the land. This was in part due to the publication of an official report in 1815 by Edward Tiffin, the commissioner of the general land office, who described the soil in Michigan as "barren, sandy land, on which scarcely any vegetation will grow, except very small scrubby oaks." For some years afterward, maps labeled Michigan an "Interminable Swamp." Interest in the region began to change later in that decade when settlers trickled into the area. They observed the land for themselves and started to dispel Tiffin's initial observations. By 1825, the Erie Canal was completed. This made travel much easier and increasing numbers of migrants chose to move to Michigan. The steady population growth continued, but was threatened by two events in 1832: the Black Hawk War and a cholera epidemic.[1]

Black Hawk, a member of the Sauk Nation, led a coalition of Indians frustrated by the increased American settlement in the Great Lakes region and the treaty-making policy of the U.S. government. For years, Native Americans had been forced to accept treaties requiring cession of land to the United States in return for a lump sum of money or goods, along with annual payments. Terms of the treaties were frequently deliberately misleading, so Indian leaders did not always understand their full content. In 1832, exaggerated stories that Black Hawk's band of warriors posed a threat to isolated settlers led to great anxiety in Michigan. In fact, stagecoach lines, which previously were overloaded, had to be canceled due to lack of passengers, many of whom returned to Ohio. By August, Black Hawk and several other leaders were captured, but not before there was a temporary reduction in the number of migrants travel-ing to Michigan.[2]

News of the Black Hawk War coincided with fears over a cholera out-break. A number of the troops mobilized to fight in the Black Hawk War were exposed to the disease. As many as half of those men died, while others pan-icked and deserted. Detroit's residents suffered greatly. In July 1832, officials reported fifty-eight cases of cholera, resulting in the deaths of twenty-eight of the community's residents. Eber Ward Sr. was traveling in Detroit during the height of the outbreak and his correspondence reflects the high level of anx-iety. Declaring that the town was "in a very sickly state," he encouraged his daughters to relocate temporarily to the country, where scattered populations "seldom suffer from the cholera, but they will be very likely to have more or less of it in every village, and where the steamboats have stopped." Fear that his daughters would be exposed to the sickness prompted him to warn that "by no means" should you "nurse those who have the disease; only your sisters." Cholera tended to run its course very quickly, within three to five days, but its deadly nature left a lasting impression on survivors.[3]

While the cholera epidemic and Black Hawk War affected Michigan's set-tlement in the short run, their impact was only temporary, and by 1834 white settler colonialism was back in full force. Most migrants tended to be young, neither very rich nor very poor. They had enough resources to invest in their journey, but were not yet established financially and sought an opportunity to improve their lot in life with an eye toward the future. They arrived in droves because Michigan had abundant land where families could establish their own farms. Not only could this allow for financial independence, the Erie Canal created the potential for cash crops to be transported cheaply and easily to eastern markets for profit. Numerous migrants came from the New England states, but many also hailed from New York. Speculators purchased land when banks issued easy credit, although records also show a significant number settled in Michigan permanently. According to historians Willis Dunbar and George May, "From 1830 to 1837 Michigan was the most popular destination for west-ward moving pioneers." Census data and records of land sales support their conclusions. In 1830, the territory's population was 31,639; by 1840, after Michigan had become a state, its population reached 212,267. This represented a seven-fold increase, the largest percentage increase of any state or territory in that era. Land sales rose steadily, from 147,062 acres in 1830 to 498,423 acres in 1834. "Michigan Fever" and land sales peaked in 1836 when nearly 4.2 million acres sold for more than $5.2 million. To provide perspective, the 1836 land sales in Michigan were so large, they surpassed those for the entire nation taken collectively as recently as 1833. Eber B. Ward even commented on the phenomenal land rush in a letter to his father and sister during the summer of 1836: "Business continues active in Detroit" as the "floods of immigration [into Michigan] have not subsided."[4]

Often, the city of Detroit was the "door" through which migrants were transported to their ultimate destination in Michigan or other parts of the Great Lakes region. Sometimes, those with the goal of settling in Illinois or Wisconsin arrived in Detroit, only to change their plans once promoters and speculators convinced them of Michigan's advantages. Some chose to remain in the city, while others explored options in communities outside Detroit or other regions of the state. The land office in Kalamazoo was so busy processing purchases for property in western Michigan during the land rush of the 1830s that officials had to close their doors several times to catch up with their paperwork. Ultimately, many residents of eastern communities came down with "Michigan Fever," which led to the population explosion and shaped the state's development.[5]

## Captain Eber B. Ward

Samuel Ward, operating out of his base at Newport, reaped the benefits of Michigan's population boom. By the early 1830s, he owned a line of schooners and operated a lucrative business taking passengers and their belongings to and from their desired destinations. In 1832, his ships included the old *St. Clair*, which he previously had taken through the Erie Canal, the *Albatross*, and the *Marshall Ney*. Of these three, the *Marshall Ney* was his flagship, at seventy-three tons. Samuel Ward also served as its master, transporting travelers and goods from east to west and throughout the Great Lakes. In 1833, Captain Samuel added the sixty-five-ton schooner *Elizabeth Ward*, named for his wife. By 1835, he built a new flagship, the *General Harrison*, in honor of William Henry Harrison, whose military conquests over Indians during the War of 1812

Michigan's Lower Peninsula. Samuel and Eber Ward developed a fleet of vessels throughout the Great Lakes, with operations based in Newport, now called Marine City. (Courtesy of Rebecca J. Mott)

facilitated the expansion of the American empire westward. The famed military commander eventually was elected president of the United States. The *General Harrison* earned a reputation as one of the fastest schooners on the Lakes. In addition to his ships, Samuel also owned farm property and a store with large warehouses stocked with goods for sale. In 1837, E.B. estimated the value of his uncle's assets to be, at a minimum, $41,400 ($960,401.07 in 2020 dollars). The expansion of Samuel Ward's fleet of ships and other properties in the 1830s reflect the profitability of his operations, which coincided with Michigan's rapid population increase.[6]

In the fall of 1832 when he was just shy of his twenty-first birthday, Eber Brock Ward went to work for his uncle Samuel in Newport, leaving his father behind on Bois Blanc Island. E.B. did not have much formal schooling growing up, nor did he ever attend college, but when he began working as a clerk in his uncle's general store, he continued the education begun when young Eber worked as a cabin boy on one of his uncle's ships. This apprenticeship was destined to shape his future. Samuel Ward and his wife Elizabeth had only one biological child: Jacob Harrison Ward, born in 1815. Considered "mentally incompetent," Jacob would never be able to follow in his father's footsteps and run the business he had created.[7]

Eber already knew the value of hard work, but his uncle taught him how to interact with customers, to identify the correct inventory of goods to keep in stock, and to keep a watchful eye on costs; essentially, it was while he worked for Samuel that Eber learned how to run a business. Eber flourished in this role, and he became like a son to Samuel. Eber's correspondence often reflected the close personal and professional relationship that developed between the two. Shortly after he began clerking for his uncle, he commented, "Uncle S. and family are very friendly to me." Within a few years, E.B. had assumed additional responsibilities, purchasing lots in Detroit or engaging in other transactions on behalf on his uncle. Several years later, Samuel Ward commented on the bond that developed between the two in his will, thanking Eber for the "faithful care over my interests, for his advice, assistance and good judgement" over the years.[8]

Eber Brock worked as a clerk in his uncle's store through the winter and early spring of 1832 and 1833; however, by the summer of 1833 he served on the *Marshall Ney*. At the time, it was the largest of Samuel Ward's ships. The position provided E.B. a greater opportunity to facilitate his father's trade in fish and other supplies. Mr. Ward was in his third year as the lighthouse keeper on Bois Blanc Island and his trade network had expanded successfully. He sent barrels of fish to numerous ports throughout the Great Lakes to be sold on consignment. Mr. Ward's correspondence helps to provide insight into his activities and the rudimentary function of commerce in this era. For example, Mr. Ward sent a memo, similar to a modern-day invoice, to a merchant in Portland, New York, outlining, "You will receive by the *Marshall Ney* Capt. Ward 21 Bbls [barrels] of Trout & Whitefish to sell at Eight Dollars per Bbl." He was "at liberty to sell as low as Seven Dollars per Bbl." If anything was to change, "my son E. B. Ward I expect will be about the shores of Lake Erie for the fish when sold or to give any new instructions when necessary." Mr. Ward traded additional items as well. Butter, flour, pork, salt, and countless other products were in demand in the isolated settlements forming throughout Michigan. E.B. served as an intermediary who arranged for these supplies to be sent to Bois Blanc Island for his father's use or for trade. Throughout the summer of 1833, he also sought a boy, or even a man, to serve as his father's assistant on the island to help with the lighthouse duties or at least provide some company.[9]

Events progressed rapidly for E. B. Ward under his uncle's tutelage. The *General Harrison* was Samuel Ward's leading vessel in his growing armada beginning in 1835. An unnamed sailor familiar with the ship described it as "exceedingly long and narrow, and somewhat crank, but she was a good sailer, being the best then on the lakes." E. B. Ward served as first mate. Initially, the captain was B. F. Owen, who was married to Eber Brock's sister Abba. At times, Samuel himself captained the ship; within a few years Eber Brock would be at its helm. E.B.'s time aboard the *General Harrison* during the 1835 season and his stint on the *Marshall Ney* the previous year allowed him to gain more experience handling a sailing vessel. He was becoming more comfortable on the waters each year.[10]

Eber spent the following year on shore, returning to clerking for the 1836 season, and by the end of the summer, he oversaw the shore end of their activities almost exclusively. Eber made the most of his opportunity. Previously, his uncle had sold his store in Newport as it became difficult for him to oversee both the store and his expanding shipping business. Eber bought out the investors and took over the store himself. He constructed a larger warehouse and considered opportunities to increase his inventory by purchasing goods in New York and other areas. He also engaged in land speculation; the last opportunity to purchase property at bargain prices was coming to a close, and 1836 would be the peak year for land sales in the territory. Even in the community of Newport, the price of real estate had risen considerably in a short time period, and several villagers were buying and selling land for profit. E.B. had caught this speculative fever and informed his father, "I shall go into the woods again to look for lands—shall probably go to Detroit again the latter part of this week." To purchase the land, he borrowed money from his father and uncle. He worked hard that season, challenging himself to learn how to manage such a complicated business. Eber was successful in his endeavors, foreshadowing the internal drive that would enable him to become the wealthiest man in all the Great Lakes. Furthermore, his increased responsibilities indicated that over time, Samuel began increasingly to rely heavily on the judgment of his nephew. Previously, Eber showed that he could successfully lead a crew on board a ship operating in the Great Lakes, but after he oversaw a prosperous shipping season from shore, he demonstrated the business acumen required to engage in long-range planning and management of the day-to-day office environment.[11]

By 1837, E.B. was back on the Great Lakes in command of the *General Harrison*. E.B. was excited when he informed his father that his uncle Samuel "is determined to have me sail the *Gen. Harrison* next season." He did not receive a set salary when he assumed this role; instead, he purchased a 25 percent interest in the ship, taking on some of its costs as well as a share of the revenue, earning Eber the title of Captain Ward. Samuel Ward's health may have been a factor that influenced E.B.'s sudden elevation to command this ship. David Ward, E.B.'s cousin and another of Samuel's nephews, observed his uncle was "in chronic poor health" at that time.[12] Eber Brock commented, "Uncle Samuel is not much better of his disease yet." The exact malady he suffered is unclear, but he was under the care of a doctor. Fortunately, his health seemed to improve over time. Samuel's decision to hand over control of the *General Harrison*, and particularly Eber's investment in the ship, was a key turning point in the relationship between Samuel and his much-younger nephew. Eber's investment represented the first step toward becoming Samuel's partner, rather than simply serving as his uncle's protégé, a transition that would be complete by the 1840s.[13]

Eber was only twenty-five years old at the time he assumed control of the *General Harrison*. Over the course of the sailing season that year, he would navigate the vessel between the ports of Buffalo, Detroit, Green Bay, and Chicago, with stops at smaller harbors in between. As a result, he gained more intimate knowledge of the Great Lakes and the communities where he made frequent visits. He noticed one location in particular, located on some high ground just south of Milwaukee with a natural harbor to allow for the ease of shipping. In later years, Eber would remember the site and establish an iron mill at this location, which would be renamed Bay View. As captain and part owner of the *General Harrison*, Eber also carried on a side trade delivering beef, fish, oats, flour, or other items on consignment for individuals from the different ports. The season began slowly, and he expressed frustration in May, writing from Cleveland, because he had been unable to see his father. Shipping had been light, so he had been traveling only between Detroit, Cleveland, and Buffalo "to ensure even a tolerable business for the spring." He hoped to clear for Green Bay or Chicago soon, but expressed concern over the spreading national economic downturn that would eventually be referred to as the Panic of 1837. He feared the impact on shipping "must be severe this season."[14] That August, E.B. purchased numerous supplies for his father in Buffalo. He planned to deliver them to Bois Blanc Island upon his return to Lake Huron. The economic depression continued, however; as he observed, "Many of the largest class of sailing vessels are laid up." Nonetheless, he was doing relatively well: "I shall have the best load out of any vessel that has left here for some time—and with ordinary luck shall clear expenses and perhaps some more."[15]

While demand for shipping improved for E.B. as the season progressed, he met with near disaster on the Lakes later that year. That fall, Captain Eber had a full load of freight as he headed toward Green Bay and Chicago on the *General Harrison*. As he later recalled, "I owned most of the cargo and expected to make a big profit from it." The ship's journey began well enough, but when Eber sailed into Lake Michigan a heavy windstorm suddenly developed. The crew reefed and close-hauled the sails, but the wind pushed the ship, "scudding along at a furious rate with almost bare poles." Captain Eber did not initially anticipate disaster, but "the wind suddenly veered to the east and blew harder than ever." Thirty minutes later it struck again and it seemed as if the waves were determined to destroy the ship. "The fury of the storm burst upon us. I could see that unless the wind changed, we were lost. . . . My precious boat would be battered to pieces, her cargo lost, and perhaps, if the worst happened, her crew would be too!" There wasn't much they could do other than ride out the storm and hope for the best. About midnight, the vessel began to approach the shore and two hours later, they struck a reef. Ward and his crew managed to launch their yawl boats and clear away from the ship. He remembered, "How we contrived to get to shore I could never tell. The yawl was constantly full of water. . . . But somehow or other the waves finally deposited us on the beach, and we found shelter in a fisherman's cabin."[16]

The next morning, Eber Brock awakened from his nightmare experience to discover his ship was damaged and his cargo scattered across the shore or lost at sea. He feared "I was a ruined man." Upon closer examination, he determined the *General Harrison* could be repaired, but much of the cargo was a complete loss. He traveled to Detroit to make arrangements to fix things, but he had no money; he already had extended his credit to invest in his portion of the ship, along with the cargo that was now on the bottom of Lake Michigan. Uncle Samuel was unable to advance him any cash either. Samuel's loans were set to come due soon and Eber feared his own credit would be ruined. He recalled, "I believe I suffered more in those few weeks than I have over all the other business disasters that came in later years." He did not know where to turn, and the stress became so intense he had trouble sleeping at night. One morning, as he was walking in town, deep in thought, he was surprised when "a hand touched my shoulder and a friendly voice said, 'What in the world is the matter with you Eber? I've shouted your name three times and you haven't heard. Come back to my hotel.'" His friend had received a package from Eber's father and Emily. When they arrived at the hotel room, his friend locked the door and handed the package to him. "Father and Emily had heard of my embarrassments and had sent me fifteen hundred dollars to help tide me over." He was shocked to see the contents of the package. The money would cover all his debts. He later reminisced, "What I would have done without that fifteen hundred dollars I have never liked to think about!"[17]

The near disaster involving the *General Harrison* demonstrated the precarious nature of shipping on the Great Lakes. Eber nearly lost everything, including his own life. Yet with the aid of his father and sister, he emerged battered but unbroken. The unexpected and critical support of his family helped restore his confidence, and his interminable will allowed him to rebound. Other than the debt to his father and sister, he was becoming more financially independent. Their help came at a crucial moment in his career. He was able to repair the *General Harrison* and pay for the lost cargo. Furthermore, this served to bind the trio together more closely than before. Soon, he encountered new challenges, some of which involved additional members of his family.

## Family Ties and Marriage

Although Eber Brock was separated from his father and sisters while working for his uncle, he maintained ties with them. Sally Ward was the first of E.B.'s siblings to marry when she wed Melchiah Brindle in June 1833. The pair settled on a farm in Springfield, Pennsylvania, near Melchiah's family. The marriage started well and the two appeared to be happy, but the couple's relationship, and Sally's health, deteriorated over time, particularly after the birth of their first two children. Eber Brock blamed "Sally's fiery temper and reckless disposition" for the couple's problems. At one point, she considered living apart from her husband and relocating to Bois Blanc Island. But Eber Brock advised his father that due to her temperament, "you cannot live with her on the Island."[18] E.B. visited Sally periodically, but on one occasion he found she had "salivated herself with calomel," a purgative commonly prescribed by doctors in the nineteenth century as a cure-all for numerous ailments. E.B. later described Sally as a "miserable woman" who "manifests in doing wrong" in a letter to his sister Emily. Eventually, there would be an explanation for Sally's behavior. She suffered from mental illness. When she was in her thirties, Sally became a patient in the New York State Lunatic Asylum in Utica. Unfortunately, as time progressed, it was apparent that mental illness ran in the family. Some of Eber's own children eventually struggled with the illness.[19]

Abba, Eber's youngest sister, married Benjamin Franklin Owen in late 1833. The couple lived in Newport, where B. F. Owen became involved in the shipping business; at times, he collaborated with Samuel Ward and even served as captain of the *General Harrison*. The couple would have four children who reached adulthood. E.B.'s fondness for his sister and family is reflected in his concern over their welfare following an accident involving the schooner *Savannah*. In September 1841, the entire family was aboard the ship, with B. F. Owen serving as captain, when it was struck by another vessel. In a rushed letter to his father, E.B. wrote, "I am waiting with the greatest anxiety for news." While the ship was a total loss, Abba, her husband, and their children all survived what must have been a terrifying experience. Eber Brock sent money and clothing to his sister.[20]

Emily Ward was the oldest of the Ward children; while she never married or had children of her own, in later years she would be known affectionately as Aunt Emily to the dozens of children she took under her care. Her status as a single woman made her unusual in her day. According to Catherine A. Fitch and Steven Ruggles, in 1850 only 7.3 percent of white women in the United States between the ages of forty-five and fifty-four were single. After spending some time teaching in Conneaut, Ohio, Emily came to live with her father on

Bois Blanc Island after Eber Brock left to work for Uncle Samuel. Life on the island was peaceful, albeit lonely. The only inhabitants other than Emily and her father were an old French man and his Native American wife. To break the monotony of life on the island, she enjoyed reading books and magazines, but it was while on the island that she decided to focus on the education of children as her vocation in life. Some of her students were her nieces and nephews. Both Abba and Sally died far too young, and Emily helped to raise their children. In 1837, Simon Bolivar Brooks, the orphaned son of family friends, was adopted by Emily and her father. Bolivar, as he was more commonly called, was nine years old when he came to live on the island, and he was present when Emily showed great courage and quick thinking during a frightening series of events concerning the lighthouse tower.[21]

The lighthouse on Bois Blanc Island was placed too close to the water when it was originally constructed in 1830. Rising lake levels and the constant winds had washed away much of the sandbank in front of the tower. In the fall of 1837, Eber Ward Sr. informed the superintendent of lighthouses, Abraham Wendell, of the precarious situation that was developing. He believed the high water threatened to destroy the lighthouse. Later that December, when Mr. Ward left the island for the day to gather some much-needed supplies, an unexpected storm arose. Emily was left with young Bolivar alone on the island. Over the course of the day, as the storm increased its intensity, Emily noticed the water begin to surround the lighthouse tower; the building creaked and groaned with every crashing wave. She and Bolivar watched the progress from the keeper's house, and when Emily saw the brick walls begin to crack and buckle, she presumed the tower was about to fall soon. She was determined to save as much as she could of the lamps and reflectors inside. Thinking quickly, she left Bolivar in the house and climbed all 150 steps to gather the valuable supplies. She later recalled, "When I reached the top what a magnificent sight met my gaze . . . ! It seemed as if then, indeed, God in his majesty, was sweeping the earth and the seas, and I felt that I also was part of the great universe that existed under that awful power." She was afraid when she observed "the mad waters leap and roar and dash with all their mighty force against the frail structure that supported" her, but she was determined to save the valuable items inside. She made five trips up and down the steps, carrying lenses, reflectors, and lamps safely away from the tower. Later that night, she and Bolivar left the lighthouse keeper's residence and went into the woods, fearful the tower would fall on the house. They watched it fall, but luckily, it did not damage the dwelling. Emily lay awake most of the night wondering whether her brother Eber was safely ashore or in the middle of the raging storm.[22]

After the storm subsided, Mr. Ward returned to the island to assess the damage. He reported to Mr. Wendell the lighthouse had fallen December 9 and he was concerned "the dwelling house appears now to be in danger of sharing the same fate." He described his situation as "unpleasant . . . in this wilderness of snow and water." While he understood there was nothing to be done that winter, it must have been frustrating to know he, Emily, and Bolivar would be stuck on the isolated island to wait until spring to make any improvements. The lighthouse was rebuilt the following year in a more suitable location, and Mr. Ward, along with Emily as his assistant, remained as the lighthouse keeper on the island until 1842. He then was transferred to Fort Gratiot, where he served as the keeper for several years. Emily and the various children under her care lived with Mr. Ward and assisted him in his duties for each of his tours as a keeper. Over the years, she took on more of the lighthouse keeper's responsibilities when her father's health began to fail. As shown by her ability to handle potential disaster when the Bois Blanc tower fell in 1837, she was up to the task.[23]

Emily and Eber Brock had a special relationship. Eber demonstrated deep respect for his sister in a revealing letter from June 1839, the tone of which was unlike most others he penned. He began with an apology for neglecting to reply to her recent letters, and he agreed to do a better job of maintaining their correspondence. He then admitted, "I am not much of a sentimentalist. . . . I generally feel a reluctance in expressing honest emotions and sentiments of my heart." It will be recalled that Emily had been selfless in caring for each of their siblings, and their father, following their mother's sudden death. He recognized their unique relationship. "You and I have lived together more than any other two of the family, have seen trials, troubles and prosperity together and enjoyed the unlimited confidence of each other. . . . As a wayward boy is inclined to neglect those to whom he is under the greatest obligations as he grows old . . . I have unwittingly neglected many of the social duties which belong to my situation." In his own way, Eber Brock tried to let his sister know how much she meant to him.[24]

It is likely Emily needed the support of her brother at that time because she was frustrated, fearing she was destined to become an "old maid." She had just reached the age of thirty and had no prospects for marriage. About the same time E.B. sent his revealing letter of contrition, Emily received another from Orson Brooks, a close family friend, and the brother of Bolivar. His letter is a reply to one of Emily's now missing. He tried to cheer her up by teasing her about "sliding into 'Old Maidish habits,'" declaring she was not thirty "but thirteen." Another factor that clearly must have upset Emily concerned Bolivar. The letter from Orson Brooks hints that a rumor had spread claiming Bolivar was her son, conceived out of wedlock. With her honor and virginity questioned, one could understand why she was upset. Orson offered to "go the rounds"; if her "integrity should be in jeopardy, from the raillery of unprincipled Devils then *I* can give his true parentage no mistake."[25]

It is not surprising that Emily would be sensitive about her status as a single woman and angry at the insinuation Bolivar was her son. Historian Barbara Welter argues that a cult of "True Womanhood" emerged in the United States during the nineteenth century. Popular women's magazines, catalogues, and religious literature of the era presented women as protectors of domestic life. Throughout her lifetime, a true woman was expected to be a "mother, daughter, sister, [and] wife." Emily was a daughter and a sister. Over the course of her lifetime, she also acted as a mother, helping to raise fourteen children to adulthood, while overseeing the education and proper care of many others. But she never had any children of her own, nor was she a wife. While the society in which she lived judged her as lacking in the virtues and attributes it held in high esteem, Emily excelled in other fields. For many years, she oversaw the furnishings to be included in the interior cabins of the ships Eber built in Newport, and Eber had great confidence in her judgment. Additionally, in later years she would serve as her brother's conscience, encouraging him to contribute to causes that improved the life and welfare of many in need of assistance.[26]

Eber's life changed dramatically when he married Maryell McQueen in 1837. Maryell, who sometimes went by Mary, or more often Polly, was the eldest of the four daughters of Daniel McQueen and Catherine (Lamberson) McQueen. A contemporary described her as "a fine looking, intelligent young lady." Polly's mother Catherine was the sister of Elizabeth Ward, Samuel Ward's wife. For a time, the McQueens worked as cooks on Uncle Samuel's boats; when

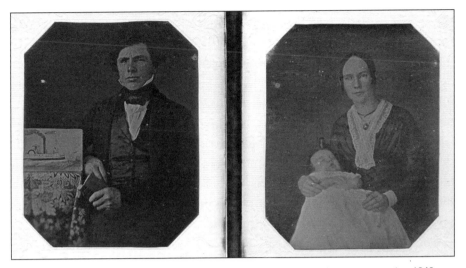

Eber Brook Ward (*left*); Polly (Maryell) McQueen Ward and infant (*right*). These daguerreotypes, circa 1842, are possibly the oldest photographic images of a Michigan subject taken in Michigan. (Courtesy of the William L. Clements Library, University of Michigan)

the two died, Elizabeth and Samuel adopted the orphaned girls and raised them as their own. E.B. would have known Polly while they were growing up. She was well liked in Newport, and the match was popular.[27]

A photo taken about five years after their marriage, believed to be from 1842, shows Eber Brock and Polly in what is possibly the oldest daguerreotype produced in the state of Michigan. Eber sits in a chair, dressed in a suit coat and tie, wearing a white ruffled shirt beneath a vest. His hair is parted on his left, and one of his eyes is opened a little wider than the other. He holds a book in one hand while his other arm rests on a table. On the table is a picture of a steamboat—the photo was taken about the time Eber and Samuel expanded their line of vessels to include steamboats. Captain Eber appears confident and self-assured, prepared to overcome any obstacle placed in his path; here is a young, successful businessman proud of his accomplishments. Polly is wearing a lace fichu with her hair pulled back and parted in the middle. She wears a ring on the index finger of her right hand and has a necklace drawn tightly around her neck. Polly is portrayed as a young woman with great pride in her role as a mother: the epitome of "True Womanhood" as described by Barbara Welter. Polly gently holds a sleeping baby in her lap. The child is likely Henry, the couple's second child, who was born in 1841. There are no other visuals in the background of her photo, emphasizing her portrayal as a nurturing mother. Interestingly, the couple chose not to be photographed together as a family. Whether this was a conscious decision or not, it may indicate that Eber placed his business interests ahead of his family obligations. Eber and Polly were married for thirty-one years and the couple had eight children, five of whom outlived Eber. Ultimately, their marriage ended in divorce.

Eber Brock's choice of mate would be questioned by some; did he marry for love or for money? Shortly after the divorce was final in 1869, Eber married a much younger woman from a family with powerful political connections. It is possible Eber was in love with Polly and her relationship to Samuel Ward was simply irrelevant. Their love could simply have weakened over time. Alternatively, maybe Eber married Polly to enhance his claim to his uncle Samuel's property. Eber's cousin David certainly believed Eber married Polly for money. In his autobiography, David claimed Eber married Polly "in order to manage and scoop Uncle Sam's property by will or otherwise." Given that Samuel Ward's only biological child was "mentally incompetent," and E.B. was Samuel's protégé and emerging business partner, it is possible David Ward was correct. Eber understood the value of marrying into Samuel Ward's family. He even commented on it once when he declared that Jacob Wolverton's marriage to Electra Andrews took place "in order to secure as much favoritism as possible at the Brick house [Samuel Ward's home]." While it is impossible to know for certain, it is unlikely that Eber married Polly strictly to "scoop" Uncle Samuel's money; after all, the couple remained together for over thirty years. However, it is also likely that money was a factor that prompted Eber Brock to choose Polly, who was Samuel's niece and ward, as his wife. If this was true, it certainly was a shrewd move. It also would fit a pattern that governed much of Eber B. Ward's behavior over the years. He often made calculated decisions, many of which were quite ruthless, that served his own economic self-interest.[28]

## Whig Politics

About the time E.B. was expanding his business interests, he became interested in politics. He and his uncle Samuel were staunch supporters of the Whig

Party, which emerged in the 1830s in opposition to the policies put forward by President Andrew Jackson. In November 1837, during a spirited election, E.B. arrived at Newport just in time for every man in his crew to vote the "Whig ticket"; it is unclear if the crew members were pressured to vote for the slate of Whig candidates. Samuel Ward was agitated when E.B. arrived on the *General Harrison* so late. He feared the votes of Eber and his men might be lost. E.B. was eager to depart after the votes had been cast, but Samuel would have none of it. The ship remained in port until after the election results could be tallied.[29]

One of the main areas of E.B.'s frustration in regard to politics involved the chaotic Michigan banking system. The chaos had its origins in President Andrew Jackson's war on the Bank of the United States. Jackson and his supporters in the Democratic Party believed the Bank of the United States empowered wealthy easterners to the detriment of the common people and those living in the West. In 1832, Jackson vetoed the renewal of the bank's charter. Although its existing charter allowed the bank to remain in operation for another four years, Jackson was determined to kill it sooner. He authorized all new government revenues to be deposited to what critics labeled "pet banks," as opposed to the Bank of the United States. The response was an expansion in the number of state banks, many of which were poorly regulated and undercapitalized. Banks issued their own notes, extended easy credit, and pumped large amounts of currency into the economy. This was one factor that influenced Michigan's land rush in the 1830s. Many settlers, as well as speculators looking to make a quick profit, took advantage of the easy credit to purchase land. Unfortunately, the easy credit and expansion of currency had a negative result: runaway inflation. In an effort to curb inflation, President Jackson issued the Specie Circular in 1836. Jackson's policies mandated that anyone purchasing government land had to pay in specie—that is, gold or silver. This requirement raised fears the president's new policy would make it more difficult for people to purchase land.[30]

Michigan joined the Union amid the controversy over the Bank of the United States and the Specie Circular. Although there were several banks in the state already, politicians in the newly formed state believed the continued expansion of the economy depended upon ensuring that residents and potential settlers had access to banks in Michigan and to easier credit. Accordingly, the state legislature passed the General Banking Law of 1837 in March to facilitate the creation of local banks throughout the state. The law permitted any twelve landowners to form a banking association as long as they completed paperwork with their county treasurer or clerk. The bank was allowed to begin operating once capital stock of at least $50,000 was raised; at least 30 percent of the capital had to be in the form of gold or silver. While the capital requirements appeared to be enough to ensure the banks would be sound, enforcement was lax and fraud was common. Forty banks opened under these regulations. Many were unscrupulous and worked to deceive inspectors: for example, lending coins or other specie between banks in advance of a state official's visit. Inspectors were shown strongboxes filled with nails, which then were topped with gold and silver coins to make it appear as if the bank held enough gold and silver to maintain its operations. In the short run, these "wildcat banks" prospered, but the house of cards upon which the system relied eventually began to topple. Numerous banks failed and depositors lost their savings; it was a mess. Ultimately, according to historian Susan E. Gray, the General Banking Law "had the effect of destroying Michigan banking for the better part of the 1840s."[31]

Eber Brock's correspondence is littered with complaints concerning wildcat banks, the lack of sound currency, and corrupt politicians. In early 1838, he declared Michigan's banking problem "will long be remembered for the imbecility of the Legislature that passed the law—and of the wickedness of these wholesale swindlers who grasped at the vile machine to ruin and oppress the simple and heedless laborer." Later that year, he expressed concern because "banks are failing in rapid succession and the prospect is that few, if any, will weather the storm." He had confidence only in chartered institutions, such as the Detroit City Bank.[32] Due to the nature of their business, Eber Brock and Samuel took as payment cash or notes from numerous institutions within and outside of Michigan. The actual value of these varying currencies could fluctuate tremendously from day to day. To address the issue of fluctuating currencies, over the years, they "started a relative [Gleson F. Lewis] in business as a 'curb-stone broker.'" He specialized in finding the best way to exchange "'wild-cat' and 'red dog' currency" of questionable value to receive as much in return as possible. Lewis was one of many members of their extended family who worked for Eber and Samuel Ward. He eventually established his own office in Detroit. In later years, Ward even served as a director on the board of the Second National Bank of Detroit in an effort to facilitate his banking needs.[33]

Eber Brock continued supporting the Whig Party through the late 1830s. He was attracted to the party due to its opposition to Jackson's banking policies and its promotion of a development agenda friendly to business. Among other issues, the Whigs supported a high protective tariff and funding for internal improvements to enhance the nation's transportation infrastructure. These policies aligned with Ward's belief that the government should be supportive of American business interests. The Democrats were favored to win in the election of 1838 and Eber observed, "Locos feel stiff & saucy enough, their prospect is too good. . . . I feel afraid for the result." He often used the nickname, common at the time, "Loco" or "Loco Foco" to refer to the Democrats. The Loco Focos, a segment of the Democratic Party originating in New York City, earned the nickname during a party meeting at Tammany Hall in 1834. A group sympathetic to the plight of workingmen used the newly available friction matches, called "loco focos" or "Lucifers," when party regulars cut the lights during a meeting in an attempt to silence their cause. Thus these radicals within the Democratic Party were labeled Loco Focos. The name stuck. The Loco Focos would remain an influential part of the Democratic Party for the years to come. While members of the group took pride in their name, individuals such as Eber Ward used it mockingly.[34]

By 1840, prospects of a Whig victory in that year's presidential election grew. The economy continued to suffer from the financial controversies of the 1830s in what began as the Panic of 1837. Many blamed Democratic president Martin Van Buren, who had succeeded Jackson in the White House, for their financial woes. E.B. felt enthusiasm for the Whig ticket, particularly after he attended a political rally at Fort Meigs, where the Whig candidate for president, William Henry Harrison, delivered a rousing speech to a throng of supporters. Eber described the event as "a great one—and a more orderly and respectable assemblage of human beings probably never met in the United States." Throughout Harrison's speech, "the close of every sentence was responded to by the assembled crowd with cheers that made the ground tremble." E.B. was excited as "the hurrah is on one side, Matty [President Martin Van Buren] is short of friends, the Locos are discouraged, thousands are deserting their ranks and the 4th of next Nov. will tell a sad story to the feeble hopes of a corrupt and wicked administration."[35]

It is not surprising that E.B. and his uncle Samuel would support the candidacy of William Henry Harrison, for they had actually named their flagship, the *General Harrison*, in his honor. While E.B. was excited by the prospects of Harrison's victory in the November election, he did not hold the same faith in the changes he believed necessary in the state of Michigan. He acknowledged the state legislature was attempting to bring about reforms, but "I do not expect our code of laws will be revised sufficiently for the good of the community." Harrison went on to win the presidency that November. With his victory, Eber Brock believed, "pretended democracy is on the decline." Unfortunately for supporters of the Whig Party, Harrison died about one month into his presidency from pneumonia after catching cold following the delivery of a long inaugural address the day he took the oath of office in March 1841. His successor, John Tyler, had numerous conflicts with members of his own political party as they accused him of abandoning their principles.[36]

E. B. Ward continued to identify with the Whig Party for many years, and later joined the Republican Party. By the 1850s Eber emerged as an effective civic leader who was willing to take action. While he never held public office, his influence was felt on many topics. His involvement in politics will be discussed in more detail in chapter 5.

## The *Huron*

As events progressed in the 1830s, Eber's business partnership with his uncle Samuel expanded. The decision to build and operate the steamboat *Huron* provides perhaps the best example of the collaboration between the two. For years, the only vessels owned and operated by Samuel Ward were sailing vessels. Steamships were expensive; often they required a collection of investors to cover costs, whereas an individual frequently could fund a schooner independently. The first steamer to operate in the upper Great Lakes was *Walk-in-the-Water*, the same vessel young Eber had ridden when he was a boy. It was built in 1818 and carried passengers to and from ports such as Detroit and Buffalo until it was wrecked in 1821. While steamships were faster and did not have to rely on prevailing winds for power, Samuel Ward was not initially interested in owning one due to the substantial cost. Samuel hesitated to become involved in steamships until he chose to make a small investment in the *Michigan* with Oliver Newberry, one of Detroit's leading businessmen. Newberry owned several vessels and operated a large warehouse of goods in Detroit. George Catlin, historian and librarian of the *Detroit News*, labeled Newberry the "Admiral of the Lakes" and identified him as Detroit's first millionaire. Samuel's partnership with Newberry to operate the *Michigan* began in 1833, shortly after Eber Brock came to work for his uncle. This timing of these two events may have been coincidental, but it is possible young Eber persuaded his uncle to invest in the relatively new enterprise of steamships as he noticed his uncle's schooners were slowly losing business to the increased number of steamers on the Lakes. Samuel already was a successful businessman, but at nearly fifty years old, he had become reluctant to take risks. In subsequent years, his nephew Eber consistently sought out the latest innovations. Maybe it took Eber's prodding to convince his uncle to take this step.[37]

Samuel's investment in the steamship *Michigan* proved to be so successful he decided to embark on the construction of a similar vessel with his nephew as a partner. Construction on their first steamer began in February 1838. Eber Brock informed his father, "We are about commencing a small steam boat at this place for the Detroit and St. Clair trade." He estimated it would cost about $14,000 and planned to "take as much stock as I can conveniently." In addition to his uncle Samuel, Eber's uncles Zael Ward and Amasa Rust also planned to invest. Eber believed he could purchase at least $500 or $600 in stock at that time, but he hoped to invest more in the future.[38] Unfortunately, it would take nearly two years to finish the vessel. In December 1838, Eber Brock observed the progress on the ship's construction and declared, "She is a good specimen of modern boat building and fully satisfies our expectations." At that point, over $4,500 was invested in the *Huron*, but Eber believed they would require an additional $2,500, not counting the engine.[39]

It would take another year to secure an engine for the *Huron*, but in the meantime, E.B. oversaw a successful shipping season in 1839; he estimated in early 1840 that he held assets of $4,845 ($127,472.61 in 2020 dollars), with $980 in liquid cash. Undeniably, his partnership with Uncle Samuel had become very lucrative. When he visited Detroit in January 1840, he "found the engine for the boat progressing nicely." By March, it was nearly ready and Eber expected

The *Huron* was the first of many steamboats operated by Samuel and Eber B. Ward. (Courtesy of the Historical Collections of the Great Lakes, Bowling Green State University)

it to be "as fast as any of the small boats in these waters and as well guarded against fire." In May, Samuel took the ship, full of soldiers and provisions, for a test run to Mackinac. While Eber was still trying to determine the best way to ensure the *Huron*'s steadiness, it already had begun its inaugural shipping season, which would provide its owners with significant profit.[40]

The final cost to build the *Huron* was $16,520. E. B. Ward eventually invested $2,000 in the ship. Samuel Ward was the largest investor at more than $8,000. Samuel had other debts as well and clearly served as the senior partner in the pair's relationship. As the *Huron* was near completion, Samuel grew concerned he may have overextended himself. Eber related to his father, "Uncle feels afraid he will not be able to get along with his debts coming due in June and I am willing he should think so." In reality, E.B. had "full faith" Samuel could easily meet these debts, but he was hoping to squeeze a little money out of his uncle. Anxious for money, Samuel had offered to sell the *General Harrison* for $3,000 cash, but there were no offers. E.B. offered to purchase five-eighths of the ship for $1,200, but Samuel turned him down. Because E.B.'s father had some cash to spare, Eber asked his father to "oblige me by making a proposition to me when you write again saying you will give at the rate of $2,500 (for the whole vessel). . . . The prospect of cash may have some influence on the acquisitiveness of Uncle S——." In other words, E.B. thought his father might be able to purchase the ship outright for only $2,500 or Samuel might be encouraged to sell E.B. five-eighths of the ship for his original offer of $1,200. The prospect of cash payments, particularly when Samuel was nervous about repaying his loans, might prompt him to agree to the proposal. Furthermore, Eber Brock wanted to hide the fact that he possessed some extra cash from his uncle; as he confided to his father, "It will operate to my disadvantage if they know I am flush" with money.[41]

Such comments from Eber Brock provide a window into how his business mind operated. He was calculating and detail orientated, even when dealing with his own partner and family. He consistently worked to devise new ways to increase profits, even if the steps he undertook would lead to marginal returns or cost savings. In 1840, there was a shortage of cash money; E.B. and his father had liquid cash, and Eber explored ways to use this to his advantage by leveraging one of their assets to increase their capital. When considered under this single set of circumstances, the money he could potentially make was small, but if applied on a larger scale, it could increase profitability by a large amount. Samuel Ward's holdings were vast. He likely had a fortune worth more than $300,000, but much of his assets were tied up in ships and other properties. He would not suffer if he had to pay a little interest on a loan; in fact, some of his anxiety could have been lifted if he accepted one of the offers Eber and his father were discussing. At the same time, Eber's actions are terribly unsettling, particularly since he was actively attempting to deceive his uncle, the man who had mentored him and welcomed him as his partner. One wonders why Eber would attempt to "nickel and dime" his uncle for such small sums of money. While it's true he wasn't trying to outright steal from his uncle, his actions clearly were deceitful. But Samuel had been absent or unable to work due to illness for long stretches of time. Meanwhile, Eber was assuming more day-to-day oversight of their operations. It is possible Eber came to resent his uncle's absences. The following June, E.B. once again conspired with his father: "I have now on hand a considerable sum of money that I do not want to use and I shall not want to keep it to protect uncle's credit." Instead, he wanted to loan it to Samuel, but suggested to his father, "He will be more willing to pay you interest than he would me. I do not wish him to know that I have any on hand—but you can write to me that you have, say $300 to lend and say you will send it to me at Detroit where I can get it & let Uncle have it on interest."[42]

This appears to be an example of Eber Brock making calculated financial decisions designed to benefit himself, although in this case he also hoped to benefit his father. Likewise, it reflects the special and very close-knit relationship between the trio of Mr. Ward, Emily, and Eber Brock. Maybe Eber was trying to repay his father and sister for the $1,500 they had provided just a few years previously when the *General Harrison* lost its cargo and had to be repaired. In the past, Mr. Ward had advised Emily to "put implicit confidence in none but your own family." It is likely that Eber Brock received similar guidance from his father, and he believed the family tie with his father and sister was of more value than the tie to his uncle. In subsequent years, Eber Brock seemed to reinforce this closeness with his father; when faced with a business problem, he confessed, "You are the only person to whom I am willing at present to give such an opinion."[43] Regardless of his motivation, Eber Brock's correspondence clearly shows he was willing to deceive his uncle Samuel in an effort to improve himself financially. This would not be the last example of his ruthless business practices.

Once the *Huron* was fit for duty, it was placed on the "through trade" from Buffalo to Detroit, with the possibility of going on to Chicago. Eber Brock served as captain. The *Huron* was relatively small for this route. An exhaustive study undertaken in 1839 by the German railroad engineer Franz Anton Ritter von Gertsner showed that the largest twenty-five ships operating on the Great Lakes had an "average capacity of 364 tons" and had cost $50,000 to build. Furthermore, the dimensions of the smallest ship included in his study (the *Charles Townsend*) were 136 feet in length, 24 feet wide, with a depth of 10 feet. The *Huron*'s capacity was 147 tons and cost $16,520; with a length of about 117 feet, width of 18 feet, and depth of 8 feet. E.B. and his uncle Samuel hoped the *Huron*'s speed would make up for her smaller size.[44]

In preparation for his trip to the Whig Party convention in Ohio at Fort Meigs, Eber Brock was looking forward to "an opportunity of trying the speed of our boat" against several others, declaring, "Our boat has improved within the last three days about two miles per hour." At the convention, the *Huron* was very competitive, defeating several ships in a race, but was outpaced by another vessel, the *Erie*. Over the course of the summer, Ward continued to push the *Huron* and believed she was gaining speed. By August, Captain Eber observed, "Our boat runs fast & I think will beat the *Erie* in a short race." E.B. probably pushed so hard with the racing because he was competitive, but it also provided valuable publicity. According to historian T. J. Stiles, boat racing in this era "created a craze for competition" and "captured the public imagination, as each vessel attracted dedicated adherents." Newspapers described the races and the speed of each steamship while crowds attended the competitions. Although Stiles was commenting on the intense rivalry on the East Coast, positive publicity for the newly launched *Huron* would surely lead to increased revenues, so E.B. worked hard to improve the speed of his vessel.[45]

The *Huron*'s placement on the Buffalo to Detroit route was somewhat surprising. Not only was it smaller than other steamships, the *Huron* faced stiff opposition from the Lake Steamboat Association, a cartel formed in 1839 by the owners of thirty steamers in response to the increased competition in the 1830s. Due to the high profitability of the industry, between 1836 and 1838 the tonnage of ships engaged in trade nearly doubled on the Lakes, from 9,017 to 17,429. As more ships became involved, competition drove the price of freights downward. The association was formed to eliminate competition and ensure profits. A board of directors headquartered in Buffalo managed it. They were empowered to determine rates for passengers and freights and required members to observe coordinated schedules. Initial arrangements called for two daily trips from Buffalo to Detroit, one leaving during the day and one at night. The steamer assigned to the night passage continued to Chicago on alternate days. Ships were expected to complete a round-trip voyage from Buffalo to Detroit in six days, or sixteen days from Buffalo to Milwaukee and Chicago.[46]

As the sailing season progressed in 1840, the *Huron* began a brisk business. The *Huron*'s speed and the low fare Eber charged cut into the profits of the "Steamboat Combination," as critics referred to it. An article in the *Daily Cleveland Herald* later described the situation. "The managers of that powerful monopoly [the Lake Steamboat Association] saw in Capt. Ward the elements of a dangerous rivalry, and resolved to 'subdue' him," but E.B. and Samuel were determined to continue their ship on the disputed line. Eber was willing to discuss matters, but declined to be intimidated by the combination. Eventually, following a spirited negotiation, a contract was developed between the association board members and Eber and Samuel. The Wards agreed to take the *Huron* off the Lake Erie route in return for a payout of $10,000 ($263,101.35 in 2020 dollars). This was a large sum of money, but not unheard of for the increasingly cutthroat steamship industry. It is possible the $10,000 was paid over a series of years. Steamship associations operating on New York's Hudson River in the same era also engaged in price setting and occasionally paid significant sums of money to ship owners to abandon specific routes. For example, in the aftermath of a furious fare war with the Hudson River Steamboat Association, Cornelius Vanderbilt received the sum of $100,000 plus a yearly payment of $5,000 to leave a route to Albany. The stakes in the Hudson River traffic were much larger than that of the "through traffic" from Detroit to Buffalo, but they show how the concept of paying off rivals to maintain a monopoly was not unusual in the steamboat industry.[47]

The *Huron* may have been removed from Lake Erie, but that did not mean the ship was idle: it was placed on the St. Clair River route. This meant Eber would captain the ship as it traveled from Detroit and along the St. Clair River to Newport, Port Huron, Goderich, Ontario, and other smaller ports as necessary. He was busy that summer, commenting, "My time is about all occupied as I am confined to the boat & running to Goderich takes all of Sunday." The ship did a brisk business the rest of the year, finally earning a dividend of $3,520 ($92,611.68 in 2020 dollars). It remained on the St. Clair route the following year as well. In addition to transporting passengers and freight, Eber made a brisk business towing vessels. Eber predicted there was enough potential profit that "one boat can be constantly employed next year towing." Additionally, the *Huron* was contracted to serve as a light ship, or a temporary floating lighthouse, outfitted with a light positioned at the top of its mast along with bells and whistles to warn of impending danger when the fog became dense. By November, the river business was "quite dull" but once again, the *Huron* produced a handsome dividend for its owners: $3,250 ($85,507.94 in 2020 dollars).[48] See table 1 for specific details concerning the ship's finances.

## TABLE 1. Steamship *Huron* finances

| Year | Cost ($) | Stock ($) | Cash receipts ($) | Expenses ($) | Dividends ($) |
|------|----------|-----------|-------------------|--------------|---------------|
| 1840 | 16,520 | 13,000 | 8,246 | – | 3,520 |
| 1841 | | | 11,023 | 7,773 | 3,250 |
| 1842 | | | 10,009 | 8,709 | 1,300 |
| 1843 | | | 10,843 | 6,943 | 3,900 |
| 1844 | | | – | – | 2,340 |
| 1845 | | | – | – | 3,400 |
| 1846 | | | – | – | 3,500 |
| 1847 | Sold for | | | | 4,000 |
| | Total revenues | | | | 25,210 |
| | Original cost of boat | | | | 16,520 |
| | Net profit | | | | 8,690 |

*Source*: Ledger Private Accounts, 1849–1866, 18, Eber Brock Ward Papers, Burton Historical Collection, Detroit Public Library.

Over the following two years, the *Huron*, captained by Eber Brock, operated in Lake Michigan in coordination with the state's Central Railroad, which was under construction. Passengers took the train from Detroit and traveled westward until they arrived at the end of the railroad, which was planned to be completed at St. Joseph. Until the rail line was completed, migrants finished the next leg of their journey via stagecoach. Once they reached St. Joseph, they embarked on the *Huron* to complete their voyage. Not only did the Wards partner with the Central Railroad to transport passengers, they also secured the contract to carry mail between St. Joseph and Chicago. The state's Central Railroad was superseded by the privately financed Michigan Central Railroad in 1846, but the partnership with the Wards to transport the mail and passengers continued. It was a mutually beneficial enterprise for both partners for many years to come.[49]

Running the *Huron* between St. Joseph and Chicago proved to be a lucrative business for the Wards. Even if the passenger service and freights were light, a portion of the Wards' costs was always covered by the funds received from the mail contract. Although the enterprise was a financial success, it involved hard work. Writing from Chicago in June 1842, Eber related, "Our daily trips over and back the same day and night" between St. Joseph and Chicago "makes very busy work for us and gives about 11 hours in port out of 24." In the same letter, he provides a clue as to how they received the mail contract, as previous efforts to provide mail service between Chicago and St. Joseph had been unsuccessful. Chicago's harbor was problematic—while light vessels could enter the harbor easily, those with a deep draft, or those heavily loaded, often had difficulty navigating the bar. The *Huron's* shallow draft and light weight, as compared to many other Lake vessels, worked to her advantage in this case. Eber explained, "We assisted in getting off and towing in two vessels that ran ashore in the last blow." Towing vessels that were stuck on the sandbar provided another opportunity for Eber to charge for the ship's services and thereby increase revenues.[50]

Eber often traveled the route between St. Joseph and Chicago as captain of the *Huron*. At times, he left the ship to check on business back at Newport or Detroit. Feedback from government officials concerning the mail was positive; as Eber commented, "Prominent post office agents here . . . talk quite favorable to me in relation to our mail contracts." As time went on, business continued to improve. Revenues were so generous, in fact, that beginning in 1844, the Wards launched a new and much larger ship, the *Champion*, which replaced the *Huron* traveling between St. Joseph and Chicago. Meanwhile, the *Huron* returned to its previous route along the St. Clair River where it operated on and off until it was sold in 1847. An advertisement in the *Detroit City Directory* for 1846 indicated the *Huron* sailed on a fixed schedule that season, led by Captain E. L. Rose, between Detroit and Port Huron. Mondays, Wednesdays, and Fridays it left Port Huron at 8:00 a.m.; Tuesdays, Thursdays, and Saturdays it left Detroit at 9:00 a.m.[51]

An incident involving the *Huron* demonstrates the extent to which Eber Brock would use ruthless tactics to defeat his business competition. A banker named Mr. Truesdill was a frequent passenger on the *Huron*, as he was doing a great deal of business in both Port Huron and Detroit. At the time, the steamboat traveled regularly between the two communities; it took two days to complete the round trip. One day, Truesdill suggested to Ward that he should receive a free ticket, since he was making so many trips on his ship. According to Dr. E. D. Burr, who was familiar with the incident, Eber "replied that he 'couldn't see it.' Mr. T. said he would try to make him see it." Shortly thereafter, another ship was advertised to run between Port Huron and Detroit the same day as Ward's ship. E.B. contacted the ship captain and suggested this new ves-sel could go up the river the same day his went down, in order to complete a daily line. Ward was informed the ship's schedule would not be altered and that Mr. Truesdill "intended to run him off the river." Ward prepared for a fight and humorously challenged, "I think you will have a good time of it."[52]

Ward immediately asked several merchants with whom he did business to exchange any notes they held for Mr. Truesdill's St. Clair bank. After acquiring a large sum, Ward called at the bank several days in a row and demanded to be paid in specie (gold and silver) in return for the notes he held. Shortly there-after, Mr. Truesdill confronted E.B. and inquired why he was doing this. Ward replied, "I intend to run on your line just so long as you do mine." Truesdill eventually backed down and ended his competition with Ward. The interaction with Truesdill provides an example of how Captain Eber was willing to instill fear and intimidate a rival to protect his business interests. By employing such practices, E.B. and his uncle Samuel were able to conduct a virtual monopoly on the St. Clair River trade.[53]

It is possible that Eber's hard-nosed business tactics went too far. In 1841, there was an attempt upon the lives of both Samuel and E. B. Ward in what Eber described as the "Powder Plot." The apparent mastermind of the scheme was Henry A. Caswell, a Newport tavern keeper. Caswell's motivation remains unclear, but his plot was hatched sometime in early October when he paid some men $100 each to place two kegs of gunpowder in the cellar of Samuel Ward's home and another two kegs under Eber's home. A witness familiar with events related that the plotters then were directed to "fix a train thereto and place a slow match to it that would burn out in fifteen minutes from the time it was set on fire and explode at 12 o'clock at night on the 27th of Oct[ober]." Additional gunpowder was purchased to set fire and blow up other buildings owned by Samuel and Eber, as well as the *Huron*. Fortunately, the plan fell to pieces when one of the criminals involved was apprehended, but not before one of Eber and Samuel's warehouses was destroyed by fire.[54]

As one would expect, Eber was incensed. He was convinced Caswell was behind the conspiracy and was determined to seek justice and vengeance. Describing those involved as "rogues and blacklegs," he declared to his father that if he got his hands on Caswell, "the next letter you receive from here you may expect to hear of . . . some lynching." Ultimately, at least one of the men involved received a twelve-year prison sentence. Caswell also ended up in prison, but it is unclear how much time he spent behind bars. Eber and Samuel were victims of this potentially deadly plot, but there must have been a reason why Caswell and his accomplices would take such drastic measures to attack the Wards. Unfortunately, the record of their motivation is lost to history, but Eber or his uncle must have done something to rile such anger. Eber's furious response is understandable, but his willingness to meet violence with violence by suggesting he would lynch Caswell represents a dark side to his personality. In the past, he had taken aggressive steps to protect his monopoly on the St. Clair River traffic and had even deceived his uncle Samuel for profit. Possibly the best insight into Eber's character provided by the event was his desire to take action himself to resolve the situation, as opposed to waiting for the authorities. Throughout his lifetime, he was a man of action who took matters into his own hands to resolve a crisis; he was never one to wait for others to act.[55]

## A Year in the Life of the *Huron*

Eber and Samuel's investment in the *Huron* proved to be a great success; it was in many ways the foundation for the Wards' expanding line of steamships. Records from the mid-nineteenth century are not always available; fortunately, a ledger recording each trip undertaken by the *Huron* in 1844 has survived, providing a window into the operation of a small steamship in this era. The *Huron* began its navigation season that year on April 14 as it traveled from its winter home in Newport to Detroit. Over the course of the next eight months, the *Huron* would make 200 trips, each centered on the key city of Detroit; the most common was from Detroit to Port Huron. That season, the *Huron* completed 134 voyages (or 67 round trips) between the two cities (via car today, this would be 63 miles each way). The second most common route, involving 52 voyages (or 26 round trips), was much further; it stretched from Detroit to Goderich, Ontario (via car today, this would be 139 miles each way). The ship would stop at many additional local ports along the way, as needed, to pick up passengers, freight, or wood. Samuel Ward is identified as the captain for the first 27 trips. It is unclear who captained the ship on the following voyages, but it is possible that he continued as captain, though he may have partnered with one or more others to share the work.[56]

The business began slowly in April, with only twelve trips, but it nearly doubled by May to twenty-three and peaked in July and October with twenty-eight each. Between July 1 and October 31, the ship was idle only 13 out of 123 days. The most popular customer was Reuben Moore; his name appeared on ninety-six trips included on the ledger. In some cases, he was listed more than once for a specific voyage, as he sometimes was registered as a passenger and also shipped some freight, but more often, he was charged for freight alone. Moore must have been a fur trader or trapper, as he often was charged for shipping animal hides. For example, on a voyage from Detroit to Port Huron on June 4, Moore was charged for nineteen hides (4 cents each), twenty-two calf skins (2 cents each), and five barrels (25 cents each), for a total of $2.45. Apparently, he did not accompany his freight on this trip. In addition to passengers, the *Huron* regularly transported a range of different items. Examples include, but are not confined to fish, salt, flour, beer, potatoes, wheat, potash, horses, oxen, nails, and lumber. On June 29, one traveler was charged $7.50 for thirty barrels of salt and $5.46 for ninety empty barrels.[57]

A set amount was charged for freight as well as passengers. Full barrels, whatever they were filled with—fish, wheat, salt, and so on—cost 25 cents; half barrels were 13 cents. Those who transported animal hides paid 4 cents for each, while a side of leather was 2 cents. Passengers were charged 25 cents if they chose to purchase a meal. They paid $1.75 for passage between Detroit and Port Huron; the fare between Detroit and Goderich was $2.50, but passengers rarely traveled the full distance. Often, they stopped at Port Huron, Lexington (Michigan), or another smaller port along the way. Reuben Moore or one of his associates was often left at "Moore's place." Most male passengers were identified by their full name, although the popular Mr. Moore was usually recognized as "R. Moore." Women were sometimes identified by name, but more often, their identity was lost and they were described simply as "Lady." A married couple with the last name of Gurney was traveling July 4 from Detroit to Goderich. Their names were entered into the ledger as "James Gurney & Lady G." Others were identified as "Sailor," "Boy," "Lady and girl," or even by their ethnicity—such as "Irishman," "two Scotchmen," "Dutchman," "Frenchman," "Indian"—or were identified by their religion and/or profession: "Catholic," "Catholic Clergyman," "Dutchman Peddler."[58]

Early in the season, primarily in April and May, the *Huron* made additional money towing other ships, such as the *Asa Wilcox* on April 29. Its owner was charged $10 to have his vessel towed "up the rapids" as it traveled from Port Huron to Detroit. Towing picked up again in the fall. Charges varied depending upon the size of the vessel to be towed and the distance traveled. The brig *Robert Hunter* was charged $20 on November 18 while the steamer *Emigrant* was charged $200 on November 6—the largest single charge for anything that season. Interestingly, twenty-two trips were made in November, historically a month filled with storms on the Great Lakes. However, this was the month with the largest total receipts: $1,166.92. Freight was heavy this month because the crops were harvested in the fall and provisions were required for the winter. Shipping shut down for three to four months each winter. It would be difficult to send or receive any items, meaning distant settlements became even more isolated. The *Huron's* last voyage of the year was undertaken on December 9; after that, the ship likely was put away for the winter. For specific detail on the *Huron's* voyages each month, see table 2.[59]

### TABLE 2. Monthly trips for the *Huron* in 1844

| Month | Number of trips | Total receipts ($) |
|---|---|---|
| April | 12 | 360.17 |
| May | 23 | 785.30 |
| June | 26 | 943.97 |
| July | 28 | 1,039.48 |
| August | 26 | 763.14 |
| September | 27 | 1,101.46 |
| October | 28 | 1,023.22 |
| November | 22 | 1,166.92 |
| December | 8 | 477.76 |
| Total | 200 | 7,661.42 |

*Source*: *Huron* Ledger, Samuel Ward Papers, Burton Historical Collection, Detroit Public Library.

The *Huron* may have been the first steamship Eber Brock and Samuel Ward built together, but it would not be the last. Over the course of her seven-year sailing history, the *Huron* paid its owners dividends of over $21,000; by the time it was sold in 1847 for $4,000, its total revenues reached $25,210. Subtracting the original cost of the boat, the *Huron's* net profit was $8,690 ($245,130.87 in 2020 dollars).[60]

# Conclusion

Eber Brock Ward's life was transformed between the time he began to work for his uncle Samuel in 1832 to the launching of the *Huron* in 1840. He began as his uncle's employee, emerged as his protégé, and then became his partner. Just as the state of Michigan expanded its population and achieved statehood in 1837, the partnership between Samuel and Eber provided each with tremendous financial success. Eber's relationship with his uncle was a key to his advancement, but in this era he also married and maintained close ties with this father and sister Emily. We also see some examples of the ruthlessness of Eber's business activities; he even went so far as to deceive his own uncle and benefactor, Samuel Ward. The "Powder Plot" demonstrates some of the conflict the partners experienced and Eber's response showed his instinct to act, rather than allow others to intercede on his behalf. Once the steamboat *Huron* was launched in 1840, there was no going back for the Wards; they would build and run one steamboat after another in the 1840s and 1850s, expanding their growing steamship empire to develop one of the largest fleets operating on the Great Lakes.

# 3

## Steamboat Kings

*There cannot be any doubt of the business shrewdnesss of*
*Capt. Sam Ward, but it is just as evident that in this line he was*
*discounted by his nephew Eber, and would not have amassed the*
*wealth he did had it not been for the stirring qualities of he who*
*afterward became one of Michigan's most prominent citizens.*
—Rev. Thompson, November 18, 1881

The success of the *Huron* convinced Eber and Samuel to continue investing in additional steamboats. Eber oversaw this expansion of their fleet as he assumed more control over the partnership with Samuel, while his uncle increasingly considered retirement. The expansion, while a risk, was profitable. Their success was due in part to connections Eber developed with the Michigan Central Railroad, but E.B. also effectively lobbied government officials to receive favors and to reduce regulations on their operations. Although Eber spent countless hours overseeing the business, he also took time to appreciate museums and unique architecture. This represented his continual thirst for knowledge, which was distinctive, given that his formal schooling was so limited. Operating their fleet of ships could be complicated, and although the Wards possessed a strong reputation for safety, tragedies involving their vessels did occur on the Great Lakes. Over time, additional traits in Eber's character emerged, such as an intense competitiveness, which helps to explain his motivation to amass a large fortune. When Samuel Ward died in 1854, Eber Brock lost a partner and mentor. However, Eber inherited his uncle's fortune, worth as much as $1 million, a vast sum of money in that time period. By the time of Samuel's death, the pair had owned and launched fourteen steamers and boasted what was reputed to be the largest fleet of vessels on the Great Lakes. Eber and Samuel had truly become Steamboat Kings.

## Expanding the Fleet of Steamers

The profits from the *Huron*'s first two years of operation exceeded Eber's and Samuel's expectations. The $10,000 buyout from the Lake Steamboat Association and profits from the *Huron* provided Eber and Samuel Ward with enough capital to build an additional steamboat, and they continued to add another nearly each year. This reinvestment of profits back into business operations was a pattern that would govern E.B.'s business practices throughout his entire career. Work on their second steamer, the *Champion*, commenced as early as the summer of 1842, just two years after the *Huron* was launched. The *Champion* was constructed in Newport, but the engine was purchased in New York. It was commissioned in August 1843, partway through that year's shipping season, at a final cost of $22,500. The *Champion* was much larger than the *Huron*, with a length of 145 feet and a capacity of nearly 270 tons. Initially, it was placed on the through trade between Buffalo and Detroit, in opposition to the Lake Steamboat Association. Its members protested that the Wards had violated their previous understanding not to run on this route. However, the only vessel identified in the initial agreement had been the *Huron*. While E.B. and Samuel were ready to entertain offers to vacate the trade once again, no payment was offered by the Steamboat Association board. Furthermore, it is likely they had another vision in mind for the *Champion*. In 1844, it replaced the *Huron*, which had been operating on Lake Michigan the previous few seasons, taking passengers to and from St. Joseph, Michigan, to Chicago.[1]

The *Champion* operated on Lake Michigan for two years and then continued on additional routes over the next several years. In its time of service for the Wards, between 1843 and 1851, the ship earned a handsome profit of $62,668 ($1,978,031.85 in 2020 dollars).[2] Those profits from the *Champion* lay the foundation for the tremendous fleet of ships constructed by E.B. and his Uncle Samuel over the next several years. Each of the next five years following the *Champion*'s initial launch in 1843, E.B. and Samuel built and operated a new vessel: the *St. Louis* (1844), the *London* (1845), the *Detroit* (1846), the *Sam Ward* (1847), and the *Pacific* (1848). These vessels were much larger than the *Champion*. The smallest was the *Detroit* at 352 tons and the largest was the *St. Louis* at 618 tons.[3] At various times, individual ships operated on routes on Lake Erie and/or Lake Michigan, but some would be placed on a bold new venture entered into by Eber and Samuel Ward.

In the early and middle 1840s, a rush of prospectors flocked to Michigan's Keweenaw Peninsula of Lake Superior in search of copper. It was not unlike California's famous gold rush of the late 1840s. Interest had been sparked by a report submitted to the state legislature in 1841 by Dr. Douglass Houghton indicating there were significant deposits of copper along portions of Lake Superior's shoreline. The rush peaked in 1846 as copper hunters sought quick wealth while fighting the elements in Michigan's Upper Peninsula. Eber Ward, always ready to take action on a perceived business opportunity, capitalized on the burgeoning interest in the region by creating the Ward Lake Superior Line. This fleet of vessels was fashioned in preparation of the increased traffic Eber envisioned between Detroit and Sault Ste. Marie. It was a gamble that would pay dividends for many years. The flagship for the new line of steamers was the *Detroit*, and Eber Brock served as its captain. The ship made its initial voyage between Detroit and Sault Ste. Marie in 1846. An advertisement in the *Detroit Free Press* that May captured the energy linking the new vessel to the exciting copper rush. "The splendid new Steamer *Detroit*, Capt. E. B. Ward, leaves this morning at 8 o' clock for the Sault Ste. Marie (or copper mines). The *Detroit* is one of the fastest and strongest boats on the Lakes." The *Detroit* was still operating on the line in 1850, making regular round trips each week between Detroit and Sault Ste. Marie.[4]

Events progressed so well that in 1849, the Wards ushered in another new era in their fleet of ships with the steamer *Atlantic*, the largest—and most expensive—vessel the partners had built up to that time. The *Atlantic* was 267 feet long and 33 feet wide with a tonnage of 1,155; its cost was $105,000. It represented the Wards' entrance into the so-called age of the palace steamer. According to historian Joel Stone, *palace steamer* was a "romantic appellation

Launched in 1849, the *Atlantic* was Ward's first palace steamer, known for its elegance and speed. Just two years later it would be involved in a deadly disaster on the Great Lakes. (Courtesy of the Historical Collections of the Great Lakes, Bowling Green State University)

adapted to the megaships" of the 1840s and 1850s. It referred to the "largest, purpose-built, side-wheel or stern-wheel passenger vessels of post-Jacksonian America. More than twice as long as most other vessels—longer than a city block—the Great Lakes version stood out gloriously in any harbor. . . . Nearly all were topped with two smokestacks set athwart the ship and employed a walking beam engine." The first palace steamer on the Great Lakes, *Empire State*, was nearly 300 feet in length. Others included the *Western World* and *Plymouth Rock*, two of the largest steamboats in the world.[5]

Construction of such large steamers was a reflection of American society in that era. Americans sought to create an identity independent from Europe. Intellectuals such as Ralph Waldo Emerson encouraged a new generation of writers to leave European standards behind with orations such as "The American Scholar." Many in the United States looked to the west as the nation expanded its boundaries to the Pacific Ocean. In addition to overland routes such as the Oregon Trail, travelers ventured westward on large passenger steamers, built to accommodate the tremendous numbers of native-born Americans and recently arrived immigrants as they journeyed to lands in the Midwest or along the Pacific coast. Furthermore, the rich and poor alike sought new and exotic forms of entertainment in the 1840s and 1850s. P. T. Barnum opened his American Museum, which included curiosities and oddities, and also sponsored a popular traveling show featuring performers with a range of talents. Large cities boasted theaters catering to those who wished to experience their entertainment in comfort and elegance. The interior of palace steamers sometimes imitated these facilities, with their spacious cabins known for their beauty and opulence. At times, steamship lines competed with one another to produce the most stylish and sophisticated vessels.[6]

The *Atlantic* was the Wards' contribution to the genre. In 1849, it transported passengers and freight between Buffalo and Detroit on Lake Erie. An article in the *Detroit Free Press* in May 1849 described the *Atlantic* as a "splendid steamer" and "a fine craft, designed expressly for passengers, . . . [that] can accommodate 300 well, in her cabin. The owners and public may be justly proud of her as an ascension to our Lake Commerce." The ship was propelled by a low-pressure engine, built in New York, of great capacity, which included a "60 inch cylinder, 11 feet stroke with two boilers 10 feet in diameter and 34 feet in length." It also was very fast. In its inaugural year, it established a new speed record, taking only sixteen hours and thirty minutes to complete the voyage from Buffalo to Detroit. Passengers traveled in luxury. The ship included two cabins below the main deck. One aft was reserved for "gentlemen," while steerage passengers occupied the forward cabin. The upper cabin was 240 feet long, lined with a total of seventy staterooms on either side and was recognized for its "convenience, beauty, and comfort. . . . The ground work is pure white, and the ornaments, gold moldings, and caps, imparting a very rich and pleasing effect." The roof was circular and lined with stained glass. The rooms and larger cabins included elegant furniture made of rosewood designed with intricate patterns. Plates, dishes, and glassware were manufactured in Liverpool and included a print of the boat and its name on each piece. Safety concerns also were reflected in the ship's design. The engine room could be flooded at a moment's notice to ensure "ample security against fire," and as early as the 1852 navigation season, the ship was equipped with several tin-bottomed stools that could serve

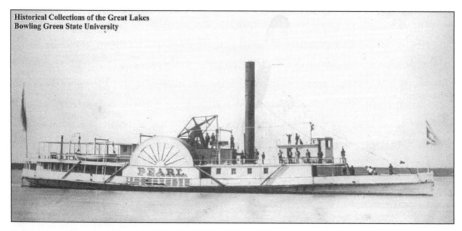

The *Pearl* was another vessel in the fleet owned and operated by Eber and Samuel Ward. (Courtesy of the Historical Collections of the Great Lakes, Bowling Green State University)

as flotation devices in case of disaster (no mention was made of the number of lifeboats).[7]

The Wards continued to construct additional large steamers in successive years, including the *Ocean* (1850), the *Caspian* (1851), and the *Arctic* (1851). Each of these vessels was built in Newport, which had a thriving shipbuilding industry known for its design and craftsmanship. Between 1820 and 1900, nearly 250 ships were manufactured in the city, where several hundred men earned good wages in the community's principal industry. The ships' hulls, masts, and cabins were constructed in Newport. Steamers then were taken to Detroit, where their boilers and engines would be installed.[8] For many years, the Wards relied on William Gallagher and Jacob Wolverton, to construct a majority of their ships. Both Gallagher and Wolverton were nephews of Samuel's wife Elizabeth. William L. Bancroft, a local resident familiar with the Ward shipbuilding operations, declared that Wolverton "was a genius in his chosen vocation." The Wards' ships always employed the latest technology and none failed. The *Ocean* was unique because the first iron originating from the Lake Superior mines was used for its walking beam. By 1852, the Wards boasted a fleet of ships valued at $475,000 ($14,992,741.58 in 2020 dollars), including two under construction.[9] For a sample of the ships owned and operated by Eber Brock and Samuel Ward in 1851 and 1852, see table 3.

## TABLE 3. Inventory of ships owned by Eber Brock and Sam Ward in 1851 and 1852

| Name | Year built | Tonnage | Value in 1851 ($) | Value in 1852 ($) |
|---|---|---|---|---|
| *Champion* | 1843 | 266 | 8,000 | |
| *St. Louis* | 1844 | 618 | 13,000 | 15,000 |
| *London* | 1845 | 432 | − | 10,000 |
| *Detroit* | 1846 | 352 | 18,000 | 15,000 |
| *Sam Ward* | 1847 | 433 | 22,000 | 25,000 |
| *Pacific* | 1848 | 462 | 25,000 | 30,000 |
| *Atlantic* | 1849 | 1,155 | 60,000 | 60,000 |
| *Telegraph* | 1849 | 181 | 10,000 | 10,000 |
| *Ocean* | 1850 | 1,052 | 75,000 | 75,000 |
| *Pearl* | 1851 | 251 | 20,000 | 20,000 |
| *Caspian* | 1851 | 921 | 90,000 | 90,000 |
| *Arctic* | 1851 | 861 | 50,000 | 60,000 |
| *Huron II* | 1852 | 348 | − | 23,000 |
| *Tecumseh* (propeller) | | | | 7,000 |
| Two new boats unfinished | | | | 35,000 |
| Total value of ships | | | 391,000 | 475,000 |

*Sources*: Ledger Private Accounts, 1849–1866, 28, 66, Eber Brock Ward Papers, Burton Historical Collection, Detroit Public Library; Jenks, *History of St. Clair County*, 1:405, 406; Great Lakes Collection, GLMS 101—Kenneth R. Hall Collection at Bowling Green State University, Eber Brock Ward, box 1, folder 31, Research Notes: vol. 14, vessels owned by Ward family.

## Eber's Ambitious Leadership

The consistent expansion and success of the Ward fleet of ships in the 1840s and 1850s was due almost entirely to the energy and vision of Eber Brock Ward. As the number of ships and complexity of the Wards' business activities increased, the involvement of Samuel Ward conversely decreased, although he occasionally spent time in the shipyards, offering his thoughts on new vessels under construction. However, his contributions lessened over time and he left the operation of the steamship lines to Eber Brock. When the *Champion* was launched, Samuel was on the eve of his sixtieth birthday. St. Clair County historian William Jenks argued that at that time, Samuel "naturally was becoming more conservative, but Eber B. brought to the firm an optimism, push and vigor which were irresistible." Samuel hoped to retire to his brick mansion in Newport and leave the stress and long working days behind. At one point, he asked Eber to buy him out. Samuel declared he did not need much, requesting "only enough to live on." No settlement was reached. Samuel simply turned more of the active oversight of their joint holdings over to Eber. It's possible that Eber refused to settle and provide his uncle with "only enough to live on" because he did not want to abandon his aging uncle and benefactor. However, it is more likely that Eber did not buy out his uncle because his vision of their partnership required his uncle's resources. Eber wanted to create one of the largest fleets of ships on the Great Lakes—perhaps *the* largest. This required him to consistently reinvest each year's profits back into the construction of larger and more elaborate vessels. If he had purchased half the value of the ships and other assets they jointly held, he would not have had the capital necessary to expand the fleet in the manner he envisioned.[10]

Eber's tremendous energy enabled him to remain alert to new ways to save or make money, resulting in many additions to his business enterprises. For example, during the winter of 1841–42, he sought to corner the market on wood in Newport. With the expansion of steamboats operating on the Great Lakes, the demand for wood, the preferred form of fuel, escalated. On average, a ship might consume one cord of wood for every four miles it was running. For one round-trip voyage of 720 miles between Buffalo and Detroit, that could mean a ship might consume 180 cords of wood. Often, ship captains would stop at smaller ports to drop off or pick up passengers, but they also did so to replenish their supply of wood. In January 1842 Eber noticed the price of wood was exceptionally low and there were very few harvesting it that winter. He considered, "I shall make an effort to get as much wood into my possession and control as I can." His goal was to acquire 2,500 or 3,000 cords so he could "control the price after the middle of July." He estimated it would cost between $6 and $8 to buy a cord of wood and place it near the docks. He then planned to sell it for $12 per cord during the heart of the shipping season when demand for wood was at its height.[11]

Another factor contributing to Eber's financial success involved the relationship he shrewdly cultivated with the Michigan Center Railroad. Eber was the driving force as he worked with the rail's general council, James F. Joy, and superintendent, John W. Brooks. Most other steamship operators viewed the railroad as competitors. Instead, Eber recognized the advantage not only of cooperating with the railroads but of linking the rails with his shipping business. The Michigan Central received its charter from the state in 1846 with the charge to construct a rail line from Detroit west to a terminus along the Lake Michigan shoreline. Ultimately, Joy and Brooks hoped to extend the line through to Chicago. Eber knew that once this line was completed, he would lose freight and passengers to the railroad, but the project to construct the rail line would take several years to complete. Meanwhile, there was a great deal of profit to be made by developing a partnership. Therefore, he chose to collaborate, rather than to compete, with the railroads.[12]

The alliance between the Michigan Central and Ward steamers was complicated, and it evolved over time. Initially, in 1846, the partners coordinated efforts to facilitate travel between Detroit and Chicago. An advertisement for the Michigan Central Railroad in the 1846 *Detroit City Directory* announced that a train car would leave Detroit every morning at 8:00 a.m. By 6:00 p.m. passengers would arrive in Kalamazoo, where they would be taken by coach to St. Joseph. From there, they would be transported "by Capt. Ward's boat *Champion*, built expressly for this route to Chicago, 70 miles in 5 hours, weather permitting." The entire journey, from Detroit to Chicago, a distance of 270 miles, could be completed in about thirty hours.[13] By 1850, the alliance was expanded to facilitate travel from Buffalo all the way to Chicago and Milwaukee. Travelers could board one of three vessels (*May Flower*, *Ocean*, or *Atlantic*) in Buffalo, from which they would cruise to Detroit and then be transferred to a train car, which they would ride to New Buffalo. From there, they connected with one of the line's steamers (*Canada*, *Pacific*, or *J. D. Morton*) and traveled to Chicago or Milwaukee. The Michigan Central advertised it had "a continuous line from Buffalo to Chicago and Milwaukee [that was] safe, expeditious, comfortable, and cheap. Travelers by this, instead of the Lake, or Mackinac route, save 500 miles distance and 2 1/2 days' time."[14]

Eber Ward's relationship with the Michigan Central's John Brooks and James Joy was unique. According to an article in the *Daily Cleveland Herald*, the complicated business agreements between the men often involved millions of dollars, yet their "transactions were all based on a verbal agreement between Mr. Brooks, the Superintendent of that road and himself [Eber Brock Ward]. No written contract ever existed between them, each relied upon the honor and integrity of the other, and neither were disappointed."[15] Communication between Ward and Brooks was just as important as the coordination of their complex operations. In a detailed letter Brooks wrote in 1848, he stressed the importance of organizing their activities and cooperating with one another because "where there is business to do, there are people enough to do it." Brooks suggested the partners should coordinate their activities on Lake Erie by creating a line of three boats traveling "on the shortest route without stopping between Detroit and Buffalo." Another line "should go on the South shore, stopping at the principal ports and should consist of five boats." Many of Brooks's proposals were adopted. For example, three ships eventually were placed on the northern line. The Wards built two boats while the Michigan Central purchased one.[16]

To facilitate the complex operations and enhance the relationship with the Michigan Central, Eber moved to Detroit in 1850 with his wife and children.

Ward's vessel the *Reindeer* docked next to a warehouse owned by E. B. Ward. (Courtesy of the Historical Collections of the Great Lakes, Bowling Green State University)

Samuel remained in Newport. This move was both symbolic and strategic. It was symbolic because it signified Eber's business activities had grown to the extent that he was required to relocate to Michigan's largest city and commercial center. It was strategic because it allowed him easier access to his associates at the Michigan Central. By the early 1850s, Eber maintained two offices in Detroit; one was located in the Michigan Central Railroad Depot, indicating the special nature of his relationship with the railway.[17]

Under the forceful and innovative management of E. B. Ward, the number of steamboats owned and operated jointly with his uncle Samuel steadily increased, as did their profits. By 1851, they operated twelve steamboats, which earned a profit of $240,444.03 ($7,589,295.17 in 2020 dollars). In a testament to the value of the relationship between the Wards and the Michigan Central Railroad, the four ships with the highest level of profit were linked to the railway's operations. These included the *Ocean* and *Atlantic*, which transported passengers from Buffalo to Detroit on Lake Erie, while the *Arctic* and *Pacific* operated on Lake Michigan between New Buffalo and Chicago.[18] See table 4 for specific details concerning receipts and disbursements for their ships operating in 1851.

## TABLE 4. Receipts, disbursements, and profits for steamers in 1851

| Name | Total receipts ($) | Total disbursements ($) | Net profit ($) |
|---|---|---|---|
| Arctic | 52,992.68 | −28,221.46 | 24,771.22 |
| Atlantic | 112,886.41 | −64,424.05 | 48,462.36 |
| Caspian | 16,362.44 | −12,286.25 | 4,076.19 |
| Champion | 14,227.13 | −9,539.17 | 4,687.96 |
| Detroit | 27,369.04 | −12,792.22 | 14,576.82 |
| Morton | 17,213.76 | −14,800.64 | 2,413.12 |
| Ocean | 106,636.95 | −54,875.76 | 51,761.19 |
| Pacific | 70,354.89 | −32,228.41 | 38,126.48 |
| Pearl | 8,558.32 | −7,663.55 | 894.77 |
| St. Louis | 46,406.51 | −22,401.65 | 24,004.86 |
| Sam Ward | 43,246.92 | −19,981.60 | 23,265.32 |
| Telegraph | 7,047.72 | −3,643.98 | 3,403.74 |
| Total | 523,302.77 | −282,858.74 | 240,444.03 |

*Source*: Ledger Private Accounts, 1849–1866, 64–65, Eber Brock Ward Papers, Burton Historical Collection, Detroit Public Library.

The steamers represented the greatest capital investment and yearly profits for Eber and Samuel Ward, but they were not the only assets the partners owned. The Ward ledgers provide a detailed understanding of their holdings. The value of all their properties jointly owned in 1852 was $555,800 ($17,543,085.83 in 2020 dollars). In addition to their ships, they owned Michigan Central Railroad stock valued at $27,500 and maintained an inventory of $12,000 in "goods and provisions" at their warehouses. The entry outlining their combined assets for 1852 also makes clear that by that year, or earlier, Eber Brock and Samuel were equal partners: "E.B. & Samuel Ward's Property, Owned on Equal Joint Account." The ledger also indicates that Eber had an additional $7,000 in assets, independent from his uncle. These included a home and lot in Detroit, property in Newport, and stock in a farm.[19] See table 5 for more detail.

### TABLE 5. Eber Brock and Sam Ward properties owned on equal, joint account

| Asset | Value in 1851 ($) | Value in 1852 ($) |
|---|---|---|
| Ships | 391,000 | 475,000 |
| Land, machinery, stocks, and other properties | 60,500 | 80,800 |
| Total value of all assets | 451,500 | 555,800 |

*Source*: Ledger Private Accounts, 1849–1866, 28–29, 66–67, Eber Brock Ward Papers, Burton Historical Collection, Detroit Public Library.

## Eber's Travels and Competitiveness

Although Eber devoted the bulk of his energy to business activities, he also took time to pursue additional interests. Often, he was able to combine business with pleasure. While on a trip to New York to purchase supplies in October 1840, he visited many of the city's sites. His trip included a visit to a museum where he marveled at the skeleton of an old elephant, viewed large alligators, snakes, and many additional items he found thrilling and strange. While at the museum, he had his skull examined by British phrenologist George Combe. "I had my skull overhauled again," Ward wrote to Emily, admitting this was not his first exposure to phrenology. "He gave my character more accurate than any other professor that has examined it." Interest in phrenology, the study of the skull to determine an individual's intellectual capabilities and character traits, was growing in the United States in the 1840s, and George Combe was "the most prolific British phrenologist of the nineteenth century," according to researcher John van Wyhe. Phrenologists claimed to have special knowledge about people, and their readings have been compared to those of psychics or mystics. Later in life, Ward would become deeply involved with spiritualism. His interaction with Combe represents Eber's interest in the field of clairvoyance when he was in his late twenties.[20]

Eber continued his tour of New York by visiting many of the city's public buildings. He was impressed with the "many grand theaters," but declared that "there is nothing in the city to compare in beauty, strength or expense with the new Custom House," built entirely of stone and iron. Ward also was impressed with the Custom House's interior, dominated by white marble. He described the Merchant's Exchange as another "elegant & costly building," but was unimpressed with the Astor House. It was very large, and visitors could look out over much of the city from its top, but the view was an unappealing series of housetops and chimneys, with only an occasional church steeple or spire to please the eye. He visited the harbor as well. Ward acknowledged the vessels were large and seaworthy, but he also observed, "I have seen no boats equal [to] our lake boats for strength and beauty." He was critical of New York City's residents, observing, "All species of business is carried on here," including "swindling, robbing, stealing, trading, etc. etc. all to great perfection."[21]

Over the next decade, as his fleet of ships increased along with his wealth, Ward was required to visit other cities to look after his business interests. Often, these trips took place during the winter months, following the close of the shipping season. In December 1842, he traveled between Detroit and Washington, DC, and informed his father, "I have spent all my leisure time in examining the natural and artificial curiosities in the several cities—months could be spent in this way." He professed, "The Patent Office alone would occupy a close observer many weeks." He preferred Philadelphia to the nation's capital, calling the city "neat, chaste, new, and in all respects superior in appearance to those of any other city." He labeled Washington, DC, the "seat of corruption" but admitted the Washington Monument, which was under construction, to be a "handsome ornament."[22] In January 1850, he commented on a New York museum's "beautiful representation of the river Nile and the interesting monuments along its banks." While growing up, Eber did not have much of a formal education, but as an adult he was a voracious reader with an appetite for knowledge, particularly of history and technology. His comments over the years on such topics represent an individual who was interested in the world in which he lived, rather than someone narrowly focused on his own activities.[23]

While he considered Washington, DC, the "seat of corruption," Eber's travels regularly took him there, as he sometimes lobbied to protect or enhance his business interests. Ward had previously garnered the contract to transport mail between St. Joseph and Chicago, but at times, due to lack of business, his ships failed to transport the mail across Lake Michigan, and he was fined. In December and early January 1843, Ward met with the postmaster general seeking to have his fines waived. He also lobbied to receive an increase in pay for his mail contract. His efforts were partially successful. He informed Emily, "I was not successful in my efforts to get my mail pay increased, but made other desirable arrangements," including the elimination of the fines. Another example of Ward's successful lobbying came in 1850. That year's navigation season had been particularly deadly. The most famous disaster came when the steamer *G. P. Griffin* caught fire in Lake Erie, resulting in the deaths of 286 passengers and crew. As a result, Congress considered legislation to improve safety on the Great Lakes by requiring steamers to carry additional lifeboats. Ward traveled to Washington, DC, in an attempt to block this legislation because it would significantly increase his costs and limit the number of passengers and freight his ships would be able to carry. In a letter to J. W. Brooks, he described his efforts. "I have arrived here just in time to save us the trouble from carrying twelve to fourteen boats on our large steamers. Congress is determined to punish all of us for the loss of life on the Lakes." While Ward was successful in his lobbying efforts, the lack of lifeboats on vessels likely led to an increased loss of life. His actions avoided an increase in costs and allowed for higher revenues, but were detrimental to the overall safety of passengers and crew traveling on the Great Lakes.[24]

Politically, Ward continued to identify with the Whig Party. Whigs supported an active government to promote legislation such as higher tariffs to protect American businesses and federal funding for internal improvements such as canals, roads, and harbors to develop the nation's transportation network. As the conflict over slavery escalated, Whigs also opposed slavery's expansion.

Ward was drawn to and maintained his allegiance with the party due to these issues. Following the sudden death of William Henry Harrison in 1841, his vice president, John Tyler, a former Democrat, assumed the presidency. Tyler was an advocate of states' rights and vetoed legislation funding internal improvements, putting him at odds with others in his party. Clashes with other Whigs continued during his administration, and Tyler eventually was disowned by the party. Ward was opposed to President Tyler's actions. While in Washington, DC, in December 1842, Ward received an invitation to visit Tyler in the White House. Initially he refused. As he informed his father, "I had an invite to go to the president's last evening. But, I declined going as I dislike the man, and of course, he don't care a fig for me."[25]

Ward's traveling companion on this visit to the nation's capital was William Duane Wilson, the general superintendent of lights on the northwestern Lakes. Wilson eventually persuaded Ward to meet with the president. Ward recalled, "I was induced by Mr. Wilson to visit the president. He received us very politely." The meeting left Ward somewhat sympathetic to the embattled president. He observed that President Tyler "looks much more care worn and I think his disappointment wears on his mind. I cannot envy him."[26] Eber and Samuel Ward developed a close working relationship with Wilson, over the next several years, even allowing Wilson to live in one of Samuel Ward's homes. As a result, Eber confided to his father that Wilson "will be considerable help to us in many matters." While the full scope of Wilson's "considerable help" is unclear, Wilson did facilitate the transfer of Eber Ward Sr. from the lighthouse keeper's position on Bois Blanc Island to Fort Gratiot during the summer of 1843. The posting at Fort Gratiot was more attractive to Mr. Ward due to its proximity to family and friends in the area of Newport. It is also likely that Eber and Samuel lobbied Wilson for additional favors to benefit their shipping interests. It is unlikely that Ward would have recognized the hypocrisy of labeling Washington, DC, the "seat of corruption" while simultaneously allowing Wilson to move into Samuel Ward's house, presumably in return for Wilson looking after Eber's and Samuel's business interests.[27]

In addition to politics, Eber Ward at times commented on religion. Eber's grandfather David Ward had been a Baptist minister. Although Eber often attended church services and eventually identified as a Unitarian, he was skeptical of those who professed their faith for the wrong reasons. When a religious revival created excitement and a flurry of new converts in Newport, he informed Emily, "Many of the basest characters . . . have left off getting drunk, gambling, cheating, etc. for a short time." While he hoped their change in behavior would be permanent, he feared "a relapse into former habits." Ward remained convinced "the hard times make people religious. Hundreds have joined the churches here who in flourishing times thought of nothing but money."[28]

As Eber became more successful with his business enterprises, he voiced his contentedness, although with some underlying contradictions. In January 1840, Eber expressed personal happiness and "universal joy of the day" to Emily as he reflected on the start of a new year. "I have everything that is necessary to make a man happy and I think I am quite content—I do most of my own chores, saw wood for the fires, feed my cows, read the news when it gets here and visit my neighbors when I wish." At the time, he had just turned twenty-nine, was in the third year of his marriage, and had one son. That winter he also was on the eve of launching the *Huron*, his first steamboat. Three years later, in 1843, he wrote to his sister again, reflecting on his financial situation and the true cause of happiness. He and Emily, along with their father, had struggled financially in the past, yet he did not believe money brought contentment. Instead, he declared, "I am firmly persuaded in the conviction that those who have the most *real* friends, those who are friends in all weathers under all circumstances are the happiest men—Wealth, and station cannot make a man happy."[29] Following the discovery of gold in California in 1848, he expressed concern over the "millions of wealth in the vaults of a few, rendering many happy and thousands miserable." Both passages written by Ward confirm his belief that money does not buy happiness. Yet he was working day and night during the navigation season to build a business empire worth a great deal of money; $500,000, by his own estimation.[30]

At this point in his life, Ward was not necessarily driven to succeed by a goal to amass a large fortune for himself so he could live an extravagant lifestyle. In fact, he criticized as "foolish" a woman who spent money frivolously on clothing and jewelry in an attempt to show off her wealth. Instead, Ward was driven by an intense competitiveness. He wanted to build a successful business second to none, crushing any competition that came across his path. His rivalry with the Steamboat Combination and his actions to defeat a competitor who attempted to run his steamer *Huron* off the St. Clair River route offer good examples of his competitive nature. A series of races between Ward's steamer *Ocean* and the *Empire State* in 1851, when he was thirty-nine years old, provide additional insight into Ward's character and motivation.[31]

The steamer *Ocean*, launched by Ward in 1850, was placed on the Buffalo to Detroit route as part of the connection with the Michigan Central Railroad line. The *Ocean* and the *Atlantic* were Ward's two palace steamers. In 1851, Eber Ward challenged the rival palace steamer *Empire State* to what historian Joel Stone labeled "the World Series of steamboat races." A contemporary observer described the race as "the most thoroughly contested, exciting and spirited contest in a trial of speed between steamboats which I ever witnessed."[32]

The contest began on a Wednesday evening in April 1851. The initial challenge was a race from Cleveland to Buffalo. The prize was $10,000 but, more important, the winner would receive bragging rights. At 7:00 p.m., the *Empire State* left Cleveland's harbor for Buffalo. The *Ocean* gained on her and eventually pulled ahead, completing the journey of some two hundred miles in eleven hours and fifteen minutes, twenty-nine minutes ahead of the *Empire State*. The officers and owners of the *Empire State* declared it had not been a fair contest as their leader, Captain Hazzard, had not been on board. A second race was conducted the following evening, this time from Buffalo to Cleveland. For more than one hour, the boats were side by side, but the *Ocean* pulled ahead and reached Cleveland thirty-four minutes ahead of its rival. Following the arrival of Captain Hazzard, a third contest was arranged to settle the matter conclusively. The day of the final race both crews worked to prepare their vessels to reach top speeds. When the steamers embarked, shortly after 7:00 p.m., spectators lined the shoreline for more than a mile; many had waged bets on their favored vessel to win. A little more than one hour into the contest, the *Ocean* pulled into the lead, eventually arriving in Buffalo eighteen minutes ahead of the *Empire State*, with a time of ten hours, forty-eight minutes. For some time, the owners of the *Empire State* had claimed their boat to be the fastest on the Lakes, but the *Ocean* emerged as the new champion, having defeated its rival three times in a row.[33]

Throughout the entire conflict, Eber Ward served as the primary aggressor, becoming belligerent at times. The Saturday prior to the series of contests, Ward had challenged Captain Hazzard to race the *Empire State* against the

*Ocean*, and Ward promised he "would continue to do so until the end of the week." Ward implied Hazzard was a coward who manufactured excuses for his defeats and "always claimed a victory after his boat was beaten, and that one whipping was not sufficient to satisfy him." Ward finished by declaring, "If Capt. Hazzard should refuse to acknowledge *the corn* if fairly beaten, I will run a boat in opposition to his until he does so." (Common in the nineteenth century, the expression "acknowledge the corn" meant to acknowledge or admit to a mistake or misdeed.) Ward's interactions with Captain Hazzard were very public. The initial challenge was made in front of several witnesses and the insults were included in a letter to the editor of the *Detroit Free Press*. That Ward would engage with Captain Hazzard and the owners of the *Empire State* in such a public manner shows he could be terribly antagonistic toward anyone he perceived as an adversary. During each race, he stood in the engine room ensuring the steamer was operating at maximum capacity, as the boilers were pushed to their very limits. Ward even placed sailors armed with mops down in the hold to mop out the bilge water to eliminate any ounce of extra weight that might slow his vessel's progress. He would stop at nothing to defeat a rival in a steamboat race. He applied the same cutthroat attitude when he faced business competitors in the future.[34]

The victory of the *Ocean* brought Eber the prize money of $10,000. He distributed half the amount to his crew and donated the other half to charity. Furthermore, his ship was awarded a broom, signifying the superiority of the vessel. It was purely symbolic, but in later years a broom became a symbol for his iron- and steel-producing blast furnaces. Historian Bernhard C. Korn observed, "For years thereafter, whenever a furnace completed a successful blow, and after the molten iron had been poured, a large steel broom was hoisted to the top of the structure." Residents of Milwaukee and Chicago, where E. B. Ward's steel mills were located, grew accustomed to seeing the broom, indicating his furnace had completed a successful "clean sweep."[35]

## The *Atlantic* Tragedy

The ships operated by Eber and Samuel Ward were known for their speed, but they also earned a reputation for being safe and reliable. In fact, for nearly two decades, they never were involved in a serious accident involving the destruction of a vessel or loss of life. Unfortunately, the partners lost three ships in 1852. The steamer *Caspian*, valued at $90,000, was tied to a pier July 1 outside Cleveland's harbor. The ship came loose from its moorings during a sudden and violent storm. As the wind continued to sweep it brutally against the pier, the crew was unable to safely resecure it, and the vessel broke in half. Other than the engine and boilers, which were salvaged, the ship was a total loss. The *St. Louis*, an older steamer valued at $15,000, was wrecked off the coast of Sandusky late in the shipping season. According to an article in the *Detroit Free Press*, it was dashed to pieces during a storm, "leaving nothing of her wreck but a few timbers." Although losing the two steamboats was costly financially, the destruction of the palace steamer *Atlantic* was devastating, given the loss of life involved with the wreck of this vessel.[36]

At approximately 2:00 a.m., August 20, 1852, the *Atlantic* was cruising from Buffalo to Detroit on Lake Erie when it was struck by the propeller *Ogdensburg*, heading north toward Canada. Within thirty minutes of the collision, the *Atlantic* would sink. Immediately following the crash, J. Byron Pettey, captain of the *Atlantic*, made toward shore, hoping to run the vessel aground to prevent loss of life, but the engines became flooded and stopped. This left the steamer stranded in the water. Between 500 and 600 passengers and crew were crowded onto the *Atlantic*, along with their baggage and other traveling goods. A large number of passengers, about 130, were immigrants, primarily from Norway, but some also came from Germany. About 250 passengers and crew died in the horrible disaster, making it one of the deadliest in the history of the Great Lakes.[37]

In the aftermath of the collision, there was tremendous confusion aboard the *Atlantic*. Most of the vessel's passengers had been asleep before being awakened by the loud crash and commotion. The crew attempted to calm the passengers, issuing commands to follow safety protocols, but a large number could not understand English. Some jumped into the water directly following the crash; most who did so drowned. While attempting to lower one of the *Atlantic*'s lifeboats into the water, Captain Pettey fell eleven feet and hit his head, cutting it badly and suffering a concussion. This led to even more confusion as the crew attempted to manage a life-threatening situation without the ship's leader.[38]

There were several instances of terror and heroism involving the passengers and crew. Survivor Amund O. Eidsmoe, a passenger on board the *Atlantic* who had left his home in Norway and was on his way to begin a new life in Manitowoc, Wisconsin, recalled that when the *Ogdensburg* first struck the *Atlantic* "we were awakened by a loud crash and saw a large beam fall down upon a Norwegian woman of our company. It crushed several bones and completely tore the head off a little baby that lay at her side." Panic set in as water rushed into the steerage cabin where so many immigrants had been crowded together. As people rushed from one end of the boat to the other, Eidsmoe and his family were able to escape; after "much swimming around with my wife and children on my back, we were picked up by the other ship." Luckily, after the *Ogdensburg's* crew realized the *Atlantic's* distress, the ship circled back to save several passengers stranded in the water.[39] According to an article in the *New York Times*, Mr. Dana, one of the crew of the *Atlantic*, "was very efficient in saving the lives of passengers and exhorted them to cling to life preservers, when in the water." Unfortunately, he was lost when he "took a settee and jumped overboard," only to be followed by twenty or thirty others who jumped over him—he went under. When the *Atlantic* was sunk other than her stern, one of the last individuals to leave the boat was Mr. Givan, the clerk. As he prepared to jump, Givan heard the voice of a young boy who was clinging to a rope. "The little fellow, talking to himself, was saying 'Oh! I can't hold on much longer. If papa was here, he would hold me up.'" A nearby passenger heard the boy and seized him as he was about to sink. Givan helped to alert a nearby lifeboat and the eight-year-old boy was saved.[40]

Subsequent investigations assigned blame to the crews of both the *Ogdensburg* and *Atlantic*. De Grass McNell, the first mate of the *Ogdensburg*, testified that he first saw the *Atlantic* when she was about three miles away from his ship. When she changed course he feared she would cross the bow of the *Ogdensburg* as she came closer. He ordered the engines to be stopped and then reversed. Under cross-examination, he admitted that if he had given the order to reverse sooner, the collision would not have taken place. Additionally, it was reasoned that if the *Atlantic* had altered its route when the crew first observed the *Ogdensburg*, the collision could have been avoided. The *Daily American Telegraph* summarized the initial inquiry into events, which placed primary responsibility for the tragic events on the *Ogdensburg*. "Last night evidence was brought forward which strongly inculpates the officers of the propeller *Ogdensburg*, leaving no doubt that she violated the rules of navigation." The paper also reported, "The *Atlantic* was well provided with life preservers."[41]

A majority of the catastrophe's survivors, however, blamed the captain and crew of the *Atlantic*. A few days after the disaster, several met and passed a resolution criticizing the "inefficiency of so-called life preservers, which are totally useless." They expressed indignation at the insufficient number of lifeboats and accused the vessel's owners, Eber and Samuel Ward, of "gross neglect and criminal misconduct." Eber Ward called for an investigation to determine what had happened. He also defended his crew in the *Detroit Free Press*, declaring, "They could not have done more, and all acted like heroes." In a private letter to his wife, he wrote, "The calamity is a dreadful one for many of those on board." He also argued, "The Propeller [*Ogdensburg*] was entirely in the wrong." While sympathetic to those who lost their lives, he continued, "They could nearly all have been saved if they had been calm and self-possessed. But, they rushed overboard without the least consideration. Many of them taking cane seat stools, instead of life preservers, and of course, found them useless."[42]

Eber Ward continued to defend his crew in a letter to the *Detroit Free Press* on August 28, 1852, eight days after the disaster. He argued if the *Ogdensburg* had "put her wheel aport" or if "her engine had been stopped one minute" earlier, the collision could have been avoided. He declared the *Ogdensburg*'s crew acted "contrary to all law and well established custom, rendering the collision inevitable." He also defended the safety devices available on his steamer. "The *Atlantic* had on board her ample means for sustaining every person." In addition to a yawl boat and two lifeboats, there were "two hundred fifty stools with airtight double tins in the bottom." He also defended his safety record, reminding readers this was "the first and only disaster involving loss of life, that has ever occurred on any of our boats." Ward additionally pointed out his personal financial loss would be at least $75,000 and declared the "calamity was not our fault."[43]

Ellett Titus, a survivor of the *Atlantic* disaster, responded directly to Ward's letter with his own. He questioned the actions of the captain and crew, but was particularly critical of the ship's life preservers, or tin stools, mentioned by Ward. The night of the accident, Titus took one with him into the water but discovered "it was of no assistance to me whatsoever—worse than useless and I am willing to swear to the fact that I saw a dozen persons jump overboard with those Stools in their hands and drown." He also criticized Ward's complaint about financial losses: "I consider neither his loss [of money], or my own, is of any moment when put in comparison with the many invaluable lives that so miserably perished."[44]

Ward's combativeness emerged as he would not allow Titus to have the final word on the issue, even though Titus was a survivor of a great tragedy. Ward's defensive response in the next day's *Detroit Free Press* appeared to blame the victim for using the tin-stool life preservers improperly. Ward argued that any "reasonable man" should be able to understand how to use the life preserver effectively and was willing to wager Mr. Titus, or anyone else, up to $500 to test the preserver. No one took him up on his offer. Given the panic and the communication problems, it was inevitable that numerous passengers would be unable to follow commands or understand how to properly identify and use the life preservers. Others mistakenly gathered the cane stools, thinking they were flotation devices. Unsurprisingly, Ward's response to Titus did not include Eber's visit to Congress just two years earlier when he successfully lobbied to limit the number of lifeboats on steamers operating in the Great Lakes. Could more passengers have been saved had there been additional lifeboats on board the *Atlantic* the night it was struck by the *Ogdensburg*? The answer to that question will never be known.[45]

In later years, Eber Ward refused to publicly comment on the tragedy. No criminal charges ever were brought against the crew of either vessel. The Wards did file a formal complaint arguing the *Ogdensburg* was at fault. The Northern Transportation Company, owner of the *Ogdensburg*, filed its own suit, blaming the *Atlantic*. Ultimately, the courts ruled both boats were at fault and the damages should be equally divided. Because the *Atlantic* was much more valuable than the *Odgensburg*, the Wards were awarded damages of $41,200 in 1859, bringing to a close litigation that had been ongoing for several years.[46]

Despite the *Atlantic* disaster, Ward continued to move forward to expand his shipping empire in the Great Lakes. This is further demonstrated by his work to promote a canal to facilitate the passage of ships into Lake Superior. His efforts, along with those of many others, resulted in the opening of the Soo Locks in 1855.

## Soo Locks

The rapids of the St. Mary's River had been a barrier to navigation between Lake Superior and the lower Great Lakes for many years due to a geologic event that left Lake Superior twenty-one feet higher in elevation than Lake Huron. The elevation drop in the St. Mary's River, which connected the two lakes, occurred in a short, narrow, three-quarter-mile stretch of the river, with rock ledges and turbulence making navigation difficult, if not impossible. At the time of European contact, the Ojibwa (commonly referred to as Chippewa) were famous for their ability to fish in the dangerous waters of the St. Mary's River. Fur traders from the North West Company built a small lock in the 1790s to allow canoes and other small vessels to travel between Lake Superior and the other lakes. In 1837, the State of Michigan became interested in a canal enabling ships to enter Lake Superior in hopes of promoting a potentially lucrative fishing industry. Unfortunately, progress halted when conflict arose with the national government as the canal's proposed route ran through a military reservation. After the discovery of copper in Michigan's Upper Peninsula in the 1840s, E. B. Ward became a champion of a canal to traverse the treacherous waters of the St. Mary's River.[47]

Ward was not alone in his support for a canal, but funding remained a major obstacle to its construction. The issue of federal funding for internal improvements such as canals, railroads, and harbors divided many politicians. In 1847, supporters of federal aid for such projects gathered in Illinois for the Chicago River and Harbor Convention. The meeting was called, in part, because of President James Polk's opposition to a Rivers and Harbors Appropriations Bill, which he had vetoed the previous year. Over ten thousand individuals descended on Chicago, including interested citizens, members of the news media, and politicians from the Democratic and Whig Parties. Eber Ward was unable to attend the convention, but paid close attention to its proceedings, and his longtime associate William L. Bancroft served as a delegate. Although the meeting did not have an immediate impact on legislation, it was important because it brought together a group of like-minded individuals who would work together in the future to secure federal funding for internal improvements in their states. It also raised the awareness of eastern capitalists whose investment would prove crucial to the development of such projects.[48]

When Millard Fillmore, a member of the Whig Party and former delegate to the Chicago Convention, assumed the presidency in 1850, supporters of internal improvements mobilized to secure funding for projects in their respective states. Ward served as a key member of a delegation from Michigan that spent much of the winter of 1851–52 in Washington, DC, lobbying for legislation favorable to a canal. Others involved in the lobbying efforts included Sheldon McKnight, another steamboat operator, and John W. Brooks, Ward's associate from the Michigan Central Railroad. Their efforts were successful. In 1852, President Fillmore signed legislation whereby 750,000 acres of public land was granted to the State of Michigan to help finance construction of the canal. This would be a "floating grant" of property that included public land in any part of the state. Eventually, a great deal of valuable public land was part of the grant. Not all of the property was of exceptional value, but some was heavily timbered pineland, and some contained valuable mineral deposits. The pinelands would have a future impact on Eber Ward's lumber holdings along the Pere Marquette River near Ludington, Michigan.[49]

With funding secured from the federal government in the form of the land grant, the State of Michigan was authorized to award a contract to a company to build the canal. James F. Joy, who had partnered with Eber Ward and the Michigan Central Railroad, lobbied to shape parameters set by the Michigan state legislature for the canal. In February 1853, a bill was passed specifying that the canal must include locks 350 feet long and 70 feet wide. A commission soon thereafter awarded a contract to build the canal to the St. Mary's Falls Ship Canal Company.[50]

Initially, Eber Ward objected strongly to the requirement the locks had to be at least 350 feet long. Historian John N. Dickinson argued, "Ward thought that 260 feet would be an adequate length—and for *his* ships, it would have been." In a letter to William Burt, a member of the Michigan House of Representatives, Ward expressed "deep anxiety" at the prospect of the locks measuring 350 feet. He believed they would be too long and contended, "The crooked, narrow, shallow and rocky channels in the St. Mary's River will forever deter the largest class of steamers from navigating these waters." Ward also was concerned that if the locks measured 350, rather than 260 feet, the cost of construction would increase substantially and the money raised by the sale of Michigan's public land would not be enough, in which case the project might never be finished. Ultimately, Ward was proven wrong. When the locks were completed, they did measure 350 feet, and those became too small, even for Ward's own ships, within just a short time. Despite Ward's initial reservations, both he and Samuel became stockholders in the St. Mary's Falls Ship Canal Company.[51]

Construction on the canal began in earnest during the spring of 1853 under the supervision of Charles T. Harvey, superintendent of construction. Eber Ward had met with Harvey at least once before on one of Harvey's visits to Detroit. Presumably, the two collaborated on the best way to secure public funding for the project. The work to construct the Soo Locks was difficult. Harvey consistently dealt with a lack of supplies and men to complete the project. Weather conditions only allowed for a working season of approximately seven months. Workers suffered through long hours and difficult working conditions. A cholera outbreak in 1854 further decimated morale and led to the deaths of as many as 10 percent of the workforce. However, in May 1855 the project was completed, with a cost of just under $1 million. Operation of the Soo Locks passed from the State of Michigan to the federal government in 1881. It has been expanded beyond the original two locks of 350 feet each and today it is considered a marvel of American engineering. Its importance is difficult to overestimate. It allowed Lake Superior's rich beds of iron ore to be transported to the nation's steel mills. At one time, the Soo Canal handled more shipping tonnage than the Suez or Panama Canals. Each year, nearly seven thousand ships use the locks to haul 86 million tons of cargo.[52]

Eber Ward eventually purchased a great deal of valuable land that originally had been granted to the State of Michigan to fund the construction of the Soo Locks. While the land grant included some of the best timber and mineral lands in northern Michigan, initial sales of the public land were slow as a result of a financial depression in 1857 and then the outbreak of the Civil War in 1861. This forced stockholders in the St. Mary's Ship Canal Company to front much of the money used for the construction of the canal. Both Eber and Samuel Ward owned stock, but among the largest shareholders were eastern financiers. To stimulate interest in the land, a catalogue was produced in 1863 prior to a public auction, dividing the remaining property available for purchase into 744 unique parcels. The catalogue included a description and minimum price for each parcel. The land sale was coordinated under the direction of Cyrus Woodman, a veteran land agent. The last of the pinelands were not sold until 1874. But in 1864, Eber Ward completed the purchase of forty-seven thousand acres of land along the Pere Marquette River for $200,000.[53] The catalogue described the property as "one of the finest points for a large lumbering establishment on the coast of Lake Michigan" ending at what was then known as the community of Pere Marquette. Today it is the city of Ludington. The land included a "large and compact body of pine, embracing some of the best timber in the State," with "easy and natural access to the water." Ward paid an average of $4.25 per acre for the valuable parcel of land. The other pinelands at the public auction sold for an average of $2.20 per acre, signifying that the value of Ward's parcel must have been considerable. Ward would not develop the property until the 1870s, but when he did, he constructed two enormous sawmills. When he died in 1875, the Ludington mills and timbered properties constituted some of the most valuable assets included in his estate.[54]

Interestingly, Ward's purchase of this property likely put him at odds with his cousin David Ward. Both men attended the auction where, according to the *Detroit Free Press*, the bidding "was more lively than had been anticipated." David had previously surveyed the Ludington property and was familiar with its value. The cousins were intensely competitive and it was clear the property along the Pere Marquette River had the potential to make its owner a great deal of wealth. It is likely the two clashed when those parcels came up for auction. Although Eber was able to successfully purchase this property, David became a very successful timber baron in his own right, eventually amassing more than 800 million acres of valuable pineland in Michigan and a substantial fortune.[55]

## Death of Samuel Ward

Samuel Ward was a proponent of the Soo Locks and stockholder in the St. Mary's Falls Ship Canal Company, but he did not live to see the completion of the canal. Samuel's health had been poor at times over the years and as he grew older, an associate described him as "somewhat bent in form and furrowed in feature." In 1852, a group of employees presented Samuel, then sixty-eight, with a cane made from the rudderpost of the *Huron*, Samuel's first steamer. Samuel was deeply touched by the gift and often was seen with the cane walking the streets of Newport thereafter. He died only two years later, just shy of his seventieth birthday, on February 1, 1854. His obituary in the *Detroit Free Press* chronicled his lifetime of achievement. "Capt. Samuel Ward, whose name, in connection with steamboating in the west is well known throughout the country, died at his residence in Newport. . . . His death is lamented by a large number of relatives and acquaintances." The obituary also mentioned Samuel's partnership with Eber Brock and the "large numbers of steamers" owned by the pair. Samuel initially was buried in Newport, but Eber eventually had his remains relocated to Detroit's Elmwood Cemetery. The inscription on his tomb reads, "A True Sailor."[56]

Samuel Ward's will had been drawn up in 1847. It ensured his wife Elizabeth and son Jacob Harrison would be able to live comfortably in the family's brick home. Jacob Harrison was an adult, but he was cognitively impaired, so his mother, E. B. Ward, and David Gallagher, another relative, were named his joint guardians. Special provisions totaling about $5,500 in cash or property were distributed to several other individuals. Most receiving money or property were family members; others were close business associates. Eber Brock Ward received the bulk of his uncle's estate, including all the steamboats and other properties associated with their joint business operations. No inventory of the property was ever filed, so the exact value of the estate was unclear, but it was estimated to range between $300,000 and $1 million ($8,767,685.14 and $29,225,617.12 in 2020 dollars). Eber was already very wealthy before the inheritance, but after his uncle's death, he likely had assets totaling more than $1 million, making him one of the richest men in Michigan.[57]

Eber's cousin David resented the fact that Eber inherited the lion's share of Samuel's estate. David, eleven years younger than Eber, was the son of Nathan Ward, Samuel's brother. While David had been born in New York, he had lived for many years in Newport, and the cousins knew each other well. David believed Eber married Polly, Samuel's niece, simply to gain access to Samuel's money. David also charged that as Samuel lay on his deathbed, Eber "placed sentinels at the outer doors of Uncle Samuel's residence" to prevent anyone other than Emily, Eber, or Eber's lawyer to enter the house. Presumably, this was undertaken to alter the will in Eber's favor. David further charged that Samuel's will left out "entirely the sisters, brothers and other relatives . . . some of whom were poor invalids, unable to obtain the necessaries of life." Despite these allegations, the will was not contested.[58]

There had been hard feelings between Eber and David going back many years. David argued that Samuel Ward treated him and his father poorly when they lived in Newport. David even claimed that Emily slandered his character when David was working as a teacher in Port Huron. In a letter to his father in 1838, Eber wrote that the reputation of David and his family in Newport had "depreciated fast in public opinion." Eber also privately declared they were "Lying Fools." Two years later, Eber described David and his family as lazy. As adults, the two men became rivals in the lumber industry and had likely clashed over the purchase of valuable pineland along the Pere Marquette River near Ludington. David also was a member of the Democratic Party, while Eber was a Whig, and then a Republican. It is probable that their competing business interests and political views, along with the hard feelings that began in childhood, strained their relationship. While some of David's criticisms of Eber had merit, others were unfounded. For example, several of Samuel's relatives, in addition to Eber and Emily, were included in Samuel's will. Furthermore, the will that granted Eber so much of his uncle's fortune had been drawn up and finalized seven years prior to Samuel's death. Therefore, no last-minute modifications were made in Eber's favor while Samuel was on his deathbed. Ultimately, it is easy to understand David's frustration at being left out of his uncle's substantial will, but his accusations are suspect—they were published posthumously in his autobiography and were not corroborated by other family members. In the end, as he put it himself, David was forced to bitterly recognize that, as a result of the inheritance, Eber "largely monopolized" the steamboat routes for both freight and passenger service which, "fairly managed, were worth another million or two dollars"—while he received nothing.[59]

## Conclusion

When Eber Ward first began working for his Uncle Samuel as a cabin boy at the age of eleven, he certainly never could have envisioned the empire the two would build by the mid-1850s. At the time of Samuel's death in 1854, Samuel and Eber Ward had either built or operated fourteen steamers, six smaller sailing vessels, and numerous tugs. The foundation of their enormous fleet was laid with the steamer *Huron*, followed shortly thereafter with the *Champion* and numerous additional ships. As their empire grew, Eber Brock took on more of the management of their affairs as Samuel eased into retirement. Perhaps the *Daily Cleveland Herald* summarized Eber's style and accomplishments best when it declared he had the "dauntless energies of a young and vigorous mind" whose steamboat "enterprises were crowned with success."[60] As Eber moved forward following the death of his uncle, he would expand beyond the steamboat industry into manufacturing and other enterprises, thereby making him deserving of the designation Michigan's pioneer industrialist.

# 4

## A Man of Iron and Steel

*Captain [Eber Brock] Ward was the most prominent of all
the pioneer iron manufacturers of Michigan, his enterprise
in this respect extended to other States than his own.*
—James M. Swank, 1892

Years of market analysis had informed Eber Ward that traffic on some of his steamboat lines would suffer by the mid-1850s due to competition from railroads. He knew steamboats, but understood the industry was changing, and he had to change with it or become obsolete. Accordingly, Ward began to divest gradually from his operations on Lake Michigan, concentrating on his steamboat lines running between Detroit and the northern and eastern Great Lakes. Railroads arguably would be the key industry driving the American economy in the years immediately before and after the Civil War. Ward invested heavily in railroads, but he also became engaged in the iron and steel industries. Railroad construction required a great deal of iron and steel. Iron manufacturing in the United States was concentrated primarily in the East, and steel was also imported from England. Eber Ward's vision was to establish the iron and steel industry in the Great Lakes and Midwest to end American dependence on foreign imports. Additionally, he hoped to diversify the economies of states located in the "Old Northwest," which previously had been dominated by agricultural production. Ward began to manufacture iron following his investment in 1853 at a facility located just south of Detroit, in Wyandotte, Michigan. Soon, his facility became the largest employer in the region. He later expanded his operations into Chicago and ultimately into Milwaukee. Eventually, his mills produced the first Bessemer steel in the United States.

Eber Ward's success in business was multifaceted, but it was characterized by some commonalities. For years, he showed an uncanny sense of timing. He was a visionary with an ability to look toward the future and determine precisely when he should invest in a new enterprise or cut ties with a steady partner and adopt a new business strategy. His decision making was informed by careful study. Another important factor in his success was Ward's ability to partner with talented individuals, or recognize the talent in others and effectively recruit those men to work with or for him. Ward also was an excellent organizer. He employed vertical integration, whereby he maintained control over the raw materials, transportation, and manufacture of the products his mills produced. These traits, along with the driving ambition and sense of competitiveness he had previously demonstrated, facilitated Ward's expansion into iron and steel in the 1850s. He began the era overseeing one of the largest fleets of steamboats operating on the Great Lakes. Within two decades, he was a pioneer business leader in an entirely new industry that drove the nation's economy into the future.

Even as Ward expanded his business ventures, he continued to rely on his sister Emily for moral support. In turn, she relied on her brother for financial support. In 1845, she returned to Newport and established an academy for local schoolchildren. Eber funded her school, which was very successful. These actions facilitated the development of another side of his personality. Emily prompted Eber, so hard-nosed in his business dealings, to become a philanthropist. Even though he lived in Detroit, while Emily remained in Newport, the two corresponded regularly and met when possible. The bond between the two remained strong, reinforced following the deaths of several close family members, including their two sisters and father. It was in the aftermath of the loss of those close to him that Eber began to explore a movement that had gained popularity in the 1850s: spiritualism.

# Reorganizing the Steamboat Fleet

On May 21, 1852, Ward ended what had been a lucrative route on Lake Michigan transporting passengers from New Buffalo to Chicago. He acted because the Michigan Central Railroad had completed its line of tracks across Michigan and into Illinois. This allowed travelers to ride from Detroit to Chicago in comfort, without having to transfer from a railcar to a steamboat to finish their journey. For several years, Ward's partnership with the Michigan Central had been mutually beneficial, but now it was clear passenger traffic on the steamers was bound to drop significantly. Ward had been preparing to make this move for some time. He understood that once the rail line was complete, passengers would prefer to travel via train, and his steamships on that route would be seriously marginalized.[1]

For the remainder of the 1852 season, he ran a limited number of steamers between Chicago and Milwaukee and smaller ports on Lake Michigan. Ward then informed his employees that his vessels would be leaving Lake Michigan altogether. Instead, he would focus operations on Lakes Erie, Huron, and Superior. A group of eleven Ward employees jumped at the chance to form their own line on Lake Michigan. Initially, they were led by Stephen Clement, a longtime Ward employee. By the 1850s, Clement had worked his way up to serve as a ship captain who eventually married into Ward's family. Following his first wife's death in 1853, Clement married Susan McQueen, the younger sister of E. B. Ward's wife. Within a short time another Ward employee, Captain Albert E. Goodrich, formed his own line as well. Although these men no longer worked for Ward, an important business relationship developed between them. Beginning in 1853, Ward began to lease, and then sell, some of his steamboats to groups led by both Clement and Goodrich. This benefited Ward because he had a ready market for his surplus ships. Rather than having his vessels remain idle, he could make money leasing or selling them. It also benefited Clement and Goodrich because they could lease or purchase older ships while they worked to build enough capital to develop their own fleets on Lake Michigan.[2]

Although Ward temporarily abandoned his passenger lines on Lake Michigan, he continued to operate his other steamship lines. The Ward boats were popular due to their speed and high quality. Several routes were maintained and even continued into the 1870s. Most originated from Detroit. One primary line connected with the eastern end of the Michigan Central Railroad and transported passengers to and from Detroit and Buffalo as well as Detroit and Cleveland. Another included two round-trip voyages each week between Detroit and Saginaw. Advertisements in the *Detroit Free Press* indicate that Ward maintained his Lake Superior Line, which traveled between Cleveland, Detroit, and several ports on Lake Superior. This line was profitable throughout the 1850s, although for years, his most lucrative passenger runs remained between Detroit and Cleveland, and Detroit and Buffalo.[3]

Eber Ward's intense competitiveness materialized when a rival vessel, the *Canadian*, began operating on the St. Clair River in the summer of 1855. This placed the *Canadian* in direct competition with Ward's steamboat *Forrester*. For years, Eber and his uncle Samuel had held a virtual monopoly on this route, and Eber was not about to let an upstart rival steal business away from him. Shortly after the *Canadian* began running, Ward responded by lowering the regular fare from $1.75 to 25 cents. For a limited time, he even allowed certain passengers to ride free on the *Forrester*. Passengers continued to purchase tickets on the *Canadian* as a protest against Ward's monopoly, although their numbers dwindled over time. Ward defended his monopoly by arguing that in the past only one vessel out of fourteen had been able to cover its costs servicing the St. Clair River route. Meanwhile, as long as the fare remained 25 cents, the *Forrester* operated at a loss. The *Canadian* operated for a short time into the 1856 shipping season, but the low fares offered by Ward proved to be too attractive to passengers. In the short run, Ward lost money because of the rivalry with the *Canadian*, but due to the depth of his resources, he could withstand these losses. After the *Canadian* left the St. Clair River, Ward raised the fare to the original price of $1.75. This conflict with the opposing steamboat line reveals Ward's combative nature and demonstrates the steps he would take to crush a business rival. His pragmatism enabled him to protect his monopoly and the long-term profits that came with it, to the detriment of passengers who would have benefited from lower fares if the competition had continued.[4]

While the incident involving the *Canadian* demonstrates the extreme steps Ward was willing to take to maintain his monopoly, another incident shows there were limits to his ruthlessness. In 1859, a local diver in Cleveland, James Cooley, approached Ward and commented on the intense rivalry between Ward's steamers and a competitor. Cooley suggested he had a solution to Ward's problem. For a tidy sum, he could blow up the *City of Buffalo* and *Western Metropolis*, two steamers operated by his rival, the Michigan Southern Railroad. Initially, Ward thought Cooley was joking, but soon realized he was serious. After further discussion, Ward arranged to meet with Cooley at a later time, then excused himself to attend to a pressing business matter. Instead, Ward immediately sent for the city marshal, James A. Craw, and informed him of the plot. Marshal Craw encouraged Ward to continue the negotiations with Cooley to determine his exact plans. When Ward met with Cooley again in his stateroom, a witness hid under the bed and overheard the entire scheme. Cooley explained he could descend into the water and secure a torpedo to one of the ships; an accomplice would detonate the explosive several minutes later by use of a safety fuse. Ward agreed to pay Cooley $500 to carry out this plan and gave him a $25 deposit. Soon thereafter, a search warrant was issued for the homes of Cooley and his accomplice. The police discovered a large tin that could have been used as a torpedo containing twenty-five to thirty pounds of powder along with a long coil fuse. Cooley ultimately was arrested. A local newspaper commended "the shrewdness of Captain Ward," who "nipped in the bud . . . a hellish plot to blow up the magnificent steamer *City of Buffalo*, and perhaps destroy a number of lives."[5]

Ward's response to the *Canadian* showed his aggressive treatment of rivals he viewed as a threat, while his reaction to Cooley's offer demonstrated an unwillingness to use violence to counter another competitor. When it worked to his advantage, Ward also partnered with other steamboat lines. Just as he had worked with James Joy and John Brooks with the Michigan Central Railroad in the past, Ward associated with John Owen and the Detroit and Cleveland Navigation Company. Ward and Owen had a great deal in common, making collaboration seem natural and mutually beneficial. Each had been born in Canada and each had lost a parent when young. Both were Whigs and later became prominent supporters of Lincoln and the Republican Party. Owen was the leading figure in what was popularly known as the D&C Line; eventually, he was named president. Beginning in 1852 and continuing as late as 1868, Ward and Owen jointly operated several steamers, such as the *Forrest City*, *May Queen*, and *City of Cleveland*, among others, that plied the waters between Cleveland and Detroit ferrying passengers. About 1874, Ward would form his own Central and Pacific Lake Company, considered "one of the largest and most popular lines," which boasted ten first-class steamers that year serving Buffalo, Cleveland, Detroit, and Duluth.[6]

At times, Ward had so many ships in his fleet he offered special excursions for passengers interested in traveling to unique locales in the Great Lakes. In August 1853, several guests boarded the steamer *Samuel Ward* for a tour of Lake Superior. The region was still very isolated outside of a few mining communities, as this was two years prior to the completion of the Soo Locks. The passengers began their "pleasure excursion" in Sault Ste. Marie and were treated to a "bountiful supply of creature comforts" as they toured the spectacular sites and natural beauty of Lake Superior. Members of the press were also invited. It appears that Ward devised the excursion to make money, but also to encourage interest in the region. At the time, he had been actively promoting the construction of a canal at Sault Ste. Marie to facilitate travel into Lake Superior, and this may have been an effort to generate support for the project.[7] Nearly ten years later, in 1862, a group of over three hundred passengers were treated to a ten-day cruise of Lake Superior on the steamer *Planet*. This voyage placed greater emphasis on creating a "champagne atmosphere" to meet the desires of wealthy clients on a tourist excursion. Passengers were treated to delightful entertainment, including live music and dancing, as well as extravagant meals highlighted by freshly caught whitefish and trout. Members of the group enjoyed the steamer's commodious cabins in a setting where each passenger's individual wish was addressed with "courtesy and promptness."[8]

It is unlikely that Ward would have had enough steamers to operate excursions had he not liquidated his operations on Lake Michigan. Furthermore, ending his Lake Michigan routes provided the flexibility to switch his steamers around to different runs based upon passenger demand and changing economic conditions. The timing of his decisions was crucial. Ward's instinct of knowing the correct moment to change a business practice served him well. About the time he began to lease and sell his Lake Michigan steamers to a group of former employees, he also invested in a venture located in Wyandotte, Michigan.

## Eureka Iron Company

Competition from railroads had prompted E. B. Ward to liquidate his steamship holdings on Lake Michigan, but Ward recognized the importance of the railroad industry in the growing industrial economy of the United States. Rather than fight the railroads, he would produce the iron (and later steel) the railroad industry demanded. In 1840, there were three thousand miles of railroad track nationwide. By 1860, there were thirty thousand miles of railroad track in the United States. Passengers had the ability to travel speedily and in comfort to many areas throughout the country. Prior to the Civil War, the nation's railroads used iron, rather than steel, rails. Often, these could wear out within two years. With the extension of new rail lines increasing at a steady pace each year, and the demand for iron rails seemingly endless, Eber Ward chose to capitalize on this opportunity and became the lead investor in the Eureka Iron Company in 1853. When it was completed, Ward's operation was the first iron mill west of Pittsburgh. Timing for the soon-to-be forty-one-year-old business leader was a key factor. This was the same year he began to liquidate a portion of his fleet of ships. Ward was willing to part with his Lake Michigan line of steamers to ensure he had enough capital to invest in the iron company.[9]

Articles of association for the Eureka Iron Company were filed in Wayne County, Michigan, on October 27, 1853. The company was capitalized at $500,000 ($15,781,833.24 in 2020 dollars) for the purpose of "mining, smelting and refining iron and copper ore and other metals and metallic ores." Ward was the largest investor, with $50,000 in stock, and was named one of seven members of the board of directors. For many years, he served as both president and treasurer of the board as well as the driving force at the company. One of the other founding board members, U. Tracy Howe, served as the treasurer of the Michigan Central Railroad, which would become a key customer for the iron company in the future. Notably, Eber's uncle Samuel Ward, who was still living, was not involved in this venture. For some time, Eber had been the more aggressive innovator of the pair. Eber's involvement in this endeavor demonstrates his willingness to assume risks, contrasting with Samuel's business instincts, which had become more conservative over time.[10]

One of the first major decisions the Eureka Iron Company board undertook was to determine where to establish the company's blast furnace. The partners chose to establish their operations in Wyandotte, twelve miles south of Detroit. In 1854, Ward negotiated the purchase of twenty-two hundred acres of heavily wooded land for $44,000. A significant portion of the property was along the Detroit River, allowing for the easy transportation of iron ore to the area and for finished products to be shipped to customers. The forested parcel also was attractive because it ensured long-term access to trees, used for making charcoal, the principal fuel for the furnace at that time. The purchase of the property put the company well on its way to producing iron.[11]

In October 1855, the *Detroit Free Press* reported that Eber Ward's steamer *Samuel Ward* transported thirty tons of iron ore from the company's Eureka mine on Lake Superior to its facility in Wyandotte. The company hoped to extract five thousand tons of iron ore each year from the mine, which was located near Marquette. Unfortunately, the Eureka mine did not possess the expected levels of ore initially estimated by company officials. While the mine did provide several hundred tons of ore used in the initial trial blast of the company's furnace in 1856, it eventually had to be abandoned. Although the mine investment was an ultimate failure, the newspaper article helps to understand Ward's business practices. He sought to control as many aspects of the production and distribution of iron as possible. Ward's ships, like the *Samuel Ward* and in later years the *Planet*, the *Montgomery*, and other vessels, transported the iron ore to his mills. Eventually, he would invest in additional iron mines. Later, by the 1870s, he had significant interest in three separate iron and steel mills. Ward also would serve as president of three railroads while serving on the boards of others. These railroads purchased the rails and other materials manufactured at his mills. This meant Ward either owned or had a major influence over the mining of iron ore, its transportation, the mills where it was transformed into marketable products, and the companies that purchased those products. This type of vertical integration sought by Ward was unusual for his time. While he did not own every aspect of the companies involved in the production and distribution of the iron and steel, he did have a controlling influence in them. His business model foreshadowed the actions of others who would follow in the late nineteenth century, such as Andrew Carnegie, the future giant in the steel industry.[12]

Following the purchase of the twenty-two hundred acres of property, company officials set about the task of surveying the village of Wyandotte and recruiting a labor force. In some ways, this was difficult as the property initially was primarily unbroken forest rather than a developed community. The company placed advertisements in multiple newspapers and even had materials posted in New York City to encourage newly arrived European immigrants to relocate to the area. These drew laborers to Wyandotte. Prospective workers initially lived in boardinghouses, but the company also constructed several homes for employees and their families. The company owned most of the land in and around Wyandotte, so it sold lots at reasonable prices to employees, who then could build their own homes. A pamphlet created by the company in 1856 advertised, "Lots are sold from $100 and $300; 20 percent of the purchase price to be paid down and the balance in four annual installments." Lots for places of worship and schools were either donated by the company or sold at the reduced rate of $25.[13]

Individuals who purchased property had to agree to a provision insisted upon by the company. E. B. Ward was very much opposed to alcohol use by his employees, and in the communities where he established a business he often attempted to curtail alcohol consumption. The purchase agreement of one employee, Henry McCloy, offers a relevant example. After reading a Detroit newspaper advertisement calling for men to work in the mills, he arrived in Wyandotte in the late 1850s. Within a short time, he had enough money to buy lot 5 in block 71 in the village of Wyandotte in November 1860. One provision of McCloy's purchase agreement included the statement "No intoxicating liquor [is] to be sold on premises except for medicinal and mechanical purposes, and with written consent of said trustees." If an owner was caught selling alcohol without permission, the property could revert back to the company. McCloy apparently never had to be held accountable to this provision. Once he bought the lot and built a home, he lived there for many years. He had to walk only a few blocks to his position at the iron works, where McCloy worked for approximately twenty-seven years.[14]

The Eureka Iron Company also constructed company housing. By doing so, it could maintain a level of control over its workforce. Workers with families living in company housing were unlikely to leave. Attempts to maintain control also were signified by the provisions prohibiting the sale of alcohol. Employees seeking greater independence from the company purchased property and built their own homes very near the iron works. If employees had a mortgage and family to support, company officials believed they would be more diligent in their work habits to ensure they maintained their positions. Ward's actions to dictate aspects of his employee's lives by developing company housing and limiting their access to alcohol mirror his efforts to maximize profit by governing all aspects of the manufacturing process through vertical integration. The Eureka Iron Company adopted these practices in the 1850s. In subsequent years, many steel manufacturers, such as the Apollo Iron and Steel Company, Granite City Steel Company, and even Andrew Carnegie's operations at Homestead, would adopt similar practices to maintain greater control over their workforce. Although this often led to greater profits for investors in those firms, it contributed to tension between labor and management, particularly in the years following the Civil War.[15]

Once the village had been platted and a labor force secured, work began to clear the forests and build a blast furnace. Ovens were constructed to burn the wood taken from the surrounding forests to create charcoal. Eventually, consumption of charcoal at the facility reached a high of six thousand bushels each day, 2 million bushels per year, and fifty thousand cords of wood per year. Following several months of work, the furnace was completed. Originally, it was only equipped to produce charcoal pig iron. Ward convinced several Eureka Iron Company board members to expand the operations to include a rolling mill when one became available in 1855. Therefore, a new organization, the Wyandotte Rolling Mill Company, which included many of the same investors as the Eureka Iron Company, was formed in 1855. Ward was also the dominant figure in the new company, serving as its president and treasurer. The rolling mill, constructed just south of the original furnace, was expected to produce ten tons of finished iron per day. The *Detroit Free Press* reported that once the machinery for the new mill arrived, the company planned to produce T-iron rails, which could be produced and shipped wherever needed. Before long, a second rolling mill was added.[16]

By 1860, the factory was the largest in the state and Ward's mill was a dominant force in the state's economy. Its workforce had grown significantly, employing seventy-five men at the original Eureka mill and more than two hundred at the rolling mills. The iron company produced about sixteen hundred tons of pig iron and the rolling mill manufactured products worth $425,000. A third rolling mill was added, enabling the production of railroad items such as spikes, boiler plates, and heavy shafts. Due to the increased demand for the company's products, a new, more efficient furnace was built at Eureka. This was completed in 1863 and was a personal venture of Ward's undertaken independently of the company, as only Ward was able and willing to invest the resources necessary to fund this expansion. What came to be known as the "Ward Furnace" was capitalized at $100,000 and was so efficient it paid for itself within its first year of operation.[17]

An advertising pamphlet published by the Eureka Iron Company and Wyandotte Rolling Mill in 1860 described the company's operations and touted the strength of the Lake Superior iron used and the products created by the company. The pamphlet argued that government tests demonstrated Eureka's rails were stronger than those produced by its competitors, and outlined the company's planned expansion. Numerous testimonials from customers highlighted the high-quality products. George Wallace, the road master for the Sandusky, Dayton & Cincinnati Railroad, wrote, "Your iron rails both in quality and pattern, are the best we have ever had on the Road." S. Sharp from the Great Western Railway declared, "Car Axels supplied to us two years ago, by your firm, have given us perfect satisfaction." Additional testimonials promoted the quality of car wheels, chain link, and other items produced by the Eureka Iron Company.[18]

As a result of both the high quality of its products and its promotion of them, the Eureka Iron Company rapidly increased its profits and stockholders received substantial dividends. Detroit historian Silas Farmer noted that another factor in the company's success was the favorable location of the complex: "its splendid river frontage, with its facilities for receiving ores by water from northern Michigan." Further expansion came about as a result of the Civil War. Near the end of the conflict, an article in the *Detroit Advertiser and Tribune* described the rolling mill as having "more capital" and providing more "employment to a larger number of working people, than any other in the State." The facilities grew rapidly due to the tremendous increase in demand for iron. During the war, the output of iron nearly doubled, and its price jumped from $18.60 to as much as $73.60 per ton.[19]

## Transforming Iron Ore at Wyandotte

A comprehensive article in the *Detroit Daily Post* explained how iron ore was transformed into workable iron products at Ward's Wyandotte facility. First, iron ore from Lake Superior or other locations was brought to the wharf in front of the Eureka works whence it was taken to a "crusher." There it was reduced to smaller particles that could be handled more easily. In quantities of four hundred to five hundred pounds (called "charges"), it then was taken to a furnace where forty to fifty pounds of limestone was added and the entire mixture was heated to "separate the cinders and dross [waste material] from the pure metal." There were two furnaces creating pig iron at the iron works by 1866. One was owned by the Eureka Iron Company and the other owned exclusively by E. B. Ward. Each furnace held the capacity to produce ten to twelve tons of pig iron per day. Once the ore was transformed into pig iron and cast into bars, it was taken to the rolling mills.[20]

By 1866, the rolling mills were capitalized at $700,000 ($12,555,633.50 in 2020 dollars) and employed about four hundred men with a payroll of $20,000 each month. The pig iron was taken to puddling furnaces in "heats" of approximately 450 pounds. There it was stirred or puddled for about two hours until it became wrought iron. The work was difficult, the fumes were dangerous, and the heat could be overbearing. Experienced puddlers were important because they determined the proper time to remove the product, which was now wrought iron. Once removed, it was taken in "balls" of about 110 pounds to a "squeezer," where it was formed into a shape and made easier to handle. Next, each ball was sent through a set of cast iron rollers where it was reduced in thickness and its length extended into bars two or three inches wide and one inch thick. Bars then were cut into small pieces of various sizes to create a shaft, axel, or other products. Visitors to the iron works experienced clouds of black smoke, sooty buildings, sparks and flames like fireworks, the hissing of steam, the roar of machinery, explosions of red hot iron, "and another hundred comingled sounds." While those unfamiliar with the facility would describe it as chaotic, order was maintained by a series of skilled workers who ensured each step at the various stages of production was followed properly. John Van Alstyne eventually served as general manager of the Eureka Iron Company. He also was elected Wyandotte's first mayor in 1867. Often, Ward placed members of his extended family into positions of trust at his businesses. Van Alstyne was unique in this regard as he was not related to Ward by blood or marriage. Initially, Van Alsytne was hired to manage the company's real estate holdings, but Ward recognized his talent, mentored him, and then empowered him to lead the facility.[21]

The complex was comprised of several interconnected buildings. The rail mill was 140 feet by 200 feet and contained eight furnaces with the capacity to reroll twelve thousand tons of railroad iron per year. Brand-new rails were not produced at the facility. Rather, old, worn-out rails were cut and rolled into slabs where they were overlaid with Lake Superior iron and converted into reconditioned rails. Each day, the facility had the capacity to produce 250 rails, weighing a combined fifty-five tons. Rails were sold to the Michigan Southern, Michigan Central, Flint & Pere Marquette, and Detroit & Milwaukee railways. The complex also included a merchant mill and boiler plate mill where one thousand tons of spikes, four hundred tons of boiler rivets, and thirty thousand feet of chain were made each year. By the early 1860s, Ward's Wyandotte works included a laboratory where William F. Durfee was recruited to conduct experiments to improve product quality and overall efficiency. Eventually, this made history when steel was manufactured at the facility, the first steel produced in the United States using the Bessemer process.[22]

Conditions for workers at the iron works and rolling mills were difficult and dangerous. When the mill was at full capacity, the furnace operated round the clock throughout the year. This led to very long shifts for laborers, who often were required to work twelve hours each day. Superintendents at other iron mills allowed employees to drink beer in moderation while at work. This was not so for Ward's employees. Workers drank oatmeal water with lemon juice to remain hydrated and avoid cramps. Accidents, however, could—and did—occur. On the afternoon of Friday, April 12, 1857, an employee at the rolling mill noticed one of the machines begin to falter. Investigating the reason, he was shocked to find the mangled body of a coworker who had been crushed to death. No one had seen exactly what had happened, but the unnamed victim, an engineer, appeared to have been oiling some of the machinery "when he was caught between two large cog wheels and literally crushed to a jelly." Work at the facility came to a halt and the next day "all hands attended the funeral." Although there had been accidents leading to injuries over the years, this was the only fatal injury reported at the facility during Eber Ward's lifetime. Unfortunately, in 1888, thirteen years after Eber Ward's death, an explosion at the mill killed three men. One of the victims was Henry McCloy, the same man who had purchased property from the company in 1860 to build his family home.[23]

Although there is no record of conflict between workers and management on Eber Ward's steamships, the same is not true for his iron and steel mills.

The Civil War sparked union activity throughout the United States as laborers protested the long hours, poor working conditions, and inflation brought on by the war. Employers fiercely opposed the emergence of various trade unions. Michigan was no exception to this growth in labor conflict. Richard Trevellick emerged as Detroit's leading labor reformer following his arrival in the city in 1862. He initially organized employees at a Detroit dry dock company where he worked, then in 1864 he founded the much larger Detroit Trades Assembly. In time, due to his effective oratory skills, the Detroit Trades Assembly boasted as many as five thousand laborers in a range of professions. Trevellick's chief objective was the eight-hour day. By 1866, there were twenty-five local eight-hour leagues in Michigan.[24]

It was within the context of this increasing union activism that tension grew between laborers and administration at Ward's Wyandotte mill. In 1865, employees went on strike over disagreements concerning working conditions and compensation. In this era of early iron production, prior to the mechanization of the industry, skilled employees, such as puddlers, held a great deal of power. They often determined the pace of work as well as how the work was to be conducted. It was common for other skilled workers, like rollers and heaters, to hire, train, and supervise the unskilled members of their crews. These skilled employees acted with a strong sense of independence and felt beholden to no one. This conflicted with Ward's need to control conditions at his facilities; power sharing was not in his DNA. Yet, considering the nature of the industry in this era, he had little choice but to do so, given his reliance on those employees whose skills were rare. Further complicating matters was his desire to drive down costs and develop efficiencies. The union's protection of these workers' jobs and resistance to mechanization were obstacles to both these goals.[25]

In what could be considered a patronizing tone, Ward addressed the striking workers' concern over wages, explaining that "wages, like everything else, were regulated by the law of supply and demand." Ward claimed he could not afford to raise wages at that time because demand for iron products lessened near the end of the Civil War and the industry experienced a recession. Like other steel producers, he took an unsentimental approach to labor, viewing employees not in humanitarian terms but from the perspective of a business manager. As the labor historian David Brody argued, for iron and steel manufactures, "labor was primarily an item of cost," and costs had to be kept low to maintain profits.

Clearly, Ward wanted to maintain control over his employees' wages, just as he controlled other aspects of his manufacturing operations. While the men were on strike that summer, the facility was forced to shut down.[26]

Perhaps Eber felt his hard-nosed negotiations with ironworkers were justified because he offered employment to so many men who could then support families. As an observer commented, Ward "believed that the best philanthropy of the age was that which gave the greatest amount of remunerative labor to the working men of the country." Ward expressed concern about the power of labor unions to a friend. "If I should hand over all the iron mills to them tomorrow, they would run them to ruin in a year or two." He admitted there was value in protecting workers from injustice, but described unions as "wrong and tyrannical" when they attempted to dictate wages. Fortunately, by August 1865, he was able to reach a settlement with his employees at Wyandotte, thus allowing the region's largest employer to resume its operations.[27]

The specific details of the settlement are unclear, but they appeared to be beneficial to both parties. An article the following year (1866) in the *Detroit Advertiser and Tribune* outlined the wage scale for workers, which showed that employees at the Wyandotte Rolling Mills earned the highest wages of any laborers in the state of Michigan. Specific compensation for workers varied, but unskilled workers identified as "Laborers" earned $1.63 per day. Other unskilled workers, such as "Carpenters" and "Catchers," earned $1.88 and $2 per day respectively. A "Boiler Plate Roller" earned the highest wage at $13.00 per day. Other skilled workers, such as "Cold Straighteners," "Boiler Plate Hammerers," and "Merchant Mills Rollers," earned between $10 and $12 per day. A total of twenty-eight classifications were included in the company's wage scale. As a point of comparison, according to government reports, in 1866 unskilled laborers in Michigan could expect to earn $2 per day on average, while farm laborers earned $2.20 per day during harvest times and $1.49 at other times of the year.[28]

Employees were most often paid in cash. For many years, there was no bank in Wyandotte, so the company's financial transactions had to be conducted in Detroit. This meant that the company's paymaster, Sylvester Pray, was required to travel by horseback to and from Detroit before each payday. For years, it was his custom to sleep with a revolver under his pillow after he had received the necessary funds for payroll. This all changed in 1871 when the

The corner of Biddle and Elm in Wyandotte, sometime between 1860 and 1871. The Eureka Iron Company works are in the background; the company's offices are in front. Beginning in 1871, the Wyandotte Savings Bank also occupied the building, which is still standing. Banking business was conducted on the north side, and Ward's iron company offices were on the south side. (Courtesy of the Wyandotte Historical Museum)

Wyandotte Savings Bank was founded by John Van Alstyne, the manager of the Eureka Iron Company. The bank was located in the same building that housed the company's offices. Banking business was transacted on the north side of the structure, while the company's offices were located on the south side.[29]

Ward always sought to employ the latest technologies at his businesses, and his operations at Wyandotte were no exception. By 1872, many of the trees around his facility had disappeared, and charcoal had to be imported by rail, sometimes from as far away as 150 or 200 miles. These transportation costs cut into profits as other iron producers used much better sources of fuel, such as coal, coke, or natural gas. Ward's facility was also nearly twenty years old at that time, while his competitors' facilities were more efficient and could produce products at a much lower cost. A news article in the *Detroit Daily Press* highlighted Ward's vision to "increase the capital stock to $1,000,000" to rebuild and expand the facility. For years, he had been the driving force at Wyandotte, but in this case, Ward's partners hesitated. They were unwilling to invest the capital necessary to modernize their facility. Seeing their lack of enthusiasm for renewed investment at Wyandotte, he sold his Ward Furnace to the Wyandotte Rolling Mill Company. He then began to focus more of his attention on his other iron and steel facilities, which had been founded previously.[30]

Eber Ward's transition from the steamboat industry into iron and steel production is representative of his tremendous ambition. Furthermore, his successful foray into an entirely different industry demonstrates his exceptional business expertise. It took intelligence, drive, and daring to determine the proper time to expand his investments and then take action. The relationship between Eber and his uncle Samuel had facilitated Eber's rise in the business world, but Samuel was noticeably absent among the investors of the Eureka Iron Company. Eber's activities at Wyandotte showed he was an innovative entrepreneur independent of his former mentor. Eber continued to rely on his father, and particularly his sister Emily, for support. Emily remained his most trusted confidante. As his business empire continued to grow, she persuaded him to contribute to a philanthropic cause dear to her.

## "Aunt" Emily Ward and Newport Academy

Beginning in the mid-1830s, Emily had joined her father while he served as the lighthouse keeper at Bois Blanc and Fort Gratiot. When Eber Sr. retired from his position in 1845, he and Emily relocated to Newport to be close to family and friends. Emily was thirty-six years old by that time, and because she remained unmarried, she would have been referred to as a spinster. It is unclear why she never married. Men likely were intimidated by her strong personality and sober sense of purpose. She had been forced to assume adult responsibilities at an early age following the sudden death of her mother. Surviving photos show that as an adult she had long hair, which she preferred to part in the middle, with ringlet curls on either side of her face. She was tall, broad-shouldered, and gave the impression she was not afraid of hard work. As she grew older, her reddish hair began to gray and she became a big woman. By the time she reached the age of forty-five, Emily seemed to come to terms with her appearance; in a self-deprecating letter to her niece she described her own "freckled, wrinkled & pale face—her turn[ed] up nose, her frizzled red & gray hair, her unwieldy figure, her stiff awkward manners [and] her limping headlong gait."[31]

"Aunt" Emily Ward. Throughout his lifetime, Eber's sister remained his closest adviser and confidante. (Courtesy of the Seitz family)

Following her return to Newport, Emily found great happiness and fulfillment in life. With the help of her brother Eber, she took up her long-held dream to care for and educate children. In 1845, she founded Newport Academy, which had the mission of providing expanded educational opportunities to children living in the community. Two years later, Emily built a schoolhouse for her academy. She hired a college graduate to teach the students, and the school was equipped with globes, charts, and other equipment to supplement the learning environment. Eber paid for everything, including the teacher's annual salary. The curriculum went beyond the commonplace rote memorization, and students studied disciplines such as Latin, chemistry, astronomy, and philosophy. Just as her brother controlled all aspects of his manufacturing enterprises, Emily administered the school with an iron hand. As one community member observed, "'Aunt' Emily had charge of the schoolmaster, the schoolhouse, and the pupils, and was a board of education of one, with original and appellate jurisdiction." Emily managed the school for over twenty years, until she moved to Detroit in 1867.[32]

Any child in the community was welcome to attend Emily's academy for $3 per year, plus an additional 25 cents if the student was to study languages. Dozens of academy graduates went on to successful careers, becoming lawyers, manufacturers, ship captains, and physicians. One, Don M. Dickinson, served as postmaster general of the United States, and two were elected to Congress. James J. Hagerman was a pupil of Emily's who later worked for Eber Brock in Milwaukee and eventually became a railroad president. Students remembered the curriculum as rigid, and Emily did not allow for gossip or idle play. If they finished their studies, students might be sent to weed a strawberry patch, clean the horse stalls, cut and stack wood, or complete another necessary chore. With Eber's financial support, she also occasionally enrolled and boarded students who could not afford to pay the tuition fees. Once a ragged boy from a poor family approached her and asked, "Aunt Emily, you take all good children; I

Emily founded Newport Academy in 1845; this building was constructed two years later. The school offered expanded educational opportunities to children in the community. Today it houses the Marine City Pride and Heritage Museum. (Author's collection)

wish you'd take me." Emily enrolled the boy in her school and he was one of many who lived under her care, in her own home, for a time.[33]

One can imagine Emily regularly contacting her brother to ask for money to purchase additional textbooks, desks, or other necessary supplies for her academy. Eber was proud to support Emily's academy and was interested in the students' welfare. He even took the time to visit Girard College in Philadelphia to observe its programs to determine how they could be implemented in Newport. The philanthropist Stephen Girard had founded the school in 1833 to provide an education for poor, disadvantaged, orphaned boys. Eber saw the institution as a "living monument of his [Girard's] foresight and benevolence." It is not hard to imagine that Eber saw himself as a kindred spirit to Girard. He wanted to provide the same benefits to the community of Newport that Girard had contributed to Philadelphia. As long as Emily was associated with the school, Eber remained the primary benefactor of Newport Academy.[34]

Although these were some of the happiest times of Emily's life, they were darkened by the deaths of both her sisters. Sally (Ward) Brindle, who was one year younger than Emily, had suffered from ill health and anxiety for many years. Emily later recalled that "Sally died insane, the disease having developed in her about the age of thirty years." At some point in the 1840s, Sally was committed to the New York State Lunatic Asylum in Utica, New York. She died there September 12, 1847. Two of Sally's children came to live with Emily and Eber Sr. in Newport. Three years later, the children's father, Melchiah Brindle, died. Soon thereafter, the remaining orphaned children moved in with Emily as well. Abba (Ward) Owen was Emily and Eber's youngest sister. She was married to the ship captain B. F. Owen and lived in Newport. She was in good health until she gave birth to a son on February 1, 1854. While her child, Orville, survived, Abba died two weeks later on February 14. Because Captain Owen was absent much of the year sailing the Great Lakes, the care of his four children, including the infant Orville, fell to Emily. Although she had no biological children of her own, Emily found herself as the primary caregiver of ten children; eight were sixteen or younger.[35]

Emily readily agreed to care for her nieces and nephews. One might ask, how did the death of his sisters affect Eber Brock? Without hesitation, he expressed his desire to "furnish the means for their support and education" and told Emily that she "might draw upon him for whatever she wanted for their maintenance." He also remarked that since the children would live under

This image of the Ward family shows Emily (*front row, second from right*), most likely accompanied by her sister Sally's children: Asa, Emily, Elizabeth, Francis, Florence, and Mary. (Courtesy of the William L. Clements Library, University of Michigan)

her roof, Emily had "the hardest part of the bargain."[36] Eber's willingness to assume the financial burden of raising his orphaned nieces and nephews was generous, yet his reaction to his sister Sally's death represented a coldness not reflected in his attitude toward her children. In the same letter of 1847 in which he informed Emily their sister Sally had just died, he also described a recent "pleasant passage" on a steamboat. He then commented about some freight being loaded on one of his ships. Eber's apparent unemotional reaction to his sister's death is striking. Previously, Eber had complained about Sally's fiery temper and unstable nature. This correspondence indicated he had already severed the emotional connection with his sister, even before her death.[37]

## Eber's Interest in Spiritualism

Eber's correspondence relating to Abba's death has not survived; however, the timing of her death, and the loss of additional family members shortly thereafter, may represent a turning point in Eber's life. On the same day Abba's son Orville was born, Samuel Ward died. Losing his sister and uncle within two weeks must have been quite a blow to Eber. The deaths of other close figures in his life followed. The next year, Eber's aunt Elizabeth, the widow of Samuel Ward, died. Although she was not a blood relative, Eber had lived with or near his aunt Elizabeth for years. Finally, following an extended illness, his father Eber Ward Sr. died on June 1, 1855. This series of losses certainly affected E. B. Ward deeply and were likely factors that prompted him to pursue spiritualism in his grief. In subsequent years, Ward attended séances and sought mediums who claimed to facilitate interaction with the spirit world.[38]

It is not necessarily surprising that Eber was drawn to spiritualism for solace. By the mid-1850s, it was a broadly popular movement that had spread across much of the country. The movement arose, in part, after two sisters living in Hydesville, New York, Kate and Margaret Fox, began to hear mysterious rappings in their home in March 1848. The noises were reported to have come from a murdered peddler who once had lived there. The girls and their supporters believed Kate and Margaret had become conduits allowing for communication with those who had died. Within months, many Americans throughout the northern states and the eastern seaboard gathered in their own homes to determine if they could reconnect with deceased family members or friends. Interest in spiritualism attracted notable persons as well as average Americans. Following the death of her son Willie, Mary Todd Lincoln held séances for political figures at the White House. The publisher Horace Greeley and author Harriet Beecher Stowe also attended séances. While historians remain unable to determine the exact number of Americans who considered themselves spiritualists in the 1850s, supporters and detractors estimated their numbers ranged from a minimum of a few hundred thousand to as many as 11 million (although the latter figure is likely exaggerated), out of an overall population of 25 million.[39]

A number of factors contributed to the rise of spiritualism in the mid-nineteenth century. Social upheaval caused by the slow but steady industrialization and urbanization of the country prompted interest in reforming society's ills. Spiritualism was linked with popular movements to reform prisons, improve the educational system, and to stem alcohol abuse. Other reformist movements sought the expansion of women's rights and the abolition of slavery. As America became more industrialized, family size decreased and fewer children were born. Parents placed increased value on their individual children, including the fate of those who had died. The ferocity with which diseases such as cholera, typhoid, and tuberculosis struck urban communities could be sudden and deadly. Death was a part of daily life as bereaved families lost loved ones. Intricate mourning rituals became common, and communities created expansive cemeteries similar to beautiful parks to celebrate those who had died. Social changes, immigration, and increased interest in science weakened the traditional authority of Christian denominations as people sought new avenues to answer questions about the afterlife. The movement also attracted consumers looking for a new form of popular entertainment. Thousands paid entrance fees to hear public lectures by spiritualists or to attend private séances. Such gatherings often resembled revival meetings, where large crowds of spectators became new converts to the movement. Additionally, new technologies such as the telegraph, which allowed for communication across cables, or the camera, with its ability to capture images, seemed to provide modern-day glimpses into what was once impossible. Spirit rappings like those of the Fox sisters were like a spiritual telegraph providing a portal through which to communicate with the unknown.[40]

Even prior to the death of his family members, Eber Ward held many beliefs in common with those involved with spiritualism. In 1840, Eber had visited the famed phrenologist George Combe to have his personality read. This experience was significant because many who embraced phrenology also became involved with spiritualism; as the scholar Robert Cox contends, experience with phrenology "was one of the most consistent waymarkers on the path to spiritualism." Eber's support for reforms such as the abolition of slavery and temperance demonstrated some of the values he shared with supporters of spiritualism.[41] Ward's own writings express an openness to spiritualism and the possibility of life after death. In an 1852 letter to his father, Eber related his potential belief in spiritualism. "I have no fixed views as to the habitation or powers of the spirit. But, I do not believe he loses at his death a single desirable attribute he possessed while on earth." Eber recognized his views might be shocking, but he assured his father he was never more "clear, calm, or stronger." Given the sudden loss of four intimate family members in the span of eighteen months, it is not surprising their deaths could have deepened Ward's interest in spiritualism. Studies of the movement show that individuals often turned to spiritualism in a desire to cope with bereavement. Although Emily experienced the same loss of family members as Eber, she was not drawn to spiritualism like her brother.[42]

Eber's wife Polly is noticeably missing from much of Eber's correspondence in this era; however, he does mention Polly in one surviving letter to Emily. Polly suffered from acute anxiety beginning about the mid-1850s and sought treatment. In 1856, Eber accompanied her to New Orleans for what was likely a holiday to help her take some time for herself. There is no indication that Polly shared Eber's interest in spiritualism. The lack of reference to his wife and children in his correspondence appears to indicate the importance Eber placed on his business activities, to the detriment of time spent with his wife and children. It is also possible that due to Polly's condition, he relied less on her support than he did on that of his sister. The siblings remained close, even though each had their own interests: Emily remained consumed by Newport Academy and Eber focused his energies on the expansion of his business interests, which took him to the city of Chicago in the late 1850s.[43]

## North Chicago Rolling Mill

Even prior to the Civil War, the facilities at Wyandotte were so successful that Ward explored the possibility of establishing another facility to manufacture iron. He determined Chicago was best situated for his new investment. E.B. was familiar with the city and its harbor due to his many visits to Chicago ferrying passengers and freight as a ship captain. Prior to 1857, the manufacture of iron in the city was insignificant, although its potential was seemingly unlimited. Chicago benefited from its central location between the iron ore deposits of Michigan and the coalfields of Pennsylvania and Illinois. Furthermore, by the 1850s, it was emerging as a hub for railroad traffic. Ward chose wisely when he decided to place his new facility in Chicago.[44]

In May 1857, Eber Ward and two others established the Chicago Rolling Mill "just outside the city" on the north side of the Chicago River. Eber and his partners invested $225,000 in the facility. The original mill did not include a blast furnace. It was built exclusively to reroll old iron rails for the railroads.

Soon, Eber and his partners employed about two hundred men and were able to produce about one hundred tons of iron rails each day. Ward turned to members of his extended family to occupy key positions. He chose his brother-in-law Captain Stephen Clement to oversee the operations in Chicago. Clement was the veteran ship captain who had originally gone into business for himself when Ward abandoned his shipping lines on Lake Michigan. Clement knew little about the steel industry, but Ward recognized Clement's natural leadership abilities and brought him onto his management team. Within a few years, due to the steady growth of the railway system surrounding Chicago, Ward's mill had a backlog of orders, ensuring it would operate at peak capacity for quite some time. By 1864, the rolling mill had grown so rapidly that it was reorganized as the North Chicago Rolling Mill Company with a capital stock of $500,000. Stephen Clement was named president of the new company, while Orrin W. Potter was named superintendent. Potter, Ward's second cousin, had lived for a time during his childhood with Eber's sister Aunt Emily. He had attended Newport Academy and later worked for Ward as a clerk in Wyandotte. He initially served as bookkeeper and paymaster in Chicago. Potter also was married to Eber Ward's niece Ellen (Owen) Potter. Clement and Potter would lead the Chicago operations on a day-to day basis for many years.[45]

Although the facilities in both Wyandotte and Chicago proved to be successful, Ward still faced challenges. Beginning in the summer and fall of 1857, shortly after the investment in the Chicago Rolling Mill was undertaken, the nation experienced an economic downturn commonly known as the Panic of 1857. This was caused by a range of factors, but one key element was the expansion of railroad construction at a much too rapid pace. In the 1850s, more than twenty thousand miles of railroad line had been built. Operators of these lines struggled to repay their loans as receipts from passenger and freight traffic did not reach expected levels. Conditions were exacerbated when European investors, who supplied much of the funding, began to call in their loans with the onset of the Crimean War. With foreign investment in the United States withdrawn, the value of American stocks and bonds fell sharply. Furthermore, the influx of gold into the economy due to the gold rush in California led to a speculative boom in the early 1850s involving western land. This boom turned to bust when the Crimean War ended and Russian wheat flooded international markets as American exports dropped. These events staged a ripple effect through the American economy. Access to credit suddenly dried up and railroad construction temporarily came to a halt. Unemployment rose nationwide and several businesses failed.[46]

By the fall of 1857, orders for new rails and other materials had dropped significantly due to the Panic. Cash flow became a problem for Ward, worsened by his recent investment in the Chicago mill. It was clear Ward had become overextended. For once, his sense of timing appeared to be faulty and threatened to endanger his expansion into Chicago and his successful Eureka Iron Company at Wyandotte. However, Eber Brock Ward was not one to make rash decisions under pressure. With a steady hand, he devised a plan to overcome the financial crisis. He gathered as much capital as he could and made small payments to his creditors, which he recognized satisfied them in the short run. He then authorized the Wyandotte Rolling Mill to pay its employees with company-issued scrip instead of cash. Employees could redeem their payment in six months at 7 percent interest. Another example of his pragmatic shrewdness, this scheme helped Ward address the short-term problem of meeting his payroll, but it came at the expense of his employees. Most businesses in Wyandotte accepted the company scrip at face value, but some men sold their bills to speculators, who paid only 60 cents on the dollar. The *Detroit Free Press*, a publication that would be critical of Ward over the years, condemned the practice, describing the bills as worthless shinplasters. The newspapers' editors declared Ward's actions were "against law and against good public policy." Fortunately, the economic upheaval caused by the Panic, while significant, was short-lived, and by 1858 Ward returned to paying employees in cash.[47]

Another struggle, possibly related to the issuance of scrip, involved the lack of a skilled workforce in Chicago. Advertisements in eastern cities for experienced ironworkers as well as company housing attracted some employees, but not enough. To remedy this, on more than one occasion Ward transported nearly his entire workforce from Wyandotte to Chicago to complete a large order. Ward's nephew Asa Brindle, who worked as a bookkeeper in Wyandotte, commented on the arrangement, expressing his frustration: "The rail mill has not been in operation for some time" because all the men "have two tons of iron to roll in Chicago which will take six or eight weeks." Once they completed the contract, they returned to Wyandotte. This exchange of personnel between Wyandotte and Chicago happened more than once in the late 1850s.[48]

While Ward's North Chicago Rolling Mill struggled in some areas, the company continued to receive orders for its products and ultimately prospered. One of the best customers was the Chicago and Northwestern Railroad Company, which maintained a steady demand for car axles and rails. According to an article in the *Detroit Post*, by 1866 the mill processed seventy-five thousand tons of iron annually, employed about five hundred laborers, and consumed thirty thousand tons of coal to run its furnaces. Many of the employees lived in what the company called a "Mill Colony, in which there are some 60 tenant houses, many of which are neat and tidy homes." Most employees were prosperous and had money in the bank, but the surrounding community did not contain any churches or schools. The paper lamented the fact that "children grow up in idleness and ignorance, while the adults go onward toward the grave with few if any of the cultivating and generous influences of religion to cheer and console them." This lack of amenities was in contrast to the conditions in Wyandotte, where Ward's company offered lots free of charge or at a reduced price for churches and schools. As an absentee owner (Ward continued to live in Detroit), he treated his Chicago operations differently than those nearer to his home.[49]

Less than ten days following the publication of the article highlighting his successful Chicago operations, on June 19, 1866, a fire broke out at Ward's facility in Chicago. It began about 10:30 p.m. in one of the puddling houses on the south side of the complex. By the time the fire department arrived to fight the flames, the blaze was out of control. It took all the firefighters' efforts to prevent the fire from spreading. The next day, it was determined that the entire original building, first constructed in 1857, had been destroyed. The structure, some 210 feet by 180 feet, had been filled with valuable machinery, including eleven boilers and four powerful engines. Everything inside was a total loss. The estimated value of the damages was at least $200,000, and the insurance on the property only amounted to $40,000. Another building containing the newest machinery had been saved by the heroic efforts of those fighting the blaze. Ward called for the immediate reconstruction of the destroyed mill. As he planned the new facility, Ward required the latest technologies to be adopted to ensure the greatest efficiencies. When it was complete, the new machinery installed was so advanced it more than doubled the facility's original production capacity. Just three years later, in 1869, the North Chicago Rolling Mill

Company received a special charter from the State of Illinois. It was reorganized once again, with a capital investment of $1 million. The following year, two blast furnaces were added, allowing the facility to produce its own pig iron, which previously had to be purchased in Pittsburgh.[50]

Ward's response to the fire and his leadership as he rebuilt his mill demonstrate remarkable resilience. The incident also exhibits an ability to plan for the future. He saw the reconstruction of his Chicago iron works as an opportunity to employ the most advanced technology in his new mill.

## Conclusion

Eber Ward's transition from the steamboat industry to producing iron was not without difficulties, but ultimately it was successful. His facilities in Wyandotte and Chicago put him in the forefront of iron manufacturers throughout the Midwest and even the country. Ward showed determination and grit as he expanded his business holdings during a difficult economic era. At the same time, he was forced to address the loss of several close family members. Fortunately, Emily remained a constant in his life, acting as his conscience and encouraging him to contribute to her Newport Academy. Driven by intense ambition, Ward also demonstrated a willingness to employ shrewd tactics to defeat rivals. His decision to vertically integrate production at his iron mills helped to keep costs low, and his ability to handle crises such as the financial Panic and fire at his Chicago facility shows he was an effective business leader with vision.

In a letter to his family in January 1858, Ward reflected on the economic hardships he and others faced during the Panic of 1857. His belief in the nation and his faith that conditions were certain to improve encouraged him to keep moving forward during troubled times. "Hundreds have been swept off by the financial turmoil that has traversed the lands of civilized man like the plagues of Egypt engulfing fortunes and hopes with a rapidity and certainty such as man had never known before. Like the terrible plague of London, it spared neither high nor low, strong or weak." He believed that humanity needed to learn from the events: "So evil is sometimes inflicted upon us for our own good both as nations and as individuals. Our duty is to make use of all these good and evil things so far as we can for our own advancement and happiness in this world." At the same time, he criticized the "besotted drunkard with his glass in hand" and those guilty of "wicked perfidy." Ward looked to the future and believed in the progress of humanity. "Thus one year succeeds another, let no one desire to stay the progress of time for with it comes more good than evil, more happiness than misery." Surely, it was much easier for Ward to maintain this positive attitude as he had amassed a great fortune as opposed to those who lost their livelihood and struggled through the economic depression. However, his words help to explain his philosophical outlook and belief in progress.[51]

Just as Eber shared with his family his belief that the nation could overcome the financial difficulties many were experiencing, he also strove to address the political divisiveness facing the country. Ward always had been interested in politics, but by the late 1850s, he became more politically active. He eventually was drawn to the policies championed by the newly formed Republican Party and the first Republican president, Abraham Lincoln.

# 5

# Anti-Slavery Politics and Civil War

*I have now on hand a sufficient quantity of iron to make seven hundred heavy cannon and twenty thousand stand of rifles. I will sell the whole of it to the state of Michigan or the United States on twenty years' time if they will use it in making guns for the maintenance of, and in obedience to the present constitution and laws of the country; and rather than have the constitution altered to favor slavery and corruption, I would make it an unconditional contribution to the cause of freedom.*
—Eber Brock Ward, letter to the editor, *Detroit
Daily Advertiser*, January 5, 1861

*I see it stated that [Secretary of State William] Seward proposes to settle with the southern traitors and practically give them all they ask. . . . Such a settlement would ruin the hopes of the friends of the administration. . . . Rather than live to witness any other settlement than the unconditional surrender of armed rebels and scoundrels, I would sink myself and estate into the middle of the ocean.*
—Eber Brock Ward, letter to Abraham Lincoln, July 11, 1863

Ever since Eber was a boy, his father had preached about the evils of slavery. His father's sojourn in Kentucky back in 1817 made a lasting impression on the elder Mr. Ward. He appreciated the beauty of the land and fertility of the soil, but he could never forget the "sufferings, the tears, and the prayers of those desponding slaves"—permanent reminders of slavery's evils. However much E. B. Ward was indifferent to the working conditions and sufferings of those he employed in his iron mills, he maintained a staunch opposition to slavery. The "seed" of this belief was likely planted by his father during young Eber's formative years. As Eber grew into adulthood he developed working relationships and close friendships with other opponents of slavery. These dealings undoubtedly deepened his hostility to slavery. The institution of slavery also impacted the nation, becoming a more divisive issue in the late 1840s and into the 1850s as the question arose of whether or not the "peculiar institution" should expand into new regions of the country.[1]

For many years, Ward had supported the Whig Party. He was attracted to its pro-business positions, such as federal support for internal improvements and a high tariff to protect American manufacturers, as well as its opposition to slavery. When the party disintegrated in the 1850s over the issue of slavery, Ward quickly transferred his allegiance to the newly formed Republican Party. He also developed alliances with powerful Republicans such as Senator Zachariah Chandler from Michigan and Ohio's Senator Benjamin Wade. Soon, he gained statewide and even national attention by contributing to anti-slavery causes and vocally opposing the expansion of slavery. During the Civil War, Ward was a vocal supporter of the Union, which sometimes put him at odds with Peace Democrats, also referred to as Copperhead Democrats. Copperheads supported the war only insofar as its aim was the preservation of the Union. They were opposed to emancipation and did not view blacks as equal to whites. Historian Paul Taylor has demonstrated that although Michigan as a whole supported Lincoln and emancipation, the city of Detroit was "a Democratic island surrounded by a sea of Michigan Republicanism." Following Lincoln's assassination, Ward joined other Radical Republicans who were critical of Andrew Johnson, the new president. As Ward achieved a national reputation in Republican circles, his name was mentioned as a possible candidate for treasury secretary, but it was a position he would never hold.[2]

# Ward and the Underground Railroad

Eber Ward contributed to the anti slavery movement in many ways. One involved his participation in the Underground Railroad. Due to its geographic location and proximity to Canada, Ward's home state of Michigan served as a gateway to freedom for many slaves seeking to escape. Writer Carol Mull has explained that by the 1850s the Underground Railroad in Michigan had evolved from an irregular organization into a "highly adaptable network of operators assisting freedom seekers." At least three vessels owned by Eber Ward were known to be sympathetic to runaways (the *Pearl*, *Forest Queen*, and *May Queen*), and at times transported escaped slaves to freedom. Ward also employed runaway slaves on his ships. Once, in the early 1850s, a slave catcher came to Michigan looking for a slave who had escaped and was working as a chef on Ward's steamer *Pearl*. Ward facilitated the runaway's escape to Canada and then led a group that negotiated with the slave's former owner to purchase his freedom. The freed man continued to work for Ward and eventually purchased his remaining family members, thereby securing their freedom and uniting his family once again.[3]

Possibly the best examples of Ward's involvement in the Underground Railroad were provided by G. L. Heaton, who worked for Ward as a freight agent on his steamships between 1852 and 1858. Heaton declared that Ward's vessels "formed a very important link in the Underground railroad" and described Ward as "a radical on the question of slavery. Whenever the subject was broached in his hearing he did not hesitate to let his views be known. . . . If there was ever a human being on earth that he [Ward] despised, that he had utter contempt for, it was the person who bought and sold human chattels." Shortly after being hired by Ward, Heaton was introduced to two men who worked as "conductors" facilitating runaways on the Underground Railroad. Ward directed Heaton to allow any fugitive slaves brought to the boat by either of those men to ride free. Often, there might be ten or twelve runaways on board the ship. Heaton recalled that once there were close to thirty on board fleeing from bondage. The runaways frequently hid in an aft steerage cabin.[4]

Sometimes Heaton asked the runaways to tell stories about their lives. One he remembered clearly was told by an old man from Kentucky in the summer of 1854. The unnamed runaway had escaped his owner's plantation with his family of twelve, ranging in age from one to sixty. He and his family traveled only at night. Luckily, they encountered another African American man who took them to the home of a Quaker, where they received their first hot meal in days. They were led to a series of safe houses along the Underground Railroad until they arrived at Ward's steamboat. The man had become determined to escape after his twelve-year-old daughter was whipped by their owner. His goal was to "reach a country where a man can protect his own children . . . against the brutality of an unprincipled licentious drunken white man" despite his African ancestry. With the help of Heaton and Eber Ward's vessel the man and his entire family landed safely in Canada.[5]

Heaton described another incident that involved Eber Ward directly. In September 1856, Heaton was approached by one of the Underground Railroad conductors and was told there were three runaways from Lexington, Kentucky, looking for passage, but their owner and some other slave catchers were right on their trail. Heaton and the captain devised a plan whereby the runaways would hide near some large piles of lumber by the river. When the ship was ready to leave, the crew would signal the runaways with a lantern to take a row-boat to the steamer and climb aboard. All went well—those escaping reached the ship just as it pulled away from the dock and were hidden in the aft cabin. Unfortunately, the slaves' owner also made it to the vessel. He questioned several members of the crew, and an Irish fireman working on the ship betrayed the escapees, showing their owner the hiding place. The Kentucky slaveholder mocked the runaways and informed them that once they reached shore, they would be placed in irons and taken home, where they would each receive one hundred lashes. Fortunately for them, Eber Ward was on board the steamer that night.[6]

Once Ward was informed of the situation, he considered, "I think we can thwart this slave holder's plans." While the vessel was still in Canadian waters, Ward had the captain take the steamer as close to the Canadian side of the Detroit River as possible. Then he was to drop the anchor and lower a small boat with the runaways on board—they would be taken to Canada and free-dom. Ward also directed his crew to "give each of the men a dollar so that they should not be turned loose without means to obtain a breakfast." When the Kentucky slaveholder noticed the ship had stopped, he left his stateroom to investigate. He soon realized what was happening, but by then the boat with the runaways was halfway to the Canadian shoreline. The slaveholder became "frantic with rage" and "belched forth in language that would astonish the most depraved." The man threatened to sue Ward, blaming him for the loss of his property, but he was not heard from again.[7]

These events demonstrate the concerns and involvement of Ward as he dealt with the issue of slavery on a personal level. The debate over slavery also dominated the national political scene and transformed the country.

# Debate over Slavery in the United States

American expansion westward heightened the debate over slavery. In the 1840s many in the country embraced Manifest Destiny, the belief the United States should, and would, extend its empire across the North American continent to the Pacific Ocean. The Mexican-American War (1846–48) was arguably the culmination of this movement. As a result of the treaty that ended the war, the United States acquired vast territories in what is now the American Southwest, including the present-day states of California, Nevada, New Mexico, Utah, most of Arizona, and portions of other states in the region. James K. Polk was the president who put Manifest Destiny into action and oversaw this expansion. He hoped the land acquisition would unite the nation. Instead, it ignited a debate over the issue of whether or not slavery should expand into this new territory. Members of Congress attempted to compromise on the issue of slavery's expansion, but less than ten years after the end of the Mexican-American War, the nation became increasingly divided along sectional lines. Conflict heightened following the passage of the Kansas-Nebraska Act in 1854.

Provisions of the act called for the organization of two new territories in the West, Kansas and Nebraska. The legal status of slavery in the new territories would be determined by popular sovereignty, a vote by the region's inhabitants. In hopes to satisfy both supporters and opponents of slavery, it was presumed that residents of Kansas would vote to protect slavery due to its proximity to the slave state of Missouri, while opponents would vote for its prohibition in Nebraska. Debate over the bill caused a firestorm of protest by slavery's opponents, in part because the legislation repealed a longtime understanding that slavery would never expand into those newly organized areas Ultimately, the proposal became law, but it reinforced the deep divisions within the country and ended the two-party system of politics featuring the Whigs and Democrats. Passage of the Kansas-Nebraska Act led to the disintegration of the Whig Party, which split into Northern and Southern wings over the possibility that slavery might expand into new territory. These national events had a deep impact on Eber Brock Ward as he transferred his political allegiance to a newly formed political party.[8]

The Whig Party's demise left a void for those opposed to the Democratic Party and its support for slavery's expansion. Accordingly, a convention was held in Jackson, Michigan, in July 1854, and a brand-new organization, the Republican Party, was born. It represented a combination of former Whigs and Free Soil Democrats with a disparate set of values. Some were reformers who previously had supported the temperance movement, or prohibition of alcohol. Others were nativists opposed to the influence of the Catholic Church and Irish immigration. Although there were different wings to this new coalition, all were unified in the goal of "preventing the further extension of slave territory." The convention nominated a slate of candidates for that fall's election in Michigan, including Kinsley S. Bingham for governor. Eber Ward quickly joined the new Republican Party and lent his support for the cause. That fall, Bingham was elected governor, and a Republican majority was elected to the state legislature.[9]

Ward reinforced his opposition to slavery after scores of pro-slavery advocates made their way to Kansas in 1855 to vote—illegally—in that territory's election to determine the status of slavery. The constitution implemented in Lecompton, Kansas, not only protected slavery but limited officeholders to only those who would swear loyalty oaths upholding slavery. Following the passage of these and similar provisions, opponents of slavery made their way to Kansas and adopted their own constitution. Violence erupted between the two groups in what was referred to as "Bleeding Kansas." Events in Kansas captured the nation's attention and struck Michigan's residents, including Eber Ward, personally. In the aftermath of the violent encounters in Kansas, Detroit's residents held a rally on June 2, 1856. Ward attended the gathering, during which the "wrongs of Kansas" were discussed. Speakers challenged the crowd to contribute funds to ensure Kansas Territory would be free from slavery. Ward demonstrated his support for the anti-slavery cause by donating $10,000 ($292,353.23 in 2020 dollars).[10]

Even prior to the rally in 1856, E.B. worked to cultivate relationships with other like-minded business leaders, many of whom became prominent members of the Republican Party. Soon after relocating to Detroit in 1850, he had joined the Fort Street Presbyterian Church, one of the largest and most influential churches in the city. The congregation at one time boasted several influential political figures, including three members of Congress and five senators. Among these were Zachariah Chandler, who was elected Detroit's mayor for one term and later served eighteen years in the U.S. Senate. Ward developed a close relationship with the influential Chandler. The two had much in common. They were both successful business leaders in Detroit who were opposed to slavery and had been Whigs before joining the Republican Party. The two also served on the Detroit Fire and Marine Insurance Company board together.[11]

Ward's decision to join a Presbyterian congregation was significant as the Presbyterians had a strong tradition of condemning slavery. In fact, at the Presbyterian's General Assembly meeting in 1818, it adopted a resolution declaring, "We consider the voluntary enslaving of one part of the human race by another, as a gross violation of the most precious and sacred rights of human nature; as utterly inconsistent with the law of God." It called for the "complete abolition of slavery throughout Christendom." However, another resolution passed at the same General Assembly meeting declared emancipation could not take place immediately due to the "ignorance" and "vicious habits" of slaves.

Pew assignments at Detroit's Fort Street Presbyterian Church. Notice "Capt. Ward" at pew 66 and Senator "Z. Chandler" at pew 68. (Courtesy of the Burton Historical Collection, Detroit Public Library)

Condemnations of slavery among Presbyterians were strongest in Northern regions of the country; many who lived in the South continued to own slaves. By the start of the Civil War, the Presbyterians were deeply divided on the slavery issue, and the church eventually split into Northern and Southern denominations. Ultimately, Ward was likely drawn to the Fort Street congregation due to the church's opposition to slavery as well as the business connections he hoped to cultivate with other powerful church members.[12]

As the decade of the 1850s continued, the nation became increasingly divided. Two events demonstrate these divisions. In 1857 the Supreme Court announced its decision in the Dred Scott case. Dred Scott was a slave transported by his owner from a slave state to a territory and state where slavery was prohibited. Scott sued to obtain his freedom. The Court ruled against him, arguing that blacks, whether free or enslaved, were not citizens and therefore had no citizenship rights. The Court also determined that Congress had no authority to prohibit slavery in any territory; only states had such power. These decisions frustrated Eber Ward and other opponents of slavery, because they seemed to validate arguments made by Southern slaveholders. Just two years later, the abolitionist John Brown attempted to start a slave rebellion. Previously, Brown had been connected to the murder of five pro-slavery supporters in Kansas during the Bleeding Kansas conflict. His action was popularly known as the Pottawatomi Creek Massacre. His goal in 1859 was to capture the federal arsenal in Harper's Ferry, Virginia, use it as a base to free slaves, and lead a slave revolt. Brown's attempt failed—he was arrested, convicted of treason, and executed. Southerners proclaimed justice had been served, but some in the North treated Brown as a martyr. As the country headed into the campaign for the 1860 election, the debate over slavery posed the greatest threat to the Union the nation had ever faced.[13]

Events progressed rapidly as voters prepared to choose a new president in 1860. Delegates from the Republican Party gathered in Chicago that May and nominated Abraham Lincoln. He pledged to allow slavery to remain where it already existed, but opposed the expansion of slavery into any new territory. Delegates to the Democratic Party's convention in South Carolina that year were divided. Eventually the party split into two factions. The Northern Democrats chose Stephen Douglas as their nominee, while the Southern Democrats picked John C. Breckinridge. Douglas wanted popular sovereignty, or the voters, to decide if slavery should expand, while Breckinridge supported the expansion of slavery into new areas. Eber Ward emerged as a vocal lobbyist in this campaign and an ardent supporter of Abraham Lincoln.[14]

In August 1860, Ward published a pamphlet outlining the reasons why working people, farmers, and all those who supported freedom should vote for the Republican Party in the upcoming election. The pamphlet presented both an economic and moral argument. First, E.B. argued in favor of a protective tariff to encourage manufacturing in the United States. He maintained this would lower unemployment and revive the nation's economy because Americans imported millions of dollars' worth of iron, silks, and other finished products from Europe. He believed consumers should purchase their goods from American companies. "A protective tariff will give the work to our own people, instead of people in Europe." He tried to keep his message simple. "If we elect the Republican ticket, we shall have a protective tariff. If we get a protective tariff the country will prosper." Ward reminded his readers that he was not running for public office and therefore he was not advocating for himself—he supported these policies in the interests of all common people. Of course, what he failed to mention was that if the United States adopted a protective tariff, Ward would stand to benefit personally, as it would protect his iron manufacturing plants from European competition.[15]

Ward continued by equating slavery with sin. He declared that slavery's extension was one of the "great besetting sins of public theft" and a "national folly." The Republican Party was firmly opposed to any expansion of slavery. Furthermore, he explained that slavery and the Democratic Party "debased, degraded" and were "infamous enemies to the human family." He encouraged voters to support Abraham Lincoln's candidacy due to his positions on both slavery and the tariff question. Such arguments prompted historian Ronald Formisano to describe Ward's views as providing "a classic example of the fusion of economic interest, sectional consciousness, and moral passion" that emerged as the driving force in Michigan's Republican Party and throughout the Midwest in this era.[16]

The pamphlet also hinted at an economic policy Ward would develop more fully in subsequent years. He argued that in order for a nation, or a region, to be truly prosperous, its economy should be diversified to include both agriculture and manufacturing. Specifically, Ward contended that the Midwest's economy was too reliant upon agriculture and therefore would remain dependent upon the manufacturing centers of the New England states and Europe until its economy became more varied. He maintained that the government should favor policies that facilitated the construction of factories, which would benefit the Midwest and the nation by providing additional employment opportunities for laborers. Eventually, Ward would argue that the enhancement of manufacturing, combined with the region's robust agricultural base, would provide a "New Manifest Destiny" for the Midwest.[17]

An Abraham Lincoln victory in the 1860 election was by no means a foregone conclusion. Detroit had been a Democratic Party stronghold for years; the party was particularly popular among the city's large immigrant population. Ultimately, Lincoln and the Republican Party did prevail in the elections that November. Lincoln carried the state of Michigan with 57 percent of the vote. He was even able to capture a majority in Wayne County, which included Detroit. Republicans also won all four of the state's congressional races. Partially because the Democratic Party had split into Northern and Southern factions, Lincoln emerged victorious at the national level as well. Ward celebrated Lincoln's win as a "victory over the most terrible enemies that ever combined against the happiness and prosperity of man." He saw it as a triumph for freedom, truth, and intelligence. He cast the victory in biblical terms, declaring Christians could rejoice because "Satan is once more rebuked." He continued, "*The people have said, 'let there be light,' and there is light.*"[18]

Almost immediately, the states of the Deep South reacted negatively to Lincoln's victory. His candidacy had been so unpopular in that region that Lincoln's name did not even appear on the ballots of several Southern states. The state legislature in South Carolina was the first to consider secession. In an effort to prevent the state from taking the radical step of leaving the Union, Ward wrote to South Carolina governor William Gist. Ward admitted that he and other Republicans were opposed to the extension of slavery into new territory, but had no plans to prohibit slavery where it already existed. He assured Gist, "There are but very few persons in the North who are really abolitionists." He encouraged the governor to meet with the newly elected Lincoln. Ward also suggested that Gist and members of South Carolina's legislature should take a tour of the Northern states, even offering to pay for such an excursion. This was likely an honest attempt to promote dialogue, but he also probably wanted to intimidate the secessionists by showing off the mines, factories, and railroads that were more plentiful in the North than the South. His message also contained a warning, should conflict develop. "The free states will be a formidable competitor in case of a hostile collision." There is no record that Governor Gist responded to Ward's proposal. On December 20, 1860, South Carolina's legislature voted to secede from the Union. Six more states followed suit, even before Lincoln's inauguration. The question remained, how would those living in Northern states react? Eber Brock Ward was unwilling to surrender.[19]

Using Detroit's Republican newspaper the *Daily Advertiser* as a loudspeaker for his message, Ward called upon those living in the North to wake up and take action to "save our government and crush disunion." Rejecting compromise, he called upon the Northern states to raise and train an army of five hundred thousand, if necessary, to show "the South that the Constitution and laws shall be obeyed."[20] The following week he continued the call to arms, professing to have enough iron at his mills to make "seven hundred heavy cannon and twenty thousand stand of rifles." He was ready to sell the iron to the federal government and allow the U.S. Treasury to take twenty years to pay him back to prevent the Constitution from being altered to protect "slavery and corruption." He also wrote a private letter of encouragement to Abraham Lincoln, relating that he and others, such as Senators Zachariah Chandler and Benjamin Wade, continued to support him. Ward predicted, "Your administration will be one of the great periods of history." In a sadly prophetic passage, he also expressed concerns for Lincoln's safety, warning, "Do not allow yourself to be assassinated."[21]

Although Lincoln and the Republican Party took the state of Michigan in the 1860 election, conditions within the city of Detroit were complicated in the succeeding years. E. B. Ward continued to operate his businesses as well as generate support for the war effort. At times, due to his vocal advocacy for Lincoln and the North, Ward stood out as a polarizing figure in the community.

## Civil War and Detroit

The Civil War began April 12, 1861, when Confederate forces fired on Fort Sumter in Charleston, South Carolina. The fort's commander surrendered the next day. President Lincoln then called for seventy-five thousand volunteers from the states loyal to the Union to suppress the rebellion. Efforts to fill Michigan's quota of soldiers were successful—there was a surge of patriotism and volunteers joined several units. Support for the war remained strong as long as residents believed the war would be short and war aims focused on preservation of the Union. Nevertheless, as the fighting dragged on and the Union's war aims began to shift, support weakened in some areas. The majority of Michigan's residents were opposed to slavery, but that did not mean they believed in racial equality. To further complicate matters, many immigrants feared that if slavery was abolished, newly freed black laborers would rush to Northern cities to compete for jobs. This was particularly true for the Irish, who often were relegated to the most menial jobs available. At the start of the Civil War, immigrants, many of them Irish, comprised nearly half of Detroit's population. In July 1862, Abraham Lincoln called for an additional three hundred thousand troops. When the City of Detroit staged a rally at Campus Martius to generate enlistment of volunteers following Lincoln's request, conflict emerged, with Eber Ward at its center.[22]

The gathering began innocently enough, with pro-Lincoln orators rallying support for the war effort. Before long, however, those in attendance began to jeer and taunt the speakers. When Ward rose to speak, some in the crowd rushed the rostrum and attempted to attack him. Ward and several other speakers were quickly rushed to safety inside a nearby hotel. Although E.B. dismissed the mob as a "drunken rabble," the attempted assault exposed deep divisions within Detroit's community.[23] Rumors had spread that Lincoln was ready to implement a military draft—and the laboring classes were more likely to be drafted. Ward's vocal support of Lincoln and his position as the city's wealthiest man prompted the crowd to target him. Additional fears arose from the belief that war aims might expand to include emancipation of the slaves. Abraham Lincoln had yet to announce the preliminary Emancipation Proclamation, but he did so in September 1862. Not everyone approved of such a policy shift. As expressed by the *Detroit Free Press*, the city's Democratic newspaper, many Detroiters would support the war effort only so long as war aims were limited to preventing the "dissolution of the Union," which it considered "armed treason." Residents were firmly opposed to a "Negro war" devoted to abolition. Other rumors circulated that Ward had dismissed white employees in favor of African Americans. Ward denied the charges in a letter he wrote in the *Advertiser and Tribune*, Detroit's newly organized Republican newspaper. E.B. claimed that he employed about 850 men, 25 of whom were black. Each black man he employed worked in some capacity on one of his ships. He defended his right to "employ just such persons to do my work as I choose," including black laborers.[24]

Despite the ugliness of the previous gathering, efforts to recruit volunteers to serve in the Union army continued. One week after the riot at Campus Martius, a second rally was held at the same location. Eber Ward was noticeably absent. Patriotism was widespread at this second meeting, and Michigan's regiments grew, as Detroit's Common Council offered bounties to volunteers who lived in the city. To ensure there were enough soldiers to continue the fight, Congress authorized a draft in 1862, which was expanded in 1863. Men between the ages of eighteen and forty-five were subject to service, although there were exemptions for those who were infirm or who had dependents. The most controversial exemption allowed a draftee to avoid service if he paid a $300 fee to the national government. The new law was terribly unpopular in Detroit and it, along with a trial involving a "mulatto" man accused of raping two white girls, sparked a race riot in March 1863. The results were devastating. Mobs of whites attacked dozens of blacks. Two people were killed, over thirty buildings were destroyed, and many of the city's residents, primarily African Americans, were left homeless. Such upheavals demonstrate the diversity of opinion Michigan's residents held concerning emancipation, the war, and who should serve in the military.[25]

Eber Ward did not serve in the military during the Civil War, nor did any of his sons who would have been eligible for the draft. It is unknown if Ward ever paid the $300 fee so that his boys could avoid the draft. He did contribute significantly to Detroit's bounty fund, which provided a cash bonus to residents who volunteered to serve in one of Michigan's regiments in an effort to boost enlistment. Ward's nephew Asa Brindle, who had been working at the Eureka Iron Mill in Wyandotte, quit his job to volunteer. He served in the Twenty-Fourth Michigan and eventually was promoted to sergeant. He saw action at more than one engagement, and was killed by a cannonball in the Chancellorsville campaign on April 30, 1863.[26]

Despite the loss of his nephew, Ward remained determined to defeat the Confederacy. In a letter to his niece Florence Mayhew, he related, "Our war news is good, but we are not quite through yet. We need two more important victories before we can destroy the piratical confederacy." Even following the battle of Gettysburg in July 1863, where the combined Union and Confederate casualties totaled more than fifty thousand, Ward was resolved to continue the fight. He was furious when he heard a rumor that Secretary of State William Seward might support a negotiated settlement with leaders of the Confederacy. Ward fired off a letter to Abraham Lincoln objecting to anything other than the complete capitulation of the South. "Rather than live to witness any other settlement than the unconditional surrender of the armed rebels and scoundrels, I would sink myself and my estate into the middle of the ocean."[27]

Somewhat surprisingly, Eber Ward was supportive of the income tax passed by Congress to raise funds for the war effort in 1862. This tax on individual incomes was the first of its kind in American history. It levied a 3 percent tax on those earning between $600 and $10,000, the rate growing to 5 percent on incomes over $10,000. Additional legislation two years later increased rates so individuals with incomes above $5,000 paid a 10 percent tax. Ward handed over a lot of money to the federal government as a result of the new tax. According to IRS tax records, in 1864 Ward paid $4,501.95 in taxes on his income of $90,039 ($1,513,093.91 in 2020 dollars). In the summer of 1863, some manufacturers complained about the tax and invited Ward to help them lobby to eliminate or reduce it. Ward declined the invitation and responded with a public letter in the *New York Daily Tribune*. He argued that all manufacturers must guard against oppressive governmental taxation, but their personal business concerns should be balanced with the interests of the country. Ward wrote, "I am willing to continue to pay my income tax" and called upon others to do the same "not grudgingly, but cheerfully, promptly, and with a hearty good will." As the nation faced a true crisis, he viewed it as his patriotic duty to pay his taxes. If the tax became too oppressive or if there were not enough protections for American businesses, he was willing to approach Congress in the future, but was not disposed to do so at that time.[28]

Ward also contributed to the war effort as Detroit's residents grew concerned the Confederates might stage an invasion of the city from Canada. In November 1863, rumors spread that rebel forces planned to invade Detroit via Sandwich (today's Windsor) and use it as a base to attack communities in the Great Lakes. Panic struck the city as local officials took steps to defend against any such offensive. Ward cooperated by allowing his steamship *Forrester* to be used for scouting missions to determine if rebel gunboats had entered the area. As a precaution, a battery of four guns was placed on the *Forrester* as the vessel prepared for its mission. Additionally, as the *Detroit Free Press* noted with appreciation, Ward had some of his small boats patrol the Detroit River near Wyandotte to spot any enemy vessels entering the waterway. It turned out the rumors were to some extent true. In September 1864, a group of Confederate spies and sympathizers boarded the steamer *Philo Parsons* at Detroit. Additional conspirators joined at the Canadian port of Amherstburg. The rebels secreted a large trunk with revolvers and axes on board the vessel. Armed with these weapons, the plotters commandeered the *Philo Parsons*. Their ultimate goal was to seize the USS *Michigan*, a warship patrolling Lake Erie, and free Confederate prisoners of war detained on Johnson's Island, just outside of Sandusky, Ohio. They succeeded in taking over an additional vessel, the *Island Queen*, but abandoned their plans when they failed to receive a signal from their accomplices that the USS *Michigan* had been captured. While the Confederate scheme was thwarted, rumors of additional plots remained as the presidential election of 1864 drew near.[29]

Throughout 1864, Confederate leaders became increasingly anxious. They were unable to launch a successful invasion of the North. Among other Union actions, General William T. Sherman led a march of destruction from Atlanta to the sea. The possible disruption of Lincoln's bid for reelection in November that year offered an opportunity to return to the offensive. About one month prior to the election, evidence circulated indicating that the rebels were planning to attack and destroy the homes of several prominent Republicans living within Detroit, including Eber Ward's. On Saturday, October 30, Henry N. Walker of the *Detroit Free Press* traveled to Ward's home to determine if E.B. had any information concerning the alleged plot. There was no love lost between the two men—they had battled one another ever since Walker had purchased the paper a few years earlier. After discussing matters for a time, Walker offered his opinion that a riot was imminent unless residents were guaranteed that the draft would soon end. Ward responded with a ruthlessness reminiscent of his business practices, declaring that if a riot did occur, he would ensure that Walker's newspaper offices would be burned to the ground. Walker was shocked. Then Ward invited Walker into his home, where eighty employees of Ward's Wyandotte plant, armed with over three hundred rifles, hand grenades, and other weapons, stood ready to defend against an attack. Ward also showed Walker a letter from Michigan's governor Austin Blair. If an attack did occur, Detroit would be placed under martial law, with Ward serving as provost marshal. Ward vowed that the instant any rebels "begin to carry out their plans to burn and shoot, I will act with authority" and Southern sympathizers in the city "will be taught a lesson." Fortunately, no attack occurred and the election took place without any problems. Abraham Lincoln was elected to a second term in office along with his new vice president, Andrew Johnson.[30]

Although Ward never served as provost marshal, E.B. did receive an honor from the state due to his support for the Union during the war. In February 1863, the First Michigan Colored Infantry Regiment was formed. Eventually, some fourteen hundred African American soldiers volunteered to serve in its ranks. Most came from Detroit, but many hailed from Canada. About one thousand had been born slaves in the United States. The facility where the First Michigan soldiers received their training was named Camp Ward in honor of Eber Brock Ward's leadership in the city and his support for emancipation. White officers commanded the unit, which later became the 102nd United

Ward was an ardent opponent of slavery and a strong supporter of the Union during the Civil War. (Author's collection)

States Colored Infantry. Troops saw action in South Carolina, Georgia, and Florida, where they acquitted themselves well.[31]

As Lincoln declared, "With malice toward none; with charity toward all" in his second inaugural address on March 4, 1865, the war was heading toward its ultimate conclusion. Less than six weeks later, Robert E. Lee surrendered his forces to Ulysses S. Grant on April 9, 1865. The next day a gathering was held in Detroit's Campus Martius to celebrate the exciting news as total victory for the Union appeared to be just around the corner. Then tragedy struck: Eber Ward's fear of a Lincoln assassination came true when the president was shot at Ford's Theater in Washington, DC, on April 14, 1865. Lincoln died the following day and Vice President Andrew Johnson assumed the presidency. Initially, Ward was supportive of Lincoln's successor, but then he, along with many other Republicans, came into conflict with Johnson as the new president did very little to protect the rights of former slaves.[32]

## Radical Republicans

At first glance, Andrew Johnson seemed an odd choice to serve as Abraham Lincoln's vice president. He was a life-long Democrat who at one point had owned slaves. He had served in a range of elected positions, including governor of Tennessee and U.S. senator. However, when his home state chose to secede, Johnson was the only senator from a Confederate state to remain loyal to the Union. Lincoln tapped Johnson to be his running mate in 1864 in an effort to broaden his candidacy and unify the country. Shortly after Johnson assumed the presidency, the *Detroit Advertiser and Tribune* expressed its support for him, praising the "favorable impression" Johnson made in several speeches as the nation grieved the fallen Lincoln. But before long the Republican paper came to sharply criticize Johnson's policies. While Johnson was opposed to secession, he vetoed civil rights legislation and other proposals designed to provide aid to former slaves. These actions put Johnson directly at odds with Eber Ward, who was an advocate of freedmen's organizations, which provided a range of amenities, such as food, shelter, and established schools, for former slaves. For a time Ward even served as the president of Detroit's Freedmen's Relief Association. The *Advertiser and Tribune* issued sharp rebukes of the president, citing his "reckless disregard of historical truth" when he ignored black codes passed in Southern states that established conditions very similar to slavery and severely limited the rights of African Americans.[33]

Johnson's actions also put him at odds with congressional Republicans, often referred to as Radical Republicans. These were members of the Republican Party who sought to punish the South for causing the Civil War and who supported legislation to protect the rights of former slaves. Eber Ward sympathized with the Radical Republicans, and two of his close friends, Senators Zachariah Chandler of Michigan and Benjamin Wade of Ohio, were vocal members of this group. The last straw for Johnson in his battle with the Radical Republicans came when he fired his secretary of war, Edwin Stanton. This violated the Tenure of Office Act, which prohibited the president from removing a cabinet member without Senate approval. As a result, Johnson was impeached by the House of Representatives in February 1868. Three weeks later, a trial was held in the Senate to determine if he would be removed from office.[34]

Ward supported Johnson's removal from office for political reasons—he disagreed with the president on many policy issues—but he also had personal motives to support Johnson's removal. If events proceeded as some predicted, it was possible that Ward could find himself named to a position in a new presidential administration. Because Johnson had assumed the presidency as a result of Lincoln's assassination, he had no vice president. According to the line of succession at that time, if Johnson was removed, Benjamin Wade would become the next president, since he held the office of president pro tempore of the Senate. Wade had risen to a leadership position within the Republican Party due to his staunch anti-slavery views and his unwillingness to compromise with secessionists during the Civil War; yet he had enemies, too. He could be outspoken and aggressive to those with whom he disagreed. He also supported high tariffs, women's rights, and voting rights for former slaves, which put him at odds with moderates even within his own party. Benjamin Wade and Eber Ward had been friends for some time. The two were so close that Ward even named one of his vessels *B. F. Wade* in his friend's honor. According to speculation at the time of the impeachment trial, Wade was so convinced that Johnson would be removed he already had picked out his cabinet. His choice for treasury secretary was Eber Brock Ward.[35]

Johnson's trial in the Senate, which lasted several weeks, captured the nation's attention. E.B. followed the proceedings closely; about one month into the trial, he related to his niece that "impeachment goes bravely on" and the "galleries of the Congress are filled every day" with observers. He also shared the public's "fixed belief in the conviction of the president." Ward expected to remain in Washington, DC, for some time while the proceedings continued. If he did become treasury secretary, Ward hoped to repeal the income tax, since he believed the wartime measure was no longer necessary, and to increase the tariff on imported goods. If both goals were achieved, Ward would stand to benefit substantially. Ultimately, Ward was denied the position he sought. Andrew Johnson was not removed from office; the Senate vote was one short of the required two-thirds majority needed to do so. The result surprised many in the United States. There weren't enough votes for removal because some senators were concerned Johnson's removal might weaken the presidency and therefore damage the balance of power in the nation's capital. Other senators simply did not like Benjamin Wade and would not vote to grant him the presidency. Wade's connection with Eber Ward did not help either. Rumors about Ward's possible selection as treasury secretary "deeply disturbed" some in the business community who worried that Ward's advocacy for a higher tariff would result in increased costs for consumers and damage the overall economy. The result likely stung Ward personally, as it dealt a blow to his ambition, but he remained committed to the Republican Party.[36]

In 1868, Republicans nominated Ulysses S. Grant for the presidency. Ward actively supported the campaign of the former Union commander, who was elected that November. In subsequent years, Ward was consumed by the active management of his business enterprises, but continued to advocate for a higher tariff. When Ward split with Grant on some fiscal policies during his first term, there was speculation Ward might join with a group of liberal Republicans to challenge Grant's nomination for a second term. Ward scoffed at the idea, declaring in an editorial, "I am mortified to think that my worst enemies should think so meanly of me as to believe me capable of deserting a party which has crushed secession [and] abolished slavery." Grant was successfully reelected to a second term, and Ward even served as a presidential elector in support of Grant that year. For the remainder of his life, Eber Ward remained a loyal and active member of the Republican Party.[37]

Ward's actions and writings make it clear he supported the presidency of Ulysses Grant, but his positions concerning other causes promoted by the Republican Party in this era are more difficult to determine. Yet a careful reading of a newly formed newspaper, the *Detroit Post*, can help to offer insight. According to Detroit historian Silas Farmer, the *Detroit Post* was a fiercely "Radical Republican organ" when first published in 1866. Senator Zachariah Chandler and Eber Ward were "large shareholders," and both used the paper as a mouthpiece to promote their own causes and those championed by the Republican Party.[38] For example, discussing a range of potential vice presidential candidates during the 1868 presidential campaign, not only did the newspaper argue in favor of a loyal Republican, it supported "a Radical candidate *from a Radical state*." The paper also labeled President Johnson "blind, deluded, and apparently insane" due to his policy decisions. Editorials consistently argued in support of Johnson's impeachment and removal from office.[39]

E. B. Ward often submitted letters to the paper advocating cuts in taxes and spending as well as a higher tariff to protect American manufacturers. These regularly were followed by editorials in support of the positions Ward promoted.[40] The *Detroit Post* also took a strong stance on the issue of voting rights for African American men, often referring to the topic as "equal suffrage." The paper argued that black men should have the right to vote based upon "the doctrine of Equal Rights for all men before the law, according to the principle which is the basis of the Declaration of Independence" and criticized Democrats for "insisting upon the principle of an aristocratic governing class." The paper's editors also noted that free blacks could vote in some of the original colonies and they had contributed in many ways to the fight for independence. The *Detroit Post* continued in support of equal access to the ballot box by arguing, "Justice and Equal Rights are Republican principles" opposed by the Democratic Party, which "appeals only to prejudice . . . injustice, oppression and wrong." The paper even invoked the Christian faith by arguing that the "Golden Rule of Christianity, of doing unto others as we would that they should do unto us" provided justification for "equal suffrage."[41]

Some of the most powerful letters included in the *Detroit Post* in support of voting rights for black men were written by African American residents of Michigan. Rather than include their name, the author of each letter was identified simply as "A Non-Voter." One letter thanked the *Post* for its "outspoken ess" support "upon the question of suffrage for the negro." Another declared, "No people have been more anxious to secure the franchise than the colored men of Michigan and none would use it more contentiously in sustaining the Government in all just measures." The author maintained that "neither ignorance, cowardice, nor barbarous instincts disqualify white men" and questioned why blacks were denied the right to vote simply based upon the color of their skin. An editorial accompanying one letter commended the author for its "calm temper, its fair use of language, its literary style and merits and its just political expression." It declared the fear raised by some whites who believed that if blacks had the right to vote, they would rule over whites was "self-evidently absurd" and only "weak, ignorant, inferior men" would have such fear.[42]

Although Ward and his associates at the *Detroit Post* supported equal suffrage for black men, that support was not extended to women. The question of extending voting rights to women actually split the Republican Party in this era. A scathing editorial in the *Detroit Post* in 1869 offered several arguments opposing women's suffrage. The editors claimed women were "very quarrelsome in disposition without the capacity to bear arms, and thus the women will force the country into wars, while they will make the men do their fighting." They contended that "women possess a power over men" and "they might use this power to drive men to war, by threatening non-intercourse, if they refused to fight." The paper also used religious arguments to support its opposition to women's suffrage: "All our troubles have come from Adam's yielding to his wife" and "It is the will of God that man should rule. Whoever says that women shall vote goes against the will of God, and will go down."[43]

The presence of such letters and numerous articles in the *Detroit Post* is significant, reflecting a range of topics supported, and opposed, by the Republican Party in this era. Eber Ward was a large shareholder in the *Post*. His outlook is clear in many of his own writings that appeared in the paper as well as in the positions taken by its editorial staff. Given the level of control Ward maintained over all aspects of his other companies, it would be hard to fathom his opposition to positions taken by the *Post*, such as the expansion of voting rights to African American men in Michigan, and ultimately the nation, with the Fifteenth Amendment.[44] Taken collectively, they indicate Ward's continued support for the Republican Party and the agenda promoted by Radical

Republicans in Congress. However, they also indicate the limit of his beliefs; it is very unlikely he supported voting rights for women.

## Ward's Attitudes about Race and Abolition of Slavery

For years, Ward had been interested in politics. Given his views, it was natural for him to gravitate to the Republican Party. He was a strong supporter of the Union during the Civil War and he emerged as a prominent, if polarizing, figure. The war complicated conditions within the state of Michigan. Although a majority in the state supported Lincoln and emancipation, the same was not true for all living in the city of Detroit. Regardless of the controversy caused by issues such as the draft and emancipation among Detroit's residents, Ward continued to be a vocal advocate in favor of Lincoln's policies and the war effort. Economic issues, such as a protective tariff, attracted Ward to the Republican Party, but he also stood firmly in favor of the party's position on slavery. Although by the end of the Civil War he believed slavery had to be eliminated, there was nuance to his beliefs.

Eber Ward's record demonstrates that he actively opposed slavery, but was he an abolitionist? Given his actions and writings, it seems unlikely. The abolitionist movement came about in the 1830s, along with many other reform movements. Its chief proponent and most militant advocate was William Lloyd Garrison. He, and others with like-minded views, rejected arguments put forth by supporters of gradual emancipation, instead demanding "an immediate end to slavery" without compensation for slave owners. Additionally, they called for the "incorporation of the freed slaves as equal members of society." Prior to the 1830s, there had been opponents of slavery, but most called for its gradual elimination and asked owners to free their slaves voluntarily. Many also supported the removal of free blacks to regions outside the United States, like Liberia. After all, the Constitution protected slavery, and eight of the first twelve presidents had owned slaves. Abolitionists were radicals who condemned slaveholders and branded slavery as a cruel and barbaric system. For years, abolitionists were very small in number, although throughout the 1850s, as the nation became increasingly divided over slavery, their members grew.[45]

In many ways, Ward's views of slavery paralleled those of Abraham Lincoln. Both Ward and Lincoln were morally opposed to slavery and had adopted this viewpoint at an early age. Both had been Whigs and then joined the Republican Party, which opposed the expansion of slavery into new territories. When Lincoln took the oath of office in March 1861, he reinforced his position that he had no intention "to interfere with the institution of slavery in the States where it exists." For some time, he even supported a program of gradual emancipation with limited compensation to slave owners. During the early stages of the Civil War, he famously wrote, "My paramount object in this struggle is to save the Union. . . . If I could save the Union without freeing any slave I would do it, and if I could save it by freeing all the slaves I would do it . . . if I could save it by freeing some and leave others alone I would also do that." However, by the summer of 1862, his views began to change. In September 1862, he issued the preliminary Emancipation Proclamation, which went into effect January 1, 1863. Lincoln's foremost military concern was to maintain the allegiance of the border states (Missouri, Kentucky, West Virginia, Maryland, and Delaware) in which slavery was legal but the governments remained loyal to the Union. The Emancipation Proclamation reflected those concerns. It declared that slaves living in states rebelling against the Union, a region where Lincoln had no authority, were free—but it did not free any slaves in the border states. Yet it was an important military and political document that helped to unify Union war aims and ultimately led to the freedom of nearly 4 million enslaved African Americans. Lincoln's actions and statements over the years demonstrate that his views of slavery had evolved over time.[46]

Statements included in E. B. Ward's letter to Governor William Gist, written prior to South Carolina's secession, sound very similar to Lincoln's comments early in the war. Ward's message was conciliatory, declaring the willingness of Northerners to respect "all your historic rights" (such as owning slaves) and maintaining that he and others objected only to the expansion of slavery. He also assured Gist, "There is not one in two hundred in our population who favor the abolition of slavery in the Southern states."[47] These are not statements that would be made by an abolitionist demanding an immediate end to slavery. Just as Lincoln's views evolved over time, so did Ward's. As the war continued, Ward's rhetoric became stronger and the conciliatory tone was replaced with statements such as "Our antagonists are traitors—enemies of the human race. . . . They will be scattered to the four corners of the earth, hated . . . and scorned." He also called for the "destruction of slavery" and the "freedom of the blacks at the South" along with the elimination of the Southern aristocracy.[48]

Ward and Lincoln also likely held similar prejudicial attitudes. Bias toward non-whites, particularly blacks, was commonplace in nineteenth-century America. Historian Eric Foner has commented that Lincoln "shared many of the prejudices of the society in which he lived. . . . He may not have fully embraced racism, but he did not condemn it."[49] The same was true for Eber Ward. He aided the efforts of the Underground Railroad, yet African American workers were relegated to second-class status when it came to employment in his businesses. When he was criticized for hiring blacks, Ward admitted that although they were employed on his ships, "I have not one now employed on land, and do not know that I ever had." Some worked as cooks, barbers, or firemen on his vessels, but often they were confined to jobs that offered low pay under difficult conditions.[50] This was particularly true for those who worked on the *Sam Ward*, a steamboat nicknamed Old Black Sam due to its unique black coloring. A crew of twenty or more African American men was often picked up in Detroit and taken to Lake Superior's Keweenaw Peninsula, in the heart of Michigan's copper country. Once there, the men loaded the ship with copper or iron ore by hand, using wheelbarrows. It took two or three days to load the ship with cargo, which then was unloaded when the *Sam Ward* reached its expected destination. While pushing their heavy loads, the men sang a tune with several verses, some of which have been captured using the workers' dialect.

> *De cap'-n's in de pilot house ringin' de bell,*
> *Who's on de way boys, who's on de way?*
> *'N' de mate's down 'atween decks giv'n de niggas hell!*
> *Tell me whar yo' goin!*

There were many verses to the song; some related to a specific storyline or character. They often provided insight into the conditions faced on Ward's ship. At times, the workers' frustration was reflected in the lyrics.

> *Ah'd rudd'r be daid 'n' a'lyin in de san',*
> *Dan make a'nudda trip on de "Old Black Sam."*

*It's wo'k all night an' wo'k all day,*
*An' all yo' get am not half pay.*[51]

The work was difficult and tedious and the men received substandard wages, typically 50 cents a day—much less than wages earned by Ward employees who worked on land at his iron mills in Wyandotte or Chicago. Overall, Ward's opposition to slavery and involvement in the Underground Railroad demonstrate true compassion for those living in bondage. Yet there were limits to his concerns. He treated white employees differently than black ones. Black workers were hired to labor on his ships, where they were confined to subservient positions with low compensation, keeping their advancement in check. Ward's attitudes and actions followed a pattern adopted by many of his contemporaries in the business world.

# 6

## A New Vision for the Midwest

*Diversified industry is the "manifest destiny" of the Northwest.*
—Eber Brock Ward, October 1, 1868

*Most of the domestic life of Eber B. Ward was unsatisfactory,
much of it disappointing. In fact it is only in his later
years that he devoted himself to his home.*
—William L. Bancroft, 1894

The years between 1864 and 1869 provide unique perspective into Eber Ward's accomplishments and influence not only as a business leader but as a man of vision. Beginning in 1864, he served as the president of the American Iron and Steel Association. He used this position as a pulpit to promote American manufacturing and to lobby Congress on a range of issues that ultimately helped to shape the post–Civil War American economy. He also expanded his iron and steel empire, taking it to new heights by becoming the first in the United States to manufacture steel using the modern Bessemer process. The subsequent legal battle to protect his patent rights to produce Bessemer steel provides another example of Ward's intense competitiveness, yet also demonstrates limits to his competitive nature. In contrast, when Ward clashed with James Ludington in an attempt to establish lumber operations in Pere Marquette (today's Ludington, Michigan), he demonstrated the full extent of his willingness to take brutal steps to crush a rival. For the majority of Ward's adult life, business interests had taken precedence over his relationship with his wife and children. This took a toll; in early 1869 his marriage ended in divorce. Shortly thereafter, Ward married Catherine Lyon, a woman thirty years his junior. Several events culminated in the fall of 1869, a key year in his life, when Ward suffered an apoplectic stroke that nearly killed him.

## A New Manifest Destiny

In November 1864, several leading producers of iron and steel from different regions of the country gathered in Philadelphia to create the American Iron and Steel Association. The organization's purpose was to address how "the whole American iron interest might be promoted, and each branch known and cared for." E. B. Ward attended this meeting, and was elected the association's first president. He served in this position until February 1869. Ward's ascension to the presidency of the organization reflected his emergence as a major player in the industry and as an important figure nationally. Additionally, Ward also was a leading member of the National Manufacturers Association, which represented several other industries nationwide. He even served as the organization's secretary.[1]

Following his ascension to these positions, Ward lobbied Congress on a range of issues in support of the iron and steel industries and all manufacturers in the United States. He also promoted a new vision of expanded manufacturing for the Midwest. Ward argued in support of new measures he believed would benefit the American economy and consumers. If enacted, his proposals also would benefit his own business interests.

In a message delivered to the National Convention of Manufacturers in May 1868, Ward explained his struggles to bring about legislative change after spending two months lobbying in the nation's capital. "Our first efforts on arriving at Washington were directed to the repeal of the 5 per cent manufacturing tax." Members of Congress resisted the tax cuts because taxes could not be lowered without a corresponding reduction in government spending. To do so threatened the status quo. Ward explained, "The moment you trench upon any of the expenditures of the Government, you are met with those who have been profiting by these expenses, and you have not only their opposition, but the opposition of all who are conscious that their services, or their contracts could be profitably dispensed with by the government." He argued that money could be saved by streamlining processes to avoid the "plunder, waste and corruption" commonplace throughout the nation's bureaucracy. Ward also believed military spending could be cut now that the Civil War was over. He maintained that if the government reduced expenditures and implemented reforms, "our import duties" and taxes on "whiskey, ale, tobacco, stamps and licenses will pay all the expenses of the government." Ward's support for these "sin taxes" is not surprising, given that he neither drank nor smoked. It also fit in with some of his past attempts to control aspects of his employees' lives by taking steps to limit their access to alcohol. These lobbying efforts in the nation's capital met with some support, but Ward soon realized members of Congress were unlikely to implement the changes he wanted without additional pressure. Therefore, he circulated twenty-five thousand copies of a pamphlet in the form of a letter to the media and general public outlining what he believed was excessive government spending and "oppressive taxation." Ward's letter was a direct appeal to individual taxpayers encouraging them to contact their senators and representatives to bring about the necessary changes.[2]

Furthermore, a form letter dated January 16, 1868, and signed by Ward was sent to every member of the House and Senate. The letter repeated many of his previous arguments. Addressing the issue of military spending, Ward asked, "Why does this country, in time of peace, with no prospect of war, require five times more expenditures, in proportion to its population, for the Army or the Navy, or of the civil list, than before the rebellion?" He continued, "The people demand an early repeal of all taxes on American productions except luxuries, and such an adjustment of the revenue laws as will secure to American citizens, the benefits of National Industry." By 1868, his advocacy aligned with congressional leadership and the 5 percent tax on manufacturers was repealed.[3]

Ward also sought civil service reform. In some ways, this was linked to the reduction of government expenditures, as Ward believed reform could reduce governmental spending and create efficiencies by firing inept individuals and hiring only those who were qualified. Critics charged that unqualified or incompetent individuals received government positions simply due to their support for a political party or a successful candidate in an election.

Ward and others sought to end the system whereby politicians rewarded their cronies with jobs in the federal government. He advocated requiring people to be appointed or removed from their positions based upon their qualifications and job performance. Ward admitted, "Some worthy men obtain office, but it is notorious that worth and fitness are the exceptions." He supported a system of exams to determine the "moral and educational fitness" of government employees. He lobbied members of Congress to support legislation commonly known as the Jenckes' Civil Service Bill. Although the bill never became law, in 1872 a Civil Service Commission was created, which established rules for examining all applicants for government positions.[4]

The most important issue Ward advocated for was tariff reform—which, if enacted, had the potential to benefit his business interests tremendously. As early as 1860, Ward had emerged as a leading advocate for a protective tariff when he wrote a pamphlet on the eve of the presidential election that year. He argued the government should sponsor legislation designed to diversify the nation's economy and encourage manufacturing. Ward built upon those recommendations in subsequent years. In an address to the Iron and Steel Association in 1865, he pushed Congress to pass legislation protecting American manufacturers from foreign competition. That same year, he published another pamphlet aimed at the farmers and laborers of the western and northwestern states. He declared, "A protective tariff encourages the building of manufacturers in the United States instead of Europe," which would lead to more jobs for American workers. This would positively affect society: "If those now unemployed could be profitably occupied, it would lessen crime and poverty, increase morality, and infuse comfort and happiness in thousands of families now poor and destitute." Ward warned that if the United States adopted free trade policies and refused to pass legislation to encourage manufacturing, individual laborers would face poverty and bankruptcy. However, if the proper policies were adopted by officials in Washington, DC, these, combined with the country's vast natural resources, would mean that the nation could "soon become the first power on earth."[5]

Three years later, in an address to the Wisconsin State Agricultural Society, Ward offered his most sophisticated arguments to date regarding the American economy, the Midwest, and a protective tariff. He connected with his audience at the beginning of his speech by praising the "heavy toils" of pioneer farmers "who leveled the forests, and grubbed the stumps, and broke up the prairies" while "living simply, amidst rude surroundings" to produce their extensive "products of the farm and mill." Then, he stressed the need for the Northwest* to diversify its economy, arguing, "Agriculture alone never made a country rich or civilized." He maintained that given the natural resources of the Midwest, the region had a natural capacity to engage in both manufacturing and farming. He expanded upon a commonly recognized phrase in declaring, "Diversified industry is the 'manifest destiny' of the Northwest."[6] Ward defended his arguments by warning that Wisconsin's farmland would suffer from soil exhaustion if the state continued to rely so heavily on the production of wheat and corn. He stated, "Diversified industry is the remedy" for this problem and argued that the government should sponsor legislation to promote manufacturing in the Northwest. By identifying this new "manifest destiny" and applying it to the economy of the Northwest, Ward demonstrated he was a visionary with an eye toward the long-term sustainability of the region's—and even the nation's—economy. Little did he know that by 1920, three of the nation's five largest cities would be located in the Midwest and for much of the twentieth century, the region would be considered the "nation's industrial heartland." In the past, Ward had shown he was a man of action as he operated, and even founded, several business enterprises. This address showed the far-sighted nature of his thoughts and their evolution over time.[7]

Much of the remainder of the address reinforced positions Ward had identified previously, but some was new. He warned about the dangers of a trade deficit and argued that finished products, such as clothing, could be made more efficiently if wool produced in Wisconsin remained in the state, rather than being sent to textile factories in the East. If Wisconsin had its own factories, all profits could remain in the state, eliminating the need for transportation costs, which then could be passed on to consumers in the form of lower prices. He repeated the refrain, "Protection to home industry is the business of a good government." However, Ward also offered suggestions many would find

---

* The "Northwest" Ward referred to was the "old Northwest," from the Northwest Ordinance of 1787. By 1868, this included the states of Ohio, Indiana, Illinois, Michigan, Wisconsin and northern Minnesota. Throughout the address Ward refers to additional locations in the West commonly considered part of the Midwest today.

objectionable then and today. "In Wisconsin, there are some 40,000 women and children of suitable age for light labor, willing and able to work." Their unemployment was "wasted idleness." If he had taken the time to observe peoples' daily routines, he would have understood that children, and women in particular, played an important role in the family economy and were far from "idle." Nevertheless, he believed that women and children could earn wages of at least 50 cents per day in a manufacturing plant, and $3 each week. Collectively, these forty thousand wage earners could make $120,000 weekly and $6,240,000 over the course of a year. Ward viewed these figures simply as lost wages, seemingly never questioning the morality of child labor; nor, like many of his contemporaries, did he recognize the contributions of women.[8]

Ward demonstrated his vision to promote manufacturing in the Midwest in his speeches and writings. His advocacy of a protective tariff and its potential impact on the American economy was not new. A higher tariff would benefit manufacturers in the East as well as the Midwest. However, Ward's vision of how it would influence the Midwest's economy, leading to its diversification, was original. Although Ward liked to publicly stress the altruistic arguments in favor of tariff reform, he had personal reasons to support its implementation. Ward stood to benefit financially if Congress enacted a higher tariff, particularly on steel imported from Europe. As Ward viewed the issue, he wanted Congress to pass legislation friendly to business, particularly his businesses. As far as he was concerned, conditions that were good for him were good for the nation.

E. B. Ward's actions involved more than his lobbying efforts with Congress; he also took steps to expand his base of manufacturing in the Midwest. In the past, he had established his own iron mills with the Eureka Iron Company and the North Chicago Rolling Mill. He continued this expansion into the Midwest when he built an additional facility near Milwaukee in the community of Bay View.

## Milwaukee Iron Company

Prior to 1867, Wisconsin boasted a handful of small foundries where iron was produced, but there were no large operations with a rolling mill. This changed when Ward chose to establish his third iron mill in the Badger State. During his sailing days, Ward had become familiar with numerous communities and harbors throughout the Great Lakes. He remembered the high ground just south of Milwaukee, which bisected Deer Creek on Milwaukee Bay. A facility at this location would allow for easy shipping in and out of its natural harbor. Ward also had connections with key figures in the Milwaukee area and could partner with them for his new enterprise. Most of all, the location was only forty miles from Iron Ridge, in Wisconsin's Dodge County. This mining town included large deposits of ore, which could be transported easily by rail. Additional ore, and fuel, could be supplied by ship. The community near Milwaukee, originally named Lake, was ideal for his new operations.[9]

Another factor motivated Ward to build an iron mill near Milwaukee. He was concerned about competition for his Chicago works. James J. Hagerman, who was intimately involved in the creation of what would become the Milwaukee Iron Company, later testified about the early history of the company. "A man by the name of Schofield got up a scheme to build a rolling mill in Milwaukee, which was, of course, adverse to the Chicago Mill." In response, Ward chose to develop his own company in the area to protect his Chicago interests from a competitor. Until Ward's death in 1875, both the Milwaukee Iron Company and the North Chicago Rolling Mill were largely under his direct control. In some cases, they cooperated and invested in joint operations. Alternatively, they also often competed against each other for contracts.[10]

The Milwaukee Iron Company was incorporated on March 8, 1867. The company's initial board of directors included some of Ward's previous business associates as well as some new partners. His brother-in-law Stephen Clement, who served as president, was from the North Chicago Rolling Mill. Eber Ward served as the new company's secretary. Another director was Orrin W. Potter, who had served as superintendent of the Chicago works. Alexander Mitchell and John Van Dyke, leading citizens in Milwaukee, provided the company with a voice in the city. Mitchell served as president of the area's largest bank. Another major investor was Russel Sage, a financier from New York. Mitchell, Van Dyke, and Sage also served on the board of the Chicago, Milwaukee & St. Paul Railroad, a key railroad in the region and the most important potential customer of Ward's new Milwaukee Iron Company. While there were several investors, Ward owned more than half the stock in the newly formed enterprise.

This ensured he would be able to heavily influence—and likely control—the organization's major decisions. Another noteworthy member of the leadership team was James Hagerman, who was from St. Clair County, Michigan, and had once been a student at Emily's Newport Academy. Hagerman later put himself through college by working on Ward's steamboats. After earning a degree from the University of Michigan, he had worked at the Eureka Iron Company at Wyandotte. Ward recruited him to manage the operations located just outside of Milwaukee.[11]

Soon after the company was incorporated, 114 acres of property were purchased. Twenty-seven and one-half acres were reserved for the mill yard and buildings. The remaining acreage was divided into lots where the company built homes for employees. Plots also were sold directly to employees so they could build their own homes. Before long the community, soon to be known as Bay View, began to emerge.[12]

A provision similar to those included in property sales in Wyandotte was included in the deeds "prohibiting the manufacture or sale of intoxicating liquors on any lots sold by the company." For many years, this provision successfully curtailed the sale of alcohol within the boundaries of the community,

Ward established the Milwaukee Iron Company in 1867. The following year the company's Bay View Rolling Mill rolled its first rail. (Courtesy of the Bay View Historical Society)

although alcohol could easily be purchased in nearby villages or in the city of Milwaukee. Eber never drank throughout his entire lifetime, and both his father and Uncle Samuel had criticized excessive drinking. In fact, when Samuel Ward was asked once how his shipping interests had avoided accidents, he replied, "I never will have a man on my boat who drinks whisky or is subject to any personal dissipation." Ward followed his uncle's lead while also adopting the ban on alcohol sales as a form of social control over his workforce. He wanted his laborers to be steady and reliable, not intoxicated or hung over as they arrived to work each day.[13]

Following the purchase of the property in 1867, work to construct the mill and housing began almost immediately. Before long, a machine shop, an office, a pier extending into the lake, and twenty-four tenement houses were built. A boardinghouse, commonly referred to as the Palmer House, also was completed. The initial phase culminated in the construction of the rail mill. On April 8, 1868, Ward's Milwaukee Iron Company rolled its first rail. Once the mill was established, the company was reorganized to implement the second phase of development. Ward was elected president, Alexander Mitchell became treasurer, and James Hagerman served as secretary. The company's capital stock was expanded from $350,000 to $800,000. These actions taken by the Milwaukee Iron Company prompted the *Watertown Republican* newspaper to comment, "It will be seen at a glance that this means business for Milwaukee."[14]

Two major steps commenced in this second phase of construction. The first involved the purchase of the Swedes Iron Mine, located forty miles northwest of Milwaukee. This purchase was undertaken jointly between Ward's three iron mills: the Wyandotte Rolling Mill Company, the North Chicago Rolling Mill, and the Milwaukee Iron Company. The Chicago and Milwaukee firms owned two-fifths each, while the Wyandotte facility owned one-fifth. Iron ore recovered at the new mine would be shipped to all three facilities. According to an article in the *Chicago Tribune*, the chemical content of the iron at the Swedes mine made it unique, "imparting a steel-like toughness and hardness of fibre to the iron." Ore from the Swedes mine was "harder," and when mixed with the proper proportion of Lake Superior ore, which was "tougher," created an iron rail that was "unsurpassed—tough, durable, and of excellent wearing surfaces." The deposits at the Swedes mine were believed to be ten to twenty-four feet deep, half a mile wide, and a mile and one half long. This was enough to keep the mills operating for thirty years. The mine's proximity to Bay View made the ore more easily accessible and less expensive to operate than ore from mines located in Michigan's Upper Peninsula. Previously, Ward often had been forced to compete with pig iron and rails manufactured in Pittsburgh and Cleveland. With the increased investment in his midwestern facilities and easier access to iron ore, Ward was attempting to dominate the manufacture of iron in the Midwest and even encroach on the market ruled for years by his eastern competitors.[15]

The next step involved expanding the operations at the mill site itself. In 1869, construction of a blast furnace to enable the smelting of ore and the manufacture of new railroad rails was undertaken. The first furnace was set to blast in April and a second was complete by the year's end. William Donahoe, longtime foreman of the car shops, recalled the flurry of activity in that era, including construction of "the fish plate mill, the puddle mill, the top and bottom mill, the boiler shop, the blacksmith shop, the carpenter shop, the pumping works, and storehouse." To facilitate the shipment of iron ore, the company built a specialized dock "161 feet long, 28 feet wide and 43 feet high, having 26 bins or 'pockets' as they are called, lined with heavy plate iron, and each capable of holding 100 tons of ore." This allowed the ore to be brought by rail to the top of the docks and dumped directly into the pockets. Each pocket contained a shoot by which the ore would be deposited into the hold of a ship. Simple machinery at the top of the dock controlled the entire system. Once loaded, ships could transport the ore to Ward's facilities in Chicago or Wyandotte. Significant amounts also were sold to mills operated by other manufacturers. Before long, the facility was essentially complete, with the capacity to manufacture and reroll thirty thousand tons of rails per year.[16]

Ward discovered he would have to recruit skilled workers to help construct his modern facility. These were brought in to help design, build, and eventually work in the iron mills at Bay View. There were plenty of unskilled workers seeking jobs, but skilled workers proved difficult to find. Therefore, recruiters traveled to England on behalf of Ward to find experienced men who were willing to relocate to the United States to work for Ward. According to Bay View historian Bernhard C. Korn, who surveyed census data, "Later Bay Viewites who gave Staffordshire as their place of origin were so numerous that Ward must have materially depopulated the English blast furnaces by his draft." Many of these skilled employees lived initially in the Palmer House, but when their families arrived, they often either rented or purchased their own homes. As the mill site grew, so did the village surrounding it. Just a few years prior to the arrival of Ward's mill, the property was unsettled farmland. Within a short time, it boasted stores, shops, churches, and a new brick school with an enrollment of 120 pupils.[17]

With the support of Eber Ward, Bay View resident Beulah Brinton helped scores of newly arrived immigrant families adapt to their new lives in the United States. Beulah was Eber's cousin, and her husband Warren came to work for Ward in about 1870. Eventually, Warren Brinton would serve as mill superintendent. The couple built a colonial-style home close to the mills. Soon after their arrival, Beulah noticed that many wives and children of the mill workers struggled with the lack of basic health care and access to recreational opportunities. Beulah traveled door-to-door visiting the homes of many immigrant families, identifying their needs. She came to know the community

Beulah Brinton contributed greatly to the Bay View community. (Courtesy of the Bay View Historical Society)

intimately and invited members into her own house, where she hosted cooking classes, sewing circles, and lessons in the English language as necessary. She even served as a midwife, delivering more than one baby in the home of a local mill worker. Beulah often read aloud from one of her many books and eventually acquired quite a library. Ultimately, she wanted to establish a library for the community. Once when Eber visited, she mentioned this goal and the need for more books. Eber promised that "if she could raise a certain sum, he would double it." Soon "her parlor became the first public library in Bay View." Beulah acted as a pioneer social worker prior to the development of that profession, and her work took place more than a decade before that of Jane Addams, who established Chicago's famous Hull House in 1889. Ward, recognizing his cousin's contributions to the community, continued to fund her initiatives.[18]

The Milwaukee Iron Company dominated the community, and as long as the mills were running, times were prosperous. Mill superintendent Hagerman even served as mayor. In 1869, the company produced over forty-two thousand tons of iron rails for the railroads. The Milwaukee Chamber of Commerce celebrated the mill's success and its importance to the surrounding communities. It declared the Milwaukee Iron Company "has already become [one] of the most extensive manufacturing concerns in the Northwest, and at the rate of progress it has made thus far, it promises ere many years to become as extensive and complete as any other establishment of the kind in existence." The payroll also had grown substantially. In 1870, the company paid out $413,673.15 in labor costs while employing over six hundred men at the mill works and docks. In addition to those figures, payroll was about $12,000 per month at the Iron Ridge mine.[19]

Between 1867 and 1869, Ward founded and transformed the Milwaukee Iron Company into a huge and modern facility. It was possibly the largest in the nation when it was completed, with a furnace sixty-six feet in height and seventeen feet in diameter. Historian Frederick Merk described it as "one of the greatest rolling mills in the entire country." As demonstrated on numerous previous occasions, Eber Brock Ward was not one to jump into a project and leave it half finished. Although he achieved great success in Milwaukee and in his other business activities, Ward's family life suffered. After more than thirty years together, in 1869, Eber's marriage to Polly ended in divorce, the same year his Milwaukee facility was completed.[20]

# Eber's Divorce and Second Marriage

William L. Bancroft, a longtime associate of Eber Ward, described Ward's family life as "unsatisfactory, much of it disappointing." While Bancroft's observation was true, Eber and Polly did remain together for thirty-one years, and their marriage resulted in the birth of eight children. According to census data from 1860, all of their surviving children lived at the family home in Detroit. Unfortunately, time would show that none of these children would acquire their father's business sense. One child, Samuel, died in infancy. Others were cognitively impaired, while at least one suffered from mental illness. Henry (age eighteen in 1860) was adjudicated "an insane person"; his aunt Emily had even called him "a little insane" beginning about the age of fifteen.[21] Elizabeth, who in 1860 was thirteen years old and the only child of school age not attending school, was described as "mentally incompetent." Frederick was eight years old in 1860 and Mary was five. Frederick would later spend time at the New York Inebriate Asylum, and died at the age of nineteen, apparently of an accidental overdose of laudanum; Mary was considered very eccentric. Milton and Charles (ages twelve and ten in 1860) would be given the opportunity as adults to work with their father, but he considered them "utter failures as managers of large interests," and Eber feared they would squander any money they received due to their lack of responsibility.[22]

Polly and Eber's oldest and most promising child was John. He also was living at home in 1860, then twenty-two, and had started to follow in his father's footsteps. He worked in the shipping industry and appeared to have inherited his father's ambition—and also his ruthlessness. He earned a negative reputation, deservedly so, due to his brutality. In 1862, while serving as captain of the *Pearl*, he discovered that a poor woman with two children had boarded his vessel without paying. When they arrived at the next port, he took the woman "by the neck, and the two children by the hair," and dragged them off the ship in the middle of a storm, "keeping their baggage on board in the meantime." His actions were publicized in the *Detroit Free Press*, which made him the object of much "detestation" in the community.[23]

Three years later John was accused of rape by a fifteen-year-old girl. He professed his innocence in a letter to his family, declaring he "did not anticipate any trouble" as long as the truth prevailed. He expected the public scandal to

John Ward was Eber's oldest and most promising son, but his actions earned him a reputation for brutal behavior. (Courtesy of the Seitz family)

be "a seven days wonder & talk & then blow over." Nevertheless, there appeared to be significant evidence he had committed the crime. As John was leaving the courthouse following a preliminary hearing to address the accusation, the girl's older brother shot him in the back and through his armpit. John was taken immediately to a hotel, his condition considered critical. Eber Brock rushed to the hotel with the "best surgeons and physicians to be found" and transported his son to the family's Detroit home. He died one week later.[24]

It is unclear if Eber felt responsible for his son John's actions or for the failures of his other children. He once admitted to Emily, "Insanity might run in the family." His own sister Sally had suffered from mental illness for years before dying in a mental institution. Samuel Ward's son Jacob had been described as "mentally incompetent," while another cousin was considered "simple." According to Geoffrey Kramer, the author of a popular clinical psychology textbook, "a disposition for mental illness can be inherited. But seldom can we attribute mental illness to heredity alone—environments (family, peers, subculture) and triggering events (e.g. trauma, illness) often play significant roles, and the influence of those factors varies from one disorder to another." It is unclear what, if any, triggering events or environmental factors may have influenced the mental health of Eber's children (although Eber was gone for long stretches of time during their childhood). It does appear likely that members of his family inherited a disposition toward mental illness. Regardless of how it came to be, Ward's children were often associated with erratic behavior. The chaos within his family would make newspaper headlines after his death as family members fought over Ward's estate in a trial that captivated the public's attention for several weeks.[25]

There really wasn't much Eber could have done for his children suffering from a mental disorder at the time, given the lack of treatment in the mid-nineteenth century for such ailments. Yet one suspects that if he had spent more time at home instead of prioritizing his business interests, he could have had a more positive relationship with his children and might have better prepared John, Milton, and Charles to follow in his footsteps and pursue a business career. A friend who observed Ward's frustration at his sons' continual failures recalled that once "Capt. Ward laid down on the lounge [in his office] seemingly quite dejected. He bemoaned the fact that he hadn't a boy or relative capable of going on with his business and that they simply squandered everything that was put in their hands." It is likely that Ward felt regret as he grew older and wished he had spent more time with his children when they were young. Although Eber's father was often absent when Eber was a young boy, beginning with Eber's teen years, the two spent a great deal of time together, including their two years working together at the lighthouse on Bois Blanc Island. During those years, Eber and his father developed a close bond. Under Mr. Ward's guidance, Eber acquired a strong work ethic that served him well over the years. Unfortunately, when he became a father, Eber did not provide the same mentorship for his sons.[26]

It is possible the children's health and behaviors added stress to Eber and Polly's marriage. Family members had described Polly as having a "mental condition," the extent of which is unknown. In the past, Eber had expressed concerns about Polly suffering from anxiety. She even had sought treatment for being overly "nervous and excitable." Eber may have blamed Polly for her condition or sought an escape by seeking a relationship with another woman. Regardless of the motivation, their marriage began to fall apart. Very little correspondence has survived between E. B. Ward and Polly. If it was available, it might provide a deeper understanding of their relationship. However, a letter from Emily addressed to Eber helps to explain Emily's thoughts about Polly and therefore Eber's relationship with his wife. Emily expressed her frustration with Polly as she confessed, "I have always tried to love and respect your wife as the mother of your children," yet she was finding it difficult to do so. This must have become particularly difficult for Emily as she had moved in with Eber and Polly, at their request, to help with the household in the late 1860s. Emily had tried not to say anything for some time, but she had "put up with a thousand little Meannesses and indignities at her hand" for long enough. Emily wanted to be a "true sister" to Polly, but she could not due to the mistreatment she had received. She compared Polly to a viper ready to strike, even when treated with benevolence.[27] Although this letter was never signed by Emily and may never have been sent, it helps to show Emily's relationship with Polly. Emily was Eber's closest confidante and the two often shared their innermost thoughts. Emily later recalled that she confronted Eber about his relationship with Polly and declared that the couple did "not have an agreeable marriage" for some time prior to their divorce.[28]

Eber Brock and Polly were divorced in February 1869. Several newspapers reported that the divorce took place "on the grounds of adultery" by Eber. Polly was to receive alimony of $6,000 per year. Polly's health failed soon after the divorce; she died just two months later. This probably came about following an accident she had while visiting Castile Water Cure Sanitarium in New York, a popular facility where patients received treatment for a range of ailments. Regardless of the cause, their mother's death, following the recent divorce of their parents, must have been devastating for the couple's children.[29]

David Ward, Eber's cousin, claimed that Eber secured the divorce by use of "fraud and bribery of the judge" because he wanted to escape the marriage due to his relationship with a much younger woman. David had always contended that Eber married Polly strictly to inherit Samuel Ward's business. It is likely that Eber initially was attracted to Polly in part due to her connection with Samuel Ward, although the fact that the marriage lasted more than thirty years and produced several children would seem to indicate they were at least reasonably happy at one time. Possibly the best evidence to contradict David Ward's claim would be that Eber and Polly's divorce came fifteen years after Samuel Ward's death. If Eber had married Polly strictly to "scoop Uncle Sam's property by will or otherwise," as David contended, the divorce would have occurred shortly after Samuel's death, once Eber had secured his inheritance.[30]

Although some of David Ward's claims appear unfounded, others were accurate. Less than two months following the divorce, Eber married Catherine Lyon of Conneaut, Ohio. Eber was much older than Catherine: Eber was fifty-seven, Catherine twenty-seven. Catherine, labeled the "belle of Conneaut," was the daughter of Robert and Clarissa Lyon. Robert was a successful business leader, regarded as Conneaut's leading merchant. Some publications described Catherine as the niece of Ohio's powerful senator Benjamin Wade, but although the Lyon and Wade families were close, the senator was not Catherine's uncle—Catherine's sister Clarissa was married to James F. Wade, Senator Wade's son. Benjamin Wade was one of Ward's associates. It is likely Ward met Catherine because of his friendship with Wade and the family's connection to the senator. In later years, Catherine stated she knew Eber about a year and a half before they were married, but it is unclear exactly when their affair began. Catherine was a great beauty, described as having "the perfect complexion, yellow hair and brown eyes." She had a captivating and vivacious personality with "an intense ambition for social distinction."[31]

The marriage benefited both partners socially and politically. For Eber, the much-younger and beautiful Catherine was what modern-day observers would call a "trophy wife." It also enhanced his relationship with Senator Wade. Eber's fortune and fame provided Catherine with the social position she sought. The couple lived at Eber's mansion at 792 W. Fort Street in Detroit, considered "perhaps, the handsomest residence in the city with ample grounds and conservatories." Census data from 1870 shows three of Ward's children from his first marriage also lived at the home (Elizabeth, Mary, and Frederick). No fewer than eight staff members also resided there: one housekeeper, two dressmakers, three domestic servants, one cook, and a coachman. A neighbor described the residence as "the symbol of enormous wealth and all that wealth could procure." The property was complete with greenhouses that produced beautiful flowers and fruit. "Across the entire front of the estate stood an artistic iron fence." There was even an area to the north of the property used as a pasture for Ward's cows. Tax data from the 1860s provide a record of the luxury items Ward had accumulated. These included three carriages, a pianoforte, a gold watch, silver plate, and a personal yacht.[32]

The home, staff, luxury items, and entire grounds confirmed the neighbor's contention that Ward had surrounded himself with symbols of his immense wealth. As a younger man, Eber had declared, "Wealth and station cannot make a man happy." He had even criticized a woman who had grown suddenly rich during the California gold rush as "foolish" because she had spent more than $2,000 on jewelry and fancy clothes. At the time, he considered it a "waste

Eber Ward's mansion on Fort Street was considered one of the finest homes in Detroit. After Ward's death, this would become the House of the Good Shepherd, a shelter and home for women. (Courtesy of the Burton Historical Collection, Detroit Public Library)

of money" and "a great sin" to spend freely in this manner when such a sum could be used "to support eight poor families in comfort for a whole year." Something had changed in Eber Brock Ward's outlook. As he founded his own manufacturing facilities, amassed great wealth, and became a powerful figure in Michigan and at the national level, he surrounded himself with multiple symbols of his power and fame. Ward had succumbed to the material excesses of the era in which he lived.[33]

Eber's divorce and second marriage took place in 1869. That same year, he also became engaged in a conflict involving his Flint & Pere Marquette Railway and the pinelands he owned along the Pere Marquette River at Ludington.

## Flint & Pere Marquette Railway

Ward had begun to invest in railroads when he recognized the importance of the industry and its potential for growth. As early as the 1850s, he purchased significant shares of stock in the Michigan Central Railroad at the same time he partnered his steamboat lines with the railroad. Later in the decade, he invested heavily in the Detroit & Milwaukee Railway and served on the company's board of directors. Ward's foray into railroads coincided with his involvement in the iron industry. By investing heavily in the railroads, he hoped to influence them to purchase their rails and other necessary materials from his companies, thus furthering the vertical integration of his business operations. Ward's involvement with the Detroit & Milwaukee Railway lessened in 1857 after the company experienced some financial problems and a new group of investors assumed more control of the company's operations. While he continued to own stock in the organization, Ward stepped down as a member of the board. This allowed him to become more actively involved in another rail line, the Flint & Pere Marquette Railway. He was attracted to the Flint & Pere Marquette because he had greater control over the organization's decision making. Not only did he become the company's major stockholder, he would serve as president of the railroad until his death in 1875.[34]

The Flint & Pere Marquette Railway came into existence on January 22, 1857, when articles of association for the company were filed with the State of Michigan. This rail line would begin in the Saginaw Valley, where Ward already had some landholdings, and extend across the state to Pere Marquette (present-day Ludington) on Lake Michigan. In the summer of 1857, the 172-mile route undertaken by the railway between Flint & Pere Marquette was surveyed, although construction was delayed due to the Panic of 1857. Work on the new rail line began the fall of 1858, and the Flint & Pere Marquette Railway opened for business on January 10, 1862. The initial line extended 26.1 miles from East Saginaw to Mt. Morris. To celebrate the completion of the first line of track, Ward organized an excursion on the new line. A special dinner was prepared, complete with a series of toasts and speeches. Dignitaries included former governor Moses Wisner as well as Flint businessman and future governor Henry Crapo. The first year, gross revenues amounted to $31,764.[35]

Construction continued in earnest as the railway extended southward toward Detroit and westward to Lake Michigan. By December 1862 the railway reached Flint, at the time a thriving lumber town with eight sawmills. This was a key development, as the Flint & Pere Marquette tripled its gross revenues the following year, transporting lumber from these mills to eastern markets. Within two years, a connection was made to Detroit. This occurred in November 1864 when the company opened a line from Flint to Holly, a distance of seventeen miles. The Flint & Pere Marquette negotiated with the Flint & Holly Railroad Company and the Detroit & Milwaukee to allow passengers to travel from Saginaw to Detroit. An article in the *Detroit Free Press* celebrated that travelers "can now leave Saginaw in the morning, go into Detroit and return in the evening, having several hours here for the transaction of business." The fare was $3.50 each way, and passengers would have to transfer railcars only once. By 1868, the Flint & Pere Marquette Railway had purchased the Flint & Holly, a consolidation benefiting Ward and his fellow stockholders.[36]

The Flint & Pere Marquette expanded westward toward Lake Michigan as well. In a letter to the board of directors in April 1864, board president Ward outlined his vision to proceed toward "Lake Michigan, a distance of one hundred and forty miles, and to prosecute the work as rapidly as the money can be procured for that purpose." By the fall of 1866, the railway extended beyond Midland and continued its way toward the village of Ludington. A twelve-mile extension to Bay City was added in November 1867. As the line continued to extend, traffic and revenues increased. In 1867, gross revenues amounted to $237,958 and by 1868, they reached $381,983.[37]

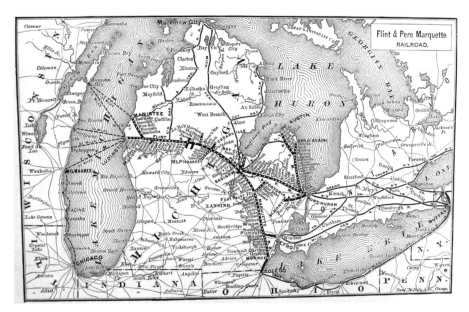

Ward served as president of the Flint & Pere Marquette Railway from 1860 until his death. By 1874 it included over 250 miles of track across the state of Michigan. (Map from *Report of the Flint & Pere Marquette Railroad Company, Including Traffic Reports of the Road for the Year 1895.* Courtesy of the Bentley Historical Library, University of Michigan)

Construction of the Flint & Pere Marquette Railway was funded in part by land grants authorized by the federal government. In June 1856, to offset the high capital expenditures involved in railroad construction, Congress passed legislation allowing states to distribute millions of acres of public land to the railroads. For each mile of track constructed, the company would receive six sections (one section was 640 acres and equal to one square mile) of land. In 1857, the Michigan state legislature identified nine railroads to be recipients of these grants. Four were located in Michigan's Upper Peninsula, while five were building their lines through northern Michigan. The land grants did not cover the full cost of construction. Instead, they were inducements to encourage the railroads to build in sparsely populated regions of the state. The Flint & Pere Marquette was identified as one of the land grant railroads. With so much land being handed out to the railroads, the *Detroit Free Press* had some reservations concerning the legislation, although its editors commented, "If judiciously used, our State must derive a vast benefit from the new roads which will be built under this law."[38]

This legislation was similar to the funding that facilitated the construction of the Soo Locks earlier in the decade. It also represented an important relationship between the government and private business in the United States. The federal government owned vast tracts of public land in each state. To promote certain industries, such as railroads, the government used the land as an incentive for companies to invest and improve the nation's transportation network. Over the next several years, more than 3 million acres of public land in Michigan was granted to railroads. The Flint & Pere Marquette Railway benefited greatly. An annual report to stockholders in 1867 highlighted the potential value of lands located in western Michigan. "The importance and magnitude of the lumber traffic on the Muskegon and Manistee Rivers urge this company to speedy construction on its road west." The report described the land as "a region of country inviting to the farmer and lumberman."[39] By 1868, the railway had received more than three hundred thousand acres. While the railroad's land department received many inquiries concerning the properties available, sales had only garnered $267,270, yet company officials were optimistic sales would increase soon. As more land came up for sale, Ward identified valuable timbered property in the Saginaw Valley and along the shore of Lake Michigan. He purchased many of these tracts of land for himself. He had no immediate plans to cut the timber on these properties, but recognized their worth as a long-term investment. He could either sell the land later or cut the timber himself. Eventually, they would prove valuable assets for his wife and children following his death.[40]

Repeatedly, the road's extension sparked tremendous business growth in communities where it ran, as sawmills, shingle mills, and related industries were erected near the line of tracks. The Saginaw River Valley in particular, where lumber and salt production flourished, used the Flint & Pere Marquette to transport products to outside markets. As historian James Cook Mills observed, "It is an unquestioned fact that no institution . . . has done so much for the material advancement of the Saginaw Valley as the Flint & Pere Marquette Railroad." This was particularly true when a road was completed south of Detroit to Monroe, Michigan, on Lake Erie, facilitating the transportation of Saginaw lumber to eastern markets. At the same time, progress of about twenty miles each year was being made as the railway extended westward.[41]

As construction of the Flint & Pere Marquette Railway neared Ludington, the community's residents grew excited at the prospect of this major rail line ending at their town. An article in the *Mason County Press* in May 1869 celebrated that Ludington soon would become the western terminus. The paper predicted the railroad's presence would lead to an economic boom for the community: "Passengers destined for Detroit and . . . lumbermen's supplies for the upper Muskegon country will also pass through this place by this Rail Road." At the time, Ludington was a small village centered on the lumber industry with a population of fewer than one thousand. The completion of a railroad linking it with the rest of the state had the potential to transform the community. However, a dispute between E. B. Ward and James Ludington threatened to derail the entire project.[42]

## E. B. Ward versus James Ludington

James Ludington never lived in the town that eventually would bear his name, but he had been a key figure in the community's development ever since he'd gained control of the region's largest sawmill in 1859. The settlement originally was known as Pere Marquette, named in honor of the French missionary and explorer who died in the area.[43] The community was officially renamed Ludington in 1873, although it had already been known by that name when the post office was first established in 1864. In addition to his mill, James Ludington owned extensive tracts of forested land near the mouth of the Pere Marquette River as it entered Pere Marquette Lake near Lake Michigan. These holdings were uniquely strategic to facilitate the transportation of logs down the river and included the best locations to establish mills for cutting logs. Ward engaged in negotiations with Ludington to purchase property along Pere Marquette Lake. Ward sought a terminal site for his railroad, and he hoped to buy land to establish a sawmill. As early as 1852 Ward had been purchasing pinelands on either side of the Pere Marquette River, and by 1869 he had amassed some seventy thousand acres. He was ready to cash in on his investment and engage in the lumber industry.[44]

Negotiations between Ward and Ludington began as early as 1866 and continued for several months. Before long, it became apparent that Ludington was unwilling to sell Ward a mill site regardless of the price. Ludington hesitated, in part, because he feared Ward would threaten his position as the leading figure in the community's economy. Most important, Ludington appeared to purposely allow the discussions to drag on because he coveted Ward's valuable pineland and hoped Ward might eventually sell it to him. Ludington confided his strategy in a letter to his brother William: "There is more money in the 'Ward' lands than in a California gold mine . . . my opinion is that if we could get them we would own the finest lumbering property in America." Ludington's comment speaks to the tremendous value of Ward's holdings in the region. After nearly three years of discussions, the negotiations came to a standstill. Ludington refused to sell a mill site, and Ward was unwilling to part with his pineland.[45]

By 1869, E. B. Ward, Michigan's leading business kingpin, had had enough of Ludington's stalling. When he learned that some of Ludington's men had illegally (possibly accidentally) cut the timber on several sections of his property, Ward developed a scheme to intimidate Ludington and force his hand. The next time Ludington visited Detroit, Ward had him arrested and thrown in the Wayne County jail, charged with trespassing and stealing timber. Ward did not stop there. A subsequent announcement in the *Detroit Free Press* outlined his next move. The Flint & Pere Marquette Railway filed a lawsuit against James Ludington in the U.S. Circuit Court "for a large amount for trespass claimed to have been committed on their lands on the west coast of this state." Additionally, Ward filed his own suit against Ludington for damages totaling as much as $650,000.[46]

A settlement was reached following Ludington's release from jail, and Ward's legal proceedings against his rival eventually were "discontinued." In May 1869, Ludington met with Ward and other officials from the Flint & Pere Marquette Railway. Ludington recalled, "They agreed to locate the western terminus of the road at Ludington . . . & I agreed to give them ample depot grounds & right of way through my lands." James Ludington had capitulated; Eber Ward emerged the victor. Ludington subsequently sold his lumbering operations to a group of local investors for $500,000 in July 1869.[47]

Ward returned to Ludington later that summer, along with several company officers, to make connections with people in the community and to announce formally the location of the railroad terminal. Eber's wife Catherine, his son Henry, and a niece accompanied him. Several community leaders met with Ward, and treated the entire group to a party. While on the visit to Ludington, Ward finalized the purchase of a mill site on Pere Marquette Lake. This would be perfectly situated to receive logs cut from his property along the Pere Marquette River, while also allowing for an outlet to Lake Michigan through Ludington's harbor. Finished lumber then could be sent with ease to the growing markets of Chicago and Milwaukee. Before long, work commenced on the first of two enormous sawmills Ward would build in the community.[48]

The agreement with James Ludington also paved the way for the completion of Ward's Flint & Pere Marquette Railway. Unfortunately, it would take five more years to finish the line all the way to Ludington as another financial panic hit the nation in 1873, causing a significant drop in revenues. Company records show that during the ten-year period from 1862 to 1872, net revenues had increased from less than $10,000 to $455,118. But then, between 1873 and 1876, revenues dropped by nearly $90,000. The financial panic slowed the rate of growth, and there simply wasn't nearly as much traffic generating the same level of revenues as in previous years. Frustration was apparent as Ludington's residents waited for the "long expected" railroad to arrive. Finally, by the first week of December 1874, the trains reached Ludington. This meant that Ward now controlled one continuous line of track, 253 miles in length, running across the state from Ludington on Lake Michigan to Monroe on Lake Erie. Additionally, by 1875, there were over thirty miles of branch lines and sixty-two miles of sidings, to make a total of 346 miles owned and managed by the railway.[49]

James Ludington suffered permanently because of Ward's ruthless tactics. Within a short time, Ludington became ill; he probably suffered a stroke. Soon thereafter, he was forced to retire from all his business activities due to failing health, although he was only forty-two years old. The use of harsh strategies to defeat a business rival was part of a pattern of behavior conducted by Ward in the past, although in this case his actions were particularly excessive. Ward was not alone among businessmen employing ruthless schemes in the Gilded Age. As one biographer observed, Cornelius Vanderbilt was willing to "prey on the weak and vulnerable" as he undercut competitors and sought revenge against his rivals to build his transportation empire. John D. Rockefeller callously engineered shortages of railcars and purchased all available barrels to disrupt his opponents' ability to produce and distribute oil. Nevertheless, conspiring to have a competitor thrown in jail as a negotiating ploy was extreme, even for Ward. His actions provide justification for his cousin David Ward's criticism of Eber as a "tyrannical, vindictive . . . selfish man, largely devoid of conscience."[50]

The late 1860s saw Ward embroiled in another controversy with a completely different set of business competitors involving patent rights to produce steel; in this case, he did not emerge as the victor.

## The Fight to Produce Bessemer Steel in the United States

Historian Thomas J. Misa has stated, "The Bessemer process was the most important technique for making steel in the nineteenth century." The method was named for Sir Henry Bessemer, an English inventor who experimented with iron to make improvements for a firearm. In the course of his trials, he discovered a way to create steel by blowing the impurities out of molten iron by using air or steam to strengthen it. This method is often called the pneumatic process. The value of railroad rails made of steel, as opposed to iron, was well established in the United States. Iron rails often required replacement after two years, whereas steel rails had a much longer lifespan. The problem was that steel rails had to be imported from England. Bessemer conducted his experiments in England beginning in 1854. In 1856, he received a patent for his process in the United States. Shortly thereafter, his patent was challenged by an American iron maker named William Kelly, who had conducted similar experiments in Kentucky. In 1857, Kelly successfully secured the patent in the United States for manipulating iron in this manner, although historians have since debunked Kelly's claim of priority over Bessemer. The product made using Kelly's pneumatic process was superior to other iron, but it was not as strong as needed. Another inventor, Robert F. Mushet, discovered an additional process that added strength and hardness: once all the carbon had been blown out of the iron, a precise amount was then reintroduced. The resulting product was steel, much favored by American railway companies.[51]

As early as 1861, E. B. Ward and his partner Z. S. Durfee had acquired the rights to Kelly's patent. Ward then hired William F. Durfee, a cousin of Z. S. Durfee, to establish an experimental laboratory in Wyandotte, adjacent to Ward's Eureka Iron Company, to develop a process for producing steel using the pneumatic method. By 1864, Ward had successfully secured the rights to Mushet's patent and formed the Kelly Process Company. This combined the rights to Kelly's patent and Mushet's. Several investors, led by E. B. Ward, were involved in the organization. One key partner was Daniel J. Morrell, the general manager of the Cambria Iron Company of Johnstown, Pennsylvania, one of the largest producers of iron in the country. Armed with the pair of patents, Ward strove to create a facility for the large-scale production of steel. However, there was one additional piece required to produce steel successfully on a large-scale basis. Ward's group required the patent for a Bessemer tilting converter. The egg-shaped converter was necessary in the steel-making process. Once molten pig iron was poured into it, a blast of air was blown through its base, resulting in a spectacular explosion of flames bursting from the top of the converter. Then the converter was tilted down and the newly formed steel was emptied out. Because the converter was necessary for the success of their operations, Z. S. Durfee traveled to England to investigate facilities that already had implemented the Bessemer process and began negotiations to secure an additional patent from Bessemer for the use of the tilting converter.[52]

Z. S. Durfee was unable to secure the patents for the Bessemer tilting converter, but William F. Durfee continued his experiments at Wyandotte. He started construction on his own uniquely designed converter, or "blowing engine," to avoid a patent challenge during the winter of 1862–63, but his work took time. Durfee remembered being interrupted on several occasions; between the "[Civil] war, strikes, and the fact that part of my time was occupied in supervising at Chicago, the engine was not completed until the spring of 1864." Durfee continued his experiments and reported some success that summer, but then was called away to help with a project at Ward's Chicago mill, so he left his assistant in charge to make some repairs. His absence nearly resulted in a great tragedy. While Durfee was away, he received a message from Ward indicating something had gone terribly wrong.

> Dear Sir—I wish you would come immediately to Wyandotte and look after that man X—— of yours. He will kill somebody by-and-by.
>
> (Signed) Yours, truly,
> E. B. Ward[53]

Unbeknownst to Durfee, Ward had invited a group of dignitaries to observe the "new process" his employees had been working on to make steel at the Wyandotte experimental laboratory. The visitors included judges, bankers, and other business leaders, with Republican senators Benjamin Wade of Ohio and Zachariah Chandler from Michigan leading the group. Both Wade and Chandler were close associates of Ward. Unfortunately, Durfee's assistant had forgotten that a barrel of water was in a reservoir meant to capture any steel that might remain fluid from the casting ladle. This mistake nearly led to the deaths of the entire entourage, because at a crucial point in the demonstration, two tons of fluid steel were dumped onto the barrel of water, which resulted in "a terrible explosion, the metal flying in all directions." Senator Chandler was thrown to the ground and "prostrated at full length . . . ; Senator Wade was projected upon a pile of sand in the corner of the casting house . . . while Capt. Ward himself was blown bodily through the open doors of the building into the yard upon a pile of pig iron." Fortunately, while members of the party did suffer some burns and minor injuries, no one was seriously hurt. Durfee commented that when the visitors returned to Detroit, they were "of the opinion that they did not care to see steel made by the 'new process' again."[54]

Despite the setbacks that summer, Ward encouraged Durfee to continue his work. His efforts culminated on September 6, 1864, when laborers at Ward's Wyandotte plant produced the first Bessemer steel made in the United States using machinery Durfee designed. It was quite an accomplishment. Once they had succeeded in creating the Bessemer steel, Ward hoped they could roll the ingots into rails at Wyandotte. This was attempted, but the rollers broke under the intense pressure. Instead, Ward had the steel ingots transported to his Chicago mill. In May 1865, members of the Iron and Steel Association were gathered in Chicago for their regular meeting. On May 24, 1865, a trial run was planned to determine if the Chicago mill could handle the new steel. Only a handful of individuals were present to observe this initial experiment as Ward did not want a repeat of the near-disaster that had taken place at Wyandotte the previous year. The trial was successful, so the following day a large group from the Iron and Steel Association watched as three rails were rolled. Once again, the rails were rolled successfully. Eber Ward was ecstatic.[55]

The rails produced in Chicago replaced the existing track of the Chicago and Northwestern Railroad. They remained there for at least ten years, carrying heavy traffic without showing any wear. Additional Wyandotte steel was subjected to tests in Bridgewater, Massachusetts, where it was determined to be "very much superior to any previously made." John Bishop, a blacksmith at the

Bridgewater works, tested the welding qualities of the steel in several everyday applications, beginning with a tobacco pipe. There was no visible sign of a weld where the bowl and stem of the pipe came together. Durfee also related, "I have now two jackknifes and a razor made from this steel; the knives are rather soft, but the razor was used regularly by my father for fifteen years, to his entire satisfaction." Ward's investment and patience were rewarded. He had recruited and empowered the right individuals to produce a highly sought-after commodity. Yet, just as he prepared to produce steel in mass quantities, he found himself engaged in another legal battle.[56]

Eber Ward and his partner Daniel J. Morrell had secured the patent for the Kelly-Mushet steel-making process, but they never acquired the patent for Bessemer's tilting converter, which was held by a competitor. Their rival was headquartered in Troy, New York, and was led by the engineer Alexander Holley, who had a distinguished career in the steel industry. He eventually would be recognized as the "most deeply knowledgeable steel engineer in the country." Holley, born in Connecticut, became the first graduate from Brown University with a degree in engineering in 1853. He brought tremendous energy to his work and was blessed with a brilliant mind. Holley had spent significant time studying the Bessemer process in England and endeavored to establish a Bessemer steel plant in the United States. Following months of trial and error in which he experimented with the Bessemer method at a facility in New York, he was able to successfully produce high-quality steel. By April 1865, his company was accepting orders for steel rails, axels, and boiler and ship plates, as well as numerous additional products. It would be difficult to overstate Holley's contribution to the steel industry. According to Jeanne McHugh, by 1866, Holley "had become the fountainhead of knowledge about every phase of the Bessemer process, and one of [only] three or four men in America who had the ability to construct and operate a Bessemer plant." Clearly, Holley's strength lay in his technical training and experience as an engineer, whereas Eber Ward had no such qualifications—but he was a seasoned entrepreneur who could organize complex business operations, develop efficiencies, and gather partners with sufficient capital to properly fund the construction of a new Bessemer facility.[57]

A standoff of sorts developed between Ward's steel allies and those of Holley's New York group. Ward and Morrell were unable to produce steel without infringing on the patent rights of Holley and his partners; neither could Holley and his associates without infringing upon the rights of Ward and Morrell. As Alexander Holley later described the situation, "Litigation of a formidable character was imminent." To avoid a long, drawn-out court battle, negotiations were undertaken starting in 1866 to determine a settlement between the two groups. Ward had never been one to back down from a fight. He had thrived on competition ever since he stood up to those who threatened to encroach on the steamboat lines he oversaw with his uncle Samuel. However, in this case, a compromise was reached with the creation of the Bessemer Steel Association. This resulted from a series of negotiations and out-of-court settlements over three years, finalized in 1869. The new organization essentially pooled the Kelly and Bessemer patents, and split the revenues generated from licensing the patents: 70 percent would go to Holley's Troy group and 30 percent to Ward and his associates.[58]

Ward's acquiescence in this case seemed to be out of character, particularly given that he was on the "losing side" of a 70 to 30 percent split. William F. Durfee was particularly upset, declaring, "In the whole history of business affairs it would indeed be hard to find a more perfect illustration of 'the tail wagging the dog' than this." However, as in most cases, events were more complicated than they appeared to be on the surface. If the litigation had moved forward between the two groups, both would have lost years and a great deal of money. Meanwhile, Ward could not have moved forward to design and construct new facilities to accommodate the production of Bessemer steel on the large-scale that he envisioned. Additionally, Ward's partner Morrell, a Quaker, was uncomfortable with lawsuits in general, and he and other investors were concerned about the unpredictability of judges and juries. Morrell also wanted to act quickly to upgrade his facilities at the Cambria Iron Works, just as Ward wanted to do in Chicago. Furthermore, the Mushet patent, which Ward held, had expired. With only the Kelly pneumatic process patent left, Ward and his associates had lost much of their negotiating advantage. An additional factor involving Eber Ward's own health likely influenced Ward's decision to compromise.[59]

Ever since Ward had taken over as the president of the Iron and Steel Association in 1864, he had been the public face of the national organization charged with lobbying the government to pass legislation favorable to American manufacturers. After nearly five years in the position, Ward stepped down in February

1869, allowing him to leave behind the stresses associated with the presidency. By 1869, his Milwaukee Iron Company boasted one of the largest facilities in the country, and Ward oversaw the successful expansion of his Flint & Pere Marquette Railway. That same year, Ward's thirty-one-year marriage ended in divorce and he remarried. He had even faced down James Ludington and forced him to sell the property he needed. The stresses of these events, and all of his other business activities, finally took their toll on Ward, who was fifty-seven years old. In September 1869, the *Detroit Post* reported, "Capt. E. B. Ward was stricken by paralysis on the morning of the 16th." The *Detroit Free Press* noted that Ward had suffered a "severe stroke of apoplexy." Both articles stated that Ward was out of immediate danger. After a recuperation of a few weeks, Ward resumed his regular business activities. Although he recovered from this health scare, it is likely this brush with death was an additional factor in his decision to compromise with his adversaries. After all, the demand for steel rails was high and the agreement allowed Ward to receive royalties for many years, thus paving the way for him to move forward and modernize his facilities.[60]

# Conclusion

Eber Brock Ward began 1869 seemingly at the apex of his power. He was the president of a national organization promoting iron and steel, had overseen the completion of a large iron mill in Milwaukee, and his Eureka Iron Company had produced the first American steel using the best technology then known. Ward also had outlined his vision for the future American economy by declaring that the nation's new manifest destiny involved the expansion of manufacturing to the Midwest. As the year continued, he successfully crushed one rival and finalized a lucrative settlement with another. His personal life had also experienced many changes. Then, in September, he almost died. Critics and supporters alike wondered how Ward might respond to this life-changing event. Would he return after his recovery as the hard-driving entrepreneur and business mogul no one dared to challenge? Or would he rest on his achievements and retire from his business empire? The business world soon would learn if Ward would return with the same resilient spirit and driving ambition to prove himself.

# 7

## Expanding an Empire

*At the time of his death, Captain Ward held the following positions:*

*President*–New England
Iron Company

*President*–The Flint &
Pere Marquette Ry.

*President and Lessee*–The
Burlington & Southern
Railway of Iowa

*President and Treasurer*–
The Wyandotte Rolling
Mills Company

*Treasurer*–North Chicago
Rolling Mills Company

*President*–Milwaukee Iron Company

*President*–The Detroit Copper
Mining Company of Arizona

*President and Treasurer*–The
American Plate Glass
Company of Missouri

*President and Treasurer*–The Eureka
Iron Company of Wyandotte

*President*–The Louisiana
Central Railroad

*President*–The Eureka Mining
Company of Utah

*Director*–The Second
National Bank of Detroit

*Director*–The Silver Islet
Mining Company

*Director*–The Wyandotte Silver
Smelting and Refining Company

—William Downie, 1941

Following his stroke in 1869, Eber Ward convalesced at home for about one month before returning to his life's work of expanding his business kingdom. He had been planning to enter the lumber industry for decades. Therefore, he began the construction of a large pair of lumber mills in Ludington and shortly thereafter built an additional lumber mill and shipyard outside of Toledo. As if that wasn't enough, Ward penetrated an entirely new industry when he founded the American Plate Glass Company outside of St. Louis. Ward also expanded his mining investments, most notably in Lake Superior's Silver Islet. This was a gamble that would pay valuable dividends.

Ward's business successes were unquestionable, yet they came with a cost. For years, Eber had focused his attentions on expanding his financial empire to the detriment of his family, denying his children the attention and mentorship they desperately needed. As his children entered adulthood, chaos characterized Eber's family life, particularly following his 1869 marriage to Catherine Lyon. Rivalry and conflict became commonplace in his household, no doubt worsened by antagonism between Eber's children and their new stepmother. This turmoil in his family life likely contributed to an uncharacteristic series of events in which Ward was swindled in a financial deal involving a silver mine.

The iron and steel mills in Wyandotte, Chicago, and Milwaukee were arguably Ward's most valuable assets. He chose to invest most heavily in his North Chicago Rolling Mill rather than those in other locations, which ultimately led to winners and losers among his businesses. A financial crisis that began in 1873 posed a serious threat to his operations and increased Ward's stress levels to near breaking point. Ultimately, this crisis, along with other events in his life, threatened Eber's health and may have contributed to a second stroke in 1875.

## Establishing Lumber Operations in Ludington

In 1869, Ward had ruthlessly pressured James Ludington to sell him property to locate a sawmill in the town of Ludington. Soon thereafter, Ward made plans to engage in the lumber industry so he could develop several thousand acres of valuable timber property he held in the vicinity. As was his usual custom, he moved forward in full force, sparing no expense. Ward's first step was to negotiate a contract with Patrick Danaher, a local lumberman familiar with logging camps, to cut 30 million feet of logs on his property for the upcoming 1869–70 winter season. In this era, cutting timber was undertaken in the winter months as the icy conditions facilitated the hauling of logs to a rollaway along rivers. Following the spring thaw, logs were released into rivers and then driven downstream by the force of water to the sawmills. Ward had no experience operating logging camps, so he chose to subcontract this aspect of his lumber operations. When word of the agreement was made public, the *Mason County Record* commented on its enormity: "This looks like business."[1]

The next steps were to plan and commence construction of the new sawmill, which eventually would be referred to as the North Mill. Much of the area where the mill would be located was a dense forest in 1870. In a little over a decade it became a thriving center of industry. Construction began in April, shortly after Eber and his son Milton made a brief visit to approve the project's final design, and work continued throughout the summer and early fall. When construction was complete in November 1870, an extensive article in the *Mason County Record* described the facility in detail. "The Mill proper is built upon 55 stone piers" constructed well out into Pere Marquette Lake, which opened up into Lake Michigan, to facilitate the collection of logs and loading of finished lumber. "These piers are placed on clumps of spiles driven closely together, and cut off 20 inches under water, and capped with heavy planking . . . and then with two feet of stone, which is thoroughly grouted with water lime up to the high water mark." The mill was 50 by 130 feet in size, including a "tightly boarded" roof covered with shingles embedded in mortar as "protection against fire." It was powered by five large boilers four feet in diameter, with a chimney ninety feet in height. The local newspaper reported that "no money" was "spared to make this a superior mill, and careful investigation has been made to find the *best* machinery" possible to ensure the greatest level of efficiency. It cost $60,000 and had a capacity to produce 100,000 feet of lumber per day.[2]

Although Ludington's residents argued Ward's mill was the finest along the east shore of Lake Michigan and rivaled any other in the state, the Detroit industrialist was not content with that achievement. In the spring of 1871, Ward purchased the property on Pere Marquette Lake between his mill and the mill operated by his neighbors, Danaher & Melendy. Eventually, Ward's operations would occupy over forty acres of land and about one-half mile of frontage on Pere Marquette Lake. Ward had a large vision for this property. Plans were developed to construct several tenant dwellings for his employees and their families, as well as a large three-story boardinghouse. A "mammoth warehouse" (50 by 20 feet) was built to store supplies and sell goods. Most

Ward's South Mill, his second sawmill in Ludington, was considered one of the finest in the state when it was completed in 1872. (Courtesy of the Mason County Historical Society)

important, the additional property would allow Ward to construct another sawmill even larger than the mill completed the previous year.[3]

Work on Ward's second sawmill, known as the South Mill, began in June 1872. It was rumored that Ward hoped to build "the largest mill in the world at Ludington." Similar to his North Mill, the new sawmill was built on a foundation of spiles and solid masonry out into Pere Marquette Lake with all the modern technologies available. However, this mill was larger than the first, 56 by 160 feet, with a capacity to produce 125,000 feet of finished lumber each day. Atop the roof was a large cupola, eighteen feet in diameter, allowing for natural light to illuminate the room beneath. Additional light entered the facility through fifteen hundred panes of glass, and it was equipped with gas lighting for work at night. The building also included fire protection. In case of fire, 1,800 feet of iron pipe could circulate water throughout the structure with numerous openings for hoses. The mill was powered by seven boilers and had a circular smoke stack 14 feet in diameter and 125 feet in height. The facility's estimated cost was $125,000, more than double that of the North Mill. When completed, it was impressive, reputed to be "the model mill of Michigan at that time."[4]

Ward was one of many business leaders who became engaged in Michigan's lumber industry in the years following the Civil War. From the late 1860s to about 1890, the state of Michigan led the nation in lumber production. In a study sponsored by the Michigan Historical Commission, historian Rolland Maybee estimated Michigan's lumber industry had greater value than all the gold mined in the California gold rush, "by more than a billion dollars." As well as Ludington's, the economies of Michigan communities such as Flint, Saginaw, Bay City, Muskegon, and Manistee were dominated by the lumber industry. By 1873, eight sawmills operated in Ludington, producing over 83 million board feet of lumber that year. Today, some might consider the sawmills as symbols of environmental destruction, but in the late 1800s they marked progress and prosperity for the areas in which they were sited. Each spring, as birds began to sing and farmers prepared their fields for crops, residents of the city awaited the sound of the mills, which signified their community's awakening from the long winter and the revival of its economy. An article in the *Mason County Record* captured this sentiment. "The first sound of the saw, announcing the early approach of the busy lumbering season, already begins to revive the life of business and quicken the pulses of trade, and its powerful influence will soon be felt and seen throughout all the avenues of our city."[5]

Although Ward had only recently established himself in the community, his operations dwarfed those of other Ludington lumber manufacturers. The assessed value of his two mills was about four times greater than those of other operators, and his mills produced far more finished products. The key markets for his lumber were Milwaukee and Chicago, particularly after the latter city's infamous fire in 1871. Ward's contributions to Ludington's development were recognized by the editors of the local newspaper, who described the "generous spirit and enterprise" and "wonderful energy" brought by E. B. Ward's investment in the community.[6]

Ward visited Ludington occasionally, but generally stayed only a short time. As an absentee owner, Ward hired an agent to represent him, as he had often done in the past; beginning in 1869, J. B. Beane oversaw Ward's interests. Nonetheless, Ward maintained strict control over the operation of his affairs.

He served as the "glue" which held his diverse business empire together. One employee recalled that Ward's correspondence "often contained a number of suggestions as to the details of managing the Ludington business." Beane continued to serve as Ward's agent until 1872, when he was replaced by Eber's son Milton, who turned twenty-four that year. Milton had been living in Ludington and working for his father at least one year prior to his promotion. Before that he had worked in Wyandotte and Milwaukee, but he "had been neglectful of his duties and couldn't be kept." He also tried attending school and working as a clerk on one of his father's ships, but neither of those efforts lasted long. In 1872, he was given "full sway at Ludington."[7]

As Milton later remembered, Eber called him into his office and informed his son "that he proposed to build the crack mill of the State of Michigan, and

Milton Ward served as his father's agent, overseeing his lumber operations in Ludington. His involvement was short-lived and unsuccessful; he left after about one year. (Courtesy of the Seitz family)

he was going to give it to his boys [Milton and his brother Charles], . . . as he thought they might well begin at once to learn the lumber business." Given his lack of success in the past, it is unsurprising that Milton failed when placed in this leadership position. Under his direction, there were numerous cost overruns and multiple conflicts with employees. Milton also was faulted for building an extravagant home and living an excessive lifestyle. His lack of experience was mocked in an article in the local newspaper titled, "An Inexperienced Lath Sawyer." Apparently, while attempting to operate a lath machine, Milton "had a narrow escape from losing an arm." Fortunately, his experience resulted only in a bad cut on his hand, requiring "tender treatment" from a local doctor.[8]

Eber Ward had placed his son in an untenable position. Milton had failed when given numerous business opportunities in the past. How could he be expected to oversee the much larger operations at Ludington? Emily recalled that Eber "was always anxious about Milton," and that Ward "would have been glad to have had Milton marry and settle down at Ludington." This was a naïve hope on the part of an inattentive parent. Milton had never had the opportunities his father had enjoyed: the education Eber had received from his own father when the two lived together on Bois Blanc Island, and the mentorship provided by his uncle Samuel Ward when Eber was about Milton's age. Instead, Eber expected his son to suddenly become an effective leader without any apprenticeship. Ward eventually came to recognize his shortcomings as a parent, confessing to a friend that "so far as his boys [Milton and Charles] were concerned, his life was a failure." Regardless, he remained deeply disappointed in his son's inability to oversee his lumbering operations in Ludington. At one point, most likely in 1873, he even confided to Emily that he had "given the boys up, and that there was no way to do but to fasten a living upon them so as to prevent them from becoming a public expense."[9]

As early as the summer of 1873, Milton left Ludington and was replaced as his father's agent by John S. Woodruff, who would serve in that capacity for the next few years. The operations Woodruff managed were quite extensive. By that time, Ward employed about four hundred men with a payroll that could reach $800 per day. In addition to his two mills, Ward had a line of six barges with an iron tugboat that transported finished lumber to Chicago and Milwaukee. He also owned a store, tenant housing, and a boardinghouse. As part of his duties, Woodruff was required to address complaints about the conditions under which the employees worked. The work environment in the mills could be dangerous. Accidents could lead to injuries or deaths. In July 1872 one employee working in the lumberyard fell from a dock and drowned. Later that year, a man working at Ward's South Mill had his foot badly crushed, while another "young man" working at the North Mill "had his hand badly mangled by a butting saw." In this era prior to the expansion of unionization, there was little, if any, compensation for employees injured or killed on the job.[10]

Eber Ward may have been an absentee owner, but he directed Woodruff to run his Ludington operations with an iron fist. In the fall of 1872, the issue of alcohol at his lumber camps emerged. Just as Ward had sought to prohibit employees from having access to alcohol at his iron mills in Wyandotte and Milwaukee, he did the same at Ludington. As the workers prepared to venture into the woods that year, Ward had the following notice posted in full view of his employees and published in the local newspaper. "Any person employed about this camp, found under the influence of liquor, will be immediately discharged; and any supply teamster bringing any liquor into camp, will also be discharged."[11]

Ward later joined other Ludington mill owners who conspired in June 1873 to lower wages by as much as 75 cents per day in an industry where the prevailing daily wage ranged from $1.50 to $4. In response, several workers went on strike. Unfortunately for those who refused to work at the reduced wages, other laborers filled their positions quickly—within a short time, the strike was broken. Mill owners collaborated to bring down wages because the lumber market had been flooded with inventory as production outpaced demand. The price they received for lumber had plummeted. Later that fall, the economic depression commonly referred to as the Panic of 1873 negatively impacted the entire nation's economy and depressed the lumber industry. Although prices recovered by the late 1870s, in the meantime, those engaged in the lumber industry often struggled.[12]

Ward continued to operate his sawmills in Ludington despite what were considered "exceedingly low prices" for lumber, in part because he needed the cash flow from lumber sales to help support his other businesses. However, just as he had done at his previous companies, he developed efficiencies to bring down costs and raise revenue. For example, he contracted with the City of Ludington to provide sawdust for the community's streets. Sawdust was a natural byproduct of any sawmill operation and Ward had no use for it. At one point in the 1870s, it was estimated that more than fifty cubic yards of sawdust from his mills was hauled and spread on the streets of Ludington each day. Ward also found a method to ensure freight would be transported on his Flint & Pere Marquette Railway. He did so when the railway entered into a contract with Ward to ship over 20 million feet of lumber per year for fifteen years from Ludington to Detroit and Toledo. Not only was Ward the president of the railway company, his mills produced the lumber. Integrating the operations of his companies in this manner helped to cut costs and ensure continued business for both the sawmills and the railroad well into the future. It also facilitated the expansion of his lumber market beyond cities to the west, such as Chicago and Milwaukee, to additional markets in the eastern Great Lakes.[13]

As a result of his careful investment over time, as well as his willingness to employ ruthless tactics, Eber Ward came to be the dominant lumberman in Ludington by the early 1870s. At the same time, he also emerged as one of Michigan's larger timber barons. Ward's activities in this community along Lake Michigan were not his only venture into the lumber industry. He became interested in a large stand of timber located in Ohio on Lake Erie. There, Ward established another large lumber operation in an area commonly referred to as the Black Swamp.

## Lumber Operations in Ohio's Black Swamp

The Black Swamp was part of a large marsh located along the western shore of Lake Erie just fifteen miles from Toledo. Although much of the area was considered desolate and isolated, Ward was drawn to it because the region beyond the marsh included what observers described as "a magnificent stand of oak, walnut, ash, elm, and cottonwood." He purchased large tracts of timbered property beginning in the late 1860s and eventually owned nearly nine thousand acres and most of what became Jerusalem Township. His timber empire in the region held great value, but the extensive marsh prevented him from cutting the timber and transporting finished lumber to market. To overcome this, Ward planned to carve a canal through the marsh. Jerome Navarre, who began working for Ward at the age of sixteen, recalled the entire project was an incredibly "ambitious piece of engineering."[14] Ward hired a team from Detroit to operate a steam dredge, which began digging on one corner of his property. The work was difficult and the machine struggled at times, but progress continued and a primitive ditch emerged from the swampland. Ward also directed his crews to straighten and widen Cedar Creek to allow access all the way to Lake Erie. The dredge machine could not be used one mile in from the lake, so that area was dug with "horse scrapers, picks and shovels." Indeed, it was an "ambitious" undertaking and proved to be more than just a large ditch. When it was finally finished, Ward's Canal was nearly three miles in length, at least thirty feet wide, and had a minimum depth of fifteen feet.[15]

By 1871, Ward built a sawmill and shipyard alongside the canal. They were connected by a wide plank road to allow wagons filled with lumber to be hauled to the shipyard. Ward also had a boardinghouse erected to house employees, who arrived in increasing numbers in search of employment. Dan Shepard, Ward's boardinghouse manager, purchased additional property, which he subdivided into plots to be sold to Ward's employees. Wells were dug to provide fresh water and other locals soon created their own subdivisions. Before long, the area had a grocery store, blacksmith shop, and other businesses as people were drawn to the area due to opportunities created by Ward's investment. The settlement was originally called New Jerusalem but eventually was renamed Bono in 1898, after a local Native American family.[16]

Before long, the shipyard became a "lively spot employing about one hundred men." Numerous vessels were built at New Jerusalem. Some were schooner barges, such as the *Mercury* (320 tons) and *Mars* (234 tons). The steamer *Leland* (325 tons) was built for Ward's new investment in the Leland Iron Furnace Company located north of Ludington along Lake Michigan. Ward's son Charles oversaw the construction of at least two vessels. These included the barge *Uranus*, which was quite large at 524 tons, and the 320-ton steamer *Music*. The *Uranus* tested the capacity of Ward's Canal as it was not only 160 feet in length, but 29.9 feet wide. An article in the *Toledo Blade* touted the *Music* as "one of the finest vessels on the lakes," featuring a cabin "entirely constructed with black walnut and handsomely ornamented." Vessels usually could make their own way through the canal, but if necessary teams of horses were used to tow ships in or out.[17]

Employees at the sawmill also remained busy. Some finished lumber was transported to market via rail, but most was shipped through the canal to Toledo, Cleveland, Buffalo, and other American and Canadian ports on Lake Erie. Some barges transported as much as one hundred thousand feet of finished lumber on a single trip. Large timbers of oak, twenty-four inches in diameter and as much as forty feet in length, were sent to the Soo. Less desirable wood, of which there was plenty, could be burned into charcoal and was sent to iron mills, including Ward's.[18]

Eber Ward also built a home for his family in the area. His former employee Jerome Navarre "remembered well all the Ward family" who spent time at New Jerusalem. They lived in a large and elegant house "constructed entirely of black walnut." Next to the dwelling was a large stable and a race track for their riding horses. Ward likely built the home, in part, as a retreat for his wife Catherine. Although he already had a grand home in Detroit, it still reflected the presence of Ward's first wife. Furthermore, according to the *Detroit Free Press*, the "matrons of Detroit were loyal to the first Mrs. Ward. They turned their backs coldly and contemptuously on her successor," treating Catherine like a "pariah." While Catherine visited occasionally with the children, the most consistent resident was Eber's son Charles.[19]

Charles H. Ward, who turned twenty-one in 1871, was two years younger than his brother Milton. Charles was given responsibility to develop operations at the Black Swamp, similar to Milton's position at Ludington. His aunt Emily remembered that Charles was studious as a youth and Eber "had more hope for him than for any other one of his boys." From 1864 until September 1866, Charles attended the State Agricultural College (which became Michigan State University) in Lansing and later graduated from Bryant & Stratton College in Detroit, where he studied bookkeeping. Once his son's education was finished, Eber had a laboratory built where Charles analyzed mineral ores for his father's businesses, but that job lasted only a few months. Charles remained restless—it appears he became more interested in drinking than working. In 1867, Emily and Eber secured a position for him at the Second National Bank in Detroit, where Eber was a member of the board of directors. At the time, Charles was only seventeen. Eber promised that if Charles worked there for one year, he would award his son a bonus of $1,800 in addition to his salary. After the year was complete, Charles received his bonus, which "disappeared in about three weeks." Eber, frustrated, complained to Emily that Charles did not understand the value of money and that his boys only wanted "fast horses, a paper kite, and for him [Eber] to furnish the money."[20]

Eber, hoping that Charles would be successful if he was removed from the temptations of his friends in the city and had a change of scenery, put his son to work in the Black Swamp beginning in 1869, and by 1871 had placed him in charge. Unfortunately, Charles was just as unsuccessful as his older brother Milton. Charles's correspondence shows that while he may have moved away from his friends, they came to him so they could drink, race horses, and generally have a good time. Reports of his heavy drinking and mismanagement of affairs made their way to his father. Eber sent an employee, Ira Lillbridge, to investigate matters. Lillbridge reported back that not only were conditions chaotic, "it was his opinion Charles was deranged." The financial downturn that began in 1873 did not help matters. The demand for and price of lumber produced in the Black Swamp tumbled just as they did in Ludington at the same time.[21]

Eber's concern for his son's situation became so dire that in July 1874 he wrote to a Toledo attorney, "I think my son Charles H. has exhibited strong evidences of slight irregularities of the mind and therefore neglects his business . . . to such an extent that failure is inevitable." He described Charles's circumstances as "a very unfortunate and sad case." Ward was unclear what should be done. At the time, he was short of cash as the Panic of 1873 had stretched his resources significantly.[22] By September 1874, Charles was forced to file for bankruptcy. Near the end of October, Ward posted a letter in the local newspaper to Charles's creditors outlining a possible settlement. In it, he offered to deed property in Michigan or Ohio if they agreed to release Charles "in full of all their claims and refrain from further legal proceedings." The fact that Ward offered land, rather than cash, to cover the remainder of Charles's debts appears to indicate he was strapped for cash by the fall of 1874 and near a breaking point.[23]

Charles's mishandling of activities in the Black Swamp, combined with the Panic of 1873, threatened Ward's activities in the region. But Eber Ward's own actions contributed to his problems and warrant criticism. He could not have predicted the financial crisis that emerged in the summer of 1873, but he never provided Charles with the preparation necessary to be successful in a position of such responsibility. Eber made the same mistake with Charles as he had with Milton. Both sons were immature and inexperienced. Neither had received the proper mentorship from their father and neither was ready to take on the task of running such complex operations. Eber previously had complained that Charles did not understand the meaning of money. Milton and Charles had grown up in a wealthy family in which money simply had been handed to them. They were more interested in spending money than earning it. This was in sharp contrast to the instincts of their intensely competitive father, whose every action was focused on the creation of a vast business empire worth a fortune.

The legacy Ward left behind in the Black Swamp was mixed. His operations provided economic opportunity for the region and employment for many families. Ward viewed the transformation of the landscape as an example of progress, although digging the canal had a major impact on the region's ecology. Previously, the marshes had provided a unique habitat for a wide range of plant and animal life. In the decades prior to Ward's activities, the abundance of game had attracted Native American, French, and American hunters and trappers to the region. The canal project and removal of the forests devastated the wetlands and the area's ecosystem. The economic boom sparked by Ward's investment was short-lived, but the environmental impact was not. In subsequent years others engaged in the lumber industry, their operations facilitated by the canal Ward had constructed. Farmers followed and later vacationers. Locals described it as "mecca for fishermen" and the canal provided access to a marina on Lake Erie. But by the 1970s, nature had its revenge and the area experienced a series of devastating floods. Today, portions of the region initially developed by Ward are included in Maumee Bay State Park, part of the Ohio State Park system.[24]

Eber Ward's involvement in the lumber industry at Ludington and the Black Swamp was not unique among Michigan's business leaders. After all, lumbering held great promise in the years following the Civil War. However, the diversification of his investments was unique. Previously, Ward had been engaged in shipping, ship building, and railroads as well as the manufacture of iron and steel. To add lumber to his growing portfolio made him distinctive. But Ward was not finished. In 1871, he became interested in the possibility of manufacturing glass at a location outside of St. Louis.

# American Plate Glass Company in Crystal City, Missouri

For years, Americans largely had relied on plate glass imported from Europe for their businesses, homes, and other structures. Beginning in the 1850s, entrepreneurs in Cheshire, Massachusetts, attempted to establish a facility to produce plate glass, but their venture failed. Successful manufacturing plants were in place by the early 1870s, but the American market could bear additional capacity. Eber Ward became interested in the plate glass industry in the early 1870s, probably due to the persistence of Dr. W. H. Bidwell, a scientist and editor of the *Eclectic Magazine*. For years, Bidwell had sought investors to exploit the high-quality sand necessary for successful glassmaking that was readily available along Plattin Creek, about thirty miles south of St. Louis. According to an 1884 government report detailing the nation's glass industry, the deposit was "one of the most important [sand] beds in the West; and is of great purity and inexhaustible in quantity, and the cost of mining is merely nominal." The snow-white sand was packed so firmly it looked like a wall of crystal, but when mined, it became "soft, clear, sparkling and beautiful, for all the world like a highly refined sugar." Its mineral content was so pure that it yielded over 99 percent silica, perfect for glassmaking.[25]

In 1871, Ward purchased 760 acres of land and organized the American Plate Glass Company with a capitalization of $250,000. About 200 acres of the newly acquired property included the vast deposits of sand. The remainder was reserved for the manufacturing plant, tenement housing, and the community set to emerge in what was then described by a local newspaper as "wilderness." Ward served as president and treasurer of his new company while Theodore Luce was named general manager in charge of operations. Luce also served on the board of directors and was one of many Michigan men sent by Ward to Missouri to help establish the new operations. Ward also recruited another key employee, Obed Blake, an experienced glassmaker from England who had produced what were reputed to be the largest pieces of plate glass in the world for a palace in Constantinople. Ward and his associates immediately set to work designing what would become, for a time, the largest glassworks in the country. In May 1872, construction of the first building commenced. Bricks, reportedly in the millions, were manufactured on-site with materials mined at the company's quarries. Dozens of skilled and unskilled workers were employed, and by

1874 an entire complex had emerged. The buildings were perfectly situated on a bluff above Plattin Creek, only half a mile from the Mississippi River. Barges could easily import necessary resources, such as coal and other materials, to the work area. Once manufacturing was underway, Ward planned to export finished glass to outside markets via the Mississippi.[26]

An article in the *St. Louis Republican* in January 1874 described the "mammoth works" constructed under Ward's direction. The main structure was the finishing hall, made entirely of brick. The hall was only one story, but it was enormous, reaching upward of 40 feet in height, and was believed to be "one of the largest, if not the largest, building in the West" at 742 by 120 feet. The architects ensured it was well ventilated and designed to take advantage of as much natural light as possible. Twelve large grinders, 20 feet in diameter, forty smoothers, and more than thirty polishers were located inside the building. These machines were designed to help shape the glass, remove scratches or roughness, and refine the finished product. Several other buildings were included in the large compound, among them a pot house for storing and mixing clays, a furnace room, and a blacksmith shop.[27]

Theodore Luce was responsible for the proper construction of the buildings whereas Obed Blake was the expert glassmaker. Ward had no experience in the glassmaking industry but, as he had often done in the past, he hired and empowered key individuals to run the day-to-day operations of his business. This allowed Ward to provide oversight for the numerous businesses of his already vast yet continually growing empire. To create glass, Ward relied on Blake, who oversaw the proper mixture of sand, soda, lime, and other fluxes in the mixing room. When ready, these were ladled into a melting pot that had been heated to the proper temperature. Then the pot, with all of its ingredients, was "exposed to an intense heat" in the furnace for about fourteen hours until the mixture was "reduced to a molten mass." Several experienced workers oversaw the process. Each pot, which could hold upward of fifteen hundred pounds of material, had to be kept at the same temperature. Sometimes the pots would boil over and would need to be refilled, or workers might be required to remove pots that were cracked or broken.[28]

When it was determined the molten liquid was ready be poured, the pots were removed by using long tongues attached to an iron carriage and taken to the casting room. There the liquid was "poured upon large iron tables to the desired thickness, then rolled with a heavy iron roller." Once completed, the table was taken to an annealing oven to be "tempered and toughened" as the temperature was lowered in a controlled environment. Each plate had to pass through the grinding machines, then the smoothers, and finally the polishers, where it attained a "perfectly polished surface." The entire operation required large amounts of capital and numerous skilled and unskilled employees. The initial $250,000 investment proved to be insufficient; Ward was forced to increase it to $500,000. Managers expected to employ "at least 1,000 persons of differing ages" when the factory began operating at full capacity. Ward visited his new facility in Missouri only occasionally, as had been his practice regarding Ludington and the Black Swamp, but he monitored progress closely from his office in Detroit. Clearly, as president of the American Plate Glass Company, he stood at the helm of this new enterprise and he offered guidance and directives accordingly.[29]

A sizable community emerged around the factory. As it grew, the "invisible hand" of Eber Brock Ward could occasionally be recognized as the settlement evolved into a true company town. Ward had a boardinghouse along with a row of two-story frame homes built on Main Street to accommodate the workers and their families. Renters paid an average of $6 per month for a three-room home. Plans for construction of a company store near the company offices, also on Main Street, were in place. This would be a two-story structure, with the second floor designed to have a reading room for the employees. Eventually, church services were held on this upper floor prior to the completion of a place of worship. One villager recalled the company street "was dubbed 'Smoky Row' by the residents because it always seemed to be in direct line with the heavy smoke coming from the plant, especially on those days when the good ladies of the village were wont to hang out the wash." Most of the managers and board members were from Detroit, so company officials named the growing village New Detroit. However, at the company's inaugural board meeting, those from Missouri declared their preference for the name Crystal City. The board of directors, led by Ward, compromised and quickly adopted the new name.[30]

Ward was unwilling to compromise on the issue of alcohol. When Crystal City was established, Ward maintained "absolute control" of the community, prohibiting the presence of any "saloon or dram shop" within its borders. These actions mirrored previous regulations implemented by Ward at his other business locations. Much to his chagrin, numerous saloons and other unsavory establishments emerged just beyond the borders of his company town. Employees looking to relax and quench their thirst began to frequent a village originally named Tanglefoot, just to the west of Crystal City. The town earned its name "on account of the whiskey that was sold to certain parties, who, in consequence, got their feet tangled in the brush returning to their homes." The town's residents later dropped the name Tanglefoot because they considered it vulgar. Tanglefoot was renamed Limitville, as the community formed a boundary signifying the limit to the company's holdings. Eventually, it was renamed Festus in the 1880s.[31]

By 1874, the furnaces were installed and enough buildings were completed and staffed to begin production. Ward traveled to Crystal City, along with many of his fellow board members, to celebrate the happy occasion. Unfortunately, the initial attempts to manufacture glass had "pathetic results." A situation emerged reminiscent to one that had taken place at Wyandotte when the new process of making Bessemer steel had been showcased to a group of dignitaries. As the furnace grew hot enough to melt the mixture of sand and other materials, it melted due to faulty construction. While no one was injured, the result was "a sad-looking mess of bricks and pots, held solidly together by a dark-hued substance that never could be called glass." Ward was furious. He had invested a great deal of time and capital in this new enterprise. Nor could he afford a setback at this time—he faced pressure resulting from the economic downturn that had started the previous year. The Panic of 1873 had threatened every segment of his financial empire. At about the same time, he also was trying to rescue his son Charles from bankruptcy. Ward recognized the glass factory would take time to become profitable, but he knew he had to produce a quality product or his investment would result in failure. After he calmed down, Ward directed his managers to build another furnace, which was completed properly. Production resumed, and within a short time, the company he founded was "producing plate-glass the equal of any made in the world."[32]

Ward's entrance into the glassmaking industry was representative of his previous business enterprises. He was willing to take risks, empowered key individuals to run daily operations while seeking to control aspects of other employees' lives, and employed a focused determination to succeed at all costs. He continued to enlarge and diversify his commercial empire, even investing in a range of copper, silver, and iron mines. Arguably the most important silver mine he developed was on a tiny, isolated piece of land located along the north shore of Lake Superior in Ontario. Ward had been born in Ontario, but he was not drawn to the place of his birth for sentimental reasons. Instead, he was lured by the potential profits to be made on Silver Islet.

## Silver Islet and Ward Is Swindled

Silver Islet is a "little rocky islet, entirely destitute of vegetation . . . lying at the entrance to Thunder Bay" about twenty miles north of Isle Royale. Beginning in 1868, a mining engineer and geologist working on behalf of the Montreal Mining Company named Thomas Macfarlane had led a group of surveyors exploring the area. They came across a tiny island of rock, located about three-quarters of a mile from the mainland, that they hoped to use as a transit base. As Macfarlane himself later described it, "The Island measured originally about ninety feet each way, rising about eight feet at its highest part above the level of the lake." Due to its shape, the surveyors initially labeled the little island "Skull Rock." When veins of native silver were discovered on the rock on July 10, they renamed it Silver Islet.[33] Over the next year men hacked out as much of the precious metal as they could using black powder, crowbars, and shovels. On calm days, they worked in the shallow waters of Lake Superior, but only for thirty minutes at a time "on account of its coldness, being like a bath of liquid ice." Regardless, in one afternoon, $6,000 worth of rich silver was taken from the rock. Macfarlane encouraged the company to invest $50,000 and establish an expanded mining operation, but it was not prepared to spend that much money on such a risky project. Instead, the company sold its entire claim to a group of American investors, led by E. B. Ward, for $225,000 on September 1, 1870.[34]

Work began immediately after the Americans gained title to rocky Silver Islet and 108,000 acres of property on the mainland. William B. Frue was named mine superintendent and charged with improving the mine. His first step was to create a breakwall surrounding the entire island. This was made with cribs of timber filled with stone. An article in the *Stark County Democrat* in 1870 offered detail. "Within these cribs a cofferdam was built, and filled with clay, having the effect of making the whole interior of the island nearly water tight, at least from the intrusion of the lake." Next, two large steam-powered pumps were set up to siphon water from the mine. After the water receded, an eight-foot-wide mine entrance was created and shortly thereafter, "six men took out $35,000 worth of silver in four days." Macfarlane estimated the cost of these undertakings was at least $80,000. By December, nearly 125 barrels of native silver had been mined, with more on the way. Once the mine began to pay large dividends, Ward must have been relieved that his investment was paying off, but perseverance was necessary. Lake Superior storms repeatedly attacked the breakwall and large segments of the cribwork were destroyed and needed to be rebuilt multiple times. Eventually, additional cribwork was constructed with a base of seventy-five feet and framed with five separate bulkheads. In some areas, the breakwall reached a height of eighteen feet above the water's surface.[35]

Miners working at Silver Islet received $40 per month, from which room and board of $14 was subtracted, for their six-day workweek. This was slightly more than the going rate for most unskilled laborers in the United States, but the work was difficult and dangerous. According to one author, for men employed at Silver Islet "working conditions were deplorable, even by nineteenth century standards." Men descended the single mine shaft down a ladder, hoping their head candles would not ignite pockets of gas that could be trapped underground. Two small airshafts were created to provide ventilation. Winters were long and tedious. Mail delivery was infrequent and the community of miners and their families was often cut off from outside communication from the fall, when the last ship left, until April, when the first vessel arrived. In their downtime, employees hunted wild game and fished in the waters of Lake Superior. The company initially prohibited the sale of alcohol, a familiar regulation at one of Eber Ward's operations. Nevertheless, several bootleg distributors arrived at the isolated hamlet to deliver their black market product to numerous willing customers. This forced the company to make whisky available to employees, although it was strictly regulated. Each man was allowed only three drinks per day, none in succession. The whisky was distributed at a company-owned building with a large bar designed to protect the bartender from the patrons. The bar and system for distributing alcohol was described in a newspaper article in 1899. "On the wall of this bar is a wide blackboard marked off into 400 little numbered squares, and on each of these a man's drinks were chalked up against him. The term 'chalking' up drink accounts is said, by the way, to have originated at this mine, and in this way."[36]

Contemporary accounts marveled at the mine's productivity. The *Islander* declared Silver Islet to be "one of the richest deposits of silver in the world," while the *Buchanan County Bulletin* reported that in July 1871 the mine yielded "an average of seven thousand dollars [in silver] a day, and stock originally worth but fifty dollars a share . . . is now rated at $1,800 per share." Ward's investment was paying off handsomely. Ultimately, in its first three years of operation, about $1.4 million ($30,701,155.51 in 2020 dollars) in silver ore was produced at Silver Islet.[37]

Progress slowed significantly beginning in the fall of 1873 as new obstacles arose. In the annual report to stockholders in 1874, superintendent William Frue declared, "Product for the mine for the year 1873 shows a perceptible falling off from the year 1872." On October 24, once the mine had reached "a depth of 292 feet, a large fissure of water was opened at the bottom of the shaft instantly driving the miners from the bottom of the mine" as they scrambled to escape with their lives. Work at the mine came to a standstill for nearly three months. From that time onward, the huge profits Ward and the other investors had earned dropped significantly. The cost of production had increased, although work at the mine continued as large pockets of silver still remained. When it was finally abandoned in 1884, the Silver Islet had generated almost $3.1 million in silver, making it one of the richest silver mines in the world.[38]

Ward's involvement at Silver Islet led directly to another investment—and it also pointed him down the road toward an embarrassing and costly mistake. In March 1871, the *Chicago Tribune* reported that Ward had formed a new company to smelt the silver ore coming from Lake Superior. The paper predicted the "smelting furnaces will cost $100,000, and will be the largest in the United States." The new facility would be located in Wyandotte, to take advantage of its location on the Detroit River to facilitate shipping. E. B. Ward was named president of the new enterprise, while Thomas Macfarlane, the initial discoverer of the silver, became superintendent. The company was named the Wyandotte Silver Smelting and Refining Works. During the first year of operations, the total value of silver processed at the facility was $504,640.13.[39]

William M. Curtis, who served as Ward's chief chemist, offered a description of the facility. "The works occupy three stone buildings. . . . The first building contains offices, laboratories, engine and boiler." The other buildings included specialized crushers and furnaces for extracting zinc, nickel, and other metals from the silver ore. The back of one building included a blacksmith and carpenter's shop. Curtis explained that the operations started slowly, "as none of the workmen employed have had any previous experience in smelting," but efficiencies were developed and quality improved over time. The capacity of the works built at Wyandotte was much larger than required to process ore from Silver Islet. Therefore, Ward formed an additional company to seek and purchase additional ore from states in the West. This resulted in Ward's investment in a range of mining operations. As events would turn out, his expansion put him into contact with Joab Lawrence, president of the Eureka Mine Company of Utah, located about seventy-five miles outside of Salt Lake City.[40]

At one time Lawrence had been a Mississippi riverboat captain, but then he moved to Utah, where he speculated in several mining operations. These were successful, and he became quite wealthy. Ward's connection with Lawrence appeared to be a perfect match. Ward looked to invest in a silver mine to meet the capacity of his smelting works, while Lawrence, claiming to be short of resources, needed an investor to provide an influx of money into his Eureka mine to gain greater access to its silver. In the summer of 1872, Lawrence visited Ward in Detroit, describing the "immense mineral wealth of the Territory, of Utah in general and the Eureka Mine in particular"—which, he argued, "would yield immense quantities of remarkably rich ore." Ward's interest was piqued by Lawrence's presentation, but he also was prudent. Later that summer, Ward sent his chemist William M. Curtis to Utah to investigate the mine and determine if Lawrence's claims were true.[41]

What happened next would become a matter of some dispute. Curtis traveled to Utah and evaluated several specimens of ore from the Eureka mine, which he determined were "unusually rich in silver." This prompted Ward to purchase a 40 percent interest in the mine for $206,000 on October 7, 1872. Interestingly, Ward paid little, if any, cash in this transaction. He forfeited large amounts of stock in his Wyandotte Rolling Mill and Silver Islet as well as some property in Detroit. He also offered three promissory notes of $10,000 each, at 8 percent interest. All seemed fine until subsequent samples of ore taken from the mine were evaluated and Ward discovered that "the new specimens were of a very inferior quality and . . . the mine would not yield sufficient silver to pay for the expense of working it." Ward seethed—it appeared he had been swindled. He charged that when Curtis gathered samples of ore on his visit to Utah, Lawrence and John Whitney, the company's vice president, had "salted" the Eureka mine—strategically placing deposits of rich silver ore in "dumps" throughout the mine to fool the inspector. Ward also alleged that some of the samples taken by Curtis had stealthily been exchanged for "rich specimens" signifying that the mine was more valuable than it was in reality.[42]

Ward developed a plan to seek retribution. According to an affidavit filed by Lawrence, Ward had his associate Allen A. Griffith approach Lawrence to determine if he would buy back the stock Ward had purchased. When Lawrence refused, Griffith threatened him, warning that "Ward was disgusted with the whole Eureka scheme and was mad. . . . Ward would give him trouble" and Lawrence "would be sorry for it." When Lawrence again refused, Griffith had him arrested. About the same time, Lawrence's partner John Whitney also was arrested. The men were charged with conspiracy to commit fraud by falsely exaggerating the value of the Eureka mine. Ward then filed an injunction in Superior Court to prevent Lawrence from selling any of the stock and properties involved in the original purchase. Ward also filed a civil suit against Lawrence asking for $100,000 in damages.[43]

Although the initial injunction preventing Lawrence from selling the stock and properties was granted, Ward never received the vengeance he sought. His actions were strikingly similar to those he took when he pressured James Ludington to sell the property he wanted for his railroad and lumber mill in Ludington. This time, Ward's attempt to intimidate a rival did not work. Whitney jumped bail and absconded to Canada. The criminal charges against Lawrence ultimately were discharged, and the judge in the civil case ruled that Ward had no legal basis for his arguments. The bottom line was that Ward had been swindled to the tune of $206,000 ($4,517,455.74 in 2020 dollars). The fraud made headlines. Ward's *Detroit Daily Post* took a sympathetic approach, labeling Lawrence and his cohorts "Slippery Speculators," experienced swindlers who used unsavory tactics in their elaborate scheme to deceive Ward.[44] The *Detroit Free Press*, an outlet that often had been critical of Ward, was merciless. The paper allowed Lawrence a platform to defend himself for his "alleged" actions and mocked Ward, sarcastically describing the "sad and touching tale" of how the "young and inexperienced" Ward had been swindled. The sarcasm continued as the paper compared Ward to a "guileless lamb" who had been "cheated by the heartless individuals who 'salted' him." Readers of the *Free Press* knew Ward was anything but a "young and inexperienced . . . guileless lamb." Eber Brock Ward was the richest man in Michigan and the region's largest employer. He was a shrewd operator who thought nothing of taking down a competitor if it would facilitate the expansion of his empire. The *Free Press* summed up: Ward had "bought a lottery ticket in a huge lottery; he drew a blank, and now he claims the intervention of the law."[45]

Eber Ward's involvement in Silver Islet and the subsequent events involving the Eureka mine swindle offer insight into his activities in the 1870s. Although Ward carried a heavy debt load for many of his businesses, the success of Silver Islet provided him with the capital necessary to expand his lumber operations into the Black Swamp and establish the glass works at Crystal City. It even directly led to the founding of the smelting works at Wyandotte. Ever since he had worked with his uncle Samuel, Eber had consistently reinvested earnings back into his businesses so as to expand his growing empire. He had hoped his investment in the Eureka mine would lead to another financial bonanza. Unfortunately, about the same time production at Silver Islet slowed, the Panic of 1873 hit, and then Ward discovered he had been fleeced by Lawrence with the Eureka mine. How could Ward have allowed this to happen?

The complexity of operating so many diverse business interests combined with the Panic of 1873 had taken a toll on Ward's health and probably his judgment. Additionally, his private life was characterized by chaos, which became increasingly convoluted following his second marriage. Ward's sister Emily attempted to maintain some stability for Eber's family after she moved to Detroit, but even she struggled to maintain her role as Eber's closest confidante.

## Chaos within the Ward Household

In 1867, Emily relocated to Detroit and moved in with Eber and his first wife, Polly, at their "earnest solicitation." According to Emily's recollection, she "had charge of his family and of his house generally." At the time, Eber's daughter

Elizabeth, who was mentally challenged, was at twenty-one the oldest child at home. Frederick and Mary, fourteen and eleven, were attending school. Henry, who was twenty-six, was away much of the time at the Castile Sanitarium in New York. Neither Milton nor Charles was living at home on a regular basis. It must have been difficult for Emily to leave her school behind and take charge of the household. In the past, there had been tension between her and Polly, but Polly appears to have become less physically able to manage the household over time and had previously struggled with anxiety and nervousness. Living under the same roof was likely a gift both Emily and Eber appreciated as the pair had resided in separate cities for decades. As he had done in the past, Eber continued to "consult her freely in regard to his business and other affairs." After she had been caring for the children and household for about three years, Eber built a home for Emily on the same block as his own shortly after his marriage to Catherine Lyon.[46]

Conditions were frustrating for Catherine as she attempted to manage Eber's domestic affairs following their wedding. At the time of her marriage, she was twenty-seven, which made her one year younger than her stepson Henry and not much older than Eber's other children. This resulted in an awkward arrangement, to say the least. Catherine oversaw the care of Elizabeth, her mentally challenged stepdaughter. Catherine's attempts to be a good stepmother ended in failure, and the household descended into chaos within a short time. Events likely started down this path following the birth of Eber Ward Jr., Catherine's and E. B. Ward's first child, in 1870. Family dynamics became even more complicated when Catherine gave birth to a second child, daughter Clara, in 1873. Catherine likely favored her own children over her stepchildren, leading to additional conflict and chaos within the family.[47]

The most tragic example of the family's disorder involved Frederick, the seventh child of Eber and Polly. Possibly as a result of his father's absence and remarriage, as well as his mother's early death, Frederick suffered from depression and alcohol abuse. He often sought comfort from his aunt Emily and spent time at her home. Early in 1872, he approached his father and asked to be sent to the New York State Inebriate Asylum as he hoped it would "cure him of his inebriety." Eber promised to pay Frederick $10,000 if he could abstain from drinking for one year. After spending several months at the asylum, Frederick returned home, but he continued to drink. He sometimes combined the

This is likely the last photo taken of Eber Brock Ward, circa 1874. (Courtesy of the Seitz family)

alcohol with laudanum. In September 1872, Frederick died of an accidental overdose of laudanum at the age of nineteen. The newspaper reported his death as a suicide but family members maintained his death was accidental. Eber was devastated by Frederick's death.[48]

The chaos continued after Frederick's death. Emily related an incident that took place two years later during an afternoon meal. As was typical, Eber was not present, but several other family members were. Just as everyone was seated and ready to begin, Henry and Milton began shouting at one another. Apparently Henry, who had spent time in and out of mental institutions, liked to carry a pistol. Milton, who had been set to carve the meat and probably had been drinking, later claimed that Henry had aimed a pistol at him. The boys (who were not actually boys; Henry was thirty-three and Milton was twenty-six), leapt up from the table and "Milton chased Henry as hard as he could jump and run with a carving knife, swearing he would kill him." Emily and the others scolded the brothers and restored calm, but the events revealed a household in true turmoil. At the time, the public knew nothing of the events taking place within the walls of Eber Ward's home, considered among the finest in Detroit. Following Ward's death, news of the bedlam inside would be released, shocking the community.[49]

Conflict also developed between Catherine Ward and her stepdaughter Mary. Catherine was accused of mistreating Mary, and attempting to remove her from the house. Furthermore, when Mary became engaged, someone tried to prevent her upcoming marriage by warning Mary's fiancé, William B. Ely, he was marrying into "a lunatic family." Ely received the warning in the form of an anonymous letter in the winter of 1874. Ely must have informed Aunt Emily of its contents, because she had possession of the letter for several months. Emily eventually traced the letter back to Catherine. Although the marriage eventually did take place, the letter surely poisoned Mary's relationship with Catherine. Catherine's motivation remains unclear. It is possible she simply wanted to inform Ely of the history of mental illness and problems associated with the family. More likely, Catherine could have been scheming in order to ensure that her own children would inherit more of Eber's vast fortune when he died; if Catherine was able to thwart Mary's marriage and prevent her from having a child, that fortune would be less dispersed. Regardless of her motivation, Catherine's actions demonstrate a very tense and strained family environment inside the Ward mansion on Fort Street. The contents of the letter probably never were revealed to Eber, as Emily was concerned it would harm Eber's relationship with his daughter.[50]

Even after Emily moved out of Eber's home and into her own, Eber continued to consult with her quite often. This was particularly true in the years immediately following his second marriage, although family members recognized that Catherine's influence over Eber became stronger with time. Nevertheless, Emily remembered Eber would "drop in almost every day to discuss with her whatever happened to be uppermost in his mind." In addition to the home and property he gave Emily, he also provided her with an income of approximately $400 per month in recognition for the life's work she had completed on his behalf. Emily and Eber discussed his business activities, but they also certainly spoke of their early lives together and of family members they had lost, both recently and long ago. It was around this time, in the early 1870s, that Eber began to investigate spiritualism more deeply. Spiritualism had interested him in the past, but his more profound involvement may have been motivated by guilt associated with his first wife's death shortly after their divorce, or from Frederick's sudden death due to overdose. It is also likely that he, like many other Americans, found it a unique form of entertainment; spiritualism had become even more popular nationally after the Civil War. Regardless of the cause, Eber attended sittings with famous mediums such as Dr. Henry Slade and even Margaret Fox Kane, one of the famous Fox sisters of New York who had influenced the spread of spiritualism beginning in the 1840s. As Eber became interested in the movement, he shared with family members his belief that "under certain conditions the spirits of the dead could communicate with the living." However, Eber declared mediums in general to be simple "money makers," many of whom had been exposed as frauds "through the papers and by word of mouth."[51]

In the meantime, Eber continued to throw himself into his work, adding even more stress to his already hectic and demanding daily schedule. As if he did not have enough investments with his shipping lines, railroads, lumber mills, glass factory, and mining operations, he decided to expand his already vast iron and steel empire. He used the profits from Silver Islet, combined with additional credit, to modernize his operations in Chicago and even purchased a facility in Leland, Michigan.

## Continued Investments and the Panic of 1873

Once the settlement to create the Bessemer Association was completed in 1869, Ward made plans to update his iron mills. Membership in the association provided access to the patent rights necessary to produce Bessemer steel. Ward approached his fellow investors at the Wyandotte plant, but they resisted the additional outlay of money necessary for capital improvements. His Milwaukee operations originally had been established to protect his Chicago mill from competition; therefore, Ward wanted the Milwaukee Iron Company to focus on production of pig iron, iron rails, and different sizes of merchant bar iron. Ultimately, he chose to produce Bessemer steel at his North Chicago Rolling Mill. The facility had been quite successful since Ward founded its operations in

1857. One factor benefiting Chicago was its status as an emerging midwestern city. It already served as a key railroad hub and had a labor force large enough to serve his needs. Back in 1865, its rolling mills also had rolled the first steel rails produced in the United States. Accordingly, Ward hired his onetime rival Alexander Holley, the nation's leading designer of Bessemer plants, to upgrade the facility. Holley predicted that once the improvements were complete, Ward's mill would produce twelve thousand tons of Bessemer steel rails each year.[52]

Construction began in 1870, but was interrupted by Chicago's Great Fire of October 1871, which destroyed numerous businesses and left thousands homeless in the city. Many of those affected were Ward's employees and their families. When leaders in Detroit called for donations to provide direct aid to Chicago's suffering residents, $25,000 was raised very quickly. Ward became the largest single contributor when he donated $5,000 to the cause. All work at his Chicago facility came to a halt. Orrin W. Potter, who served as general superintendent of the Chicago works, recalled, "The plant turned into a boarding and lodging house." One of the company's workers, an English immigrant known only as Patterson, used the company facilities to erect a "soup kitchen . . . supervising everything himself, and thus people were cared for" during the stressful days in the fire's immediate aftermath. One of the first carloads of supplies sent to help Chicago's relief efforts came from Ward's Milwaukee Iron Company under the direction of its superintendent, James Hagerman. Through the combined efforts of Ward, Hagerman, and Potter, food, water, clothing, and household goods of all kinds were distributed to many of the homeless.[53]

As soon as conditions allowed, construction resumed, and in 1872 the work was completed at a cost of $350,000. This was the eighth Bessemer facility designed by Alexander Holley. Eventually, he would oversee the construction of eleven of the thirteen Bessemer plants created between 1864 and 1876 in the United States, thereby cementing his status as the foremost steel engineer in the country. Due to his competitive nature, Ward always sought the most advanced technology at his operations. He was not disappointed when the upgrades at his Chicago facility were completed; it was considered "undoubtedly the most perfect in existence" by Robert W. Hunt, the general superintendent of the Albany and Rensselaer Iron and Steel Company of New York.[54]

Ward took two additional steps to ensure he had the raw materials necessary to expand his production of steel in the summer of 1872. First, he secured the rights to purchase a large parcel of land in Michigan's Upper Peninsula believed to be rich in iron ore. It was located about forty miles west of Escanaba. Ward moved forward with the purchase after his researchers determined the property included "iron ore found to exist in unsurpassed quantity and quality." By doing so, he prevented his competitors from accessing a much "coveted region," and he also ensured expanded control over some of the richest iron ore fields in the Lake Superior region. If Ward's mills had excess ore, he could sell it to others at a substantial profit.[55]

Ward's second action was to acquire a company located in Leland, Michigan, which had been smelting iron ore. The community of Leland is located in northern Michigan, about eighty miles from the deep-water port of Escanaba, which had emerged as an important railroad connection for the Upper Peninsula's iron ore ranges. In 1869, the Leland Lake Superior Iron Company was organized to take advantage of its proximity to Escanaba and the iron ore fields. The company also hoped to benefit from the abundant supply of hardwood in and near Leland, which was used to make the charcoal required for smelting the ore. The Leland Iron Company constructed a furnace with a seventy-five-foot brick stack, built several kilns for making charcoal, and made other necessary investments. Operations began in 1871, and the company began to ship pig iron to various locales in the Great Lakes region. Production continued until the spring of 1872, but then the furnace was destroyed by fire and the company experienced financial difficulties. Ward stepped in and purchased the company. He reorganized the firm and renamed it E. B. Ward and Company.[56]

Ward jumped at the chance to secure the company as it enhanced the vertical integration of his iron mills. He had the furnace rebuilt and funded some much-needed additional improvements. By October 1872, the reconstructed furnace was "put into blast" and began operating near full capacity within a month. According to the *Detroit Daily Post*, it was "turning out 18 tons of charcoal pig iron daily" with "a capacity to make about 6,000 tons yearly." Ward's operations brought renewed activity to life in Leland as employees were hired to work at the furnace, mind the kilns, and provide wood to be transformed into charcoal. The demand for wood was seemingly endless; each day more than 150 cords of hardwood were brought by barge to provide fuel for the furnace. Ward's Leland interests were closely tied to his other operations as the pig iron produced in Leland was shipped to his mills in Chicago, Wyandotte, and

Ward purchased the Leland Iron Company and renamed it E. B. Ward and Company. By 1872, it produced pig iron for his mills in Wyandotte, Chicago, and Milwaukee. Here we see large stacks of wood ready to be converted into charcoal in the "beehive" kilns to the right. (Courtesy of the Leelenau Historical Society, Catalog ID 1970.06)

Milwaukee. The fact that Ward owned vast deposits of iron ore, which were shipped on *his* vessels and smelted at *his* facility in Leland, and then transformed into railroad rails or other materials at *his* facilities, which were often bought by *his* railroad led to even greater efficiencies in the Ward empire, resulting in larger profit margins. This integration of processes was terribly complicated, but E. B. Ward had his finger firmly on the pulse of each aspect of these operations.[57]

Ward's steps to vertically integrate his business operations can be compared to actions taken by contemporary American business leaders. In his prize-winning biography of Cornelius Vanderbilt, author T. J. Stiles demonstrates that Vanderbilt engaged in vertical integration of his steamship empire by gaining control of shipyards and steam engine plants. Stiles continues, "Late in the nineteenth century, John D. Rockefeller and Andrew Carnegie would emerge as the leading exponents of this form of organization." Eber Ward's actions to vertically integrate his operations, which began in the 1850s, were adopted decades prior to both Rockefeller's and Carnegie's, signifying Ward's status as a pioneer of American industry. Implementation of these business practices, which cut costs and captured as much profit as possible, facilitated the continual expansion of his operations. This enabled Ward to dominate the midwestern iron and steel industry in such a way that the *Chicago Tribune* labeled him the "iron king of the West."[58]

Conditions were running smoothly, but in 1873 problems emerged. James Hagerman, the superintendent and secretary at Ward's Milwaukee Iron Company, raised some concerns that year. The works he operated produced only iron rails. While the rails the company manufactured were of high quality, they still required replacement after heavy use. Increasingly, railroads purchased Bessemer steel rails, which lasted much longer. Hagerman attempted to convince Ward to invest in the production of Bessemer steel at Milwaukee, just as he had in Chicago. Ward was unwilling to do so. It is possible that Ward's other investments prevented him from having the capital necessary to make the additional improvements. More likely, and of greater importance, was Ward's investment at his North Chicago Rolling Mill. By 1872, Bessemer steel was being produced in Chicago. Ward's facility in that city could produce enough rails to meet the demand at that time. Furthermore, although Ward essentially controlled both facilities, he encouraged the two companies to compete with one another, believing it would create efficiencies, result in greater profits, and prevent competitors from encroaching on their market. At times the competition could be fierce. Hagerman remembered that when conflicts arose between the operations in Chicago and Milwaukee, "Captain Ward, as long as he lived, although he often tried to take a neutral part in the matter, would not decide between us except when he was obliged to." While Hagerman recalled that Ward attempted to remain neutral, in many ways he favored his Chicago mill. By choosing to invest capital in the Bessemer works in Chicago and refusing to do so in Milwaukee, Ward ensured that Milwaukee would play "second fiddle" to his Chicago mill. Ultimately, this would have negative consequences for the Milwaukee Iron Company.[59]

Another problem emerged when a labor dispute brought work at the Milwaukee Iron Company to a halt in 1873. Apparently, on July 25 the night shift left work early due to the "oppressive heat" on what must have been a hot, humid summer evening. Even operating under normal conditions, temperatures near the furnaces reached 130 degrees, and employees were forced to wear leather straps around their boots to prevent burns as they worked with molten iron. For leaving their posts early, the employees were fired, a step that certainly was in line with other hard-nosed tactics E. B. Ward had supported in the past. The next day, the morning shift men refused to work unless their comrades were rehired. When superintendent Hagerman refused to rescind the order firing the men, the other employees walked off the job, leaving nearly one thousand men out of work. Short-term walkouts of skilled employees had previously occurred, but news of this general work stoppage was reported in several newspapers, and word of the conflict spread rapidly. The workers declared the conflict was not over wages, but rather "on account of the discharge of some unruly members." The matter was settled within the month, but it signified the potential for labor conflict at the facility.[60]

The strike in July was not the only work stoppage that year. On the morning of Wednesday, August 28, Hagerman called some of the men to his office to make an announcement, which came directly from E. B. Ward, to "close the mills immediately." The workers were upset and Hagerman's disappointment was clear when he was unable to offer an explanation. His only response was, "A complication of circumstances brought us to this, and I neither blame you nor am I to blame." Eber Ward must have received advance word of the rumors circulating on Wall Street—financial worries that would soon come to fruition in the Panic of 1873.[61]

Just as in 1857, the railroad industry and international events influenced a financial crisis in the United States. Ever since the completion of the transcontinental railroad in 1869, there had been a frenzy to construct new railroad lines. According to historian H. W. Brands, regrettably, by 1873 "the railroad industry was badly overbuilt, with too many lines chasing too little traffic." A financial scandal involving the Union Pacific Railroad and misuse of government subsidies did not help. Additionally, the quick end to the Franco-Prussian War led to an oversupply of grain on the world market, causing prices to plummet. This hurt western farmers in the United States and lessened interest in railroad expansion in the West. Jay Cooke, a leading railroad promoter and pillar of the financial community who had invested heavily in the railroad industry, was forced into bankruptcy in the fall of 1873. The news of Cooke's failure "staggered Wall Street. . . . If he could fall, anyone could."[62]

Just as the Panic impacted Ward's lumber operations negatively, the same occurred at his iron and steel mills, with conditions at the Milwaukee Iron

Company proving to be devastating. Hagerman recalled, "In September [1873] the panic knocked everything sky-high. Early in 1873 we sold iron rails at eighty-five dollars. Before the year closed I think forty-five dollars would have been a good price." Ward himself declared he had "never known so complete a dead lock in iron manufacture." He was stunned by the way it "stopped suddenly and completely." The impact of the crisis was felt throughout the city of Milwaukee as community officials worried for the future.[63] In response to the financial troubles, Hagerman resigned as superintendent, remaining as secretary to "devote himself to the financial business of the corporation." Work at the mill resumed, but there was very little new railway constructed in 1874. With a shortage of contracts, work at the mill was inconsistent, and at levels far below its full capacity. Ward related that between five hundred and six hundred men had been laid off, and those who continued to be employed saw their wages reduced. Frustration became commonplace among men attempting to provide for their families. In 1874, workers attempted to negotiate a pay increase to levels nearer to those previously in place. Ward directed management to respond by staging a lockout and shutting down the mills completely.[64]

Ward's mill in Chicago also suffered from the financial panic, but not as deeply as the Milwaukee Iron Company. Years later, Hagerman explained the key difference. The North Chicago Rolling Mill had engaged in "the Bessemer steel business, which had just come into vogue, and in which we [Milwaukee] had no interest, unfortunately." Ward's decision to invest in Chicago as opposed to Milwaukee led to casualties among his companies. As events moved forward, the greatest casualty of the financial crisis for Eber was his personal health.[65]

## Anxiety and Financial Stress Take a Toll

When the financial panic hit, Ward felt its impact immediately. With the sudden drop in sales from the railroads and his other businesses, he faced a serious cash-flow problem. Many of his companies already carried heavy mortgages, so he was forced to seek additional credit to continue payment on his loans and cover payroll. Unfortunately, banks were suffering too, and most found it difficult, if not impossible, to extend additional loans. Although Ward served as a director on the board of the Second National Bank of Detroit, he was unable to obtain additional funding locally. He eventually sought a loan from the banking firm of S. P. Burt & Co., located in New Bedford, Massachusetts. Samuel P. Burt later recalled that in October 1873 Ward came to him in desperation, explaining "that he was in great need of money; that his necessities were imperative, and that without aid in procuring a loan he could not meet his obligations as they matured." Ward managed to receive a loan of $100,000, but it came with an interest rate of 20 percent.[66] Even with this influx of cash, Ward still could not meet payroll, and the Wyandotte Rolling Mill was forced to issue between $80,000 and $90,000 in scrip to pay employees and other bills the following month. Individuals holding notes could redeem their value plus 7 percent interest in six months. Ward defended the issuance of scrip as perfectly legal and argued it helped to maintain employment in the area. The *Detroit Free Press* criticized it as a "new-fangled way of cutting down the wages of the men employed by the Rolling Mill Company." When payment for the scrip came due the following May, some of it was redeemed by the company, but much was renewed, at the rate of 8 percent, indicating that financial difficulties still remained.[67]

Matters in October 1873 were further complicated by events dealing with Silver Islet. In the same edition of the *Detroit Daily Post* concerning the issuance of scrip, the paper reported a "wild rumor" (which proved to be true) that work had come to a stop at the Lake Superior silver mine as water filled the mine shaft, preventing further progress. Operations were interrupted for several months, further deepening Ward's financial woes and ensuring there would be no quick influx of cash to fix his predicament. This was also about the same time Ward realized he had been swindled with his purchase of the Eureka silver mine, news of which became public that December. Charles's financial problems similarly became apparent. Concerning Charles, who would eventually declare bankruptcy, Eber confided to a business associate, "I am not clear as to what is best to do." Eber admitted that he felt "great anxiety" as a result of Charles's problems.[68]

The stress and anxiety Eber felt increased as time went on. In 1874, the same year Charles was forced into bankruptcy, Eber was set to celebrate his sixty-third birthday. Just five years earlier he had suffered an attack of apoplexy (most likely a stroke) and nearly died. Emily observed that prior to the attack, Eber's memory had been "prodigious," and although he had become more easily fatigued in recent years, his mind remained strong and was "superior in that respect to the world in general." While most business associates believed Eber to be nearly as strong as ever, he apparently nodded off at times in the afternoons, something he had never done in the past. Yet Eber continued to disregard his health and throw himself into his work as he searched for steps he could take to prop up his struggling empire.[69]

On January 1, 1875, Eber wrote his nine-year-old granddaughter Mabel, the child of his deceased son John, a touching letter beginning, "My Dear Little Granddaughter, A Happy New Year to you." He apologized for not answering her letters more quickly, but explained he had "not had time to do it until now." He promised to call on her soon. But, in an indication that his business activities continued to weigh heavily on his mind, he said he wasn't sure when he would be able to break away from his commitments to come visit her. Although it was New Year's Day, he wrote, "I have to work today as well as other days."[70] The next morning, he wrote to Emily expressing concerns about her health and living situation. He shared that although he believed his health was strong, "my own affairs are not in such a shape as would allow more quiet. My business has been so bad the last two years that I have to pay all my attention to it and cannot then sleep even." He offered, "If you stand in need of money, I can lend you a small amount, though I am badly pressed." He ended his letter, "Your affectionate Brother, Eber Ward."[71] Later that morning, walking down Griswold Street on his way to a meeting at Superior Court, Eber fell. A crowd quickly gathered, and a group of three doctors arrived to provide help, but to no avail. The medical specialists declared he had been struck with apoplexy once again. Eber Brock Ward, Detroit's famed industrialist, had dropped dead on the streets of the city.

In some ways, Eber became a victim of his own success. He had been driven his entire adult life by an intense competitiveness to build a prosperous business empire. He was successful in doing so. His realm included diverse industries, ranging from shipping and railroads to iron and steel production as well as mining, lumbering, and glassmaking. He was a visionary whose ideas influenced politics and manufacturing in the Midwest and even the nation. Yet the burden of overseeing each of the moving parts of his domain created an incredible amount of stress. He had thrived on the competition and pressures associated with his businesses for years. Nevertheless, his apoplectic stroke in

1869 should have served as a warning that he was growing older and his body and psyche were unable to handle the responsibilities he had once handled easily. The chaos in his private life and events involving the Panic of 1873 became the inevitable straws that broke and killed E. B. Ward.

Following Ward's death, an intense battle over his estate would divide his family. Furthermore, the actions of his youngest child, Clara, would capture the attention of many throughout the nation, overshadowing his accomplishments. This fight over his will and his daughter's actions would shape his legacy in the years to come.

# 8

## A Will and a Princess

*The Ward Will Case: Extraordinary Revelations of the Trial. A Case without Parallel—a Man of Vast Business Connections Who Managed His Affairs by the Advice of Mediums—a German Geological Medium Named "Cabbage John"—Idiocy and Insanity in the Ward Family.*
—Headline from the *New York Times*, October 5, 1875

*Gone with a Gypsy: Princess of Chimay Elopes with a Hungarian Fiddler. The Princess of Chimay and Caraman who was a rich American girl, has ruined her life for the sake of a wretched Hungarian musician.*
—*Ludington Record*, December 24, 1896

*Clara Ward is a shameless daughter of Michigan.*
—*Wyandotte Herald*, February 24, 1899

News of Eber Ward's death shocked residents of Detroit and those living throughout Michigan. His funeral would be the largest in the city's history up to that time as hundreds sought to pay their respects in honor of their community's business leader. Interest in Eber's achievements continued after his death as a tremendous fight over Ward's estate emerged between Catherine Ward and the children from Eber's first marriage. Catherine emerged as the "victor" in this rivalry as a resolution eventually was reached. Once the conflict over her deceased husband's estate had been finalized, Catherine sought to enhance her own legacy by having her daughter Clara marry a Belgian prince. The marriage only lasted about six years, ending in scandal when Clara left her husband for a "gypsy fiddler." The exploits of Clara Ward, the princess of Chimay, would be chronicled by the press for several years as she showed she was just as headstrong as her father, determined to live life on her own terms despite society's expectations.

## Ward's Funeral

Word of Eber Brock Ward's death spread rapidly through the streets of Detroit. The day he died, the *Detroit News* captured the mood of the city: "No event that has happened in Detroit in many years has sent such a sudden and wide-felt thrill through the length and breadth of the city. . . . The great millionaire, the great maker of men and their fortune, is himself unmade in one brief moment, his life blown out like a candle with a mere puff of the cold breath of death." Some were curious; others felt horror and sympathy. Many were left to wonder how the death of the region's wealthiest man and largest employer might impact the city's economy. Even the *Detroit Free Press*, which had been highly critical of Ward in the past, declared his death to be "a great public calamity."[1]

Shortly after the cause of death was determined, Eber's remains were taken by sleigh to his mansion on Fort Street. Catherine Ward was out of town visiting family in Ohio, so Aunt Emily took charge of the initial arrangements. A stream of friends and admirers made their way to Ward's "palatial residence," which was draped with black crepe to indicate the household was in mourning. Eber's body was placed in the front parlor. Throngs of visitors entered the home to view their leading citizen one final time. The members of the board of trade, which met that afternoon, voted to attend Ward's funeral as a group and then adjourned out of respect for the many contributions Eber had made to the community.[2]

After the shock of Ward's death began to wear off, speculation commenced as to the value of his massive estate. Guesses from people on the streets ranged anywhere from $3 million to $30 million. Those familiar with the estate recognized the latter figure was greatly inflated. Ward's railroad investments, steamboats, lumber properties, and other assets held great value. However, much of his wealth was tied to his iron and steel works. These facilities had depreciated significantly in the two years prior to Ward's death as a result of the Panic of 1873, which caused demand for new railroad rails to plummet and unsold inventories to grow. The *Detroit News* estimated that prior to the Panic the cost to manufacture rails was $40 per ton and the selling price $55 per ton, leading to a handsome profit. In recent months, the price had fallen to $30 per ton. Speculation also centered on the contents of Ward's will, which had been updated several months before his death. Details of his final wishes were not yet forthcoming, but they were expected to be made public once the will was admitted to probate. Reporters did learn that Ward had life insurance policies amounting to about $85,000.[3]

Eber's widow Catherine was informed of her husband's death via telegraph the day he died. She immediately arranged to return home from Ohio. Because there were no scheduled trains from Toledo to Detroit remaining that day, she was forced to engage a special train, and she arrived in Detroit about 3:00 the next morning. Preparations were made to hold the funeral at Fort Street Presbyterian Church the following Wednesday at 10:00. The Reverend Arthur A. Pierson of Fort Street Presbyterian prepared to conduct the service, with assistance from the Unitarian ministers Robert Collyer of Chicago and Calvin Stebbins of Detroit's Congregational Unitarian Church. Eber had not attended church services regularly for some time, but did have a pew at the Congregational Unitarian Church and prior to that had been associated with Fort Street Presbyterian for many years. Eber's remains would be buried in Detroit's Elmwood Cemetery.[4]

Interest in Ward's funeral was widespread. As early as 9:30 on the morning of the service, scores of people descended upon Ward's splendid home to meet with members of the family. His body was placed in a coffin of finely polished rosewood with large silver handles, decorated with a cross and a wreath of white flowers. The front of the casket was made of glass, showing Eber's face, which carried an expression of peace and serenity. At about 10:00 the funeral procession began; it was "one of the largest the city had ever seen—over seven blocks long" as it made its way from Eber's home to the church. Near the front of the procession were the pall bearers, led by Ward's business associate James

F. Joy and Detroit mayor Hugh Moffat. There were about 150 carriages following the hearse bearing Ward's coffin, along with numerous followers on foot.
Throngs of observers congregated along Fort Street, despite the extreme cold,
to watch the procession. The pews of Fort Street Presbyterian, the largest church
in Detroit, were nearly full when the solemn entourage arrived; more than one
thousand mourners attended the funeral, the largest in the city's history. About
three hundred in attendance were Ward's employees from Wyandotte who had
come to the service via a special train on the Canadian Southern Railroad.[5]

Those fortunate enough to gain entry to the standing-room-only facility
heard the memorial sermon delivered by the Reverend Collyer. He stressed
Ward's lifetime of achievements as well as his charity and philanthropy. The
reverend recognized that Ward could be obstinate at times and that his views
were considered controversial by some. Nevertheless, he emphasized Ward's
ability to "create new industries, new neighborhoods, new communities, to
instill life into dying enterprises that feed and clothe thousands—this is truly
a grand work." At the close of the service, the procession formed once again as
it exited the church. Detroit's city hall bell tolled for the first time in its history

E. B. Ward's gravesite at Detroit's Elmwood Cemetery. Several other family members are buried at this plot,
including Eber's sister Emily and his uncle Samuel. (Author's collection)

as Ward's body passed by on its way to Elmwood Cemetery while hundreds either participated in the cortege or watched from the streets. Once the family plot was reached, a brief service was held for the family and close friends. Then Eber's casket was placed in a marble sarcophagus and sealed. His final resting place positioned him alongside his longtime mentor and partner, Uncle Samuel, his father Eber, and a handful of other deceased family members.[6]

Once Eber's remains had been laid to rest, the fight for control over his estate began in earnest. This contest would continue for decades, ultimately resulting in deep divisions within the family.

## The Fight over Ward's Estate

Even prior to Ward's funeral, there were indications of a looming battle over Eber's will. Ever since Ward had remarried in 1869, the relationship between his second wife and the children of his first wife had been characterized by conflict. This was particularly true of Milton's and Charles's relationship with Catherine. They viewed Catherine as an interloper who attempted to control their father and favored her own children to their detriment. She considered her stepsons ne'er-do-wells whose greatest talent was spending their father's money. The actions of Milton and Charles the day Eber died only served to reinforce Catherine's beliefs. When the boys first heard of their father's death, they left the family home and dashed off in a carriage. Rushing to reach their destination, Milton and Charles observed an undertaker's wagon leaving the area where their father had just died. Rather than stop, the pair raced past their father's body, which was growing colder by the minute. Instead, their goal was the Moffat office building, where they secured the services of an attorney to contest their father's will.[7]

The will in question was developed by Eber Ward on March 12, 1874. It included two codicils, the second of which was adopted August 25. Essentially, the will provided Catherine and her two children with all the property in Ludington, including the valuable sawmills, vessels, timbered lands, uncut logs, warehouses, and so on. Aside from the distribution of small amounts of stock to several friends and family members, the remainder was to be divided equally between the five children from his first marriage and Aunt Emily. The children of his first marriage also would receive his grand home on Fort Street. Catherine's properties were to be "clear of all encumbrances." The inventory would later estimate the value of Ward's estate at $5.3 million ($126,797,686.96 in 2020 dollars), although this did not take into account the many creditors' claims. Milton and Charles feared those figures were inflated and that once their father's assets were liquidated, particularly in the aftermath of the financial panic, there might not be much left to distribute. They were troubled that Catherine would receive the Ludington properties outright, without having to assume any of the estate's debt. Furthermore, and most important, the brothers objected to the second codicil. This limited payments from the estate to "a sum not exceeding two hundred dollars per month" for each of Ward's children from his first marriage.[8]

Catherine hoped to admit Eber's will into probate quickly. The estate's debts were significant, and each month loan payments were set to come due. No one wanted the estate to fall behind and incur additional penalties, so she attempted to negotiate an agreement with Ward's children from his first marriage. According to the *Detroit Free Press*, Catherine reportedly agreed to set aside "one hundred and fifty million feet of pine lumber" from her holdings in Ludington to create "a fund of at least $300,000." The money generated from the sale of this lumber would be used by the executors to help pay the estate's debts. Once Catherine made this promise, Milton and Charles withdrew their opposition to probating the will. However, once the will was admitted to probate, Catherine reneged on her promise. She did not explain the reasons behind her decision, but it appears Catherine was just as ruthless as the husband she had recently buried. Once her stepsons dropped their opposition, she was clear to inherit a valuable set of assets. The boys objected immediately and filed a petition to contest the will. Public interest in the squabble between Ward's heirs expanded beyond Detroit; the *New York Times* commented that "protracted litigation" was very likely. The paper anticipated that extended delays and a forced sale in the midst of the financial downturn would "cause great shrinkage in the value of the estate . . . from which all parties will suffer." This prediction proved strikingly accurate.[9]

Milton and Charles filed their bill of complaint officially challenging the will on March 30, 1875, nearly three months following Ward's death. Their father's cousin, also named Eber Ward, joined the two brothers in their suit.

He became involved because he was appointed Elizabeth V. Ward's guardian by the court after she had been declared "mentally incompetent." Neither of E. B. Ward's two remaining children joined the suit. Henry S. Ward was "adjudged mentally incompetent" and Mary S. Ward was only twenty years old and therefore a minor. Noticeably absent from the filing was Aunt Emily. She was most sympathetic to the plight of her brother's children from his first marriage, rather than Catherine, with whom she had clashed at times. Emily was particularly concerned about the estate's indebtedness and feared that if the debts were not handled quickly, the bank, mining, and railroad stock used as collateral would be lost. Nevertheless, she did not support the tactics employed by the attorneys hired by Milton and Charles.[10]

Theodore Romeyn led the group of attorneys Milton and Charles secured to contest the will. The legal challenges were based upon several grounds. They declared E. B. Ward was "not of sound mind and memory" when his will and both codicils were executed. Furthermore, they claimed those papers were procured while Eber was under the "undue influence" of his wife Catherine. The filing also charged that the will and codicils contained "illegal provisions" concerning limits placed on the disbursement of funds. Romeyn requested that a receiver be appointed to administer affairs until the issues involving the will were resolved, because the estate was losing value, and he feared the initial inventory of assets was "largely exaggerated." Arguably the most serious allegation raised was that E. B. Ward was "under strong delusions controlling his mind" when he executed the will's provisions, "so that they do not express his actual unbiased wishes and intensions." This final argument foreshadowed the approach Romeyn and his fellow attorneys would take as they prepared for a trial. The "strong delusions" referred to their contention that Ward sought council from mediums and that his belief in spiritualism demonstrated he was of an unsound mind. As historian Justin Wargo attests, the attorneys in the case presented Ward as "a mentally incompetent, superstitious fool who had been easily manipulated by Catherine and the trustees." Although it was true that Ward did attend séances and was interested in spiritualism, he was far from a mentally incompetent fool when his will was developed. As events progressed, Emily would stand for none of this argument and subsequent testimony at the trial demonstrated his sound mind and mental fitness.[11]

For the next several months the parties attempted to reach a settlement, but none was forthcoming. By September 1875, a jury trial was set to commence. It would capture the attention of many Michigan residents and even people living in other parts of the country.

## Ward Will Trial

After the jurors had been chosen, the long-awaited trial over Ward's will began on September 21, 1875. The *Detroit Free Press* and other local newspapers covered the trial in great detail due to the public's interest. Wayne County Circuit Court judge Jared Patchin oversaw the proceedings. Ashley Pond, one of the attorneys for Catherine Ward, opened the case by challenging the allegation "that Captain Ward was laboring under an insane delusion and under various influences at the time of making his will and the codicils." Instead, Pond declared he would show that Ward had "exercised wisdom" by placing a $200 limit on the amount of money his children could receive each month from his estate.[12]

The first witness was Captain R. J. Hackert. He had known E. B. Ward for about twenty years and had served as a witness for Ward's 1874 will and its first codicil. Hackert testified that "he had no reason to suppose that Capt. Ward was not of sound mind" at the time Ward signed the will and subsequent codicil. Another who testified that day was Arthur Edwards, operator of a rival shipping line, who had known Ward "very intimately" for thirty years. Edwards observed that in years past, Ward had a strength of will and purpose that could be domineering. However, following Eber's first attack of apoplexy in 1869, Ward's memory was not the same as it had been. When initially questioned, Edwards offered his belief that Ward was "not a man of sound and unimpaired mind—that is he was not as competent to do business as he had previously been." Edwards continued by testifying that he had accompanied Ward to see mediums and had attended séances with him in the past. Upon cross-examination, however, Edwards clarified his previous testimony, explaining, "Ward had capacity sufficient to understand what he was doing" when the second codicil was added.[13]

Thus ended the first day of testimony, which set the stage for the remainder of the trial, which would last forty-seven days. A number of witnesses would testify as to their relationship with E. B. Ward, the attorneys attempting to influence each witness's testimony in their client's favor. Ward's interest in spiritualism would be explored to determine if he really was of sound mind when he developed his will and codicil. It was a pattern that would be repeated throughout the trial.

Most days, benches in the courtroom contained spectators as the public heard the same testimony as the jurors. At times it could be tedious, but some days included great drama. To break the tedium, audience members placed "numerous bets" as to the general outcome of the trial or on smaller issues, such as how the judge might rule on the admission of evidence. On Saturday, September 25, the courthouse corridors were packed with spectators, forcing Judge Patchin to limit attendance numbers.[14] The crowd was particularly large due to the previous day's appearance of Dr. Henry Slade, whose testimony had generated great interest. At the time, Slade was recognized as the best-known spirit medium in the United States. He had held séances and other exhibitions for over twenty years and had even hosted performances for European royalty. Dr. Slade testified that he "had been acquainted with Capt. E. B. Ward for about 12 years" and the two had participated in multiple séances during that time. At some sittings, Ward's business dealings were discussed, while other occasions concerned his children. The spirits declared there was "hereditary insanity in the family" and that Ward should "'tie up' or secure any property he might wish to bequeath to the children of his first wife in such a way as they would be unable to handle it" because they were "incompetent."[15]

Following a spirited debate between the attorneys concerning the admissibility of Dr. Slade's testimony, an incident involving Eber Ward's eldest son Henry shocked those in attendance. Just as the proceedings had adjourned, Henry sprang to his feet, yelled epithets at one of the attorneys, and threatened to "blow his head off." The attorney in question was Wirt Dexter who, Henry claimed, had defamed his deceased mother. Henry's outburst "created a decided sensation" among the observers, who learned he suffered from a "mental disease [that] has rendered him peculiarly susceptible to excitement." Henry had to be forcibly removed from the courtroom. The events involving Henry Ward, particularly in front of such a large crowd, prompted the *Detroit Free Press* to label the proceedings "the most exciting day in the progress of the Ward will case" yet.[16]

Dr. Slade was not the only one to testify during the trial who claimed an ability to converse with the spirits. Margaret Fox Kane, one of the original Fox sisters from Rochester, New York, who had popularized spirit rappings, was called as a witness. She had known E. B. Ward for seven or eight years and declared he had frequently visited "for the purpose of communicating with the spirits of his departed friends through her." Fox Kane claimed that at times she worked with Ward to facilitate a conduit between him and his deceased wife Polly. Another medium called to the stand was Miss Emma Martin. She testified that a spirit known as Cabbage John "frequently communicated with Capt. Ward" and he advised Ward "to invest in Silver Islet and the glass works."[17] Martin explained she had the ability to converse with spirits while in a trance. Asked if she would place herself in such a trance while on the witness stand, she complied. The entire courtroom became silent as "a hush fell upon the audience. Some of the ladies turned a little pale." Martin's body began to "jerk spasmodically, her lips trembled visibly and there came forth in a distinct tone the word 'Marie.'" The judge, who appeared amused, encouraged the attorney to continue his cross-examination of the witness "whether ghost or human." Martin claimed to be the spirit of Andrew Kurthaldrus. She spoke a few sentences in English and jumbled German, but then recovered her consciousness. The *Detroit Free Press* reported that the audience members, most of whom had risen from their seats, watched the events unfold "in open-mouthed wonder (some of them in awe) of the extraordinary scene." It was about this time that "gossip in Detroit surrounding the trial soon reached its zenith."[18]

Not every day proved to be quite as enthralling, but the trial continued to make headlines. Mr. E. W. Meddaugh, an attorney for the defense, offered a rebuttal to the arguments made by those who contested the will. He reasoned no testimony had been presented in the trial to prove that Ward was delusional when he developed his will in 1874. Meddaugh admitted that Ward was a follower of spiritualism, but simply following a religious belief did not mean he was of unsound mind. He declared the arguments offered thus far were "a sham," asking, "Suppose Capt. Ward had consulted half a dozen mortals and made his will in accordance with their suggestions?" If he had done so, no one would have called him delusional. He argued that those challenging the will had no case.[19]

Numerous friends and business associates of Ward were called to the witness stand. James F. Joy testified he had developed partnerships with Eber Ward going back to his time with the Michigan Central Railroad, and the two had served on the bank board together. Joy did not share Ward's interest in spirits, but observed that when he saw Ward in March 1874, he had a "perfectly sound mind"—Joy trusted Ward's judgment without reservation. Don M. Dickinson, who would later serve as postmaster general of the United States, affirmed that he had known Ward for over twenty years and had worked with him in 1873 and 1874 to lobby Congress. He contended that Ward "was a man of perfectly sound mind" and "a great man intellectually." The Reverend Calvin Stebbins stated he and Eber had had several conversations about spiritualism and religion in general. Stebbins considered Ward to be a "clear-headed and strong minded man." He recalled a conversation during which Ward also showed a sense of humor. "Ward said of one person that he was a wonderful medium and a wonderful liar; that it was with mediums as with the clergy—you could believe some things they said and some you couldn't; you had to discount both mediums and clergy, especially the latter."[20]

Witnesses also recounted their conversations with Eber about his children. Time and again Eber had expressed his frustration with the actions of Milton and Charles in particular. Tubal C. Owen, Eber's nephew, testified that he had once approached Eber on behalf of Milton, who wanted $20,000 to start a business. This was about the time the second codicil was added to the will in 1874. Eber would hear none of it, replying that he had tried over and over with his boys, yet "they squandered everything that was put in their hands. . . . He might as well throw it [the money] in the river." Even prior to adopting the second codicil, on several occasions Ward related to others that he planned to "fix the property so the boys could not squander it." Ward had never indicated he came to this conclusion as a result of consultation with mediums; instead, he designed his will as a result of his sons' actions and their inability to handle money. A letter from Milton to Charles was read into the record. It showed that Milton was scheming to maintain control over his father's properties and keep them away from Catherine. He predicted that in the future there would be a "grand fight . . . and then look out." The trial taking place demonstrated that his prediction was coming true.[21]

It is possible the trial's most important testimony came from Aunt Emily. She was not a party to the lawsuit and therefore was considered by many to be an impartial observer. Furthermore, she was a respected member of the community whose judgment concerning Eber's state of mind was expected to influence the jury. Emily took the stand on October 15 and 16. She recalled the special relationship she had with her brother over the years and outlined a number of his accomplishments. For years, "E.B. consulted her freely . . . even after he became a reputed wealthy man." She lived with Eber and his first wife prior to the divorce and recognized that insanity ran in the family. Her sister Sally "died insane," but Emily never had reason to question her brother's sanity. She flatly rejected the idea that her brother was delusional, declaring his mind was "superior" to most of the world in general, even after his first attack of apoplexy. Emily described Eber as a "most loving and affectionate father" while also outlining the "great failure" of both Milton and Charles in business. She stated that Milton was living in a "questionable quarter" of Milwaukee. She and Eber had also discussed their shared concerns about Charles's future.[22] When asked, "Do you remember saying that Capt. Ward was like dough in the hands of Mrs. Ward?" she replied, "I might," but continued, "I say that of every man who has a wife," which led the audience to laugh and applaud. Her testimony would prove to be important because she dismissed the argument that Catherine Ward had undue influence over Eber.[23]

As the trial began to wind down, it continued in a much less dramatic fashion, prompting one newspaper headline to announce, "The Sixth Week Opens with a Dull and Pointless Session." Milton and Charles both testified, albeit not as effectively as each had hoped. They did not appear to convince the jury they were anything more than the spoiled children of a wealthy man whose money they liked to spend. After overseeing forty-five days of testimony, Judge Patchin charged the jury to determine if E. B. Ward was "of sound mind and memory at the time" his will was adopted and whether the will was executed according to the law. Patchin explained to the jurors they could consider the impact of Ward's attack of apoplexy from 1869, but told them that belief in spirits did not constitute unsoundness of mind.[24]

The all-male jury began its deliberations at 11:00 on the morning of November 10. A crowd of interested parties remained in the courtroom hoping for a quick verdict, but no word came from the jury room. After two hours, Judge Patchin requested information as to how the deliberations were progressing. While no verdict had been reached, the foreman replied that "they were working quietly and encouragingly." The jurors continued to discuss the case until 11:00 p.m., when they were called to the courtroom once again. There was still no agreement, although Judge Patchin informed them a unanimous verdict "was greatly to be desired." The court adjourned until 10:00 the next morning. The jury continued to deliberate, yet no verdict could be reached the second day either.[25]

After the jury began its deliberations on the third morning, Judge Patchin announced he would reconvene the proceedings at 5:00 that evening. The *Detroit Free Press* reported that throughout the day "curiosity seekers haunted the sidewalks on the east side and south end of the City Hall, from which posts of observation they could see the jurors moving about in their room." As the 5:00 hour drew near, the courtroom became "packed to its utmost capacity." Interest in the case had peaked, and those so inclined "laid heavy wagers" on the trial's outcome. The jurors filed into the courtroom at the appointed hour. When all was settled and a silence had descended upon the room, the clerk of the court asked, "Gentlemen, have you agreed upon a verdict?" The jury foreman, Mr. Sackett, replied simply, "Have not." Upon hearing this, the judge repeated his desire that the jury reach a verdict. He then asked Sackett, "Is there any probability of an agreement?" When Sackett replied they would "never" reach a verdict, Judge Patchin discharged the jury, and adjourned for the day.[26]

Once the proceedings were adjourned, the courtroom cleared out quickly, but the corridors and porches of city hall were filled with "excited disputants" who advanced many "ridiculous" explanations as to why a verdict had not been reached. Eventually, Mr. Sackett reported that eight of the jurors believed the will should be thrown out, while four supported maintaining it. He declared the four "were as immovable as rocks" during the fifty-four hours of deliberations over three days and two nights. The *Detroit Free Press* speculated as to whether or not there would be another trial or if the parties involved would be able to reach a settlement. As events moved forward, a second trial to determine the fate of Eber Ward's will was scheduled for the following year.[27]

The second trial was set to commence in March 1876, but it was postponed more than once. There was great conjecture among the general populace concerning a negotiated settlement. An anonymous informant reported to the *Detroit Free Press*, "There is not at present the remotest possibility" of a compromise. But then, only two days after the second trial began, the newspaper ran the headline "The Great Suit Ended by Compromise." Both parties agreed to accept the will as written along with the first codicil. The second codicil, which limited the disbursements to Ward's children from his first marriage to $200 per month, was abandoned. Catherine and her children would receive the Ludington properties free from debt. In return, Catherine agreed to pay Eber's children and Emily a total of $105,000. Once Ward's estate was liquidated (the will charged the executors with doing so as quickly as possible), the debts would be paid and Eber's children from his first marriage would then divide the remaining assets among themselves.[28] The *Chicago Tribune* regarded the settlement as "a fair distribution" among the competing parties, although, the paper pointed out that a similar settlement could have been reached without a trial "had it not been for the greed and combativeness" of those involved.[29]

The agreement allowed members of Ward's family to finally move forward and get on with their lives. Nevertheless, as time progressed, it became apparent that liquidating Eber Ward's assets would be exceedingly complicated, particularly given the devaluation of his holdings as a result of the financial panic.

## Catherine Ward

Shortly after the compromise was reached, Catherine described the settlement as "splendid" in a letter to her niece. For months, she had experienced "tormenting anxiety" waiting for the fate of Eber's will, and therefore her own future, to be determined.[30] According to the inventory of Ward's assets at the time of his death, the lumber, sawmills, and other Ludington properties she inherited had a theoretical value of nearly $700,000. Yet the nation's economy was still in the midst of an economic depression, and demand for finished lumber had plummeted. Justus Stearns, Catherine's brother-in-law, who was working for her in Ludington, described the situation Catherine faced. "Although Mrs. Ward had this immense tract of timber and the two sawmills . . . she did not for four years make anything out of it and was greatly concerned fearing that she was going to lose everything." The price she received for lumber was so low it barely covered her expenses in the years immediately following Eber's death. Catherine almost sold the property for an immediate cash payment of $250,000, but did not. This proved to be fortunate, because by 1879 the price of lumber finally rose once again; according to Stearns, she began "cleaning up in profits" over the next two decades. By holding onto her properties and not selling, Catherine's actions represented a coolness of mind and shrewdness that had been characteristic of her husband. As events moved forward, she continued to show these traits.[31]

Although the will provided Catherine with the Ludington properties free from all debt, some creditors saw in Catherine's assets an opportunity to make good on their claims to the Ward estate. According to the *Detroit Free Press*, the extended trial over Ward's will had multiplied the debts owed to these creditors, which left them "clamorous for the collateral." With the pressure mounting, Catherine turned to her brothers John B. and Thomas R. Lyon for help. The trio developed a "bold experiment" that if successful would lead to great profits, but if unsuccessful would mean "ruin and poverty to themselves." Their scheme involved purchasing the claims of all the creditors to the estate of Eber Brock Ward.[32]

The Lyon brothers received credit from a bank in Chicago and then went to work buying up the claims. Negotiations continued for more than two years. Because the estate was so unsettled, combined with the nationwide downturn in the economy, the Lyons were able to purchase most claims for "anywhere from forty cents to ninety-seven and a half cents on the dollar." Although creditors were not compensated at par, they agreed to the price offered by the Lyons because they bid more than any others were willing to pay.[33] Once the Lyons had purchased all the claims to the estate, they forced the executor to put the estate's property for sale at a series of public auctions. Because they knew the assets of the estate so well and held the claims, "they had the inside track of all bidders" at these venues. As the *Detroit Journal* described it, "The whole thing was a highly successful business operation," although it came with a high risk. The Lyons calculated they would be able to purchase the claims at a low price and that the American economy would experience a revival. Their gamble paid off.[34]

Some assets bought and sold by the Lyons lost money, while great profits were made on others. For example, fifteen thousand shares of North Chicago Rolling Mill stock were purchased at public auction at $40 to $60 per share. These were later sold for $100 to $164. Additionally, the Lyons made "a clear profit of $373,030" on the purchase and subsequent sale of railroad stock. The proceeds from these and other sales were divided between Catherine, John, and Thomas. By the early 1890s, the *Detroit Free Press* and the *Detroit Journal* speculated that Catherine had amassed a fortune of about $4 million. The children from Eber's first marriage and Aunt Emily "never received a single cent" of the money from the estate because once the assets were liquidated, nothing remained. In subsequent years, Catherine made significant payments, possibly totaling as much as $210,000, to Eber's relatives when they came to her in need. Nonetheless, as one would suspect, a "bitter feeling" developed toward Catherine as this was far less than the profits she and her brothers had earned from the estate.[35]

Over time, events concerning the liquidation of the estate and the profits enjoyed by Catherine only deepened divisions within the family. Aunt Emily in particular "began to suspect that a great swindle had been perpetrated" and Catherine had conspired with the executor of Eber's will. In 1892, a petition was filed to reopen the Ward will case to determine if fraud had occurred. By the time the case actually came to trial, Emily and Eber's son Milton had passed away, and Charles was out of the country, but those contesting the will included several family members from Eber Ward's first family. The defendants included Orrin Potter, the executor of the will, along with Catherine and her brothers John and Thomas. Catherine proved to be ruthless in the defense of her and her brothers' actions. She hired a top team of defense attorneys from Chicago who successfully argued her case in the Wayne County Superior Court. After hearing testimony from all parties, the judge ruled in Catherine's favor; no fraud was uncovered. The decision was appealed to the Michigan Supreme Court, which affirmed the earlier decision.[36]

The bitterness felt by members of Eber Ward's "first family" evolved into hostility toward Catherine. Catherine, for her part, had another plan for her own family. This eventually resulted in a marriage between her daughter Clara and a prince from Belgium.

## Clara Ward, Princess of Chimay

Once the compromise was reached with her stepchildren concerning Eber Brock Ward's will, Catherine Ward spent time in Detroit and New York, with occasional visits to her property in Ludington. She and her two children also reportedly toured Europe for several months. Catherine's time in New York and Detroit brought her into contact with Alexander Cameron, a widowed attorney from Windsor, Ontario, who had amassed a fortune in real estate and banking. The two were married on November 7, 1878, nearly four years following Eber's death. At the time, Catherine was thirty-six and Cameron was fifty-two. The couple, along with the children, initially lived in Windsor, but Catherine sought an expanded social life in a larger city, so they eventually moved to Toronto, where Clara Ward lived until about the age of fourteen.[37]

Clara was known for her attractiveness, even at a young age. Ludington resident Luman Goodenough, who saw Clara when Catherine brought the children on a visit to oversee her sawmills and timbered property, recalled, "I remember vividly the rare beauty of this girl who was then little more than a child." Acquaintances in Detroit and Toronto recalled "pretty Clara Ward" who engaged in pranks and "gay larks" while growing up. She could be quite generous when she wanted. Clara was known to give her pocket money to private charities and to friends in need. However, others observed she appeared to lack any "moral sense" and "seemed to have no conception of the legal rights of others." If she wanted something that belonged to one of her playmates, she schemed and developed a strategy to acquire the object of her desire. Furthermore, when dared by a friend to attend a masked ball in a costume designed to represent Nudity, Clara prepared to accept that dare until she received "dire threats of punishment." Possibly in an attempt to refine her daughter's impulsive behavior, Catherine sent Clara to a boarding school in London when she turned fourteen.[38]

While in London, Clara became fluent in at least five languages, while simultaneously becoming "the despair of her teachers." She acted like the spoiled teen she was. Catherine's great wealth allowed her to indulge Clara's whims, which were repeatedly granted. Clara also reportedly received a yearly income of $30,000 ($876,326.09 in 2020 dollars) from Eber's fortune. She spent money lavishly on expensive clothes, jewelry, and other personal items. The cloistered nature of school seemed to bring out the worst in her, as Clara loved to shock her fellow students and teachers. She rebelled against authority figures and ended up moving from one school to another. It was while she was living in one of the schools that Clara confided to her diary, "The humdrum life is not for me. I must feel, must have emotions. Ordinary marriage and smug respectability appall me. I feel that it would be a joy to marry a murderer." Although she never married a murderer, there would be nothing humdrum about the life she eventually led, which would be based upon rules she developed, not those imposed on her by society.[39]

In 1889 or 1890, at the age of sixteen, Clara left finishing school—it remains unclear whether she left of her own volition or was kicked out. Nevertheless, before leaving England, she had an audience with Queen Victoria. She then toured southern Europe with her mother, apparently in an attempt to find Clara a husband. Initially, Clara fell in love with a German captain named Von Hessels, but Catherine was "eager to secure a title in her family" so she discouraged Clara from pursuing the alliance. Shortly thereafter, Clara and Catherine attended the opera in Nice, France. Also present was Prince Joseph de Caraman-Chimay of Belgium (his proper name was Marie Joseph Anatole Elie de Riquet, Prince de Caraman, Prince de Chimay). Prince Joseph noticed Clara when he observed members of the audience gazing up at "a young woman people thought dazzling" in one of the box seats. The prince, who had seen her previously, immediately recognized who the beautiful woman at the opera was. Shortly thereafter, he asked his sister to arrange a meeting with Clara. A marriage proposal soon followed.[40]

According to the *Sunday Vindicator*, Catherine argued in favor of the marriage, but Clara "protested that she did not love" the prince. Yet Catherine's "ambitions were too strong, and she [Clara] yielded." Joseph, "a tall, dark, fine looking fellow . . . and the heir of one of the noblest families of Belgium," was thirty-one; Clara was one month shy of her seventeenth birthday. The couple was married in Paris on May 20, 1890. Their wedding was an elaborate affair that created excitement on two continents and was considered the "most distinguished that had been celebrated in Europe for many years." The ceremony was performed by Monsignor Rotelle, the papal nuncio to Paris, and witnesses included Baron Beyens, the Belgian minister to Paris, and Whitelaw Reid, the American minister to France, among many others. Clara's gown of white satin and ancient lace reportedly cost $10,000. Excitement and wonder surrounding the marriage made it the "table talk of Paris for many a day afterward."[41]

Clara also became an overnight celebrity in the United States. She joined a small group of young American women from wealthy families who married

Clara Ward, princess of Chimay, shown here on an advertisement for cigarettes. (Courtesy of Historic White Pine Village)

into titled European families at the turn of the twentieth century. A woman who participated in such an arrangement was sometimes labeled a "dollar princess." The Americans were interested in a marriage to a member of the nobility, while the Europeans needed the bride's wealth to support their extravagant lifestyles. As one author put it bluntly in the case of Clara Ward, "The Belgian prince could provide a title for the lady, while the lady supplied cash for the prince." Contemporary reports indicated that in return for the title princess of Chimay, Clara and her family provided a payment of $100,000 to cover Prince Joseph's debts and an additional $300,000 to restore the family castle, which had fallen into disrepair.[42]

A rare photo of Prince Joseph de Caraman-Chimay of Belgium. (Courtesy of the Seitz family)

The newlyweds appeared to be happy in the first few years of their marriage. Clara became a sensation in Paris, and she reveled in the attention. The couple visited Joseph's estates and spent time at the Belgian royal court. Clara shone at social events where she was surrounded by groups of diplomats or other dignitaries, "addressing each in his mother tongue and flinging off witticisms in French, German, Spanish or Italian." Prince Joseph was not the social figure his young wife proved to be. Clara openly flouted tradition and proper etiquette. The public admired her boldness, finding it charming, although some members of the aristocracy considered her actions annoying. Clara and Joseph would have two children: Marie was born in 1891 and Joseph came three years later.[43]

Following the birth of her children, vicious rumors circulated that Clara had affairs with several men. At least one rumor was true. In January 1896, Clara's brother, Eber Jr., confided to his cousin Mabel Seitz, "Clara didn't care a rap for Chimay when she married him, & only did so to get away from her mother. She had an affair with [the Marquis de] Castellane," a member of the French nobility who had married another American, Anna Gould, the daughter of the financier Jay Gould. He declared that Clara "in fact was intimate with him & Joe [Prince Joseph] caught them, but did not challenge Castellane," who waited two days for the prince to call him out. Apparently, Joseph was indifferent to his wife's actions—neither of the two had married for love. Clara later acknowledged that the prince was "a good type of a man . . . courteous, gentlemanly, generous," but she complained he was "cold as ice. I wonder if he thinks me a woman of wood or stone to be satisfied with 'good morning' or 'good night.' I want to love and be loved."[44]

Clara began to tire of the Belgian court. According to Clara, she became a "social pariah" when Belgium's King Leopold II became "enamored" of her beauty. His attentions seemingly infuriated the queen. Clara later reflected, "I defied them, as I have all my life defied everyone." Joseph and Clara left the Belgian court and moved to Paris. Clara relished fashionable Parisian society with its nightlife of parties, drinking, and dancing. It was while visiting a night-club in November 1896 that Clara chanced to meet a musician named Janczy (Janos) Rigo.[45]

Janos Rigo was somewhat of a mysterious figure; even aspects of his physical appearance are in doubt. One contemporary newspaper described the "Hungarian gypsy" fiddler as "tall and well proportioned," about thirty-four years of age. Conversely, another described him the "gypsy musician" as "small of stature, with a face pitted with smallpox . . . noted for his winning smile." He was also married, although his wife had abandoned him some years earlier. He was working as the director of what was labeled a "gypsy orchestra" at a Paris restaurant and nightclub frequented by Clara and Joseph. Clara became so captivated with Rigo that she returned several nights in a row to hear him perform. Ten days after first hearing Rigo play his violin, Clara left her husband and children to run off with the "gypsy fiddler" who caught her fancy.[46]

Clara had become increasingly dissatisfied in her marriage, and the free-dom represented by Rigo made him attractive as she looked to escape her situation. Rigo was an exotic musician, quite the opposite of the stuffy husband she once described as "cold as ice." The *New York Times* reported that Clara's actions caused a great "sensation in aristocratic circles" as she "bade farewell to her husband" and children. Asked if she regretted abandoning her children, Clara responded, "It is too late to think of them. Let us face facts and have a good dinner on reaching Paris."[47] Joseph filed for divorce and was granted custody of the children. Clara was required to pay alimony of $15,000 per year, but she appeared unfazed as she avowed, "I am done with it all. I wanted to be free. I am at least out of the rotten atmosphere in which modern society lives. . . . We are quits."[48]

The press was merciless in its criticism of Clara. The *Ludington Record* ran the headline "Gone with a Gypsy" along with an image of the princess, opining that Clara had "ruined her life for the sake of a wretched Hungarian musician." The *Wyandotte Herald* labeled her a "disgrace to womanhood" and criticized her lack of morality. The *New York Journal and Advertiser* declared, "No individual has done more to injure the reputation of Americans abroad than Clara Ward," while Ohio's *Sunday Vindicator* reported, "All America stands ashamed—fearful of the next act in this sad and horrible melodrama."[49]

Although the American press was highly critical of Clara, reporters recognized a good story that would sell papers, so they monitored Clara's actions much as modern-day paparazzi would. The *New York Times* routinely reported on the activities of the notorious couple. Shortly after leaving her husband and children, the princess and Rigo visited his parents, who lived in a "gypsy hut." The couple hoped to marry as soon as Rigo's divorce was finalized. Apparently, passion ran hot and cold between Clara and her new lover. Less than two months after deserting her husband, Clara and Rigo were engaged in a "violent quarrel" while staying at a hotel in Milan. Guests grew alarmed over the "screams of the Princess and violent language of Rigo," fearful of what was happening behind the doors of the couple's room. Clara soon left for Monte Carlo, abandoning Rigo for a short time. Before she left, Clara paid her portion of the hotel bill, but not Rigo's, who was left to fend for himself. The couple soon reunited, but the incident caused great excitement and made newspaper headlines.[50]

The media reported that Clara's actions frustrated her mother so much that Catherine cut off Clara's annual allowance. Rigo had no money, so if such claims were true, Clara was forced to earn a living for the first time in her life. She chose to cash in on her fame in several ways. She had photos taken of her wearing a suit that clung so tightly to her body it created the appearance she was entirely naked. These images were mass-produced for sale in Paris. Upon close inspection, one could see the initial "C" and the Chimay crown had been tattooed on her shoulder. The *New York Times* reported that Clara earned a royalty for "every one of many thousand photographs, which were being eagerly caught up by the scandal-loving visitors to Paris." This generated a substantial income until the Paris prefect of police suppressed the sale of the photos at the request of the prince, who was embarrassed by his former wife and her inappropriate use of his family's name. The actions of the police only increased publicity and demand for Clara's image. The princess then allowed her portrait to be used in advertisements for cigarettes, French bicycles, and even postcards. In some cases, Clara appeared alone; in others, she was joined by Rigo.[51]

Clara also engaged in performances she labeled *poses plastiques*. For these, Clara often wore only a bodysuit of flesh-colored tights, similar to the one she had worn in the banned photos, which simulated nudity. Sometimes Rigo joined her on-stage, playing his violin, while on other occasions, Clara appeared alone. She also gave private performances, although Rigo did not approve of these. The princess reportedly earned at least $750 per night for her shows, and negotiated contracts to be paid $6,000 per month in Berlin and $8,000 for four weeks in London. A journalist described one of her performances that took place in Paris at the Folies Bergère theater. Once the lights were dimmed, Clara appeared on-stage while music played in the background. The princess then "began her dance to the weird barbaric music, softly, lightly, with a voluptuous, sensuous charm, her feet keeping time" with the music. "There was dead silence throughout the crowded theater"; "no sound could be heard save the weird chant of the gipsy's fiddle" and the rustling of Clara's dress. "Suddenly, a man sprang on to the stage, and in a loud voice cried: 'I forbid this performance in the name of the law!'" Initially, the audience cheered, believing this was part of the performance. But the man was the prefect of police, who threatened to close the theater and expel Clara from France if the proceedings were not immediately halted. Such actions only increased the public's interest in Clara's exploits, but she soon left Paris for the south of France.[52]

Princess Clara performing in a bodysuit simulating nudity with her second husband, Rigo. (Courtesy of Historic White Pine Village)

The adventures of the princess and her Hungarian fiddler continued to capture the public's attention. It is possible Toulouse-Lautrec's *Idylle Princière* was inspired by the romance between Rigo and Clara. Moreover, a decadent Hungarian cake, Rigójancsi, was named for Rigo.[53] More than once, the press falsely reported that Clara or Rigo had died. But they were thriving—Clara built a villa in Alexandria, Egypt, where the couple lived for two years. Clara bought Rigo a zoo of exotic animals, including tigers, lions, and baby elephants. They also traveled the world, vacationing in Africa, China, and parts of Europe. All the while, Clara spent money carelessly. Contrary to previous reports, Clara was not cut off from her inheritance; when she turned twenty-one, she had reportedly received a fortune of $3 million ($94,594,172.65 in 2020 dollars) in the form of a trust, from which her yearly allowance was increased to $50,000.

Clara also had earned money from her various public appearances. Nonetheless, she managed to accumulate such a large amount of debt that her uncle Thomas R. Lyon was appointed conservatory of her estate in 1901. Lyon discovered that Clara had spent as much as $750,000 between 1894 and 1901 on country villas, gifts for Rigo, travel abroad, and personal items for herself, such as diamond earrings and the latest fashions. In paperwork filed in Chicago, Clara was forced to admit she was "a spendthrift and incapable of conducting her own affairs."[54]

Clara and Rigo's passionate relationship did not last. News headlines in 1903 proclaimed that she had left Rigo for another man: "Princess Chimay Tires of Her Gipsy." Not long thereafter, the couple divorced. The following year, while Clara was on holiday in Italy, she met the man who would become her next husband. As she described it, Clara met Giuseppe Ricciardi "at the foot of Mount Vesuvius. But it was I who was the volcano. My heart took fire at the sight of Joseph. The conflagration was mutual." The two were married in 1904, about three months after their first meeting. Ricciardi, who had been an Italian railroad employee, was twenty-two; Clara was thirty-one. He was described as "youthful, regular of feature, effeminate of look, and with a curled moustache."[55]

It was about the time of Clara's third marriage that Dr. Charles H. Hughes, a noted medical doctor and psychologist, became interested in her escapades. Hughes was a member of the faculty at Washington University in St. Louis and served as superintendent of the hospital for the insane in Fulton, Missouri. He founded the journal the *Alienist and Neurologist* and often testified as an expert witness at criminal trials. In 1904, he wrote an article focused on Clara, "The Erratic Erotic Princess Chimay: A Psychological Analysis," which was published in his journal. It does not appear as if Hughes ever interviewed Clara personally, but he believed that by studying her behavior and recent interviews, he could develop a diagnosis. While Hughes stopped short of labeling her a nymphomaniac, he declared her an "erotopath," subject to "erotic impulses and blind to the ordinary restraining social, moral and organic proprieties that usually govern others of her sex." He argued her behavior was erratic and impulsive because she had never been taught restraint in her youth, yet she had "limitless financial ability for self-indulgence." He consistently criticized her behavior, particularly her "adultery with two men." He then asked why Clara was "still roaming Europe unrestrained in her morbid erotism, to the shame of society and all true womanhood and the harm of herself?" He prescribed "psychological medication and a friendly sanitarium" as a cure for the ailments from which he believed she suffered.[56]

The fact that Dr. Hughes would take the time to analyze and diagnose Clara's behavior is a testament to the diverse segments of society familiar with her actions. In the past, social columns of newspapers had included chronicles of her exploits, but here was a medical professional, with a national reputation, who chose to examine her life. Contrary to Hughes's analysis, and to those who might point to the history of mental illness in Ward's family, the actions of the princess of Chimay do not appear to indicate Clara suffered from psychological problems. Rather than mental illness, Clara's actions might best be explained by the fact she never had restrictions placed upon her behavior, either as a child or adult, with one key exception. Clara had been forced into marriage with the prince of Chimay at her mother's insistence. After a period of time, Clara rebelled. Hughes was correct to point to Clara's "limitless financial ability." Most women did not have such financial resources, which allowed Clara not only to live an extravagant lifestyle, but also to leave her husband. A strong, independent woman, Clara left the husband she did not love and chose to live her life on her own terms. She did not care about contravening the social norms of the era in which she lived. These actions showed a similarity to traits her father possessed and demonstrated throughout his professional career. E. B. Ward's independent spirit and competitive nature sometimes put him at odds with others. Yet he took steps he felt necessary to build his business empire, regardless of criticism from individual, or the press.[57]

Details of Clara's life are scarcer following her third marriage. Although the newspapers still chronicled some of her adventures, they appeared less often than previously. Clara and Ricciardi remained together about six years. In 1910, the New York Times reported that Clara had brought formal divorce proceedings against her husband. Ricciardi then accused Clara of having an affair with one of their employees, Abano Cassolota, who was either a butler or a chauffeur in their household. Sometime thereafter Clara and Cassolota were married.[58]

# The Fate of Catherine, Clara, and Eber Ward Jr.

Clara's brother Eber Jr. was also associated with scandal and at least one failed marriage. In the 1890s, Eber married Victorine Herault, a widow with a fifteen-year-old daughter. (His wife later alleged that Ward told his uncle he wished he had never married his wife—he favored his stepdaughter Blanche.) In 1900, Victorine sued for divorce after Ward abandoned her and eloped with her maid. She also accused her husband of "drinking to excess." Although the divorce was not finalized in 1900, the two lived apart from that time onward.[59]

Catherine Ward Cameron must have been disappointed in the actions of both her son and daughter, particularly the escapades of Clara. Her relations with Clara had been strained ever since she pressured her daughter to marry Prince Joseph. Catherine's goal of entering Europe's aristocracy through the marriage of her daughter did not work out the way she had planned. After Catherine's second husband, Alexander Cameron, died in 1893, she became involved in a range of charitable activities in Toronto. She then met and married John Morrow, a Montreal stockbroker, in 1896. The prospect of a third marriage excited her; as she acknowledged, "I married twice for money.... This time I'm marrying for love!" Unfortunately, while Catherine found happiness in her new husband, she was estranged from her children, and much of her family was in turmoil. Comments made by Eber Jr. to his cousin Mabel seem to confirm the chaotic state of the family. Mabel wrote that Eber had confided to her that "he thoroughly hates her [his mother], so does Clara, & he hates Clara & Clara hates him, he despises his wife & don't give a damn for his children." Indeed, these comments indicate the family members were terribly resentful of one another.[60]

In an attempt to maintain a relationship with at least some in her family, Catherine organized a living situation that would be unique in any era. She invited her grandchildren and daughter-in-law Victorine, who had yet to receive a formal divorce from Eber Jr., to live with her. For several years they lived together in Catherine's Toronto mansion. Victorine and Eber Jr. finally divorced in 1907 and shortly thereafter, Victorine remarried. Then the entire family relocated to England, where they lived until Catherine's death in 1915. When she died, Catherine had an estate valued at more than $1 million. The provisions of Catherine's will reflect both the disappointment she felt in her children and the importance she placed on the next generation. Clara and Eber Jr. received only $1,000 each. Other than some minor bequests to other relatives and a $5,000 life annuity for her husband, the bulk of her estate was bequeathed to her grandchildren. This was split between Clara's children, who were still living with their father, Prince Joseph, and Eber Jr.'s two oldest children.[61]

When Clara learned that her mother's health was failing, she attempted to reconcile with her, but the two were never reunited as Catherine's condition declined quite rapidly. Although Clara and her mother had not spoken for years, the *Detroit Free Press* reported that Catherine "never lost her love for" Clara and a "magnificent portrait of the princess always hung in the place of honor in the grand drawing room" of her home. The year after Catherine's death, Clara's own health began to fail, and in December 1916, the *New York Times* reported she had died at her villa in Italy at the age of forty-three. Family members learned of her death via a cable sent to her uncle's firm in Chicago that read simply, "Clara dead. Notify family. Cassolota." At the time, family members were unaware that Abano Cassolota and Clara were married.[62]

The intrigue concerning Clara Ward's activities did not end with her death. Initial reports indicated Clara "had been buried in a pauper's coffin and that all she had left of her millions was a case of jewels worth a few thousand francs." In reality, Clara did not die a pauper. Instead, she had a "very large income and lived in a manner befitting its possessor," according to the American consul in Venice. During her sickness, which was not identified, she received the best care possible and her funeral was "elaborate and costly." When her will was filed in a Chicago probate court, paperwork indicated she had an estate worth $1,224,935. It was divided into three trust funds: one for each of her children and one for a former husband. Interestingly, Clara's will had been written several years earlier, when she was married to Giuseppe Ricciardi; thus he, not her current husband, received one-third of her estate.[63]

Less than two years following the death of Clara, Eber Ward Jr. died at the age of forty-eight. He was survived by his wife, Luna Kunz Ward, and at least four children. Although his legal residence was Chicago, he had been living abroad for many years. The *Detroit Free Press* reported that, at his death, he had an estate worth $1,035,000. Catherine, Clara, and Eber Jr. each died with estates valued at more than $1 million ($17,504,064 in 2020 dollars), yet their interaction had been characterized by chaos and turmoil. Mabel Seitz, Clara and Eber's cousin, described their family situation quite accurately when she commented, "I guess with all their money, they are about as unhappy & unnatural a family as ever existed."[64]

# Conclusion

The business empire created by Eber Brock Ward represented a lifetime of achievement that touched the lives of many individuals. Yet, as one longtime acquaintance, William L. Bancroft, observed, "On his demise his immense estate, estimated larger than any other in Michigan, collapse like a punctured balloon." One might ask how this could have happened. Several factors led to the "demise of his immense estate," valued at $5,300,000 in 1875. Conflict between members of Ward's family was surely a key factor leading to this loss of value. Underlying tensions were exacerbated by Catherine's unexplained decision to withdraw her offer to work with members of Eber's first family and set aside $300,000 worth of lumber to help cover the estate's debt shortly after Eber's death. This led directly to the trial, which lasted nearly fifty days and ended in a hung jury. It took more than a year following Eber's death to reach a final settlement concerning his estate. In the meantime, loans were not paid, leading to additional fees and fines, which certainly took away from the estate's value.[65]

Another factor leading to the erosion of his estate related to the management style Ward employed during his lifetime. He always maintained strict control over the operations of his businesses, serving as the linchpin that held his empire together. Without his leadership, the interconnected procedures he had successfully established and maintained over time began to suffer. The death of the empire's chief executive officer led to a power vacuum plant managers were unable to fill.

A final factor involved the provisions of Ward's will. By awarding his wife the Ludington properties "clear of all incumbrances," he contributed to the conflict bound to emerge between Catherine and the children from his first family. Ward could have avoided this by requiring Catherine to pay for at least part of the debt associated with his estate. Additionally, provisions of the will called for his properties to be "sold and converted into cash, or interest–bearing bonds." By converting his properties into cash, it allowed organizations that were once included in his orbit to become their own entities, thereby leaving behind their connection to the Ward empire. Another contributing factor was the provision to liquidate his assets "as fast as practicable."[66] Ward's death took place in the midst of an economic depression when the entire American economy was suffering. Many of his assets were losing value quickly—and would have done so even if he had not died. If Ward had survived his second attack of apoplexy, he likely would have weathered the economic storm just as he had survived previous downturns in the American economy. But this was not to be.

During his lifetime, E. B. Ward was a well-known public figure: Michigan's "Iron King" and the region's largest employer. Fifteen years after his death, it was his daughter Clara who captured the public's attention with her illustrious marriage and subsequent scandals. While Clara was not driven to create a business empire like her father, she created a kingdom based upon her own set of rules, regardless of the expectations of society. Clara's goal was to live a life of excitement on her own terms. As previously stated, she once confided to her diary, "The humdrum life is not for me. . . . Ordinary marriage and smug respectability appall me." She remained true to her own convictions until she died.

# Epilogue

## *A Legacy Forgotten*

*With the fresh coats of paint has gone everything to remind
one of the days when E. B. Ward was a great power here.*
—*Detroit Free Press*, April 11, 1879

*In character he was a man of mild and agreeable manners, quick to
action, open-hearted and generous. Possessed of almost invincible
determination, if he thought his plans were unreasonably opposed,
he would brook no opposition and usually carried his point, but
in general he was far from being a difficult man to please.*
—William Downie, 1941

*E. B. Ward became an overbearing, egotistic, vainglorious, dishonest,
tyrannical, vindictive, aggressive, energetic, selfish man, largely devoid
of conscience. This tyrannical, envious, vain, selfish, grasping, energetic
man soon spread out his then comparatively vast fortune . . . mostly
in illegitimate dishonest schemes, in view of showing his financial
ability, power and consequence. His schemes were largely the grasping
of others' property, paying therefore little or no equivalent.*
—David Ward, 1912

On Christmas Day in 1871, Emily Ward hosted a party at her home in honor
of Eber's sixtieth birthday. A large number of friends were in attendance that

Portrait of Eber Brock Ward by John Mix Stanley. This painting highlights Ward's lifetime of achievements. (Courtesy of the Detroit Historical Society)

afternoon to celebrate the occasion. At an appointed time, Emily offered a signal and the doors to her back parlor were thrown open in a dramatic manner, revealing a very large full-length portrait of Eber Brock Ward. Eber had no idea Emily had commissioned the piece, described by those who viewed it as "a superb work of art." As Eber slowly walked toward the painting, he was clearly touched and nearly broke down, causing an observer to report, "For once at least in his life [Ward], gave visible tokens of being in the melting mood."[1]

The artist who produced the portrait was John Mix Stanley. In years past, Stanley had gained recognition as a chronicler of Native Americans and scenes in the American West. The *Detroit Free Press* described the painting as both "a portrait and biography." Its images celebrate Ward's long list of achievements, emphasizing his involvement in the shipping industry. Ward is depicted standing on a wharf, an anchor and compass at his feet and a globe at his side. Behind him is a collection of scientific books about mining, metallurgy, and other topics. In the background are numerous landscape scenes representing key events in his early life. On the left, a country youth is shown trapping muskrats on the St. Clair River in Newport. To the right is the old lighthouse at Bois Blanc Island. The viewer's eye is also drawn to the image of a schooner, representing another phase in Ward's life as he became master of the *General Harrison*. Toward the front of the painting is the steamer *Huron*, laden with cargo on its way into port with its captain in command. Finally, the wharf where Ward stands shows the city of Wyandotte, with heavy columns of smoke emerging from numerous smokestacks.[2]

The individual scenes are best viewed by standing close to the portrait, but from a short distance, the viewer notices how each scene revolves around its central figure. Ward's towering presence dominates the canvas just as he towered over the economy and life in his home state of Michigan. It took Stanley four months to complete his work, which was enormous: about twelve feet in height by five feet wide. According to an analysis of Stanley's work by Peter Hassrick and Mindy Besaw, it was "perhaps the largest canvas Stanley had ever painted . . . commensurate with the exalted stature of its subject." At the time of its creation in 1871, Eber Ward was at the height of his power and influence. It appeared as if nothing could stop him and his legacy would live on forever. Yet, within just a few years, the Panic of 1873 threatened his business empire, a stroke took his life, and a range of factors overshadowed his accomplishments, leaving his legacy forgotten.[3]

Certainly, the extended court battle over Ward's estate contributed to the public's perception of his legacy. Ward was presented as a fool who took advice from spiritualists and was controlled by his manipulating wife. The subsequent liquidation of his estate contributed to the public's forgetfulness as businesses once part of the Ward empire saw their stock sold to a range of buyers, thereby eliminating their connection to the man who had founded them. This disbursement of Ward's assets can be contrasted to the situation of one of Ward's contemporary business tycoons, Cornelius Vanderbilt, who bequeathed the majority of his estate to his son William, thereby keeping his empire intact. Eber had no such heir with an ability to sustain his operations.[4]

The actions of Catherine Ward also contributed to the fact that her husband's many accomplishments faded in the mind of the general public. Catherine's scheming and ruthless tactics to maintain control of Ward's wealth split the family apart and created tremendous resentment among his heirs. Rather than taking steps to maintain their father's legacy, Eber's children used their energy and resources to fight their stepmother. Catherine could have acted to preserve her husband's legacy, such as Eliza Hamilton, the widow of Alexander Hamilton, did. Instead, she was focused on preserving a fortune for herself and securing a title for her daughter Clara. Furthermore, the scandalous exploits of Princess Chimay captured the nation's attention, overshadowing her father's actions and thereby casting his accomplishments further into oblivion.

Even the physical representations of Eber's life began to crumble and disappear after his death. In 1878, a portion of the marble veneer on his Detroit mansion came loose and fell to the ground in a thundering crash. Although this soon was repaired, the following year Ward's heirs sold the home to the House of the Good Shepherd, transforming the once glorious castle of Eber Brock Ward into a shelter for young girls in need. That same year, one of the structures Ward had previously occupied along the waterfront was sold. The building had held his office, offering a view of the river: Ward could watch his steamers carrying passengers to their destinations, iron ore to his mills, or finished products to market. Each side of the building included a sign with Ward's name, such as "Ward's Lake Superior Line" and "Ward's Warehouse." The new owners chose to paint the building and make some additional improvements. As the *Detroit Free Press* observed, "With the fresh coats of paint has gone everything to remind one of the days when E. B. Ward was a great power here. . . . His private office is occupied by another man and not even a black-lettered sign is left to suggest his person and character and revive old memories."[5]

## Evaluating Ward's Legacy

Rather than fading into oblivion, Ward's many accomplishments should be recognized and celebrated. Eber Brock Ward was a man of vision and action. Possibly the best example of his vision was related by a business associate. In the early 1870s, Hamilton Gay Howard was chatting with Eber in his office as the two enjoyed the view of the Detroit River. Howard had inquired about investing in mining operations when Ward stopped him short and offered a prophecy. He predicted, "Detroit will be one of the largest manufacturing centers, if not the largest, in the world!" Ward recognized that "with iron and copper in immense quantity to the north, coal to the south, and plenty of Detroit River water in front of it . . . Detroit would be an industrial island of the greatest extent on earth." Henry Ford and other manufacturers would see to it that Ward's prophecy came true by the early decades of the twentieth century. But it was Ward who took the initial steps to put the region on a manufacturing path when he established the Eureka Iron Company just outside the city in 1853. This was only the first of his manufacturing operations, which spread throughout the Great Lakes and Midwest.[6]

Ward was able to expand operations due to his implementation of vertical integration. This allowed him to cut costs and interconnect the operations of each business he owned. He possessed iron mines where ore was extracted, owned the ships that transported the ore, built the iron and steel mills where it was transformed into railroad rails or other merchantable commodities, and operated the railroads that purchased these products. Ward adopted these practices well in advance of other, more famous business moguls such as Andrew Carnegie. Ward also was willing to invest in the latest and most efficient manufacturing practices. This led him to become the first in the United States to produce Bessemer steel, at his Wyandotte facility in 1865.

Ward also demonstrated great vision in his speeches concerning the future of the Midwest. The area had a strong agricultural basis for its economy, but given its abundance of rich natural resources, Ward believed there could be more. He argued that the diversification of the Midwest's economy would become the nation's new Manifest Destiny. He contended that if manufacturing was added to the region's agricultural base, economic development would follow. The addition of manufacturing would expand the American economy, lead to a higher standard of living, and result in a more sustainable future. He did more than talk about expanding the Midwest's industrial base; he founded the Eureka Iron Company near Detroit as well as iron and steel operations in Milwaukee and Chicago. The Windy City's North Chicago Rolling Mill eventually became an integral part of Illinois Steel Company and later U.S. Steel.[7]

At the time of Ward's death, he was the president of nine companies and served on the board of directors of many others, indicating he was a man of action, not just words. The holdings included in the Ward empire were diverse, ranging from mining operations involving silver and iron ore to railroads, lumber mills, steamboat lines, and even plate glass manufacturing. These were in addition to his three enormous iron and steel mills. Although he recruited and empowered skilled officers, many of whom were members of his extended family, to run day-to-day operations, Ward maintained absolute control over his businesses. He often owned a majority of the stock in each company to ensure his decisions were final.

While Ward's list of achievements is long, he was not without fault. Ward's combative style and ruthlessness made him enemies. He did not think twice about attacking competitors who threatened his steamboat lines. Eber success-fully pressured James Ludington to sell property he desired by having Ludington thrown in jail. Ward always aggressively defended his actions when he believed he was in the right. He demonstrated this combativeness when defending the crew of his vessel the *Atlantic* after it was struck by the *Ogdensburg*, leading to a tremendous loss of life in 1852. He was even willing to criticize victims of the disaster who mistook cane stools for flotation devices in the chaos fol-lowing the crash. Prior to this tragedy, Eber had lobbied in Washington, DC, to limit the number of lifeboats on Great Lakes vessels. It is possible some vic-tims could have been saved had there been more lifeboats, but we will never know.

Admirers such as William Downie described Eber Ward as "a man of mild and agreeable manners, quick to action, open-hearted and generous." In con-trast, Eber's own cousin David Ward declared he was, "an overbearing, egotis-tic, vainglorious, dishonest, tyrannical, vindictive, aggressive, energetic, selfish man, largely devoid of conscience." How can these assessments be reconciled? Maybe there is some truth in both statements. Downie observed that Ward was quick to act in regard to his diverse business interests. If Ward saw an oppor-tunity, he immediately took it. Yet even Downie admitted that if Ward felt strongly about an issue, "he would brook no opposition and usually carried his point." Clearly, Eber's career successes demonstrate that David Ward's descrip-tion of Eber as overbearing, aggressive, and energetic rings true. Eber's actions in 1851, when he challenged the captain of the *Empire State* to race his steamer, the *Ocean*, demonstrated he could be vainglorious. Some of Ward's employ-ees might have considered Eber tyrannical and devoid of conscience, given the working conditions and pay scale at his factories as well as his attempts to control their lives by prohibiting their consumption of alcohol. Ward did not support union organizing, and conflict with laborers over compensation led to strikes on more than one occasion. When credit became unavailable, Ward even issued scrip rather than paying his employees in cash. This undoubtedly led his employees and their families to suffer, as some recipients were forced to redeem their scrip at less than its face value. Ward furthermore demonstrated a level of selfishness as a parent and husband. He was an absent father for much of his children's upbringing. Once his sons became adults, he placed them into positions for which they had little, if any, preparation. Predictably, they failed, which led to great disappointment. Eber also abandoned his wife Polly after more than thirty years of marriage in order to marry Catherine Lyon, a much younger beauty queen.[8]

The businesses owned and operated by Ward had a major impact on the environment. The mining and lumber industries are two of the most damaging extractive industries. Regardless of whether these operations took place in Michigan's Upper Peninsula, the ranges of Wisconsin, or the banks of the Pere Marquette River, Ward's companies altered the natural landscape significantly. The algal blooms outside of Toledo on Lake Erie represent one legacy resulting from the creation of Ward's Canal in Ohio's Black Swamp and the following transformation of the area into farmland. Even the clouds of billowing smoke emerging from the factories Ward founded, shown in Stanley's great portrait, impacted life where those facilities were located. However, one must remember the context in which those businesses operated. The billowing smoke from factories or the whistle of a sawmill were symbols of economic development and prosperity in nineteenth-century America. Perhaps a description of Ward's Bay View Mill near Milwaukee can help to offer perspective. In his 1881 *History of Milwaukee*, A. T. Andreas wrote, "Smoke from the furnaces hung like a cloud over the village by day, and the light shone as a pillar of fire by night, a sign of the unceasing labor, and the unceasing reward of the industrious and prosperous villagers." Ironically, at the time, the clouds of billowing smoke from the iron mill were considered symbols of the area's progress, not pollution.[9]

While it is true that some of Ward's actions warrant criticism, he also contributed positively to the nation in many ways. He was generous with his philanthropy and took pride in his support of his sister's Newport Academy. He was a virulent opponent of slavery, the key moral issue of his lifetime. He spoke out against the peculiar institution and even directed employees on his steamers to aid runaway slaves. He corresponded with President Lincoln and was an ardent supporter of the Union.

Rather than being forgotten, Ward should be recognized as a true visionary. He was an industrial titan whose actions helped to propel the United States into the industrial age. The progressive business practices he implemented predated those of other better-known figures, such as Andrew Carnegie and John D. Rockefeller, by decades. Henry Ford often is identified as Michigan's great industrial leader. E. B. Ward was a forerunner, operating fifty years prior to the man who reportedly "put America on wheels." An article in the journal the *Valve World* may have put it best: Eber Brock Ward "stands out as a pioneer in four of our greatest fields of industrial activity, namely, water and rail transportation, lumber and the manufacture of steel and iron. . . . He was a genius and deserves to be ranked as one of the 'Real Builders of America.'"[10]

# Notes

## Abbreviations

**BGSU-Hall**   Bowling Green State University, Center for Archival Collections, Bowling Green, OH, Great Lakes History Collection, GLMS 101-Kenneth R. Hall Collection

**BHC**   Burton Historical Collection of the Detroit Public Library, Detroit, MI

**EBW-Clarke**   Clarke Historical Library, Central Michigan University, Mount Pleasant, MI, E. B. Ward Family Papers

**MCHS-Korn**   Milwaukee County Historical Society Research Library, Milwaukee, WI, Korn Papers

**NYHS-Ludington**   New York Historical Society, New York, NY, Ludington Family Papers

**WFC-MC**   Ward Family Collection, Community Pride and Heritage Museum Archive, Marine City, MI

## Introduction

1. The first quotation is from "The Poor Boy a Millionaire," *Daily Cleveland Herald*, October 4, 1856. The second quotation is from "Captain E. B. Ward's Investment in Ore-Bearing Land," *Chicago Tribune*, February 21, 1873, 3. Another source is "Progress in Western Iron Manufactures," *Chicago Tribune*, July 31, 1869, 2. The phrase "pathfinder of industry" was inspired by Bernhard C. Korn's excellent dissertation: "Eber Brock Ward, Pathfinder of American Industry."

2. The quotation is from Machiavelli, *The Prince*, 56.

3. The first set of quotations is from William Downie, "Biography of Eber Brock Ward," 1941, Eber Brock Ward Collection, 1939, Burton Historical Collection, Detroit Public Library. The other quotations are from "Capt. Ward's Faith in City Justified," *Detroit Free Press*, October 27, 1925.

4. The quotation is from "Taxing Profits Twice," *New York Daily Tribune*, June 6, 1863.

5. See Korn, "Eber Brock Ward, Pathfinder of American Industry"; Shinn, "Captain Eber Brock Ward, Ironmaster of the West." The exploits of Clara Ward are

found in Passante, "Clara Ward, Paparazzi Princess"; and "Clara Ward, Princesse de Caraman-Chimay: An American Dollar Princess," *Crowns, Tiaras and Coronets*, posted July 31, 2016, available online at http://crownstiarasandcoronets .blogspot.com/2016/07/clara-ward-princesse-de-caraman-chimay.html, accessed August 29, 2020. For Wargo's excellent articles, see "A Case Without Parallel" and "Awful Calamity!"

6  The quotation is from "Death of Captain E. B. Ward," *Detroit Free Press*, January 3, 1875, 1.

## Prologue

1  The events discussed in this prologue are taken from several different sources. An excellent analysis of the controversies surrounding Ward's death and will is found in Wargo, "A Case Without Parallel." Other sources include Eber Ward to Emily Ward, January 2, 1875, Michigan Letters, 1864–1915 folder, box 1, Ward Family Papers, BHC; "Eber B. Ward, His Death," newspaper clippings, Ward, Eber Brock, 1868–1875 folder, Eber Brock Ward Papers, 1848–1875, BHC; Korn, "Eber Brock Ward, Pathfinder of American Industry," 316–17; "E. B. Ward, He Falls Dead on the Street," *Detroit Advertiser and Tribune*, January 4, 1875; "New Year's Calls," *Detroit Free Press*, January 1, 1875, 1; "Death of Captain E. B. Ward," *Detroit Free Press*, January 3, 1875, 1; "Local Matters: Storm Signal Corps Report," *Detroit Free Press*, January 3, 1875, 1; "The Ward Will Case," *New York Times*, October 5, 1875.

2  The quotation is from Bancroft, "Memoir of Capt. Samuel Ward," 341. An additional source is William Downie, "Biography of Eber Brock Ward," 1941, Eber Brock Ward Collection, 1939, Burton Historical Collection, Detroit Public Library.

3  "Eber B. Ward, His Death," newspaper clippings; Eber Ward to Emily Ward, January 2, 1875.

4  The quotation is from "Death of Captain E. B. Ward," *Detroit Free Press*, January 3, 1875, 1; Wargo, "A Case Without Parallel," 82, 84; "E. B. Ward, He Falls Dead on the Street."

## 1. Modest Beginnings

1  The quotation is from Hurlbut, *Grandmother's Stories*, 22.

2  During the American Revolution, Asael Ward, Eber Brock Ward's great-grandfather, joined the Patriot cause; he was killed at the battle of Bennington in 1777. Asael's son David Ward, Eber Brock Ward's grandfather, became the new head of the family. This early history of the Ward family comes from a range of sources, the most important being "Family Record," Genealogy folder, box 1, Ward Family Papers, 1807–1945, BHC; "Genealogy of the Ward Family, Compiled from Family Bible Records and Various Types of Family Papers," Genealogy folder, box 1, Ward Family Papers, 1807–1945, BHC; Hurlbut, *Grandmother's Stories*, 19–23, 151; Ward, *The Autobiography of David Ward*, 1–3; Korn, "Eber Brock Ward, Pathfinder of American Industry," 3–9; Shinn, "Captain Eber Brock Ward, Ironmaster of the West," 7.

3 "Sally Potter," https://ancestry.com, accessed June 5, 2017; "Phebe Woodward," https://ancestry.com, accessed June 5, 2017; Smith and Rann, *History of Rutland County, Vermont*, 698, 707, 853–54; "Family Record," Genealogy folder, box 1, Ward Family Papers, 1807–1945, BHC; "Genealogy of the Ward Family," BHC; Carlisle, *Chronography of Notable Events*, 243.

4 The first quotation is from Hurlbut, *Grandmother's Stories*, 20. The second is from Sally Potter Ward to Phebe Wyman, November 12, 1807, Eber B. Ward Family Papers, folder 2, Correspondence, 1807–1829, box 1, EBW-Clarke. Other sources include "Family Record," Genealogy folder, box 1, Ward Family Papers, 1807–1945, BHC; Korn, "Eber Brock Ward, Pathfinder of American Industry," 6–7; Bancroft, "Memoir of Capt. Samuel Ward," 337–39. The history of salt production near Syracuse, New York, is addressed in Kappel, *Salt Production in Syracuse*, 1–2.

5 "Family Record," Genealogy folder, box 1, Ward Family Papers, 1807–1945, BHC; Korn, "Eber Brock Ward, Pathfinder of American Industry," 8.

6 The quotation is from Bancroft, "Memoir of Capt. Samuel Ward," 347. Another source is Ward, *The Autobiography of David Ward*, 2.

7 Korn, "Eber Brock Ward, Pathfinder of American Industry," 8–11; Bancroft, "Memoir of Capt. Samuel Ward," 337; "Family Record," Genealogy folder, box 1, Ward Family Papers, 1807–1945, BHC; Roosevelt, *The Naval War of 1812*, 185, 282–84. The inflation-adjusted currency values are according to https://westegg.com/inflation/infl.cgi, accessed February 5, 2021.

8 "Family Record," Genealogy folder, box 1, Ward Family Papers, 1807–1945, BHC; Hurlbut, *Grandmother's Stories*, 23–26; Bancroft, "Memoir of Capt. Samuel Ward," 337.

9 "Family Record," Genealogy folder, box 1, Ward Family Papers, 1807–1945, BHC; Eber Ward Sr. to Daniel Hubbel, July 13, 1817, Eber B. Ward Family Papers, folder 2, Correspondence, 1807–1829, box 1, EBW-Clarke.

10 The key source for Eber's time in Kentucky and for each quotation is Eber Ward Sr. to Daniel Hubbel, July 13, 1817, Eber B. Ward Family Papers, folder 2, Correspondence, 1807–1829, box 1, EBW-Clarke. Other sources used include "Family Record," Genealogy folder, box 1, Ward Family Papers, 1807–1945, BHC.

11 Boyer, *The Enduring Vision*, 301–2.

12 Korn, "Eber Brock Ward, Pathfinder of American Industry," 15–16; Hurlbut, *Grandmother's Stories*, 43–53; "Family Record," Genealogy folder, box 1, Ward Family Papers, 1807–1945, BHC; Shinn, "Captain Eber Brock Ward, Ironmaster of the West," 8–9; Bancroft, "Aunt Emily Ward," 367. Driving in a car today from Wells, Vermont, to Lexington, Kentucky, with a stop in Rochester, New York, would take thirteen hours and forty minutes and cover 850 miles, according to https://mapquest.com, accessed June 11, 2017.

13 The quotations are from Hurlbut, *Grandmother's Stories*, 50. Other sources include "Family Record," Genealogy folder, box 1, Ward Family Papers, 1807–1945, BHC; Korn, "Eber Brock Ward, Pathfinder of American Industry," 16–17; Hurlbut, *Grandmother's Stories*, 49–58.

14 Bancroft, "Aunt Emily Ward," 368; Jones, "Miss Emily Ward," 581; Hurlbut, *Grandmother's Stories*, 49–58, 60; "Family Record," Genealogy folder, box 1, Ward Family Papers, 1807–1945, BHC; Korn, "Eber Brock Ward, Pathfinder of American Industry," 17–18; Shinn, "Captain Eber Brock Ward, Ironmaster of the West," 8; Stewart, "Incidents in the Life of Mr. Eber Ward."

15 Various sources spell Elizabeth Ward's maiden name differently. These include Lammerson, Lambertson, and Lamberson. Lamberson appears most often in the sources; therefore this spelling is used in the text. The *Salem Packet* was most likely built in 1816, but not licensed until 1819. For more information, see "79-Salem Packet," Eber Brock Ward, box 1, folder 31, Research Notes: vol. 14, vessels owned by Ward family, BGSU-Hall; Bancroft, "Memoir of Capt. Samuel Ward," 337–39; Andreas, *History of St. Clair County*, 404, 687–89; Korn, "Eber Brock Ward, Pathfinder of American Industry," 14–15, 18–20; Shinn, "Captain Eber Brock Ward, Ironmaster of the West," 9–10; Stewart, "Incidents in the Life of Mr. Eber Ward"; "Family Record," BHC.

16 The first quotation is from Hurlbut, *Grandmother's Stories*, 70; the others are from Eber Ward to his children, November 4, 1820, Eber B. Ward Family Papers, folder 2, Correspondence, 1807–1829, box 1, EBW-Clarke. Other sources include Stewart, "Incidents in the Life of Mr. Eber Ward"; "Family Record," Genealogy folder, box 1, Ward Family Papers, 1807–1945, BHC.

17 Samuel Ward initially called the community along the St. Clair River Yankee Point; for a short time it was referred to as Ward's Landing. Some referred to the area as Cottrellville as it was located near Cottrellville Township. Today it is Marine City. It was commonly known as Newport until the 1860s, and Ward family correspondence in this era refers to the community most often by that name, so usually it will be referred to as Newport in the text. Jenks, *St. Clair County*, 1:111–12, 259, 303; Bancroft, "Memoir of Capt. Samuel Ward," 338–39; Korn, "Eber Brock Ward, Pathfinder of American Industry," 20–23; Shinn, "Captain Eber Brock Ward, Ironmaster of the West," 9–10.

18 The quotations are from Bancroft, "Memoir of Capt. Samuel Ward," 338. Other sources include McElroy, *A Short History of Marine City*, 6; Jenks, *St. Clair County*, 1:111, 112; Korn, "Eber Brock Ward, Pathfinder of American Industry," 21–24.

19 The quotation is from Andreas, *History of St. Clair County*, 689. Other sources include Jenks, *St. Clair County*, 1:112, 117, 132. Samuel Ward's ownership of a tavern is mentioned in "Notes," Ward, Samuel folder, WFC-MC. The "commodious" brick home built by Samuel Ward about 1832 is still standing. It is a private residence, and the exterior has been remodeled, but the original brick structure is easily recognizable. It is considered the oldest brick house north of Detroit and one of the five oldest houses still standing in Michigan. The exact date Samuel Ward's home was completed is unclear. William Bancroft argues that Ward "established a brick-yard, and in 1828 erected a commodious brick house of quite imposing proportions." See Bancroft, "Memoir of Capt. Samuel Ward," 338. Gene

and Scott Buel contend that it was built "around 1832." See Buel and Buel, *Images of America*, 10. Raymond Donahue argues Samuel Ward most likely finished his home in 1838 with bricks from his own brickyard. See Donahue, "Captain Samuel Ward," 31. A letter from Eber Ward Sr. dated June 7, 1829, might identify the year as 1829; he declared to his daughter Emily, "Your Uncle Saml. Has nearly finished his house." However, it is likely this referred to a different home built by Samuel. See Eber Ward to Emily Ward, June 7, 1829, Eber B. Ward Family Papers, folder 2, Correspondence, 1807–1829, box 1, EBW-Clarke. Possibly the best case for the 1832 date is found in McElroy, *A Short History of Marine City*, 8. Although the exact date is unclear, because the argument for the 1832 date appears to be the strongest, this was included in the text.

20 It is possible that Eber Ward Sr., along with Emily and Eber B., relocated to Newport in 1821, but it appears that the fall of 1822 is more likely. The quotation is from Hurlbut, *Grandmother's Stories*, 82. Other sources include Stewart, "Incidents in the Life of Mr. Eber Ward"; Korn, "Eber Brock Ward, Pathfinder of American Industry," 25–27; Shinn, "Captain Eber Brock Ward, Ironmaster of the West," 11.

21 The history of using hemlock in the tanning industry can be found in Canham, "Hemlock and Hide."

22 The quotation is from Stewart, "Incidents in the Life of Mr. Eber Ward," 472. Other sources include Korn, "Eber Brock Ward, Pathfinder of American Industry," 28–29; Hurlbut, *Grandmother's Stories*, 88–89.

23 Most sources argue that E. B. Ward began working for his uncle Samuel in 1823, when he was twelve years old. While it is true that E.B. did turn twelve in 1823, it was not until December of that year. Therefore, E.B. must have started working for his uncle while he was still eleven, in the summer of 1823. See Shinn, "Captain Eber Brock Ward, Ironmaster of the West," 11; Stark, *City of Destiny*, 352; Farmer, *History of Detroit*, 2:1234; William Downie Narrative, Ward, Eber folder, WFC-MC; Carlisle, *Chronography of Notable Events*, 242; "Capt. Eber Ward's Portrait Recalls Rich Saga of Early Industry," *Detroit News*, June 29, 1852. This last article was found in Local History Collection, Biography W-Y, vol. 2, Beacon Memorial District Library, Wyandotte, MI.

24 The quotation is from Bancroft, "Memoir of Capt. Samuel Ward," 339; another source is Stewart, "Recollections of Aura P. Stewart," 350. An additional description of the *St. Clair* is included in "75-St. Clair," Eber Brock Ward, box 1, folder 31, Research Notes: vol. 14, vessels owned by Ward family, BGSU-Hall.

25 The first quotation is from Burrows and Wallace, *Gotham*, 429; the second quotation is from Shaw, *Erie Water West*, 88. Other sources include Boyer, *The Enduring Vision*, 207; Burrows and Wallace, *Gotham*, 430–31. The celebration undertaken at the canal's completion is chronicled in Seelye, "Rational Exultation"; and Shaw, *Erie Water West*, 181–94.

26 The first quotation is taken from "Real Builders of America," 595; the second is from Ward, *The Autobiography of David Ward*, 35. The inconvenience of the low

bridges, which often drove passengers to remain in their cabins, is also described in Shaw, *Erie Water West*, 206. Other sources used include Korn, "Eber Brock Ward, Pathfinder of American Industry," 31–33; Shinn, "Captain Eber Brock Ward, Ironmaster of the West," 14, 15; Jenks, *St. Clair County*, 1:112; Bancroft, "Memoir of Capt. Samuel Ward," 339; Stewart, "Recollections of Aura P. Stewart," 350; Buel, and Buel, *Images of America*, 7.

27 The quotation is from Bancroft, "Memoir of Capt. Samuel Ward," 21, 340. Other sources include Korn, "Eber Brock Ward, Pathfinder of American Industry," 31–33; Shinn, "Captain Eber Brock Ward, Ironmaster of the West," 14, 15. The inflation-adjusted currency values are according to https://westegg.com/inflation/infl.cgi, accessed February 5, 2021.

28 Bancroft, "Memoir of Capt. Samuel Ward," 340; Korn, "Eber Brock Ward, Pathfinder of American Industry," 33–34; Shinn, "Captain Eber Brock Ward, Ironmaster of the West," 15.

29 Boyer, *The Enduring Vision*, 257–63.

30 Census data is found in Dunbar and May, *Michigan*, 675.

31 The quotation is from Jenks, *St. Clair County*, 1:269; "Timeline," Ward, Samuel folder, WFC-MC. Other sources include Andreas, *History of St. Clair County*, 689; Jones, "Miss Emily Ward," 581; Harrington, "Daniel B. Harrington," 141; Korn, "Eber Brock Ward, Pathfinder of American Industry," 34.

32 The quotation is from Carlisle, *Chronography of Notable Events*, 245. Other sources include Andreas, *History of St. Clair County*, 689; Jones, "Miss Emily Ward," 581. It is a bit unclear why Abba remained in Ohio while her sister Sally moved to Newport in 1826. She lived with the Thayer family and threw a fit when it was time for her to leave. See Lewis Thayer to Eber Ward, April 15, 1826, Eber B. Ward Family Papers, folder 2, Correspondence, 1807–1829, box 1, EBW-Clarke.

33 The quotations are from Hurlbut, *Grandmother's Stories*, 107. The full story is found in Hurlbut, *Grandmother's Stories*, 104–10; and Jones, "Miss Emily Ward," 584–86.

34 The quotations are from Hurlbut, *Grandmother's Stories*, 108.

35 Dunbar and May, *Michigan*, 138, 146–49.

36 The quotations are from Hurlbut, *Grandmother's Stories*, 98–99. The full story is found in Hurlbut, *Grandmother's Stories*, 97–103; and Jones, "Miss Emily Ward," 582–84. Other sources used include Stewart, "Incidents in the Life of Mr. Eber Ward," 473; Korn, "Eber Brock Ward, Pathfinder of American Industry," 34–36.

37 Eber Ward Sr.'s correspondence addresses his business activities in the late 1820s. The price of fish is discussed in Nathan Ward to Eber Ward, October 8, 1826; his attempt to be named lighthouse keeper is shown in John J. Deming to Eber Ward, January 31, 1829; collecting and selling wood is described in Eber Ward to Eber B. and Emily Ward, March 16, 1829; making potash for Captain Ward is covered in Eber Ward to Emily Ward, April 12, 1829. All letters are found in Ward Family Papers, folder 2, Correspondence, 1807–1829, box 1, EBW-Clarke. Other sources used include Korn, "Eber Brock Ward, Pathfinder of American Industry," 35–37; Shinn, "Captain Eber Brock Ward, Ironmaster of the West," 12.

38 The quotation is from Gamber, *The Female Economy*, 12. The word *milliner* derived from the earliest milliners, who sold fancy goods in sixteenth- and seventeenth-century Milan. Most milliners at that time were male; by the eighteenth century the profession was dominated by women. While it is slightly beyond the time period when Emily Ward was apprenticed in the millinery trade, it may be important to note that, by 1870, millinery and dressmaking ranked as the fourth most important occupational category for American women. For an additional source and more information, see Gamber, *The Female Economy*, 7, 12–15. The second quotation is from Maccabe, *Detroit City Directory, 1837*.

39 The first quotation is from Eber B. Ward to Eber Ward, December 22, 1828; the second is from Emily Ward to Sally Ward, January 1, 1829; another source is Eber B. Ward to Kezia (Ward) Lewis, November 28, 1828. All letters are found in Ward Family Papers, folder 2, Correspondence, 1807–1829, box 1, EBW-Clarke. Another letter that provides perspective on E. B. Ward's education and his short time in the varnishing trade is Eber Ward to Emily and Eber B. Ward, February 2, 1829, Detroit Historical Society, http://detroithistorical.pastperfectonline.com, accessed January 3, 2018.

40 The first quotation is from Emily Ward to Sally Ward, January 1, 1829; the second is from Eber Ward to Eber B. and Emily Ward, March 16, 1829, both in Ward Family Papers, folder 2, Correspondence, 1807–1829, box 1, EBW-Clarke.

41 In an era with phones, email, and instant text messaging, it may be difficult to comprehend the importance of the postal service, but during the era in which E. B. Ward was alive, it played a crucial role in enabling communication. The first quotation is from Eber B. Ward to Kezia (Ward) Lewis, November 28, 1828; the second is from Emily Ward to Eber Ward, December 22, 1828, both in Ward Family Papers, folder 2, Correspondence, 1807–1829, box 1, EBW-Clarke.

42 Hyde, *The Northern Lights*, 48, 98. Other sources include Stewart, "Incidents in the Life of Mr. Eber Ward," 473; "Family Record," Genealogy folder, box 1, Ward Family Papers, 1807–1945, BHC. Eber Ward's correspondence addresses the lighthouse position several times. See John J. Deming to Eber Ward, January 31, 1829; Thomas C. Sheldon to Eber Ward, March 20, 1829; Eber Ward to Eber B. and Emily Ward, March 16, 1829; Eber Ward to Emily Ward, April 12, 1829; Eber Ward to Emily Ward, June 7, 1829, all in Ward Family Papers, folder 2, Correspondence, 1807–1829, box 1, EBW-Clarke.

43 The first quotation is from Hyde, *The Northern Lights*, 60; the second is from Stewart, "Incidents in the Life of Mr. Eber Ward," 473; the final is from Eber Ward to Emily Ward, August 24, 1830, Ward Family Papers, folder 3, Correspondence, 1830–1832, box 1, EBW-Clarke.

44 The quotations are taken from S. Pleasanton to Treasury Department, April 29, 1835, Terry Pepper, "Keepers Instructions," available at http://www.terrypepper .com/lights/lists/instructions.htm, accessed July 7, 2017. Other sources include

Hyde, *The Northern Lights*, 48; the inflation-adjusted currency values are according to https://westegg.com/inflation/infl.cgi, accessed February 5, 2021; "Gill (Unit)," *Wikipedia*, https://en.wikipedia.org/wiki/Gill_(unit), accessed July 7, 2017.

45  The first quotation is from Eber Ward to Emily, Sally, and Abba Ward, July 10, 1830; the second quotation is from Eber Ward to Emily Ward, July 28, 1830; the third quotation is from Eber Ward to Emily Ward, November 4, 1831, all in Ward Family Papers, folder 3, Correspondence, 1830–1832, box 1, EBW-Clarke.

46  The first quotation is from Eber B. Ward to Emily Sally, and Abba Ward, June 8, 1831; the second is from Eber Ward to Emily Ward, July 28, 1830; the third is from Eber Ward to Emily Ward, March 6, 1831. Other sources include Eber Ward to Emily Ward January 23, 1831. All these letters are included in Ward Family Papers, folder 3, Correspondence, 1830–1832, box 1, EBW-Clarke. Another source is Hyde, *The Northern Lights*, 54.

47  The first quotation is from Korn, "Eber Brock Ward, Pathfinder of American Industry," 47; the second quotation is from Eber B. Ward to Emily, Sally, and Abba Ward, June 8, 1831; the third quotation is from Eber Ward to Emily Ward, July 7, 1831. The price of fish is discussed in, among others, Eber Ward to Emily Ward, July 28, 1830; Eber Ward to Emily Ward, October 6, 1830; Eber Ward to Emily Ward, October 31, 1830; Eber Ward to Emily Ward, May 31, 1831. Other sources include Eber Ward to Emily Ward August 4, 1831; Eber Ward to Emily Ward, October 27, 1831; Eber B. Ward to Emily Ward, November 20, 1831. All of these letters are in Ward Family Papers, folder 3, Correspondence, 1830–1832, box 1, EBW-Clarke.

48  Mr. Ward complains of missing mail and failed deliveries in the first months of his time on Bois Blanc Island. See Eber Ward to Emily Ward, July 30, 1830; Eber Ward to Emily Ward, August 14, 1830; Eber Ward to Emily Ward, August 24, 1830. The first set of quotations is from Eber Ward to Emily, Sally, and Abba Ward, July 10, 1830; the second set is from Eber Ward to Emily Ward, May 13, 1832. All of these letters are included in Ward Family Papers, folder 3, Correspondence, 1830–1832, box 1, EBW-Clarke. Stewart, "Incidents in the Life of Mr. Eber Ward," 473, mentions that mail delivery was "regular" once per month. An additional source is Korn, "Eber Brock Ward, Pathfinder of American Industry," 47.

49  The first quotation is from Eber Ward to Emily Ward, January 23, 1831, Ward Family Papers, folder 3, Correspondence, 1830–1832, box 1, EBW-Clarke; the second is from Kezia Ward to Eber Ward, June 20, 1827, Ward Family Papers, folder 2, Correspondence, 1807–1829, box 1, EBW-Clarke.

50  Information concerning *Godey's Lady's Book* is available at http://www.accessible-archives.com/collections/godeys-ladys-book/, accessed July 17, 2017; additional sources include Gamber, *The Female Economy*, 111, 135; Eber Ward to Emily Ward, April 5, 1831; Eber Ward to Emily Ward, May 27, 1831. Both letters are in Ward Family Papers, folder 3, Correspondence, 1830–1832, box 1, EBW-Clarke.

51 The first quotation is from Eber Ward to Emily, Sally, and Abba Ward, July 10, 1830; the second is from Eber Ward to Emily Ward April 5, 1831; the third is from Eber B. Ward to Emily, Sally, and Abba Ward, June 8, 1831, all in Ward Family Papers, folder 3, Correspondence, 1830–1832, box 1, EBW-Clarke.

52 The first quotation is from Eber Ward to Emily Ward, July 7, 1831; the second is from Eber B. Ward to Emily Ward, November 20, 1831. See also Eber Ward to Emily Ward, April 5, 1831. All of these letters are in Ward Family Papers, folder 3, Correspondence, 1830–1832, box 1, EBW-Clarke.

53 The first quotation is from Eber Ward to Emily Ward, January 16, 1831; the second is from Eber Ward to Emily Ward, July 7, 1831; the third is from Eber Ward to Emily Ward, November 12, 1830, all in Ward Family Papers, folder 3, Correspondence, 1830–1832, box 1, EBW-Clarke.

54 The first quotation is from Eber Ward to Emily Ward, August 4, 1831; the second is from Eber Ward to Emily Ward, November 12, 1830; the third is from Eber B. Ward to Emily, Sally, and Abba Ward, June 8, 1831, all in Ward Family Papers, folder 3, Correspondence, 1830–1832, box 1, EBW-Clarke.

# 2. From Protégé to Partner

1 The quotation is from Fuller, "An Introduction to the Settlement of Southern Michigan," 546. Another source is Dunbar and May, *Michigan*, 675.

2 Dunbar and May, *Michigan*, 178; Fuller, "An Introduction to the Settlement of Southern Michigan" 547. For the anxiety concerning how the Black Hawk War might influence immigration, see A. Dart to Eber Ward, June 21, 1832, Ward Family Papers, folder 3, Correspondence, 1830–1832, box 1, EBW-Clarke.

3 The quotations are from Eber Ward to Emily Ward, July 12, 1832, Ward Family Papers, folder 3, Correspondence, 1830–1832, box 1, EBW-Clarke. Other sources include Dunbar and May, *Michigan*, 178–79; Fuller, "Settlement of Michigan Territory," 33, 34; Fuller, "An Introduction to the Settlement of Southern Michigan," 547. It was not uncommon for individuals to flock to the country, if they were able, to avoid a cholera outbreak. B. F. Cozens, a friend of Eber B. Ward, worked in New York when the disease spread to the city. He wrote, "As soon as the cholera became alarming in New York, I took my leave," instead enjoying "the pure and wholesome area of the country." When the cholera had run its course, he returned to the city, "which was crowded with citizens returning to their homes who had fled like myself to avoid the disease and were now returning to mourn the loss of friends." A "gloom and dread" spread over the city where previously "the hum & jostle of the business would be so great that it would be difficult" to travel the streets. For more information, see B. F. Cozens to Eber B. Ward, October 12, 1832, Ward Family Papers, folder 3, Correspondence, 1830–1832, box 1, EBW-Clarke.

4 The first quotation is from Dunbar and May, *Michigan*, 675; the statistics concerning population and land sales, as well as the profile of migrants, are also from that source, 164–69. The second quotation is from Eber B. Ward to Eber

and Emily Ward, June 18, 1836, Ward Family Papers, folder 4, Correspondence, 1833–1837, box 1, EBW-Clarke. Another source is Fuller, "An Introduction to the Settlement of Southern Michigan," 547, 556.

5  Fuller, "An Introduction to the Settlement of Southern Michigan," 547, 556; Dunbar and May, *Michigan*, 164. For the land rush and periodic closures at the Kalamazoo Land Office, see Gray, *The Yankee West*, 43–46.

6  Korn, "Eber Brock Ward, Pathfinder of American Industry," 38–40; Donahue, "Captain Samuel Ward," 39, 40; Shinn, "Captain Eber Brock Ward, Ironmaster of the West," 15; Jenks, *St. Clair County*, 1:405; Eber B. Ward to Eber Ward, February 16, 1837, Ward Family Papers, folder 4, Correspondence, 1833–1837, box 1, EBW-Clarke. The inflation-adjusted currency values are according to https://westegg.com/inflation/infl.cgi, accessed February 6, 2021. Detailed descriptions of Samuel Ward's schooners are included in "23-Elizabeth Ward," "33-General Harrison," "48-Marshall Ney," "75-St. Clair," "Albatross," all in Eber Brock Ward, box 1, folder 31, Research Notes: vol. 14, vessels owned by Ward family, BGSU-Hall. While Hall does not include the schooner *Albatross* in his tabulation of vessels owned by Ward because Samuel Ward may not have been its owner, several sources indicate the ship was built at Marine City (then known as Newport) and operated by Samuel Ward.

7  In his biographical study of Samuel Ward, Donovan uses the phrase "mentally incompetent" to describe Samuel Ward's son Jacob Harrison, but fails to offer any additional detail. See Donahue, "Captain Samuel Ward," 63. Korn writes (incorrectly) that Jacob Harrison was "a sickly lad who died at an early age." See Korn, "Eber Brock Ward, Pathfinder of American Industry," 39. Other sources include Stewart, "Recollections of Aura P. Stewart," 349; Korn, "Eber Brock Ward, Pathfinder of American Industry," 42–43; Shinn, "Captain Eber Brock Ward, Ironmaster of the West," 13–14; Donahue, "Captain Samuel Ward," 42.

8  The first quotation is from Eber B. Ward to Eber Ward, August 8, 1833; the second is from Samuel Ward's will and can be found in Donahue, "Captain Samuel Ward," 71. An additional source is Eber B. Ward to Emily Ward, June 18, 1836, both in Ward Family Papers, folder 4, Correspondence, 1833–1837, box 1, EBW-Clarke.

9  Eber Ward to Mr. Knapp, July 1, 1833; Eber B. Ward to Eber Ward, August 8, 1833, both in Ward Family Papers, folder 4, Correspondence, 1833–1837, box 1, EBW-Clarke.

10  The quotation is from Andreas, *History of St. Clair County*, 690. Other sources include Shinn, "Captain Eber Brock Ward, Ironmaster of the West," 16; Korn, "Eber Brock Ward, Pathfinder of American Industry," 43; Andreas, *History of St. Clair County*, 690.

11  The quotation is from Eber B. Ward to Eber and Emily Ward, June 18, 1836, Ward Family Papers, folder 4, Correspondence, 1833–1837, box 1, EBW-Clarke. Additional sources include Eber B. Ward to Eber Ward, July 29, 1836, Ward Family

Papers, folder 4, Correspondence, 1833–1837, box 1, EBW-Clarke; Shinn, "Captain Eber Brock Ward, Ironmaster of the West," 16–17.

12    The first quotation is from Eber B. Ward to Eber Ward, February 16, 1837; the second is from Ward, *The Autobiography of David Ward*, 39. Korn argues E.B. served as captain of the *General Harrison* beginning in 1833, but Eber Brock's correspondence places it at 1837. See Korn, "Eber Brock Ward, Pathfinder of American Industry," 43–44; Shinn, "Captain Eber Brock Ward, Ironmaster of the West," 17.

13    The quotation is from Eber B. Ward to Eber and Emily Ward, January 18, 1838. Other references to Samuel Ward's health and the status of his marriage are found in Eber B. Ward to Eber Ward, February 18, 1838; and Eber B. Ward to Eber Ward, December 26, 1838. All correspondence from Ward Family Papers, folder 5, Correspondence, 1838–1839, box 1, EBW-Clarke.

14    The quotations are from Eber B. Ward to Eber Ward, May 15, 1837, Ward Family Papers, folder 4, Correspondence, 1833–1837, box 1, EBW-Clarke.

15    E. B. Ward to E. Ward, August 6, 1837, Ward Family Papers, folder 4, Correspondence, 1833–1837, box 1, EBW-Clarke.

16    The quotations are from "Captain Eber Remembers: The Loss of the Schooner Harrison," 1837(?), Ward Family Papers, folder 4, Correspondence, 1833–1837, box 1, EBW-Clarke. The same story is also included in Hurlbut, *Grandmother's Stories*, 156–62.

17    "Captain Eber Remembers"; Hurlbut, *Grandmother's Stories*, 156–62. Not all the freight on the *General Harrison* was a total loss. E.B. salvaged as much as he could, and even repacked and salted some barrels of fish. He describes this in a letter to his father: Eber B. Ward to Eber Ward, December 18, 1837, Ward Family Papers, folder 4, Correspondence, 1833–1837, box 1, EBW-Clarke.

18    The quotation is from Eber B. Ward to Eber Ward, May 15, 1837. Additional sources include Eber B. Ward to Eber Ward, August 8, 1833; Sally W. Brindle and Abba Ward to Eber Ward, December 3, 1833; all from Ward Family Papers, folder 4, Correspondence, 1833–1837, box 1, EBW-Clarke. Another source is "Melchiah Brindle," https://www.findagrave.com/memorial/128780551/melchiah-brindle, accessed June 21, 2018.

19    The first quotation is from Eber B. Ward to Eber Ward, June 1, 1839; the second is from Eber B. Ward to Emily Ward, June 17, 1839; other sources include M. Brindle to Eber and Emily Ward, December 8, 1838—all from Ward Family Papers, folder 5, Correspondence, 1838–1839, box 1, EBW-Clarke. For the use of calomel in the nineteenth century, see Jennifer Schmid, "Beautiful Black Poison," last modified April 2, 2009, https://www.westonaprice.org/health-topics/environmental-toxins/beautiful-black-poison/, accessed June 21, 2018. Emily later declared that her sister "Sally died insane, the disease having developed in her at about the age of thirty years." See "Ward's Will," *Detroit Free Press*, October 16, 1875, 1.

20 The quotation is from Eber B. Ward to E. Ward, September 26, 1841. Other sources include Eber B. Ward to Eber Ward, September 30, 1841; E. B. Ward to Eber Ward, October 21, 1841; Abba Owen to Eber Ward, October 23, 1841; Eber B. Ward to Eber Ward, November 4, 1841; all correspondence taken from Ward Family Papers, folder 6, Correspondence, 1840–1841, box 1, EBW-Clarke. Other sources include Eber Ward to Emily Ward, February 3, 1834, Ward Family Papers, folder 4, Correspondence, 1833–1837, box 1, EBW-Clarke; "Abba Owen," https://www .findagrave.com/memorial/47167552/abba-owen, accessed June 21, 2018.

21 Hurlbut, *Grandmother's Stories*, 111–13; Orson Brooks to Emily Ward, May 5, 1836; O. Brooks to Capt. Eber Ward, September 27, 1836, both from Ward Family Papers, folder 4, Correspondence, 1833–1837, box 1, EBW-Clarke. In a reply to one of Emily's letters, Orson Brooks comments on Emily's "plan of rearing & educating children." See Orson Brooks to Emily Ward, July 16, 1838, Ward Family Papers, folder 5, Correspondence, 1838–1839, box 1, EBW-Clarke. The marriage statistic is from and Ruggles, "Historical Trends in Marriage Formation," 85.

22 The quotations are from Hurlbut, *Grandmother's Stories*, 123–24; other sources include Eber Ward to Abraham Wendell, September 17, 1837, Ward Family Papers, folder 4, Correspondence, 1833–1837, box 1, EBW-Clarke; Hyde, *The Northern Lights*, 67.

23 The quotation is from Eber Ward to Abraham Wendell, December 12, 1837, Ward Family Papers, folder 4, Correspondence, 1833–1837, box 1, EBW-Clarke. See also Hyde, *The Northern Lights*, 98.

24 Eber B. Ward to Emily Ward, June 17, 1839, Ward Family Papers, folder 5, Correspondence, 1838–1839, box 1, EBW-Clarke.

25 Orson Brooks to Emily Ward, July 4, 1839, Ward Family Papers, folder 5, Correspondence, 1838–1839, box 1, EBW-Clarke.

26 The quotation is from Welter, "The True Cult of Womanhood," 152; an additional source is Bancroft, "Aunt Emily Ward," 369.

27 The quotation is from Ward, *The Autobiography of David Ward*, 145. David Ward's complimentary description of Polly is interesting as he rarely has positive words to say about anyone in his autobiography. Additional sources include United States Census, 1860, Wayne County, Michigan, 51, https://www.ancestry .com/, accessed May 19, 2017; Farrand, "St. Clair County. Reminiscences," 564; "Mary 'Polly' McQueen Ward," https://www.findagrave.com, accessed June 22, 2018; Eber B. Ward to Eber Ward, February 1, 1840, Ward Family Papers, folder 6, Correspondence, 1840–1841, box 1, EBW-Clarke. There is some question as to whether Eber and Polly married in 1837 or 1838; the former is most likely. The Wikipedia entry on Eber Brock Ward identifies the date of his marriage as July 24, 1837. See "Eber Brock Ward," https://en.wikipedia.org, accessed June 23, 2018. Shinn argues he married in 1837 (see Shinn, "Captain Eber Brock Ward, Ironmaster of the West," 18), while Korn contends he married in 1838 (see Korn, "Eber Brock Ward, Pathfinder of American Industry," 52–53). David Ward writes, "E.B. was about twenty-five or twenty-six years of age at the time of his

marriage," which would indicate he married in 1837 or 1838. See Ward, *The Autobiography of David Ward*, 38–39, 145.

28  The first quotation is from Ward, *The Autobiography of David Ward*, 39; the second is from Eber B. Ward to Eber Ward, February 1, 1840, Ward Family Papers, folder 6, Correspondence, 1840–1841, box 1, EBW-Clarke. See also Korn, "Eber Brock Ward, Pathfinder of American Industry," 52–53. Unfortunately, it is difficult to provide much insight into Ward's first marriage. Either he did not mention her much in his correspondence, or the bulk of their correspondence has not survived.

29  The "Whig ticket" quote is taken from Eber B. Ward to Eber and Emily Ward, November 10, 1837, Ward Family Papers, folder 4, Correspondence, 1833–1837, box 1, EBW-Clarke. See also Shinn, "Captain Eber Brock Ward, Ironmaster of the West," 18.

30  Gray, *The Yankee West*, 43–46; Dunbar and May, *Michigan*, 221–24.

31  The quotation is from Gray, *The Yankee West*, 45. Other sources include Felch, "Early Banks and Banking in Michigan"; Utley, "The Wild Cat Banking System in Michigan"; Dunbar and May, *Michigan*, 221–24. An interview produced by Michigan Public Radio with Mark Harvey from the Michigan History Center provides insight into Michigan's "wild cat" banks. See "In Earliest Years of Michigan Statehood, Unregulated 'Wildcat Banks' Ran Wild," April 19, 2017, http://michiganradio.org/post/earliest-years-michigan-statehood-unregulated-wildcat-banks-ran-wild, accessed June 24, 2018.

32  The first quotation is from Eber B. Ward to Eber Ward, February 18, 1838; the second is from Eber B. Ward to Eber Ward, April 2, 1838. References to the lack of specie, or currency, are included in E. B. Ward to E. Ward, August 6, 1837; J. B. Watrous to Eber Ward, October 27, 1837, which can be found in Ward Family Papers, folder 4, Correspondence, 1833-1837, box 1, EBW-Clarke; and Eber B. Ward to Eber Ward, April 2, 1838; Eber B. Ward to Eber Ward, December 26, 1838, Ward Family Papers, folder 5, Correspondence, 1838-1839, box 1, EBW-Clarke.

33  The quotation is from Bancroft, "Memoir of Capt. Samuel Ward," 348–49. See also Korn, "Eber Brock Ward, Pathfinder of American Industry," 68–69.

34  The quotation is from Eber B. Ward to Eber Ward, November 5, 1838, Ward Family Papers, folder 5, Correspondence, 1838–1839, box 1, EBW-Clarke. See also Howe, *What Hath God Wrought*, 546; Wilentz, *The Rise of American Democracy*, 421; Morris, *The Tycoons*, 7.

35  Eber B. Ward to Eber Ward, June 25, 1840, Ward Family Papers, folder 6, Correspondence, 1840–1841, box 1, EBW-Clarke.

36  The first quotation is from Eber B. Ward to Eber Ward, February 1, 1840; the second is from Eber B. Ward to Eber Ward, October 11, 1840, both in Ward Family Papers, folder 6, Correspondence, 1840–1841, box 1, EBW-Clarke.

37  An excellent profile of Oliver Newberry is found in Catlin, "Oliver Newberry." Additionally, The *Detroit City Directory* for 1837 lists Oliver Newberry & Co. as

forwarding and commission merchants operating at 16 Woodbridge Street, and Newbury is listed as the managing owner of two steamboats (*Michigan* and *Niagara*), one brig (*Manhattan*), and four schooners (*Austerlitz*, *Napoleon*, *Marango*, and *Lodi*). See Maccabe, *Detroit City Directory, 1837*, 67, 101–2. Other sources include Korn, "Eber Brock Ward, Pathfinder of American Industry," 45–46; Donahue, "Captain Samuel Ward," 43; Dunbar and May, *Michigan*, 159.

38 The quotations are from Eber B. Ward to Eber Ward, February 18, 1838, Ward Family Papers, folder 5, Correspondence, 1838–1839, box 1, EBW-Clarke. See also Shinn, "Captain Eber Brock Ward, Ironmaster of the West," 20; Korn, "Eber Brock Ward, Pathfinder of American Industry," 51–52; Donahue, "Captain Samuel Ward," 43–44.

39 The quotation is from Eber B. Ward to Eber Ward December 26, 1838; another source is E. B. Ward to E. Ward, November 27, 1838, both in Ward Family Papers, folder 5, Correspondence, 1838–1839, box 1, EBW-Clarke. The investors in the *Huron* were Samuel Ward, Eber B. Ward, Amasa Rust, Zael Ward, and Sanborn & Gillette, each was from St. Clair County, Michigan. An additional investor was the Detroit Iron Company of Detroit. See "37-Huron," Eber Brock Ward, box 1, folder 31, Research Notes: vol. 14, vessels owned by Ward family, BGSU-Hall.

40 For the inflation-adjusted currency values of Eber's assets, see https://westegg .com/inflation/infl.cgi, accessed February 6, 2021. The first quotation is from Eber B. Ward to Eber Ward, February 1, 1840; the second is from Eber B. Ward to Emily Ward, March 28, 1840; another source is Eber B. Ward to Eber Ward, May 17, 1840. All letters are from Ward Family Papers, folder 6, Correspondence, 1840–1841, box 1, EBW-Clarke.

41 The quotations are all from Eber B. Ward to Eber Ward, February 1, 1840, Ward Family Papers, folder 6, Correspondence, 1840–1841, box 1, EBW-Clarke. Another source is Korn, "Eber Brock Ward, Pathfinder of American Industry," 52.

42 The quotation is from Eber B. Ward to Eber Ward, June 25, 1840, Ward Family Papers, folder 6, Correspondence, 1840–1841, box 1, EBW-Clarke. Korn argues Samuel Ward's fortune exceeded $300,000 by the early 1840s. See Korn, "Eber Brock Ward, Pathfinder of American Industry," 56.

43 The first quotation is from Eber Ward to Emily Ward, February 3, 1834; the second is from Eber B. Ward to Eber Ward, July 18, 1852, both from Ward Family Papers, folder 8, Correspondence, 1850–1875, box 1, EBW-Clarke.

44 The first quotation is from von Gerstner, *Early American Railroads*, 415. Other sources include "37-Huron," BGSU-Hall; Jenks, *St. Clair County*, 1:405; von Gerstner, *Early American Railroads*, 415–16.

45 The first quotation is from Eber B. Ward to Eber Ward, June 6, 1840; the second is from Eber B. Ward to Eber Ward, August 13, 1840, both in Ward Family Papers, folder 6, Correspondence, 1840–1841, box 1, EBW-Clarke; the third is from Stiles, *The First Tycoon*, 68–69. Other sources include Eber B. Ward to Eber Ward, June 25, 1840, Ward Family Papers, folder 6, Correspondence, 1840–1841, box 1, EBW-Clarke.

46 Details of the Lake Steamboat Association are discussed in von Gerstner, *Early American Railroads*, 421–23; Hilton, *Lake Michigan Passenger Steamers*, 29–33; Stone, *Floating Palaces of the Great Lakes*, 74.

47 The quotation is from "The Poor Boy a Millionaire," *Daily Cleveland Herald*, October 4, 1856, 1. The payout of $10,000 is not included in the ledgers for the *Huron*, but is addressed in several sources, including Korn, "Eber Brock Ward, Pathfinder of American Industry," 53–54; Donahue, "Captain Samuel Ward," 47–48; Andreas, *History of St. Clair County*, 690; "37-Huron," BGSU-Hall. Emeline Jenks Crampton also mentions the payout, but argues that it was $15,000. See Crampton, *History of the Saint Clair River*, 34. The inflation-adjusted currency values are according to https://westegg.com/inflation/infl.cgi, accessed February 6, 2021. The Hudson River Steamboat Association and the payout to Cornelius Vanderbilt are discussed in Stiles, *The First Tycoon*, 99–103.

48 The first quotation is from Eber B. Ward to Eber Ward, August 13, 1840; the second is from Eber B. Ward to Eber Ward, November 5, 1841; the third is from Eber B. Ward to Eber Ward, October 6, 1841. An additional source is E. B. Ward to Eber Ward, October 21, 1841. All these letters are in Ward Family Papers, folder 6, Correspondence, 1840–1841, box 1, EBW-Clarke. Additional sources include Shinn, "Captain Eber Brock Ward, Ironmaster of the West," 22; Korn, "Eber Brock Ward, Pathfinder of American Industry," 55; Donahue, "Captain Samuel Ward," 48. Light ships are described in "Huron Lightship," https://www.phmuseum.org/huron-lightship/, accessed June 1, 2019. The inflation-adjusted currency values are according to https://westegg.com/inflation/infl.cgi, accessed February 6, 2021. The figures on the *Huron*'s dividends are found in Ledger Private Accounts, 1849–1866, 18, Eber Brock Ward Papers, 1848–1875, BHC.

49 Ledger Private Accounts, 1849–1866, 58, Eber Brock Ward Papers, 1848–1875, BHC; Bancroft, "Memoir of Capt. Samuel Ward," 340; Stone, *Floating Palaces of the Great Lakes*, 70; Hilton, *Lake Michigan Passenger Steamers*, 35–36; Elliott, *Red Stacks over the Horizon*, 15–16.

50 The quotations are from Eber B. Ward to Miss Emily Ward, June 13, 1842, Ward Family Papers, folder 7, Correspondence, 1842–1849, box 1, EBW-Clarke; an additional source is Hilton, *Lake Michigan Passenger Steamers*, 35.

51 The quotation is from Eber B. Ward to Eber Ward, August 13, 1842, Ward Family Papers, folder 7, Correspondence, 1842–1849, box 1, EBW-Clarke; an additional source is Wellings, *Detroit City Directory, 1846*, 161.

52 The quotations are from Burr, "Navigation vs. Banking," 652; another source is Shinn, "Captain Eber Brock Ward, Ironmaster of the West," 22.

53 Burr, "Navigation vs. Banking," 653.

54 The quotation is from Eber B. Ward to Eber Ward, December 28, 1841. The "Powder Plot" is also described in Eber B. Ward to Eber Ward, October 29, 1841, and December 16, 1841. All letters can be found in Ward Family Papers, folder 6, Correspondence, 1840–1841, box 1, EBW-Clarke. Unfortunately, the only source for

this attempt on the lives of Eber and Samuel comes from Eber's correspondence, so the motivation for this conflict is unclear, but it does appear to be significant.

55 The quotation is from Eber B. Ward to Eber Ward, October 29, 1841, Ward Family Papers, folder 6, Correspondence, 1840–1841, box 1, EBW-Clarke. Another source is an additional note written by Samuel Ward. Although this appears to be dated January 2, 1842, it can also be found in the 1840–1841 correspondence. An interesting comment from the transcriber (identified only as C.L.S.) appears with Samuel's note. "The above is the only thing I have found in Samuel Ward's hand. It is almost illegible, but I have tried very hard to reproduce it exactly and believe I have succeeded. It evidently took nothing less than an attempt on the old man's life to spur him to letter writing!"

56 *Huron* Ledger, 1844, Samuel Ward Papers, BHC. Sean Marshall, one of the librarians at the BHC, deserves a big thank-you for locating this ledger. Driving in a car from Detroit to Port Huron would take one hour and five minutes and cover 63 miles; driving in a car from Detroit to Goderich, Ontario, would take two hours and fifty minutes and cover 139 miles, according to https://mapquest.com, accessed July 2, 2018.

57 *Huron* Ledger, 1844, Samuel Ward Papers, BHC.

58 Ibid.

59 Ibid. The *Huron* Ledger is a great resource. Unfortunately, at times it is difficult to read the handwriting. Any mistakes in deciphering the handwriting, or in the calculation of receipts, are the author's alone.

60 Ledger Private Accounts, 1849–1866, 18, Eber Brock Ward Papers, 1848–1875, BHC. The inflation-adjusted currency values are according to https://westegg.com/inflation/infl.cgi, accessed February 6, 2021.

## 3. Steamboat Kings

1 Eber mentions work on a new boat in Eber B. Ward to Eber Ward, August 13, 1842; Eber B. Ward to Eber Ward, December 25, 1842; Eber B. Ward to Eber Ward, January 21, 1843, all in, Ward Family Papers, folder 7, Correspondence, 1842–1849, box 1, EBW-Clarke. Additional sources include "13-Champion," Eber Brock Ward, box 1, folder 31, Research Notes: vol. 14, vessels owned by Ward family, BGSU-Hall; Korn, "Eber Brock Ward, Pathfinder of American Industry," 54–55, 59; Donahue, "Captain Samuel Ward," 47–48; "The Poor Boy a Millionaire," *Daily Cleveland Herald*, October 1, 1856, 1.

2 *Detroit Daily Advertiser*, July 26, 1844, 1, found in "13-Champion," Eber Brock Ward, box 1, folder 31, Research Notes: vol. 14, vessels owned by Ward family, BGSU-Hall. Data concerning the earnings of the *Champion* are found in Ledger Private Accounts, 1849–1866, 19, Eber Brock Ward Papers, 1848–1875, BHC. Other sources include *Detroit Free Press*, April 2, 1851, 1. The inflation-adjusted currency values are according to https://westegg.com/inflation/infl.cgi, accessed February 7, 2021.

3 "19-Detroit," "61-Pacific," "77-St. Louis," and "80-Samuel Ward," all in Eber Brock Ward, box 1, folder 31, Research Notes: vol. 14, vessels owned by Ward family, BGSU-Hall.

4 The quotation is from *Detroit Free Press*, May 19, 1846, 2. Other sources include Korn, "Eber Brock Ward, Pathfinder of American Industry," 60–61; Dunbar and May, *Michigan*, 251–53; Whittlesey, *Ancient Mining on the Shores of Lake Superior*, 4; *Detroit Free Press*, March 1, 1850, 2.

5 The quotation is from Stone, *Floating Palaces of the Great Lakes*, 84, 85; another source is "6-Atlantic," Eber Brock Ward, box 1, folder 31, Research Notes: vol. 14, vessels owned by Ward family, BGSU-Hall.

6 Chapter 7 of Joel Stone's excellent study of palace steamers describes this short-lived era well. See Stone, *Floating Palaces of the Great Lakes*, 117–30.

7 The quotation is from *Detroit Free Press*, May 30, 1849, 2; another source is E. B. Ward, "Steamer Atlantic," *Detroit Free Press*, September 1, 1852, 2; "6-Atlantic," Eber Brock Ward, box 1, folder 31, Research Notes: vol. 14, vessels owned by Ward family, BGSU-Hall.

8 "4-Arctic," "12-Caspian," "59-Ocean," Eber Brock Ward, box 1, folder 31, Research Notes: vol. 14, vessels owned by Ward family, BGSU-Hall. An additional source is McElroy, *A Short History of Marine City*, 10–11, 36.

9 The quotation is from Bancroft, "Memoir of Capt. Samuel Ward," 345. Additional sources include Stone, *Floating Palaces of the Great Lakes*, 121; Crampton, *History of the St. Clair River*, 39; Andreas, *History of St. Clair County, Michigan*, 689; Korn, "Eber Brock Ward, Pathfinder of American Industry," 61; McElroy, *A Short History of Marine City*, 10–11, 38, 42. The inflation-adjusted currency values are according to https://westegg.com/inflation/infl.cgi, accessed February 7, 2021.

10 The first quotation is from Jenks, *St. Clair County*, 1:304; the second is from Bancroft, "Memoir of Capt. Samuel Ward," 349. Additional sources include Korn, "Eber Brock Ward, Pathfinder of American Industry," 60; Shinn, "Captain Eber Brock Ward, Ironmaster of the West," 36, 37.

11 The estimate of one cord of wood consumed every four miles is for the steamboat *Erie*. See Klein, "Notes on the Steam Navigation," 301. The quotation is from Eber B. Ward to Eber Ward, January 7, 1842, Ward Family Papers, folder 7, Correspondence, 1842–1849, box 1, EBW-Clarke.

12 Korn, "Eber Brock Ward, Pathfinder of American Industry," 62–66; Shinn, "Captain Eber Brock Ward, Ironmaster of the West," 26, 27.

13 Wellings, *Detroit City Directory, 1846*, 159.

14 *Detroit City Directory, 1850*, 68.

15 "The Poor Boy a Millionaire," *Daily Cleveland Herald*, October 4, 1856, 1.

16 J. W. Brooks to E. B. Ward, January 8, 1848, Eber Brock Ward Papers, 1848–1875, Ward, Eber Brock, 1848–1865 folder, BHC.

17 The *Detroit City Directory* for 1852–53 includes an entry for Eber Ward's business office. It reads, "WARD, EBER B. steamboat office, M.C.R.R. Depot." See *Shove's Detroit City Directory, 1852–53*, 224. It is possible that Eber moved to

Detroit very late in 1849. Although Emily mentions that Eber has purchased a home for $6,000 and will be moving to Detroit, it's possible that he did not actually relocate until 1850. See Emily Ward to Melchiah Brindle, November 16, 1849, Ward Family Papers, folder 7, Correspondence, 1842–1849, box 1, EBW-Clarke.

18  Ledger Private Accounts, 1849–1866, 22, 28–29, 64, 65, Eber Brock Ward Papers, 1848–1875, BHC; Korn, "Eber Brock Ward, Pathfinder of American Industry," 59. The inflation-adjusted currency values are according to https://westegg.com/inflation/infl.cgi, accessed February 7, 2021.

19  Ledger Private Accounts, 1849–1866, 28–29, 66–67, Eber Brock Ward Papers, 1848–1875, BHC. The joint holdings of Eber and Samuel in 1851 were $451,500. The inflation-adjusted currency values are according to https://westegg.com/inflation/infl.cgi, accessed February 8, 2021.

20  The first quotation is from Eber B. Ward to Emily Ward, October 18, 1840, Ward Family Papers, folder 6, Correspondence, 1840–1841, box 1, EBW-Clarke. The second quotation is from John van Wyhe, "George Combe (1788–1858) Phrenologist & Natural Philosopher," Victorian Web, http://www.victorianweb.org/science/phrenology/combe.html, last modified January 6, 2017, accessed July 31, 2018. Other sources include John van Wyhe, "The History of Phrenology on the Web," http://www.historyofphrenology.org.uk/overview.htm, accessed July 31, 2018.

21  Eber B. Ward to Emily Ward, October 18, 1840, Ward Family Papers, folder 6, Correspondence, 1840–1841, box 1, EBW-Clarke.

22  The first set of quotations is from Eber B. Ward to Eber Ward, December 25, 1842; the second is from Eber B. Ward to Emily Ward, January 1, 1843, both in Ward Family Papers, folder 7, Correspondence, 1842–1849, box 1, EBW-Clarke.

23  Eber B. Ward to Eber Ward, January 9, 1850, Ward Family Papers, folder 8, Correspondence, 1850–1875, box 1, EBW-Clarke.

24  The first quotation is from Eber B. Ward to Emily Ward, January 1, 1843, Ward Family Papers, folder 7, Correspondence, 1842–1849, box 1, EBW-Clarke; the second is from E. B. Ward to J. W. Brooks, August 23, 1850, Ward Family Papers, folder 8, Correspondence to J. W. Burks [sic] August 23, 1850, box 1, EBW-Clarke. Other sources include Eber B. Ward to Eber Ward, December 25, 1842, Ward Family Papers, folder 7, Correspondence, 1842–1849, box 1, EBW-Clarke; Mansfield, *History of the Great Lakes*, 659.

25  The quotation is from Eber B. Ward to Eber Ward, December 25, 1842, Ward Family Papers, folder 7, Correspondence, 1842–1849, box 1, EBW-Clarke. Additional sources include Morris, *The Tycoons*, 8; Boyer, *The Enduring Vision*, 300–301.

26  The quotations are from Eber B. Ward to Emily Ward, January 1, 1843, Ward Family Papers, folder 7, Correspondence, 1842–1849, box 1, EBW-Clarke; another source is Mott, "William Duane Wilson," 362.

27   The quotation is from Eber B. Ward to Eber Ward, January 21, 1843, Ward Family Papers, folder 7, Correspondence, 1842–1849, box 1, EBW-Clarke. Eber Ward Sr.'s transfer from the Bois Blanc lighthouse to Fort Gratiot is addressed in Eber Ward to William Church, June 29, 1843; and Eber Ward to E. Brooks, September 1843, both in Ward Family Papers, folder 7, Correspondence, 1842–1849, box 1, EBW-Clarke.

28   Eber B. Ward to Emily Ward, March 28, 1840, Ward Family Papers, folder 6, Correspondence, 1840–1841, box 1, EBW-Clarke.

29   The first set of quotations is from Eber B. Ward to Emily Ward, January 1, 1840, Ward Family Papers, folder 6, Correspondence, 1840–1841, box 1, EBW-Clarke. The last quotation is from Eber B. Ward to Emily Ward, January 2, 1843, Ward Family Papers, folder 7, Correspondence, 1842-1849, box 1, EBW-Clarke.

30   Eber B. Ward letter to Eber Ward, January 9, 1850, Ward Family Papers, folder 8, Correspondence, 1850–1875, box 1, EBW-Clarke.

31   The "foolish" quotation is from Eber B. Ward to one of his sons, January 22, 1855, Ward Family Papers, folder 8, Correspondence, 1850–1875, box 1, EBW-Clarke.

32   The first quotation is from Stone, *Floating Palaces of the Great Lakes*, 124; the second quotation is from M.B., "Trial of Speed-Ocean and Empire State," *Detroit Free Press*, April 29, 1851, 2.

33   M.B., "Trial of Speed-Ocean and Empire State," *Detroit Free Press*, April 29, 1851, 2. Several additional articles in the *Detroit Free Press* addressed the contest between the *Ocean* and *Empire State*: April 22, 1851, 3; April 23, 1851, 3; April 24, 1851, 3; "The Ocean and Empire State," April 25, 1851, 3; April 26, 1851, 3; April 28, 1851, 3. See also Korn, "Eber Brock Ward, Pathfinder of American Industry," 266.

34   The quotations are from E. B. Ward, "Letter to the Editor," *Detroit Free Press*, April 23, 1851, 3. Additional sources are Metcalf, "Acknowledging the Corn"; Korn, "Eber Brock Ward, Pathfinder of American Industry," 267; "The Remarkable Family of Ward," 59–60.

35   Korn, "Eber Brock Ward, Pathfinder of American Industry," 267–68.

36   The quotation is from "The St. Louis," *Detroit Free Press*, December 15, 1852, 3; additional sources include *Detroit Free Press*, November 13, 1852, 3; "Steamboats and Steam Engines for Sale," *Detroit Free Press*, September 9, 1852, 3; "The Poor Boy a Millionaire," *Daily Cleveland Herald*, October 4, 1856, 1; *Grand River Times*, July 14, 1852, 2; Mansfield, *History of the Great Lakes*, 665–66; "12-Caspian" and "77-St. Louis," both from BGSU-Hall; Jenks, *St. Clair County*, 1:406.

37   The exact number of victims who died in the disaster will never be known for certain. Most contemporary sources put the figure at 250. The best single source covering the sinking of the *Atlantic* is by Justin Wargo, who cites 250 deaths, while noting that the range of estimates was between 131 and 400. See Wargo, "Awful Calamity!" 20, 27n. Mansfield argues the death toll was 131. See Mansfield, *History of the Great Lakes*, 665. Several newspapers across the nation covered the tragedy. The *New York Times* estimated 250 deaths: "Latest Intelligence," *New*

*York Times*, August 21, 1852, 2. The *National Era* reported 250 had died: "Steamboat Collision—Two Hundred and Fifty Lives Lost," August 26, 1852, 3. The *Wilmington Journal* stated that "not more than half" of the 550 passengers and crew was saved: "Awful Steamboat Disaster—At Least Two Hundred Lives Lost," *Wilmington Journal*, August 27, 1852, 2. The *Wisconsin Tribune* said, "We cannot believe the initial estimates" of 250 dead, believing the number was higher: "More of the Atlantic," *Wisconsin Tribune*, September 2, 1852, 2. The *Grand River Times* cited 250 lives lost in the incident: "If Papa Was Here," *Grand River Times*, October 6, 1852, 1. The *Vermont Watchman and State Journal* reported 250 deaths: "Terrible Steamboat Calamity—250 Lives Lost," *Vermont Watchman and State Journal*, August 26, 1852, 3. The *Wheeling Daily Intelligencer* estimated "some three hundred lives are lost": "Further Particulars of the Collision," *Wheeling Daily Intelligencer*, August 27, 1852, 2.

38 Wargo, "Awful Calamity!" 16–27. Some of the most thorough contemporary sources are "Frightful Accident. Steamboat Collision on Lake Erie," *New York Times*, August 21, 1852, 2; "Awful Calamity!" *Detroit Free Press*, August 21, 1852, 2; "Terrible Disaster," *Portage Sentinel*, August 8, 1852, 2.

39 The quotations are from "Amund O. Eidsmoe's Story of His Own Life," Norway-Heritage, http://www.norwayheritage.com/articles/templates/norwegian_settl.asp?articleid=32&zoneid=17, accessed July 9, 2018. Eidsmoe further remembered that when the panicked passengers in the steerage section of the *Atlantic* began to storm the deck, "The sailors became absolutely raving and tried to get as many killed as possible. When they saw that people crowded up they struck them on the heads and shoulders to drive them down again. When this did not help, they took and raised the stairway up on end so the people fell down backwards again. Then they jerked the ladder up on the deck. All hopes were gone for those that were underneath. Water filled the rooms and life was no more." While this may have been true, contemporary accounts do not describe the crew acting in this manner. Furthermore, while much of Eidsmoe's account is reinforced by the descriptions of others, this portion was not. An additional source is Wargo, "Awful Calamity," 18–19.

40 "The Latest from the Wreck," *New York Times*, August 21, 1852, 2.

41 The quotations are from "The Steamer Atlantic Catastrophe," *Daily American Telegraph*, August 25, 1852, 3. Additional sources include "The Catastrophe on Lake Erie," *New York Times*, August 23, 1852, 3; Wargo, "Awful Calamity," 22–23.

42 The first quotation is from "The Catastrophe on Lake Erie," *New York Times*, August 23, 1852, 3; the second quotation is from P. Homan, "The Lake Erie Catastrophe," *New York Times*, August 26, 1852, 4. Other sources include "The Lake Erie Disaster," *New York Times*, August 23, 1852, 2; "The Loss of the Atlantic," *Detroit Free Press*, August 23, 1852, 2; Wargo, "Awful Calamity," 23. The additional quotations are from Eber B. Ward to Mary Ward, August 23, 1852, Ward

Family Papers, folder 8, Correspondence, 1850–1875, box 1 EBW-Clarke. The transcribed letter is mistakenly dated May 23, 1852.

43　E. B. Ward, "Loss of the Steamer Atlantic," *Detroit Free Press*, August 28, 1852, 2.

44　Ellett H. Titus, "Steamer Atlantic," *Detroit Free Press*, August 31, 1852, 2.

45　E. B. Ward, "Steamer Atlantic," *Detroit Free Press*, September 1, 1852, 2.

46　Wargo, "Awful Calamity," 23–24; "Final Decision," *Grand Haven News*, March 23, 1859, 2.

47　Dickinson, *To Build a Canal*, xi; Dunbar and May, *Michigan*, 14, 259; Korn, "Eber Brock Ward, Pathfinder of American Industry," 81.

48　Neu, "The Building of the Sault Canal," 28; Williams, "The Chicago River and Harbor Convention, 1847," 608, 623–24; Fergus, *Chicago River and Harbor Convention*, 62.

49　Dickinson, *To Build a Canal*, 25–28; Chandler, *History of the St. Mary's Falls Ship Canal*, 5; Neu, "The Mineral Lands of the St. Mary's Falls Ship Canal Company," 164–65; Shinn, "Captain Eber Brock Ward, Ironmaster of the West," 41.

50　Dickinson, *To Build a Canal*, 45–58; Dunbar and May, *Michigan*, 260.

51　The first quotation is from Dickinson, *To Build a Canal*, 59. The following two are from White, "Sault Ste. Marie and the Canal Fifty Years Ago," 353. Additional sources include Beasley, *Freighters of Fortune*, 80–83; Korn, "Eber Brock Ward, Pathfinder of American Industry," 83–84; Shinn, "Captain Eber Brock Ward, Ironmaster of the West," 42–43.

52　Dickinson shows the weakness of Charles T. Harvey's leadership as well as other obstacles involved with construction. John W. Brooks of the Michigan Central Railroad eventually oversaw the successful completion of the project. See Dickinson, *To Build a Canal*, 59–120; Neu, "The Building of the Sault Canal," 31; Dunbar and May, *Michigan*, 3, 260–61. Statistics concerning usage of the Soo Locks today are found at "Soo Locks—A Wonder of Engineering and Human Ingenuity," https://www.saultstemarie.com/attractions/soo-locks/, accessed August 18, 2018.

53　Gara, *Westernized Yankee*, 154–74; p. 158 mentions the purchase of nearly fifty thousand acres of land on the Pere Marquette River for $200,000. Additional sources include *Catalogue of 525,000 Acres of Pine Timber Lands*, vii; Dickinson, *To Build a Canal*, 166; Neu, *Erastus Corning*, 158–59; Neu, "The Building of the Sault Canal," 46; Neu, "The Mineral Lands of the St. Mary's Falls Ship Canal Company," 180–81; Dunbar and May, *Michigan*, 261. The inflation-adjusted value of $200,000 in 1863 dollars is $4,046,048.23 in 2020, according to https://westegg.com/inflation/infl.cgi, accessed August 18, 2020.

54　The quotations are from Catalogue of 525,000 Acres of Pine Timber Lands, xix. Another source is Neu, "The Mineral Lands of the St. Mary's Falls Ship Canal Company," 45. The question of whether Ward received a "sweetheart deal" with the purchase is good one. The valuation of the Pere Marquette River property, according to the *Catalogue*, was $96,740. He ended up spending more than double the value ($200,000) as listed, leading to the conclusion he did not receive an advantage. However, as a stockholder in the company, he was required to pay only 27 percent of the amount he bid in cash. The rest could be paid in company stock, at $100 per share. While Ward was a stockholder, it is unclear how many shares he owned, or if he paid cash or in stock. If he did pay in stock, he had an advantage over nonstockholders as he did not have to raise as much cash immediately to complete the purchase. As stated in the text, Ward's Pere Marquette River property and sawmills in Ludington were valuable assets at the time of Ward's death. However, considerable capital investment had been made in the sawmills well after the land purchase. Ward likely did benefit from some advantages over the general public. First, as a stockholder in the company, he did not have to pay the full price for the property in cash. Second, it's possible he was given a discount because he was willing to pay for the Pere Marquette River property in total. It is likely very few, if any, others had the ability to raise $200,000. At the time, the investors were frustrated the property had not yet sold. The auction was set for May 1863, during the Civil War. Land speculators who might otherwise have been interested in such a potentially valuable tract of land could have been strapped for cash at the time, or even distracted by their involvement in the war. Ward also may have been in a position to negotiate for a "discount" because he was well acquainted with so many principals associated with the canal project overall, and the major stockholders of the company. Given his apparent advantages, the $200,000 he paid was quite a bit more than $96,740, the value identified in the catalogue.

55  The quotation is from "The Great Land Sale," *Detroit Free Press*, September 3, 1863, 1. Additional information is found in "Ward's Will," *Detroit Free Press*, October 21, 1875, 3; Bancroft, "Memoir of Capt. Samuel Ward," 345–46.

56  The first quotation is from Bancroft, "Memoir of Capt. Samuel Ward," 348; the others are from "Death of Capt. Samuel Ward," *Detroit Free Press*, February 7, 1854, 3. An additional source is Donahue, "Captain Samuel Ward," 63–64. Following the death of Eber Brock Ward in 1875, Samuel's body, along with his wife Elizabeth's and son Jacob Harrison's, were placed next to Eber at Elmwood Cemetery in Detroit.

57  A Ward family genealogy at the Pride and Heritage Museum in Marine City, Michigan, describes Jacob Harrison as "mentally handicapped." See "Genealogy of Ward Family," Ward, Samuel folder, WFC-MC. Other sources include Donahue, "Captain Samuel Ward," 62–63, 70–72. The inflation-adjusted currency values are according to https://westegg.com/inflation/infl.cgi, accessed February 8, 2021.

58  The quotations are from Ward, *The Autobiography of David Ward*, 4–5. Other sources include Shinn, "Captain Eber Brock Ward, Ironmaster of the West," 45–46; Korn, "Eber Brock Ward, Pathfinder of American Industry," 70–71.

59  The first two quotations are from Eber B. Ward to Eber Ward, February 18, 1838, Ward Family Papers, folder 5, Correspondence, 1838–1839, box 1, EBW-Clarke. Eber's letter describes David Ward's family as "Ly—— F——s," but it is clear he

meant "Lying Fools." Another source is Eber B. Ward to Emily Ward, January 1, 1840. The final quotation is from Ward, The Autobiography of David Ward, 4; David describes Emily's attempts to slander him on p. 52. David Ward's autobiography is interesting to read and provides helpful insight at times, but must be taken cautiously. He has something negative to say concerning just about every individual included in the book. Eber Brock is the primary target, but David is also critical of Emily, Samuel, and Elizabeth Ward. Denunciations are also leveled toward a former teacher and the philanthropist Gerrit Smith. The following passage shows an example of his attitude: "I reluctantly and with grief admit that the majority of those whom I have assisted and befriended most during my long business life have at last repaid me in ingratitude, and some with downright injury, seemingly because I may have ceased to direct the flow of favors to them." For this quotation and the examples above, see Ward, The Autobiography of David Ward, 31, 44–45, 140.

60 "The Poor Boy a Millionaire," *Daily Cleveland Herald*, October 4, 1856, 1.

## 4. A Man of Iron and Steel

1 Hilton, *Lake Michigan Passenger Steamers*, 38–41, 48; Shinn, "Captain Eber Brock Ward, Ironmaster of the West," 46; Korn, "Eber Brock Ward, Pathfinder of American Industry," 100–101.

2 Hilton, *Lake Michigan Passenger Steamers*, 48, 61–62, 256; Stone, *Floating Palaces of the Great Lakes*, 144; Elliott, *Red Stacks over the Horizon*, 21–48, 57–58; "Goodrich Transportation Co.," box 1, folder 10, Subject File Goodrich Transportation Co., 1825–1930, BGSU-Hall; *Owen vs. Potter*, 2:1281, Records and Briefs, Michigan Supreme Court, 72, April Term, 1897, State Law Library at the Library of Michigan, Lansing, MI; Korn, "Eber Brock Ward, Pathfinder of American Industry," 101.

3 A sample of advertisements, all from the *Detroit Free Press*, helps to show some of the routes undertaken by passenger ships owned and operated by Ward: March 17, 1852, 3; May 7, 1854, 1; September 6, 1855, 1; November 21, 1855, 1; August 3, 1859, 3; March 9, 1862, 2. Additional relevant articles from the newspaper include "Steamboat Change," August 3, 1859, 1; "Withdrawn," September 23, 1859, 1; "Steamboat Line to Buffalo to Be Kept Open until the Close of Navigation," September 24, 1859, 1. Additional sources include *Detroit Advertiser and Tribune*, August 16, 1859, 3; Shinn, "Captain Eber Brock Ward, Ironmaster of the West," 47–48.

4 The *Canadian* began running an advertisement touting itself as an alternative to Ward's monopoly on the St. Clair River route as early as July 21, 1855. See "Opposition Line," *Port Huron Commercial*, July 21, 1855, 2. Additional sources include "The River Steamboats," *Port Huron Commercial*, July 21, 1855, 2; "The River Steamers—Arrogance Overleaping Itself—Continued Insults to the People," *Port Huron Commercial*, August 4, 1855, 2; W. W. Erberts, "Bundle of Blunders," *Port Huron Commercial*, August 4, 1855, 2; "Flattened Out," *Port Huron*

*Commercial*, August 18, 1855, 2. Advertisements for the *Canadian* appeared in the *Detroit Free Press* into April of 1856 and then ended as early as April 25, 1856; for examples, see editions of July 18, 1855, 3, and March 22, 1856, 3. Rivalry with the *Canadian* is also mentioned in, Jenks, *St. Clair County*, 1:399.

5   The quotation and additional information is from "Diabolical Conspiracy to Blow up the Steamer City of Buffalo—Arrest of the Chief Conspirator—Seizure of His Torpedo," *Cleveland Morning Leader*, June 27, 1859, 3. Additional sources include "Diabolical Conspiracy Frustrated," *Detroit Free Press*, June 28, 1859, 1; "Convicts from Cuyahoga," *Cleveland Morning Leader*, January 2, 1860, 3.

6   The quotation is from Mills, *Our Inland Seas*, 182. Additional sources include Sibley, "A Dreamer's Vision That Became a Reality," 6; Mansfield, *History of the Great Lakes*, 462, 463; Stone, *Floating Palaces of the Great Lakes*, 151; "14-City of Cleveland," "28-Forest City," "41-Keweenaw," "49-May Queen," all from Eber Brock Ward, box 1, folder 31, Research Notes: vol. 14, vessels owned by Ward family, BGSU-Hall. Other sources are "Detroit & Cleveland Steam Navigation Co.," box 1, folder 6, Subject File Detroit & Cleveland Steam Navigation Co., 1847–1941, BGSU-Hall; Weeks, *Detroit City Directory, 1874–1875*, 558. Another possible connection between Ward and the Detroit & Cleveland Navigation Company involved the building popularly known as the D&C Warehouse. It was built by Oliver Newberry and his partner Henry Whiting, most likely in 1854. After Newberry died, Eber Ward purchased it in 1864. Following Ward's death, James McMillan and John Owen of the D&C Line became the owners. It is possible the D&C Line began to use it only after 1878, but it is also possible, given previous partnerships with Ward, that it was used by both parties. For more information, see Lorch, "The Detroit and Cleveland Navigation Company Warehouse." The interconnected and complicated relationship between the D&C Line and various steamship owners (including Eber Ward) between 1852 and when the company was incorporated in 1868 is addressed in portions of two articles. See Duncan, "The Story of the D&C, Part I," 225–26; and Duncan, "The Story of the D&C, Part IV," 175–76.

7   "Steamer Sam Ward," *Detroit Free Press*, August 29, 1853, 2.

8   The quotations are from "Excursion on the Steamer Planet," *Detroit Advertiser and Tribune*, August 18, 1862, 2. Another source is "For Lake Superior—A Grand Pleasure Excursion," *Detroit Advertiser and Tribune*, August 16, 1862, 1. Another example of a pleasure excursion, not identified in the text, is "An Evening on the Ruby," *Detroit Free Press*, June 17, 1854, 3.

9   Casson, *The Romance of Steel*, 4; Boyer, *The Enduring Vision*, 316–17. Korn addresses Ward's early involvement in the iron industry in "Eber Brock Ward, Pathfinder of American Industry," 104–19. Another source is "Real Builders of America," 596.

10  The articles of association for the Eureka Iron Company are found in DeWindt, *Proudly We Record*, 226. Several dates in the month of October have been identified as the date of the "origin" of the Eureka Iron Company. According to the articles of association, they were presented to the Wayne County Clerk October 24,

1853. But it is also said they were "Acknowledged October 25 and 26, 1853. Filed October 27, 1853, at 10:00 A.M." Because the Articles indicated they were *filed* October 27, 1853, this is the date included in the text. Additional sources include John S. Van Alstyne, "The Iron Industry: Its Rise, Progress and Decline in Wyandotte," 1901, 4–5; Johnson, *Detroit City Directory, 1853–54*, 277. The inflation-adjusted currency values are according to https://westegg.com/inflation/infl.cgi, accessed February 8, 2021.

11    Initially, the company considered placing its blast furnace in Marquette, Michigan, on Lake Superior. This was near the Eureka iron ore mine the company was set to operate. However, Darius Webb, a veteran iron producer who would serve as the organization's first superintendent, argued that Michigan's Upper Peninsula was not a feasible location, as the weather would interfere with year-round production. Barnett, "Making America's First Steel in Wyandotte," 30; John S. Van Alstyne, "Reminiscences of Early Times in Wyandotte," 1900, 5–6; DeWindt, *Proudly We Record*, 29; Burton, *The City of Detroit*, 538, 541; Christian, "Historical Associations Connected with Wyandotte," 320–21; William Downie, "Biography of Eber Brock Ward," 1941, Eber Brock Ward Collection, 1939, Burton Historical Collection, Detroit Public Library. Downie's biography is an excellent source for some items, but it also includes some factual errors, so it must be used with caution.

12    "From Lake Superior," *Detroit Free Press*, October 31, 1855, 1; "The Eureka Iron Company," *Detroit Free Press*, February 10 1856, 2; Van Alstyne, "Reminiscences of Early Times in Wyandotte," 7. Additional examples of Ward's use of his own ships to transport iron ore to his mills are found in "City Intelligence," *Detroit Free Press*, May 18, 1856, 1; "From Lake Superior," *Detroit Free Press*, June 24, 1859, 1; "54-Montgomery" and "65-Planet," Eber Brock Ward, box 1, folder 31, Research Notes: vol. 14, vessels owned by Ward family, BGSU-Hall. At the time of his death in 1875, Ward was the president of the New England Iron Company, Flint & Pere Marquette Railway, Burlington and Southwestern Railway of Iowa, Wyandotte Rolling Mills, Milwaukee Iron Company, Eureka Iron Company of Wyandotte, and Louisiana Central Railroad; he was also the treasurer of the North Chicago Rolling Mill Company.

13    The quotation is in DeWindt, *Proudly We Record*, 32. See also Van Alstyne, "Reminiscences of Early Times in Wyandotte," 8–9; DeWindt and DeWindt, *Our Fame and Fortune in Wyandotte*, 26.

14    The quotation is from "McCloy," Eureka Iron Co. Documents folder, Eureka Iron & Steel Co. box, Wyandotte Museum, Wyandotte, MI. Unfortunately, McCoy and two others were killed in an explosion at the Eureka Iron Company in June 1888. Another source is Van Alstyne, "Reminiscences of Early Times in Wyandotte," 11–12.

15    Brody, *Steelworkers in America*, 87–89. Eber Ward later built company housing for his employees in many of the communities where he established manufacturing plants.

16　Barnett, "Making America's First Steel in Wyandotte," 30, 32; "Rolling Mills at Wyandotte," *Detroit Free Press*, August 7, 1856, 1; DeWindt, *Proudly We Record*, 228–29, 231; Christian, "Historical Associations Connected with Wyandotte," 321; Van Alstyne, "The Iron Industry," 12.

17　Van Alstyne, "The Iron Industry," 10; Barnett, "Making America's First Steel in Wyandotte," 30; "Iron and Iron Manufacturers," *Detroit Advertiser and Tribune*, April 7, 1865, 3.

18　*Lake Superior Iron, Wyandotte Rolling Mill, and Eureka Iron Company*.

19　The first quotation is from Farmer, *History of Detroit*, 2:1276, 1277. The second quotation is from "Iron and Iron Manufacturers," *Detroit Advertiser and Tribune*, April 7, 1865, 3. Casson argues that as a result of the Civil War, "The output of iron nearly doubled, and the price jumped from $18.60 to as high as $73.60 per ton." See Casson, *The Romance of Steel*, 3.

20　The quotation and additional material are from "Iron and Steel," *Detroit Daily Post*, June 12, 1866, 4. Formisano argues that Ward's mill in Wyandotte was the "biggest factory in Michigan." See Formisano, *The Birth of Mass Political Parties*, 18.

21　"Iron and Steel," *Detroit Post*, June 12, 1866, 4; DeWindt, *Proudly We Record*, 32, 178. The inflation-adjusted currency values are according to https://westegg.com/inflation/infl.cgi, accessed February 8, 2021.

22　"Iron and Steel," *Detroit Post*, June 12, 1866, 4–5.

23　The quotations are from "Fatal Accident at Wyandotte," *Detroit Free Press*, April 12, 1857, 1; "The Wyandotte Disaster," *Detroit Free Press*, June 3, 1888, 9. Another source is "Long Hours, Hard Work the Custom in Iron and Steel 80 Years Ago," *Steel Facts*, no. 84 (June 1947): 6–7, found in box 4, Bay View History: Related Publications (1 of 2), folder 1, MCHS-Korn.

24　McLaughlin, *Michigan Labor*, 8–15; Taylor, *Old Slow Town*, 126–31; Montgomery, *Beyond Equality*, 97–101. Trevelleck is profiled in Yearly, "Richard Trevellick."

25　Babson, *Working Detroit*, 3–10; Brody, *Steelworkers in America*, 8–9, 31–32, 52, 77, 85.

26　The first quotation is from "The Labor Movement," *Detroit Advertiser and Tribune*, April 14, 1865, 1. The second is from Brody, *Steelworkers in America*, 27. Additional sources include "Wyandotte," *Detroit Advertiser and Tribune*, August 3, 1865, 1; Andreas, *History of Chicago*, 675; Shinn, "Captain Eber Brock Ward, Ironmaster of the West," 72–73.

27　The first quotation is from "Real Builders of America," 596. The next two are from Stebbins, *Upward Steps of Seventy Years*, 168.

28　"Wages of Iron Workers," *Detroit Advertiser and Tribune*, January 12, 1866, 2. The *Detroit Post* reinforces the idea that employees earned high wages at the Wyandotte Rolling Mill, although it noted, "Wages paid for operatives in the rolling mills varies from $1.50 to $15.00 per day"; see "Iron and Steel" *Detroit Post*, June 12, 1866, 4. It appears that the *Detroit Post*'s article used estimates of the scale used at the mill, while the *Detroit Advertiser and Tribune* used detailed data directly from the company secretary. Data concerning wages for average laborers is found in U.S. Department of Labor, *History of Wages in the United States*, 253. Data concerning farm workers is found in U.S. Department of Commerce, *Statistical Abstract of the United States*, 283.

29 DeWindt, *Proudly We Record*, 57–58. The building that housed the company offices and bank is still standing. In the fall of 1857 and again in the early 1870s, the company did pay employees using scrip, but most often they were paid in cash.

30 The quotation is from "The Wyandotte Rolling Mills," *Detroit Daily Press*, October 19, 1872, 4. Additional sources include "Sale of Furnace," *Detroit Daily Press*, December 21, 1872, 4; Catlin, *The Story of Detroit*, 498; Barnett, "Making America's First Steel in Wyandotte," 33–34; DeWindt, *Proudly We Record*, 233; Korn, "Eber Brock Ward, Pathfinder of American Industry," 147–48; Shinn, "Captain Eber Brock Ward, Ironmaster of the West," 152.

31 The quotation is from Emily Ward to Ada Brindle, December 29, 1854, Ward Family Papers, folder 8, Correspondence, 1850–1875, box 1, EBW-Clarke. An additional source is Ward, *The Autobiography of David Ward*, 147–48.

32 The quotation is from Carlisle, *Chronography of Notable Events*, 246. Additional sources include Hurlbut, *Grandmother's Stories*, 147–48; McElroy, *A Short History of Marine City*, 9, 35; Jenks, *St. Clair County*, 1:306–7; Jones, "Miss Emily Ward," 587. The building that housed Newport Academy is still standing. It was originally located at the corner of South Main and Washington Street in Marine City. In 1870, the building was moved to St. Clair Street and South Main so a new high school could be built on the original site. Since its relocation, it has served as a city hall, a jail, a fire station, and a Presbyterian church. Today, it houses Marine City's Community Pride and Heritage Museum.

33 Jones, "Miss Emily Ward," 587; Bancroft, "Aunt Emily Ward," 369; Hurlbut, *Grandmother's Stories*, 152–54. Most sources declare students attending Emily's academy were required to pay a small fee. This was likely the case. However, at least one writer argues the school "served without charge, both boys and girls." For more information concerning this source, see Dorothy Mitts, "Emily Ward Academy in Marine City," *Port Huron Times-Herald*, February 7, 1965, found in St. Clair Public Library, Michigan History Collection, Ward, Emily, 1809–1891 folder.

34 The quotation is from Eber B. Ward to Emily Ward, January 28, 1849, Ward Family Papers, folder 7, Correspondence, 1842–1849, box 1, EBW-Clarke. An additional source is "Stephen Girard's—Girard College," http://www.stephengirardsgirardcollege.com/, accessed June 15, 2019. Girard College, with a reimagined focus, is still in operation today.

35 The quotation is from "Ward's Will," *Detroit Free Press*, October 16, 1875, 1. Sally's death is also mentioned in A. Brigham to Eber Ward, September 12, 1847; and Eber B. Ward to Emily Ward, September 22, 1847, both in Ward Family Papers, folder 7, Correspondence, 1842–1849, box 1, EBW-Clarke.

36 "Ward's Will," *Detroit Free Press*, October 16, 1875, 1.

37 Eber B. Ward to Emily Ward, September 22, 1847, Ward Family Papers, folder 7, Correspondence, 1842–1849, box 1, EBW-Clarke.

38 Ross and Catlin, *Landmarks of Detroit*, 786–87; "Lot 86, Section A," 86 A folder, Historic Elmwood Cemetery & Foundation, Detroit.

39 It is unclear exactly who was considered a follower of spiritualism or how many followed spiritualism in the nineteenth century. In her extensive study of the movement, Ann Braude offers some perspective and argues that a spiritualist was "anyone participating in a Spiritualist activity or idea." She estimates the number of spiritualists to range between "a few hundred thousand to eleven million (out of a total population of twenty-five million)." See Braude, *Radical Spirits*, 8, 25. Other scholars reinforce her figures. David Nartonis argues that "thousands and perhaps millions of Americans participated in Spiritualism." See Nartonis, "The Rise of 19th-Century American Spiritualism," 361. Barbara Weisberg states that "tens of thousands of Americans" flocked to séances in the mid-1850s and that following the Civil War, "estimates of the numbers of Spiritualists in the United States would range from one million to a highly inflated eleven million." See Weisberg, *Talking to the Dead*, 3, 211. Stephen Gottschalk describes spiritualism as "perhaps the most popular occult fad of the nineteenth century," and "something of an indoor occult sport." See Gottschalk, *The Emergence of Christian Science in American Religious Life*, 141. Additional sources include Braude, *Radical Spirits*, 19, 27; McGarry, *Ghosts of Futures Past*, 5.

40 Nartonis, "The Rise of 19th-Century American Spiritualism," 361–62; McGarry, *Ghosts of Futures Past*, 20–24; Weisberg, *Talking to the Dead*, 54–58, 92–93, 118–19; Natale, *Supernatural Entertainments*, 21–41.

41 The quotation is from Cox, *Body and Soul*, 74. Additional sources include Eber B. Ward to Emily Ward, October 18, 1840, Ward Family Papers, folder 6, Correspondence, 1840–1841, box 1, EBW-Clarke; Braude, *Radical Spirits*, 3, 78, 153; Weisberg, *Talking to the Dead*, 118–19; McGarry, *Ghosts of Futures Past*, 41–43.

42 The quotations are from Eber B. Ward to Eber Ward, July 18, 1852, Ward Family Papers, folder 8, Correspondence, 1850–1875, box 1, EBW-Clarke. Ann Braude addresses the issue of Americans turning to spiritualism following the death of close family members. See Braude, *Radical Spirits*, 33–34, 49–52.

43 Emily mentions that Polly was "nervous and excitable" and sought treatment for her "mental condition," which began about ten to fifteen years before her death in 1869. See "Ward's Will," *Detroit Free Press*, October 16, 1875, 1. Eber's trip to New Orleans with Polly was in March 1856. While on the holiday, Eber related to Emily that "in case any fatal accident should occur to me before I return," he had arranged to provide her with $130,000 worth of bonds in companies he owned. It is possible that he was simply looking out for his sister's welfare, but in the aftermath of the death of so many family members, he may have been consumed with his own mortality. See Eber B. Ward to Emily Ward, March 13, 1856, Ward Family Papers, folder 8, Correspondence, 1850–1875, box 1, EBW-Clarke.

44 Andreas, *History of Chicago*, 674.

45  The quotation is from Swank, *History of the Manufacture of Iron*, 318. Additional sources include *Detroit Free Press*, May 26, 1857, 1; "New Engines for Captain Ward's Works," *Detroit Free Press*, September 9, 1857, 1; "Detroit Enterprise in Chicago," *Detroit Advertiser and Tribune*, July 27, 1864, 1; *Owen vs. Potter*, 2:1002–3; Shinn, "Captain Eber Brock Ward, Ironmaster of the West," 59–61; Korn, "Eber Brock Ward, Pathfinder of American Industry," 59–61.

46  Wilentz, *The Rise of American Democracy*, 719–25; Stiles, *The First Tycoon*, 309.

47  The quotation is from "A Good Example," *Detroit Free Press*, October 13, 1857, 2. Additional sources include "The Issue of Shin-plasters," *Detroit Free Press*, October 14, 1857, 2; DeWindt, *Proudly We Record*, 233–34.

48  Asa Brindle to his sisters, August 25, 1858, and April 24, 1859, Ward Family Papers, box 1, Michigan Letters, 1859–1863 folder, BHC; Shinn, "Captain Eber Brock Ward, Ironmaster of the West," 59–60.

49  "The Chicago Rolling Mill," *Detroit Post*, June 11, 1866, 2.

50  "Disastrous Fire," *Chicago Tribune*, June 20, 1866, 4; "Ward's Rolling Mill Destroyed," *Chicago Tribune*, June 21, 1866, 4. Additional sources include "Ward's Rolling Mill Destroyed—Loss—$200,000," *Detroit Free Press*, June 21, 1866, 2; Andreas, *History of Chicago*, 674.

51  Eber B. Ward to My Friends, 1847–1859 folder, box 1, Ward Family Papers, 1807–1945, BHC. The letter in its entirely also appears in Shinn, "Captain Eber Brock Ward, Ironmaster of the West," 48–50, although Shinn mistakenly states Ward was writing from New York.

## 5. Anti-Slavery Politics and Civil War

1  Eber Ward Sr. to Daniel Hubbel, July 13, 1817, Eber B. Ward Family Papers, folder 2, Correspondence, 1807–1829, box 1, EBW-Clarke.

2  The quotation is from Taylor, *Old Slow Town*, 108; additional information is on 63–64.

3  The quotation is from Mull, *The Underground Railroad in Michigan*, 1. Additional sources include Mull, "The McCoys," 220–21; Jenks, *St. Clair County*, 2:821; Warnes, *Ecorse, Michigan*, 34–35. According to Harlon Hatcher, the *Forest Queen* and *May Queen* "regularly took on fugitives." See Hatcher, *Lake Erie*, 237; "29-Forest Queen" and "49-May Queen," Eber Brock Ward, box 1, folder 31, Research Notes: vol. 14, vessels owned by Ward family, BGSU-Hall. While it is impossible to know the exact number of slaves who escaped using the Underground Railroad, Eric Foner argues that between one thousand and five thousand used it each year from 1830 to 1860. See Foner, *Gateway to Freedom*, 4.

4  G. L. Heaton's story first appeared in the *Fredonia Censor* on March 17, 1886, in an article written by Heaton titled, "Recollections of an Old Conductor—From Shore to Shore—Tricking the Slave Catchers." The full article, as well as some background detail, was transcribed by Douglas H. Shepard in 2013. It is available at https://chqgov.com/sites/default/files/document-files/2019-09/Heaton%20G

%20L%20and%20the%20UGRR_201401211609151483.pdf, accessed June 10, 2018.

5   Ibid.

6   Ibid.

7   Ibid.

8   For an overview of Manifest Destiny and issues involving the Kansas-Nebraska Act, see Boyer, *The Enduring Vision*, 386–92, 403–7.

9   The quotation is from Streeter, *Political Parties in Michigan*, 182. Additional sources include Formisano, *The Birth of Mass Political Parties*, 239–45. The community of Ripon, Wisconsin, also claims to be the birthplace of the Republican Party. While the community did hold the first meeting of Whigs and Democrats opposed to the Kansas-Nebraska Act, the meeting in Jackson, Michigan, was the first to adopt the name "Republican Party." See Dunbar and May, *Michigan*, 308–10.

10  The quotation is from "Gov. at the City Hall," *Detroit Free Press*, June 3, 1856, 1. Additional sources include "Aid for Kansas," *Western Reserve Chronicle*, June 18, 1856, 2; Boyer, *The Enduring Vision*, 407–9. The inflation-adjusted currency values are according to https://westegg.com/inflation/infl.cgi, accessed February 8, 2021.

11  Fort Street Presbyterian Church Twenty-Fifth Anniversary Booklet, box IV, Anniversaries, Fort Street Presbyterian Church records, 1849–1962, BHC; Pew Assessments, 1853, box VI, First Protestant Society Records, Fort Street Presbyterian Church records, 1849–1962, BHC; "Detroit Fire and Marine Insurance Co. Advertisement," *Detroit Free Press*, March 29, 1852, 3.

12  The quotations are from James Moorhead, "Presbyterians and Slavery," Princeton University, https://slavery.princeton.edu/stories/presbyterians-and-slavery, accessed November 1, 2019. Additional information is taken from American Presbyterian Church, "The Schism of 1861," http://www.americanpresbyterianchurch.org/apc -history/presbyterian-history/the-schism-of-1861/, accessed November 1, 2019.

13  Michael W. Nagle, "Impending Crisis," LecturePoint: US History, Cengage Learning, http://college.cengage.com/history/lecturepoints/, accessed July 27, 2019.

14  Ibid.

15  Ward, *Reasons Why the Northwest Should Have a Protective Tariff*. Special thanks to Sean Marshall, who searched for and found this document located in the special vault of the Burton Historical Collection of the Detroit Public Library.

16  Ibid. The final quotation is from Formisano, *The Birth of Mass Political Parties*, 294.

17  Ward, *Reasons Why the Northwest Should Have a Protective Tariff*.

18  The quotations are from E. B. Ward, "Our Victory," *Detroit Daily Advertiser*, November 9, 1860, 1. The italics are in the original. A handwritten copy of this message, apparently in Eber Ward's hand, is found in "Our Victory," Ward, Eber Brock 1848–1865 folder, Eber Brock Ward Papers, 1848–1875, BHC. Additional sources include Taylor, *Old Slow Town*, 3, 13–14, 39; Dunbar and May, *Michigan*, 317–18.

19 The quotations are from Eber Ward to William H. Gist, n.d., Ward, Eber Brock 1848–1865 folder, Eber Brock Ward Papers, 1848–1875, BHC. It is possible that Ward only drafted this letter to Gist but never sent it because the state acted so quickly to vote in favor of secession. Even if he never sent it, the document is still important because it provides insight into Ward's views concerning abolitionists. An additional source is Taylor, *Old Slow Town*, 39.

20 E. B. Ward, "Shall We Basely Surrender?" *Detroit Daily Advertiser*, December 31, 1860, 2.

21 The first set of quotations is from E. B. Ward, "Aid for the Union!" *Detroit Daily Advertiser*, January 4, 1861, 1. The second set is from Eber B. Ward to Abraham Lincoln, January 4, 1861, Abraham Lincoln Papers at the Library of Congress, series 1, General Correspondence, 1833–1916, available at https://www.loc.gov/resource/mal.0575900/, accessed September 5, 2018.

22 The first chapter of Paul Taylor's work does an outstanding job of explaining the basis for ethnic conflict in the city of Detroit. See Taylor, *Old Slow Town*, 7–39.

23 Ibid., 78–82. The quotation is from Eber Ward, "Letter from Captain Ward," *Detroit Advertiser and Tribune*, July 16, 1862.

24 The first quotations are from "The Public Meeting," *Detroit Free Press*, July 17, 1862, 2. The final quotation is from Eber Ward, "Letter From Captain Ward," *Detroit Advertiser and Tribune*, July 16, 1862.

25 The "mulatto" man accused of raping two young girls was William Faulkner. Prior to the incident, Faulkner had always maintained that he was white. He was convicted of the crime, but the girls later recanted their testimony. Faulkner then was granted a pardon, but not before he had served seven years of a life sentence. For highlights of the race riot and background to Faulkner's story, see Taylor, *Old Slow Town*, 82–103.

26 Ward contributed at least $250 to Detroit's bounty funds, possibly more. See "War Meeting," *Detroit Free Press*, July 23, 1862, 1; "Contributions to Colonel Morrow's Regiment," *Detroit Free Press*, July 29, 1862, 1; "Bounty Fund," *Detroit Free Press*, July 30, 1862, 1. Information concerning Asa Brindle can be found in Henry A. Morrow to Capt. E. B. Ward, box 1, Michigan Letters, 1863–1875, Includes Civil War Letters of Asa Brindle folder, Ward Family Papers, 1807–1945, BHC.

27 The first quotation is from Eber Ward to Florence Mayhew, July 12, 1863, box 1863–1865, Includes Civil War Letters of Asa Brindle folder, Ward Family Papers, 1807–1945, BHC. The second is from Eber B. Ward to Abraham Lincoln, July 11, 1863, Abraham Lincoln Papers at the Library of Congress, series 1, General Correspondence, 1833–1916, available at https://www.loc.gov/resource/mal.2476500/, accessed September 5, 2018.

28 Fox, "Income Tax Records of the Civil War Years"; U.S. IRS Tax Assessment Lists, 1862–1918, Provo, UT, https://www.ancestry.com/, accessed December 29, 2018; "Taxing Profits Twice," *New York Daily Tribune*, June 6, 1863. The inflation-adjusted currency values are according to https://westegg.com/inflation/infl.cgi, accessed February 8, 2021.

29  "The Rebel Plot," *Detroit Free Press*, November 11, 1863, 1; "Defensive Measures," *Detroit Free Press*, November 11, 1863, 1; "Local Intelligence," *Detroit Free Press*, November 11, 1863, 3; Taylor, *Old Slow Town*, 156–74; Dunbar and May, *Michigan*, 335.

30  The quotation is from "Captain Eber B. Ward's Fortress." Another source is Taylor, *Old Slow Town*, 175–79.

31  McRae, "Camp Ward, Detroit"; Stacy Newman, "First Michigan Colored Regiment," https://detroithistorical.org/learn/encyclopedia-of-detroit/first-michigan-colored-regiment, accessed August 3, 2019; Taylor, *Old Slow Town*, 74–75.

32  The quotation is from "Lincoln's Second Inaugural," https://www.nps.gov/linc/learn/historyculture/lincoln-second-inaugural.htm, accessed August 3, 2019. Additional sources include Taylor, *Old Slow Town*, 190–91.

33  The first quotation is from *Detroit Advertiser and Tribune*, April 27, 1865, 2; the second is from "Presidential Veracity," *Detroit Advertiser and Tribune*, April 5, 1866, 4. Additional sources include Boyer, *The Enduring Vision*, 372–73; Haviland, *A Woman's Life Work*, 279.

34  Gordon-Reed, "The Fight over Andrew Johnson's Impeachment."

35  Trefousse, *Benjamin Franklin Wade*, 7–8, 131–37, 300–301; Benedict, *The Impeachment and Trial of Andrew Johnson*, 67, 134; Trefousse, *Impeachment of a President*, 175–76; "7-B. F. Wade," Eber Brock Ward, box 1, folder 31, Research Notes: vol. 14, vessels owned by Ward family, BGSU-Hall. Ward and Ben Wade were so close that on at least one occasion when Wade visited Detroit, he stayed at Ward's spacious mansion. See "In Town," *Detroit Post*, September 8, 1869, 4.

36  The first quotation is from E. B. Ward to Mrs. Mayhew, April 4, 1868; the next two are from E. B. Ward to Florence Mayhew April 24, 1868, all in box 1, Michigan Letters, 1863–1875 Includes Civil War Letters of Asa Brindle folder, Ward Family Papers, 1807–1945, BHC. The "deeply disturbed" quotation is from Trefousse, *Impeachment of a President*, 176. An additional source is Trefousse, *Impeachment of a President*, 63, 156, 165–79.

37  The quotation is from E. B. Ward, "Capt. Ward Speaks for Himself," *Detroit Daily Post*, April 18, 1872, 2. Additional sources are, E. B. Ward, "Some of Greeley's Vagaries and Inconsistencies," *Detroit Daily Post*, July 22, 1872, 1; "Political," *Chicago Tribune*, August 2, 1872, 4.

38  Farmer, *History of Detroit, 1:684.*

39  The first quotation is from "The Vice Presidency," *Detroit Post*, February 10, 1868, 4; italics in the original. The *Detroit Post* labeled Johnson "blind, deluded, and apparently insane" after he fired Edwin Stanton as the secretary of war in direct opposition to the Tenure of Office Act. See "The News from Washington," *Detroit Post*, February 22, 1868, 4. Even prior to this, the newspaper took a very negative view of Johnson and supported impeaching the president. See, for example, "Impeachment," *Detroit Post*, December 3, 1867, 4.

40  A sample of articles included in the *Detroit Post* where Ward advocated in favor of a change in economic policy include "The Financial Question," January 22, 1868,

2; "Retrenchment," January 29, 1868, 2; "Memorial from Mr. Ward," February 20, 1868, 2; "Government Expenses: A Good Prospect for Retrenchment Efforts," March 10, 1868, 4. At times, the *Detroit Post* printed the entire text of a Ward speech. See "Speech of Capt. E. B. Ward Before the Manufacturer's Convention at Cleveland," May 29, 1868, 4. Examples of editorials in the paper in support of Ward's policy positions include "Retrenchment," January 29, 1868, 4; "Retrenchment and Economy," February 20, 1868, 4; "The Money Value of Impeachment," March 12, 1868, 4; "The Manufacturer's Resolution," May 1, 1868, 4.

41  The first quotation is from "The Main Question," *Detroit Post*, January 14, 1868, 4. The others are from "A Party Issue," *Detroit Post*, February 18, 1868, 4. Additional examples of similar arguments can be found in "Bread and the Ballot," *Detroit Post*, December 28, 1867, 4; "Conscience and Voting," *Detroit Post*, February 7, 1868, 4; "A White Man's Government," *Detroit Post*, February 14, 1868, 4.

42  The first set of quotations is from A Non-Voter, "The Franchise for the Negro," *Detroit Post*, March 17, 1868, 4. The second set is from A Non-Voter, "The Franchise for the Negro," *Detroit Post*, March 20, 1868. The quotations from the editorial are found in "Democratic Know-Nothingism," *Detroit Post*, March 17, 1868, 4.

43  "Female Suffrage: The Argument against the Extension of Suffrage to Women," *Detroit Post*, March 11, 1869, 7.

44  In 1869, the *Detroit Post* supported passage of the Fifteenth Amendment, which extended the right to vote to all adult black men. See "The Suffrage Amendment," *Detroit Post*, March 1, 1869, 4.

45  The quotation is from Foner, *The Fiery Trial*, xvii. Additional sources include Foner, *The Fiery Trial*, 20–21; Potter, *The Impending Crisis*, 39–40, 476–77.

46  The quotation is from McGovern, *Abraham Lincoln*, 55; the second is from Foner, *The Fiery Trial*, 228. An additional source is Foner, *The Fiery Trial*, 157–58, 181–96, 212–18, 240–47.

47  Eber Ward to William H. Gist, n.d., Ward, Eber Brock 1848–1865 folder, Eber Brock Ward Papers, 1848–1875, BHC.

48  "Speech of Capt. E. B. Ward," *Detroit Advertiser & Tribune*, December 18, 1863, 3.

49  Foner, *The Fiery Trial*, 120, 122.

50  The quotation is from Eber Ward, "Letter from Captain Ward," *Detroit Advertiser and Tribune*, July 16, 1862. Apparently, by 1868 Ward employed some African American workers on land, as shown in an article in the *Detroit Post* that described Mr. Johnson, "a colored man, and his boy" who worked at "Capt. Ward's kiln." See "Wyandotte—Temperance Movements—Fires—Attempts to Wreck a Railroad Train—Building," *Detroit Post*, February 25, 1868, 4.

51  Walton and Grimm, *Windjammers*, 42–43.

# 6. A New Vision for the Midwest

1 The quotation is from *Proceedings of the Convention of Iron and Steel Manufacturers*, 6. An additional source is Swank, "The Association and Its Work," 4; Hoogenboom, "Thomas A. Jenckes and Civil Service Reform," 642n.

2 The quotations are from Ward, *Address of E. B. Ward*. Additional sources include National Convention of Manufacturers, *Report of the Delegation Sent to Washington*; "To the Hon. Chairmen of Committees on Ways and Means and on Appropriations of the House of Representatives and of the Senate of the United States," n.d., Ward, Eber Brock 1868–1875 folder, Eber Brock Ward Papers, 1848–1875, BHC.

3 The form letter is found in multiple locations; two are E. B. Ward to the Honorable [blank], January 16, 1868, Ward, Eber Brock 1868–1875 folder, Eber Brock Ward Papers, 1848–1875, BHC; Ward, "Washington, January 16, 1868."

4 The quotation is from "To the Hon. Senate and House of Representatives of the United States, in Congress Assembled," n.d., Ward, Eber Brock 1868–1875 folder, Eber Brock Ward Papers, 1848–1875, BHC. An additional source is E. B. Ward, "To the Senate and House of Representatives of the United States," n.d., Ward, Eber Brock 1868–1875 folder, Eber Brock Ward Papers, 1848–1875, BHC. A complete discussion of the Jenckes' Bill is found in Hoogenboom, "Thomas A. Jenckes and Civil Service Reform."

5 The first two quotations are from Ward, *Reasons Why the Northwest Should Have a Protective Tariff*. Additional sources include Eber B. Ward, "Gentlemen of the Iron and Steel Association," Ward, Eber Brock 1848–1865 folder, Eber Brock Ward Papers, 1848–1875, BHC. The final quotation is from Ward, *Protection vs. Free Trade*.

6 The quotations are from Ward, *The Farmer and the Manufacturer*, 4.

7 Ibid., 6. The final quotation is from Nichols, *Peoples of the Inland Sea*, xii. Kristin Hoganson addresses the theme of the Midwest as the nation's heartland extensively. See Hoganson, *The Heartland*.

8 The quotations are from Ward, *The Farmer and the Manufacturer*, 13, 10.

9 Korn, *The Story of Bay View*, 49, 50–51; Swank, *History of the Manufacture of Iron*, 329–31. Korn's dissertation addresses much of the same material as his published work, *The Story of Bay View*. For information included in the dissertation, see Korn, "Eber Brock Ward, Pathfinder of American Industry," 169–80.

10 The quotation is from *Owen vs. Potter*, 2:1386–87, Records and Briefs, Michigan Supreme Court, 72, April Term, 1897, State Law Library at the Library of Michigan, Lansing, MI. Stephen Clement, who later served as president of both the North Chicago Rolling Mill and Milwaukee Iron Company, reinforced Hagerman's testimony. He declared, "The Milwaukee Iron Company was built by Captain Ward for the purpose of practically protecting the interests of the North Chicago Rolling Mill Company from a competitor as he had learned, I think, that there was other parties thinking of building at Milwaukee." See *Owen vs. Potter*, 2:1105–6.

11 Andreas, *History of Milwaukee*, 1616–17, 1619; Korn, "Eber Brock Ward, Pathfinder of American Industry," 169–71; Korn, *The Story of Bay View*, 52. Hagerman

later testified that Ward owned "more than half the stock of the company" when it was formed. In later years, Ward and members of his immediate family continued to own more than half of the company stock. See *Owen vs. Potter*, "Orrin Potter's Brief," 371. It is likely that Hagerman was enrolled in Emily Ward's school in Newport, but it is unclear when and for how many years he attended.

12  William J. Donahoe, "A History of Old Bay View," n.d., box 4, Bay View History: Notes, folder #9, MCHS-Korn; Korn, *The Story of Bay View*, 52.

13  The first quotation is from Andreas, *History of Milwaukee*, 1616; the second is from "Minutes." An additional source is Wilentz, *The Rise of American Democracy*, 679–82.

14  The quotation is from "The Iron Business," *Watertown Republican*, July 14, 1869, 1. Additional sources include Donahoe, "A History of Old Bay View"; Korn, *The Story of Bay View*, 52.

15  The first set of quotations is from "Progress in Western Iron Manufacturers," *Chicago Tribune*, July 31, 1869, 2; the final quotation is from Merk, *Economic History of Wisconsin*, 143. Additional sources include Korn, *The Story of Bay View*, 53–54; Kopmeier, *From Mayville to Milwaukee*, 7.

16  The first quotation is from Donahoe, "A History of Old Bay View"; the second is from Langson, *Thirteenth Annual Statement of the Trade and Commerce of Milwaukee*, 13. Additional sources include Andreas, *History of Milwaukee*, 1617; Kopmeier, *From Mayville to Milwaukee*, 7.

17  The quotation is from Korn, *The Story of Bay View*, 53. Other sources include Andreas, *History of Milwaukee*, 1617; Shinn, "Captain Eber Brock Ward, Ironmaster of the West," 76.

18  The quotations are from Kursch, "Beulah Brinton of Bay View." Additional sources include "Conversation with Warrant Brinton, September 19, 1935," folder 69, box 4, "Bay View History Notes," MCHS-Korn; Ilona Gonzales and John Gurda, "Brinton, Beulah (nee Tobey) 1836–1928," Wisconsin Historical Society, available at https://www.wisconsinhistory.org/Records/Article/CS5751, accessed August 8, 2020. The home built by Beulah and Warren Brinton is commonly referred to as the Beulah Brinton house and is still standing. Today, it is occupied by the Bay View Historical Society.

19  The quotation is from Langson, *Thirteenth Annual Statement of the Trade and Commerce of Milwaukee*, 13. Additional information is found at ibid., 14; Langson, *Nineteenth Annual Statement of the Trade and Commerce of Milwaukee*, 117; Korn, *The Story of Bay View*, 55.

20  The quotation is from Merk, *Economic History of Wisconsin*, 142.

21  The first quotation is from Bancroft, "Memoir of Capt. Samuel Ward," 343. The second is from "Bill of Complaint," *Owen vs. Potter*, 1:64. The third is from "Ward's Will," *Detroit Free Press*, October 16, 1875, 1. Additional sources include United States Census, 1860, Detroit Ward 9, Wayne, Michigan, p. 51, available at https://www.ancestry.com/, accessed December 17, 2019; Wargo, "A Case Without Parallel," 88.

22 The first quotation is from Wargo, "A Case Without Parallel," 88. The second is from "The Will of Capt. Ward," *New York Times*, October 11, 1875, 1. Additional sources include "Ward's Will," *Detroit Free Press*, October 16, 1875, 1; "Bill of Complaint," *Owen vs. Potter*, 1:63.

23 Thomas Finn, "Atrocious Conduct of a Steamboat Captain," *Detroit Free Press*, October 8, 1862, 1.

24 The first two quotations are from John P. Ward to My Dear Friends, n.d., Seitz Family Collection. The final quotation is from "Trial for Murder," *Detroit Free Press*, November 15, 1867, 1. Additional sources include "A Youthful Avenger," *Detroit Free Press*, October 15, 1865, 1; "Coroner's Inquest on the Body of Captain John P. Ward," *Detroit Free Press*, October 24, 1865, 1; "Closing Arguments of Messrs. Lathrop and Maynard in the Farman Murder Trial," *Detroit Free Press*, November 20, 1867, 1.

25 The first quotation is from "Ward's Will," *Detroit Free Press*, October 16, 1875, 1. The second is from Geoff Kramer, email to author, January 19, 2021. Kramer argues, "Because there was no standardized diagnostic manual at the time—the American Psychiatric Association's first Diagnostic and Statistical Manual of Mental Disorders was not published until 1952—clinicians from Eber Ward's era varied in their selection of diagnostic labels (e.g., 'insane,' 'mentally incompetent,' 'anxious,' 'simple,' 'feebleminded,' 'retarded') and in the diagnostic criteria needed to establish those labels. As a result, diagnoses of mental illness might have been too liberally applied." The textbook authored by Kramer is Kramer, Bernstein, and Phares, *Introduction to Clinical Psychology*.

26 The quotation is from "Local Matters, Ward's Will," *Detroit Free Press*, October 10, 1875, 5.

27 All quotations concerning Polly are found in "Ward's Will," *Detroit Free Press*, October 16, 1875, 1. The additional quotations are from Emily Ward to Eber Ward, March 8, 1853, Ward Family Papers, folder 7, Correspondence, 1850–1875, box 1, EBW-Clarke; the emphasis is included in the original. The letter also includes a comment from the transcriber, "This letter is unsigned, and was either never sent or was copied from this original draft." Eber expressed concern about Polly being "very anxious" in, Eber B. Ward to Emily Ward, March 13, 1856, Ward Family Papers, folder 7, Correspondence, 1850–1875, box 1, EBW-Clarke.

28 "Ward's Will," *Detroit Free Press*, October 16, 1875, 1. Emily also testified that Polly had been "nervous and excitable" for the last ten to fifteen years of her life.

29 The quotation is taken from several sources, including *Memphis Daily Appeal*, February 27, 1869; *Nashville Union and American*, February 28, 1869; *Evening Star*, March 4, 1869. Although she and Eber divorced, Polly was buried in the Ward family plot at Detroit's Elwood Cemetery near Eber and other family members. Her tombstone identifies her date of death as April 26, 1869. The exact circumstances surrounding Polly's death are unclear. But during the trial over Eber Ward's will, the *Detroit Free Press* reported that Emily testified, "When Mrs. Ward

came back from the water-cure at Castile she was in poor health, but the witness [Emily] does not know whether or not she died from the effects of an attack of paralysis received while at Castile." She must have been referring to the Castile Water Cure Sanitarium in New York. It is unclear when Polly visited this sanitarium, but Emily's answers indicate it was near the end of her life. See "Ward's Will," *Detroit Free Press*, October 16, 1875, 1. A brief overview of the Castile Water Cure Sanitarium is found in "Historical Horizons: Recollections of the Castile Water Cure," *Daily News*, November 26, 2016, https://www.thedailynewsonline.com/bdn05/historical-horizons-recollections-of-the-castile-water-cure-20161126, accessed December 24, 2019.

30 The quotations are from Ward, *The Autobiography of David Ward*, 145, 39.

31 The first quotation is from "Western Ohio," *New York Herald*, February 21, 1869, 10. The others are from "Princess Followed Mother's Footsteps," *Detroit Free Press*, December 21, 1916, 10. Eber and Catherine were married March 11, 1869. In 1897 Catherine testified she and Eber married "about a year and a half" after they first met. See *Owen vs. Potter*, 1:277. For the relationship between Catherine Lyon's family and Senator Benjamin Wade, see Lyon, *Lyon Memorial*, 164, 165, 201; Nagle, *Justus S. Stearns*, 13–14; and *Owen vs. Potter*, 1:726.

32 The first quotation is from "Captain Eber B. Ward's Fortress," 21. The other quotations are from William Downie Papers, Eber Brock Ward, box 2, microfilm reel 1, BGSU-Hall. This set of William Downie Papers is similar to William Downie's unpublished biography of Ward, but it includes additional information. Additional sources include "Eber Ward," 1865, U.S. IRS Tax Assessment Lists, 1862–1918, Provo, UT, https://www.ancestry.com/, accessed December 29, 2018; United States Census, 1870, Detroit Ward 9, Wayne, Michigan, p. 156, available at https://www.ancestry.com/, accessed December 17, 2019. The exact addresses of Eber's home and the one he built for Emily are somewhat confusing. The two lived on the same street and various sources have attributed different addresses to each. Additionally, the numbering system changed over time. But according to the *Detroit City Directory* for 1873–74, Eber's home address was "792 Fort west," while Emily's was "Fort bet Eighteenth and Eighteenth-and-a-half." See Weeks, *Detroit City Directory, 1873–1874*, 549. Another contemporary source that reinforces this address is the record of Eber's internment on January 6, 1875, where his address is listed as "792 Fort Street West." See Record of Internment, Elmwood Cemetery, August 1, 1874–August 8, 1879, Elmwood Cemetery Archive, Detroit.

33 The first quotation is from Eber B. Ward to Emily Ward, January 1, 1840, Ward Family Papers, folder 6, Correspondence, 1840–1841, box 1, EBW-Clarke. The others are from Eber B. Ward to One of his Sons, January 22, 1855, Ward Family Papers, folder 8, Correspondence, 1850–1875, box 1, EBW-Clarke.

34 According to Ward's ledger, in 1852 Eber and Samuel jointly owned stock in the Michigan Central Railroad worth an estimated $27,500. See Ledger Private Accounts, 1849–1866, 66–67, Eber Brock Ward Papers, BHC. Another source is

Korn, "Eber Brock Ward, Pathfinder of American Industry," 203. The railroad's financial difficulties are discussed in Detroit & Milwaukee Railway Company, "Report to the Stockholders," December 1, 1858, Rare Books, Library of Michigan, Lansing; "Detroit and Milwaukee Railway—Loan of One Hundred and Fifty Thousand Pounds Effected," *Detroit Free Press*, October 27, 1857, 1.

35 The first president of the Flint & Pere Marquette was George M. Dewey. Ward succeeded Dewey as president in July 1860. See Meints, *Pere Marquette*, 8. Ivey, *The Pere Marquette Railroad Company*, 215; "History, Resources, and Prospects of the Saginaw Valley. The Railroad Excursion. The Flint & Pere Marquette Rail Road," 1862, Bentley Historical Library, Ann Arbor, MI. James Cook Mills identifies Eber B. Ward as a landowner in Saginaw County's Albee Township at an "early date." It is unclear how much land he owned or when he began to purchase land in the area. See Mills, *History of Saginaw County*, 2:349–50; Korn, "Eber Brock Ward, Pathfinder of American Industry," 204–5.

36 The quotation is from "The Flint and Holly Railroad: Its History and Construction," *Detroit Free Press*, October 27, 1864, 1. Additional sources include *Annual Report of the Flint & Pere Marquette Railway Company Made to the Stockholders for the Fiscal Year Ending December 1, 1868*; Ivey, *The Pere Marquette Railroad Company*, 216–17; "Flint and Pere Marquette Railway," *Detroit Free Press*, January 3, 1863, 1; "Railway Consolidation," *Detroit Free Press*, June 1, 1868, 4; "Opening of the Flint and Pere Marquette Railroad," *Detroit Advertiser and Tribune*, December 8, 1862, 1.

37 The quotation is from *Flint and Pere Marquette Railway Company*. Additional sources include Ivey, *The Pere Marquette Railroad Company*, 218; "Railroad to Bay City," *Detroit Free Press*, January 12, 1864, 4; "Good News—F & P.M. Railway Extension," *Detroit Free Press*, September 26, 1866; "Flint & Pere Marquette Road," *Detroit Free Press*, December 3, 1867, 4. Pere Marquette was not officially renamed Ludington until 1873, but as early as the mid-1860s, many referred to the settlement as Ludington in honor of James Ludington, particularly after the post office was named Ludington in 1864.

38 The quotation is from "The Railroad Grants," *Detroit Free Press*, February 17, 1857, 2. Additional sources include *Flint and Pere Marquette Railway Company*; Dunbar and May, *Michigan*, 369–73; Ivey, *The Pere Marquette Railroad Company*, 217. The Detroit & Milwaukee Railway also became a land grant railroad under this legislation. However, its benefits were not retroactive. Land grants were awarded for rail lines constructed after the passage of this legislation.

39 Ivey, *The Pere Marquette Railroad Company*, 217–18.

40 Ibid., 219; Korn, "Eber Brock Ward, Pathfinder of American Industry," 207. Shortly before Ward's death, in December 1874, 253 miles of the Flint & Pere Marquette had been completed; it ran from Monroe on Lake Erie to Ludington on Lake Michigan. This allowed the line to receive additional government land. Ultimately, according to historian Paul Ivey, by 1899, 513,000 acres of land had been granted to the railway under the legislation passed by Congress in 1856, an

area about two-thirds the size of Rhode Island. "This land sold at an average price of $10.34 per acre or a total of $4,847,007." See Ivey, *The Pere Marquette Railroad Company*, 231, with additional information on 221.

41 The quotation is from Mills, *History of Saginaw County*, 3:275. Additional sources include "Flint and Pere Marquette," *Detroit Free Press*, May 18, 1872, 4; "Railway Matters," *Detroit Free Press*, December 23, 1871, 1; "First Shipment of Lumber by Rail," *Detroit Free Press*, January 17, 1868, 3. An additional source is Ivey, *The Pere Marquette Railroad Company*, 219–20.

42 "Flint and Pere Marquette Railroad," *Mason County Record*, May 4, 1869.

43 There is some controversy concerning the specific location of Père Marquette's death. The State of Michigan has erected two historical markers, each identifying a different site for his death. One is in Ludington and the other is in Frankfort. In 2012, the City of Manistee erected a marker claiming Marquette died at that location. Most scholars believe he died near Ludington at the mouth of the Pere Marquette River, on Ludington's Buttersville Peninsula. For more information, see Nagle, *Justus S. Stearns*, 209, 25n.

44 *History of Mason County*, 17–20, 49–50. In a letter from 1866, James Ludington wrote, "I met Ward's agent for his land & he wants me to go to Detroit & see him & says Ward is anxious to consolidate our interests or will sell his lands—so I think I will go & see him on Wednesday." See James Ludington to William Ludington, August 12, 1866, box 2, Family Correspondence, 1866–1867, folder 6, NYHS-Ludington.

45 The quotation is from James Ludington to William Ludington, August 28, 1866, box 2, Family Correspondence, 1866–1867, folder 6, NYHS-Ludington. Another source is James Ludington to William Ludington, March 20, 1868, box 2, Family Correspondence, 1868–1869, folder 7, NYHS-Ludington. By the summer of 1866, it seemed clear to Ludington that Ward was not desperate to sell his pineland; Ludington observed, "Saw Mr. Ward in regard to his lands—he is not anxious at all to sell." See James Ludington to William Ludington, August 22, 1866, box 2, Family Correspondence, 1866–1867, folder 6, NYHS-Ludington. General coverage of the controversy between James Ludington and Eber Ward is taken from several sources. These include "Ludington Is Named for Rich Lumberman," *Ludington Chronicle*, August 22, 1906, 3; a nearly identical but shorter article is "How Capt. Ward Won Out," *Detroit Free Press*, August 17, 1906, 11. See also Cabot, "A Different View of James Ludington," *Ludington Daily News*, April 25, 2002, 4; Rob Alway, "MC History Spotlight: The Origins of Ludington Carferries Nearly Killed the Town's Namesake," *Mason County Press*, April 19, 2019, masoncountypress .com, accessed August 1, 2019; Cabot, *Images of America*, 16–17; James Jensen, "The Captain and the Princess," presentation, 2018 (author's collection).

46 The quotation is from "Saginaw County," *Detroit Free Press*, September 4, 1869, 4. Another source is Cabot, *Images of America*, 16–17.

47 The first quotation is from "The Courts," *Detroit Free Press*, September 14, 1870, 1. The second is from James Ludington to William Ludington, May 24, 1869, box

2, Family Correspondence, 1868–1869, folder 7, NYHS-Ludington. The same letter suggests Ward may have even facilitated the subsequent sale of James Ludington's properties, as Ludington continued, "They went from our place to Manistee & I learned that Ward was closeted with Mr. Filer—a responsible man—very late that night—& the next morning Mr. Filer came down to Ludington. He wanted me to remain over, but I could not. He said he wanted to buy me out. I told him I would sell for $500,000 & then I left on the boat for Milwaukee. I think there is something in it. He said he would look matters over & see me soon." Additional sources include "Large Sale of Property in the Village of Ludington, Michigan," "Important Event in the History of the Village—Its Future Prospects—Personal," and "Great Sale of Property," all from *Mason County Record*, July 28, 1869.

48   "Railroad Men Coming," *Mason County Record*, August 11, 1869; "Railroad Party," *Mason County Record*, August 18, 1869; "Captain Ward Buys Two Mill Sites," *Mason County Record*, August 18, 1869.

49   The "long expected" quotation is from "F. & P.M. Railway," *Mason County Record*, October 2, 1872. Other sources include "Railroad Prospects," *Mason County Record*, March 13, 1872, October 2, 1872, August 27, 1873; *Mason County Record*, August 5, 1874; Ivey, *The Pere Marquette Railroad Company*, 221–22.

50   The first quotation is from Stiles, *The First Tycoon*, 136; the second is from Ward, *The Autobiography of David Ward*, 4. Additional sources include *History of Mason County*, 19; Brands, *American Colossus*, 87–89.

51   The quotation is from Misa, *A Nation of Steel*, 5. Casson addresses the controversy between Kelly and Bessemer and supports Kelly's claim. See Casson, *The Romance of Steel*, 4–15. Swank also supports Kelly, declaring, "Mr. Kelly claims for himself the discovery of the pneumatic principle of the Bessemer process several years before it dawned upon the mind of Mr. Bessemer. The validity of this claim can not be impeached." See Swank, *History of the Manufacture of Iron*, 399. More recently, Bessemer's priority over Kelly is addressed in Gordon, "The Kelly Converter"; Misa, "Controversy and Closure in Technological Change." Additional sources include Maw and Dredge, "The Invention of the Bessemer Process"; McHugh, *Alexander Holley and the Makers of Steel*, 112–35, 145–64; Korn, *Story of Bay View*, 51–52. Morris argues Edgar Thompson's Pennsylvania Railroad was a forerunner in the transition from iron rails to steel, beginning in 1861. Thompson eventually became convinced steel rails provided "eight times the service life at only twice the cost," even though they had to be imported from England. See Morris, *The Tycoons*, 124.

52   Swank, "The Bessemer Process in the United States"; Rogers, *An Economic History of the American Steel Industry*, 17–18; Temin, *Iron and Steel in Nineteenth-Century America*, 126; McHugh, *Alexander Holley and the Makers of Steel*, 174–79; Johnson, *The Twentieth Century Biographical Dictionary of Notable Americans*, 2012–13; Durfee, "An Account of the Experimental Steel Works at Wyandotte," 40–41; "Morrell, Daniel Johnson," Biographical Directory of the United States Congress, http://bioguide.congress.gov/, accessed October 16, 2018; "Bessemer Converter," Sheffield

Industrial Museums Trust, http://www.simt.co.uk/kelham-island-museum/what-to-see/outdoor-collection/bessemer-converter, accessed April 2, 2020.

53  The quotations are from Durfee, "An Account of the Experimental Steel Works at Wyandotte," 42, 43.

54  Ibid., 44, 45; McHugh, *Alexander Holley and the Makers of Steel*, 183–84.

55  Durfee, "An Account of the Experimental Steel Works at Wyandotte," 59. An additional source is Barnett, "Making America's First Steel in Wyandotte," 32–33. The successful production of steel at Wyandotte in May 1865 almost never happened. To continue his experiments, Durfee constructed an analytical laboratory, nicknamed "Durfee's Apothecary Shop," to further his study. This laboratory was the first of its kind connected to a steel plant in the United States. The employees at Wyandotte rejected his scientific approach, labeling him "little better than a mild sort of lunatic, or confirmed idiot" for his experimentation. The workers were likely threatened by his activities. Skilled puddlers often were considered "aristocrats" of the iron-making process. They spent hours each day stirring pig iron at a puddling, or furnace, so it could be hammered into wrought iron bars and taken to a rolling mill. Adoption of a new process might bypass these skilled workers. On another occasion, when Durfee again was forced to leave Wyandotte, a group of employees destroyed his laboratory, along with much of his correspondence. Durfee was bitter at the loss: "No person or thing was safe from the virus of their tongues or the penetration of their eyes." Eber Ward continually supported his efforts, but there is no record of his response to the actions of the other employees. See Durfee, "An Account of the Experimental Steel Works at Wyandotte," 42, 58. An additional source is McHugh, *Alexander Holley and the Makers of Steel*, 179–83.

56  Durfee, "The Development of American Industries," 27.

57  The first quotation is from Morris, *The Tycoons*, 189. The second is from McHugh, *Alexander Holley and the Makers of Steel*, 200. An additional source is "Washington Square Park, Alexander Lyman Holley," New York City Department of Parks and Recreation, https://www.nycgovparks.org/parks/washington-square-park/monuments/735, accessed June 18, 2021.

58  The quotation is from Maw and Dredge, "The Invention of the Bessemer Process," 414. Additional sources include Misa, *A Nation of Steel*, 19–20; Casson, *The Romance of Steel*, 17–18; Swank, *History of the Manufacture of Iron*, 409–11; *Owen vs. Potter*, 2:1151–52; Temin, *Iron and Steel in Nineteenth-Century America*, 127–30; Morris, *The Tycoons*, 127–28; Korn, "Eber Brock Ward, Pathfinder of American Industry," 157–58.

59  The quotation is from Durfee, "The Development of American Industries," 7. An additional source is Korn, "Eber Brock Ward, Pathfinder of American Industry," 158–61. Temin speculates that another factor weakening Ward's position was that he and his investors "were in some kind of financial difficulty and needed frequent infusions of capital to continue" their operations. He admits he does not know this for certain due to the absence of sources. See Temin, *Iron and Steel in*

*Nineteenth-Century America*, 129. McHugh argues that Ward's interest in spiritualism is another reason Ward was willing to settle so quickly. She offers the possibility that a medium may have advised Ward to settle, rather than pursue a lawsuit against Holley and his group, but sufficient evidence is lacking concerning this argument. See McHugh, *Alexander Holley and the Makers of Steel*, 206–7, 22n.

60 The first quotation is from "The City," *Detroit Post*, September 17, 1869, 4. The second is "A Stroke of Apoplexy," *Detroit Free Press*, September 17, 1869, 1. An additional source is "Ward's Will," *Detroit Free Press*, October 16, 1875, 1. When testifying at a trial later in 1897, Catherine Ward described Ward's stroke as "somewhat serious. I have always supposed myself he had heart disease, and I think so still." See *Owen vs. Potter*, 1:282.

## 7. Expanding an Empire

1 "Heavy Contract," *Mason County Record*, October 13, 1869.

2 The quotations are from "Capt. Ward's New Mill," *Mason County Record*, November 9, 1870. Several additional articles in the *Mason County Record* chronicle the progress of the North Mill's construction: "Another Saw Mill," March 9, 1870; "The Contract Let," April 13, 1870; "Personal," April 13, 1870; "New Pile Driver," May 18, 1870; "Completed," June 1, 1870; "To Begin Work," June 8, 1870; "Progressing," July 6, 1870; "Machinery Arrived," September 14, 1870. Other sources include Nagle, *Justus S. Stearns*, 16; *History of Mason County*, 50–51.

3 The quotation is from "A Fine Warehouse," November 1, 1871, *Mason County Record*. Additional sources include "Well Appointed Mill," *Mason County Record*, December 28, 1870; "A Good Purchase," *Mason County Record*, April 19, 1871; "Capt. Ward's Tenant Houses," *Mason County Record*, May 4, 1870; *Mason County Record*, May 22, 1872. *History of Mason County*, 51; Hannah, *Sand, Sawdust, and Saw Logs*, 29–31.

4 The first quotation is from *Mason County Record*, June 5, 1872. The second is in Maybee, *Michigan's White Pine Era*, 52. Additional sources include *History of Mason County*, 51; *Mason County Record*, June 12, 1872; "Mr. Ward's New Mill," *Mason County Record*, July 24, 1872; "Ward's New Mill—A Model Structure," *Mason County Record*, September 11, 1872; Nagle, *Justus S. Stearns*, 16; Peterson, *The Story of Ludington*, 15–16.

5 The first quotation is from Maybee, *Michigan's White Pine Era*, 11. The second is from *Mason County Record*, April 15, 1874. An additional source is Nagle, *Justus S. Stearns*, 16.

6 The quotation is from "Mr. Ward's New Mill," *Mason County Record*, July 24, 1872. The comparison between Ward's operations in Ludington and other lumber interests in the community is found in "Assessments," *Mason County Record*, May 7, 1873; and "Shipments," *Mason County Record*, July 29, 1874. The sale and shipment of Ward's lumber to Chicago and other markets is addressed in several articles from the *Mason County Record*, including November 29, 1871;

January 24, 1872; June 26, 1872; April 16, 1873; "Another New Lumbering Enterprise," May 21, 1873; June 18, 1873; July 2, 1873; March 18, 1874; April 15, 1874.

7  The first quotation is from "Ward's Will," *Detroit Free Press*, October 13, 1875, 3; the others are from "Ward's Will," *Detroit Free Press*, October 9, 1875, 1. Additional sources include "Personal," *Mason County Record*, December 15, 1869; "A Suggestion," *Mason County Record*, July 10, 1872; *History of Mason County*, 51.

8  The first quotation is from "Ward's Will," *Detroit Free Press*, October 21, 1875, 3. The others are from "An Inexperienced Lath Sawyer," *Mason County Record*, April 18, 1871. The home built by Milton Ward for his father is still standing in Ludington. It originally was located very near Ward's South Mill at 110 Sixth Street. It was moved to 309 South Washington Avenue in the early 1900s. Today, it is occupied by the Beacon Funeral Home and Pere Marquette Chapel. See Hawley, *Historic Mason County*, 260. The home is described as "finished and furnished in an elegant manner, is supplied with gas fixtures throughout, with speaking tubes and in fact almost everything necessary for convenience and comfort." See "Ward's New Mill—A Model Structure," *Mason County Record*, September 11, 1872.

9  The first quotation is from "Ward's Will," *Detroit Free Press*, October 15, 1875, 3; the second is from "Ward's Will," *Detroit Free Press*, October 16, 1875, 1.

10  The quotations concerning accidents are from *Mason County Record*, September 11, 1872; June 18, 1873. Additional sources include "Sad Accident," *Mason County Record*, August 28, 1872; *History of Mason County*, 51. Additional articles in the *Mason County Record* address the size of Ward's operations and wages paid. See "Michigan Lumber," May 21, 1873; July 16, 1873; and "Fourth Ward," April 29, 1874.

11  The quotation is from "Commendable," *Mason County Record*, October 9, 1872.

12  Several articles in the *Mason County Record* address the strike and problems with excessive inventory that emerged in 1873 and 1874. See "Opening of the Season's Work," May 7, 1873; "Michigan Lumber," May 21, 1873; June 18, 1873; "Lumbering—The Winter's Work," October 15, 1873; "Lumbering Interests," November 12, 1873; January 21, 1874; "The Lumber Business," February 18, 1874.

13  The quotation is from *Mason County Record*, February 18, 1874. Additional sources include Hannah, *Sand, Sawdust, and Saw Logs*, 31; *History of Mason County*, 51; *Mason County Record*, February 12, 1873.

14  The first quotation is from Carroll, "The Lake Erie Netherlands," 118. The second is from "Ward's Canal," 8. Another source chronicling Ward's activities in the Black Swamp is Fassett, *History of Oregon and Jerusalem Township*, 95–96, 171–72.

15  The quotations are from Carroll, "The Lake Erie Netherlands," 118. Another source is "Ward's Canal," 8.

16  Carroll, "The Lake Erie Netherlands," 118–19; Fassett, *History of Oregon and Jerusalem Township*, 96. According to the Jerusalem Township website, settlers

"decided to name the village Bunno after a member who was a resident of the Ottawa Indian tribe. Somehow, the spelling was changed." See "Jerusalem Township," https://twp.jerusalem.oh.us/history/, accessed May 16, 2020.

17 The first quotation is from Carroll, "The Lake Erie Netherlands," 119–21. The others are from "The Steamer Music," *Toledo Blade*, July 28, 1874, found in Eber Brock Ward, box 2, folder 41, E. B. Ward and Family, BGSU-Hall. Additional information concerning the vessels is found in "43-Leland," "47-Mars," "50-Mercury," "55-Music," and "86-Uranus," all from Eber Brock Ward, box 1, folder 31, Research Notes: vol. 14, vessels owned by Ward family, BGSU-Hall.

18 Carroll, "The Lake Erie Netherlands," 118, 121; Fassett, *History of Oregon and Jerusalem Township*, 95.

19 The first quotation is from "Ward's Canal," 8. The others are from "Princess Followed Mother's Footsteps," *Detroit Free Press*, December 21, 1916. See also Fassett, *History of Oregon and Jerusalem Township*, 95–96.

20 The quotations are all from "Ward's Will," *New York Times*, October 16, 1875, 1. Additional information is found in "Ward's Will," *New York Times*, October 27, 1875, 3.

21 The quotation is from "Ward's Will," *New York Times*, October 17, 1875, 5. Additional sources include Will Kedzie to Charlie Ward, May 22 [no year given]; and Will Kedzie to Charlie Ward, June 17, 1870; both are from the Seitz Family Collection.

22 The quotation is from Eber B. Ward to Mr. Scribner, July 1, 1874, quoted in "Ward's Will," *New York Times*, October 17, 1875, 5.

23 The quotation is from "In Bankruptcy: A Proposition Offered the Creditors of Charles H. Ward," *Toledo Blade*, October 30, 1874. Another source is "Marine News," *Toledo Blade*, September 30, 1874; both can be found in Eber Brock Ward, box 2, folder 41, Eber Ward and Family, 1855, 1874–1897, BGSU-Hall.

24 The quotation is from Carroll, "The Lake Erie Netherlands," 118; additional information is taken from the same source, 127–29. Another source is "Maumee Bay State Park," https://www.stateparks.com/maumee_bay_state_park_in_ohio.html, accessed July 31, 2020.

25 The first quotation is from Weeks, *Report on the Manufacture of Glass*, 29. The second is from "Plate Glass. A Pleasant Excursion of St. Louisiana to Crystal City," *St. Louis Republican*, October 30, 1875, 5. Special thanks are due to Dennis Northcott of the Missouri Historical Society for acquiring this and another article from the *St. Louis Republican*. The early history and development of the glass industry in the United States and Ward's activities with the American Plate Glass Company are taken from a range of sources. These include Weeks, *Report on the Manufacture of Glass*; Goodspeed, *History of Franklin, Jefferson, Washington, Crawford and Gasconade Counties*, 436–37; Roop, *Pittsburgh Plate Glass Company*; Roop, "Works No. Nine." Additionally, chapter 15 of Korn's dissertation addresses Ward's involvement in the glass industry. See Korn, "Eber Brock Ward, Pathfinder of American Industry," 232–44.

26 Some sources argue the initial capitalization was at $150,000, which was quickly exhausted and increased to $250,000. Others argue it was capitalized at $250,000 initially. Regardless, by 1874 all agree it had reached $500,000. The area that would become Crystal City was described as "a wilderness" in "Plate Glass. A Pleasant Excursion," *St. Louis Republican*, October 30, 1875, 5. Additional sources include "Plate Glass. The Works at Crystal City," *St. Louis Republican*, January 22, 1874, 1; Goodspeed, *History of Franklin, Jefferson, Washington, Crawford and Gasconade Counties*, 438.

27 "Plate Glass. The Works at Crystal City," *St. Louis Republican*, January 22, 1874, 1.

28 Ibid.

29 Ibid.

30 The quotation is from Korn, "Eber Brock Ward, Pathfinder of American Industry," 238. Additional sources include "Plate Glass. A Pleasant Excursion," *St. Louis Republican*, October 30, 1875, 5; Goodspeed, *History of Franklin, Jefferson, Washington, Crawford and Gasconade Counties, Missouri*, 438–39; Eaton, "How Missouri Counties, Towns, and Streams Were Named," 180.

31 The quotations are from Goodspeed, *History of Franklin, Jefferson, Washington, Crawford and Gasconade Counties*, 440. Another source is Korn, "Eber Brock Ward, Pathfinder of American Industry," 238.

32 The first two quotations are from Roop, "Works No. Nine," 4; the last is from Weeks, *Report on the Manufacture of Glass*, 99. Another source is Korn, "Eber Brock Ward, Pathfinder of American Industry," 240–41.

33 The first quotation is from "Silver Islet," *Detroit Post*, July 22, 1872, 3. The second is from Macfarlane, *Silver Islet*, 9–10.

34 The quotation is from "Romance of a Mine," *Spokesman-Review*, July 16, 1899, 1. The early history and development of the Sliver Islet is taken from the sources above and a range of additional sources. These include Forster, "The History of the Settlement of Silver Islet"; "A Solid Silver Island," *Stark County Democrat*, December 15, 1870, 1; "Silver Mining Location on Lake Superior," *Islander*, September 1, 1871, 1; "The Lake Superior Silver Island," *Detroit Post*, November 7, 1870, 3; "Silver Islet," *Detroit Post*, July 22, 1872, 3; Kathy Warnes, "Canadian Silver Islet—Mining Silver under Lake Superior with Backing from Detroit," *Meandering Michigan History*, https://meanderingmichiganhistory.weebly.com/, accessed May 30, 2020; Elle Andra-Warner, "Silver Islet: The World's Richest Silver Mine," https://northernwilds.com/, accessed May 30, 2020; V. C. Smith, "Thomas McFarlane," *Dictionary of Canadian Biography*, http://www.biographi.ca/en/bio/macfarlane_thomas_13E.html, accessed May 31, 2020; Waters, *The Superior North Shore*, 88–90.

35 The quotations are from "A Solid Silver Island," *Stark County Democrat*, December 15, 1870, 1. Additional sources include Forster, "The History of the Settlement of Silver Islet," 203; "Silver Islet," *Detroit Post*, July 22, 1872, 3; Macfarlane, *Silver Islet*, 20.

36  The first quotation is from Warnes, "Canadian Silver Islet." The second is from "Romance of a Mine," *Spokesman-Review*, July 16, 1899, 1. Additional information is found in "Silver Islet," *Detroit Post*, July 22, 1872, 3; Forster, "The History of the Settlement of Silver Islet," 199–200; *Annual Report of the Silver Mining Company for Silver Islet for 1873*, 11.

37  The quotations are from "Silver Mining Location on Lake Superior," *Islander*, September 1, 1871, 1; "The North Shore of Lake Superior," *Buchanan County Bulletin*, July 21, 1871, 1. Additional information is found in "Silver Islet," *Detroit Post*, July 22, 1872, 3. The inflation-adjusted currency values are according to https://westegg.com/inflation/infl.cgi, accessed February 8, 2021.

38  The quotations are from *Annual Report of the Silver Mining Company for Silver Islet for 1873*, 11–12. An additional source is Forster, "The History of the Settlement of Silver Islet," 204–5.

39  The quotation is from "Silver Mining," *Chicago Tribune*, March 9, 1871, 2. Another source is Curtis, "The Wyandotte Silver Smelting and Refining Works," 89; Macfarlane, *Silver Islet*, 23.

40  The quotations are from Curtis, "The Wyandotte Silver Smelting and Refining Works," 90, 97. Additional information is found in DeWindt, *Proudly We Record*, 249; "Michigan, Manufacturing at Wyandotte," *Detroit Free Press*, July 25, 1874, 3. Several articles in the *Detroit Post* comment on the activities of Ward's silver smelting company at Wyandotte: "Silver Islet Product," July 30, 1872, 4; "Silver Mining," November 18, 1872, 4; "Silver Smelting" and "Type Metal," November 23, 1872, 4.

41  Ward's involvement with the Eureka mine in Utah is outlined in several articles appearing in Detroit newspapers. The quotation is from "The Silver Mine Swindle," *Detroit Daily Post*, December 12, 1872, 4. The next several paragraphs in the text include information from the following newspaper articles covering the "Eureka Mine Swindle." Citations will be included only if a direct quote has been used. The following articles are all from the *Detroit Daily Post*: "Slippery Speculators," December 15, 1873, 4; "Eureka," December 20, 1873, 4; "Joab Lawrence," February 27, 1874, 4. The following articles are from the *Detroit Free Press*: "The Ward Swindle," December 13, 1873, 1; "The Salted Silver Mine," January 4, 1874, 5; "Eureka! The Story of a Lamb," February 15, 1874, 3; "Joab Lawrence Discharged," March 28, 1874, 4; "The Ward-Lawrence Case," August 3, 1876, 2.

42  "The Silver Mine Swindle," *Detroit Daily Post*, December 12, 1872, 4.

43  "The Salted Silver Mine," *Detroit Free Press*, January 4, 1874, 5.

44  "Slippery Speculators," *Detroit Daily Post*, December 15, 1873, 4. The inflation-adjusted currency values areaccording to https://westegg.com/inflation/infl.cgi, accessed February 8, 2021.

45  "Eureka! The Story of a Lamb," *Detroit Free Press*, February 15, 1874, 3.

46  The quotations are all from "Ward's Will," *Detroit Free Press*, October 16, 1875, 1. Additional sources include Jones, "Miss Emily Ward," 588; United States Census,

1870, Detroit Ward 9, Wayne, Michigan, p. 156, https://www.ancestry.com/, accessed December 17, 2019.

47 According to a letter from Mabel Ward Seitz (E. B. Ward's granddaughter) speaking of Catherine Ward, "Kate tried to be a good mother, in her own way, but made a big failure of it." See Mabel Seitz to Charles Seitz, January 6, 1896, Seitz Family Collection.

48 The quotation is from "Ward's Will," *Detroit Free Press*, October 17, 1875, 5. Additional sources include "New York State Inebriate Asylum," National Park Service, https://www.nps.gov/places/new-york-state-inebriate-asylum.htm, accessed June 18, 2020; "Another Suicide," *Detroit Free Press*, September 14, 1872, 1.

49 "Ward's Will," *Detroit Free Press*, October 16, 1875, 1.

50 The quotation is from "The Ward Will Case," *Burlington Free Press*, October 15, 1875, 1. Additional sources include "Ward's Will," *Detroit Free Press*, October 3, 1875, 5; "Ward's Will," *Detroit Free Press*, October 17, 1875, 5.

51 The first quotation is from "Ward's Will," *Detroit Free Press*, October 16, 1875, 1. The others are from "Ward's Will," *Detroit Free Press*, October 11, 1875, 5. Additional sources include *Owen vs. Potter*, 2:1529, 1536, Records and Briefs, Michigan Supreme Court, 72, April Term, 1897, State Law Library at the Library of Michigan, Lansing, MI; *Owen vs. Potter*, vol. 3, exhibit 261, 2502–3. Simone Natale argues that spiritualists provided a "brilliant form of amusement" and were associated with the "rise of the entertainment industry as we know it." See Natale, *Supernatural Entertainments*, 1, 2.

52 Potter, "Early Rail Making in Chicago," 26; Andreas, *History of Chicago*, 674; Misa, *A Nation of Steel*, 15.

53 The quotations are from Potter, "Early Rail Making in Chicago," 26. Potter had served as superintendent since the inception of the Chicago works. In 1871, Stephen Clement stepped down as president and Potter served as both president and superintendent. See Andreas, *History of Chicago*, 676. Another source is "The Sea of Fire," *Detroit Free Press*, October 10, 1871.

54 The quotation is from Hunt, "A History of the Bessemer Manufacture in America," 212. Additional sources include Potter, "Early Rail Making in Chicago," 26; Misa, *A Nation of Steel*, 22; Andreas, *History of Chicago*, 674–75.

55 "Captain E. B. Ward's Investment in Ore-Bearing Land," *Chicago Tribune*, February 21, 1873, 3.

56 Dickinson, "A Short History of the Leland Iron Works"; "A Detroit Enterprise," *Detroit Daily Post*, November 22, 1872, 4. Ward's purchase of the Leland Lake Superior Iron Company is mentioned briefly in Erhardt Peters, *Local History and Traditions of Leland*, Leelanau Historical Collection, Leelanau Historical Society, Leland, MI.

57 The quotations are from "A Detroit Enterprise," *Detroit Daily Post*, November 22, 1872, 4. Additional sources include Dickinson, "A Short History of the Leland Iron Works"; "General Items," *Detroit Daily Post*, November 23, 1872, 1.

58 The first quotation is from Stiles, *The First Tycoon*, 201. The second is from "Captain E. B. Ward's Investment in Ore-Bearing Land," *Chicago Tribune*, February 21, 1873, 3.

59 The quotation is from *Owen vs. Potter*, 2:1388. Additional information is from *Owen vs. Potter*, 2:1106–9, 1393. A good example of the shift from using iron rails to steel is demonstrated in the actions of the Milwaukee and St. Paul Railway Company, an important customer for railroad rails. In 1874, a report of the Milwaukee Chamber of Commerce declared, "The Milwaukee and St. Paul Railway Company has not built any new roads during the past year but has materially improved its main line by substituting steel rails in the place of iron, where most needed." See Langson, *Sixteenth Annual Statement of the Trade and Commerce of Milwaukee*, 18; Kopmeier, *From Mayville to Milwaukee*, 8–9.

60 The first quotation is from "The Strike at the Milwaukee Iron Works," *Chicago Tribune*, July 23, 1873, 3. The second is from "Milwaukee Iron Rollers on Strike," *New York Herald*, July 23, 1873, 7. Additional sources include *Lake County Star*, August 7, 1873, 1; "Strike at Milwaukee," *Wheeling Daily Intelligencer*, July 28, 1873, 1. These offer examples of newspapers in Illinois, New York, Michigan, and West Virginia that reported the walkout. An additional source is Kopmeier, *From Mayville to Milwaukee*, 8.

61 The quotations are from "The Closing of the Iron-Mill—An Unsatisfactory Explanation," *Chicago Tribune*, August 29, 1873, 8.

62 The quotations and additional material are from Brands, *American Colossus*, 80–82.

63 The first quotation is from *Owen vs. Potter*, 2:1399; the second and third are from "The Financial Stringency," *Detroit Daily Post*, November 3, 1873, 4. Additional sources include Langson, *Sixteenth Annual Statement of the Trade and Commerce of Milwaukee*, 31; Korn, *Story of Bay View*, 52–53; Langson, *Nineteenth Annual Statement of the Trade and Commerce of Milwaukee*, 116–17.

64 The quotation is from "Milwaukee Iron Company," *Chicago Tribune*, October 10, 1873, 8. Additional sources include "The Financial Stringency," *Detroit Daily Post*, November 3, 1873, 4; "Iron-Workers in Milwaukee," *Chicago Tribune*, March 30, 1874, 8; Langson, *Seventeenth Annual Statement of the Trade and Commerce of Milwaukee*, 99.

65 *Owen vs. Potter*, 2:1400.

66 The quotation is from *Owen vs. Potter*, 44. An additional source is "Second National Bank of Detroit," *Detroit Free Press*, November 2, 1863, 2.

67 The quotation is from "The Rolling Mill Notes," *Detroit Free Press*, November 20, 1873, 2. Additional sources include "An Elastic Currency Solved—The Problem Solved," *Detroit Free Press*, November 18, 1873, 2; E. B. Ward, "The Wyandotte Rolling Mill Notes," *Detroit Daily Post*, November 19, 1873, 3; *Detroit Daily Post*, November 19, 1873, 2; "The Wyandotte Scrip," *Detroit Daily Post*, November 22, 1873, 4; "Wyandotte Scrip," *Detroit Daily Post*, May 18, 1874, 4.

68  The first quotation is from "Silver Islet Mine," *Detroit Daily Post*, November 19, 1873, 3; the second is from "Ward's Will," *Detroit Free Press*, October 17, 1875, 5.

69  The quotations are from "Ward's Will," *Detroit Free Press*, October 16, 1875, 1. At the trial over Ward's will, Professor Allen A. Griffith testified to Ward's "sleepiness and nodding in the day"; see "Ward's Will," *Detroit Free Press*, October 1, 1875, 1. An additional source is Eliasz Engelhardt, "Apoplexy, Cerebrovascular Disease, and Stroke: Historical Definition of Terms and Definitions," *Dementia & Neuropsychologia* 11, no. 4 (October–December 2017), 449–53, https://www.ncbi.nlm.nih.gov/, accessed June 27, 2020.

70  Eber Ward to Mabel Ward, January 1, 1875, Seitz Family Collection.

71  Eber Ward to Emily Ward, January 2, 1875, January 2, 1875, Michigan Letters 1864–1915 folder, box 1, Ward Family Papers, BHC.

## 8. A Will and a Princess

1   The first two quotations are from "Dropped Dead," *Detroit News*, January 2, 1875, found in William Downie, "Scrap book," Eber Brock Ward Collection, 1939, BHC. The last quotation is from "Death of Captain E. B. Ward," *Detroit Free Press*, January 3, 1875, 1. Additional sources include William Downie, "Biography of Eber Brock Ward," 1941, Eber Brock Ward Collection, 1939, Burton Historical Collection, Detroit Public Library; Wargo, "A Case Without Parallel," 84.

2   "Dropped Dead," *Detroit News*, January 2, 1875.

3   "Capt. Ward, Reminiscences of His Life—His Wealth," *Detroit News*, January 4, 1875, found in Downie, "Scrap book," Eber Brock Ward Collection, 1939, BHC; "Death of Captain E. B. Ward," *Detroit Free Press*, January 3, 1875, 1; Wargo, "A Case Without Parallel," 85.

4   "Capt. Ward, Reminiscences of his Life—His Wealth," *Detroit News*, January 4, 1875; "Captain E. B. Ward," *Detroit Free Press*, January 6, 1875, found in Downie, "Scrap book," Eber Brock Ward Collection, 1939, BHC; Downie, "Biography of Eber Brock Ward."

5   The quotation is from Downie, "Biography of Eber Brock Ward." Additional sources include "Dust to Dust: The Funeral of Capt. Eber Brock Ward," *Detroit News*, January 6, 1875, found in Downie, "Scrap book," Eber Brock Ward Collection, 1939, BHC; Wargo, "A Case Without Parallel," 86.

6   The quotation is from "Dust to Dust: The Funeral of Capt. Eber Brock Ward," *Detroit News*, January 6, 1875. Additional sources include Downie, "Biography of Eber Brock Ward"; "Captain E. B. Ward: The Last Offices of the Living for the Dead," *Detroit Free Press*, January 7, 1875, found in Downie, "Scrap book," Eber Brock Ward Collection, 1939, BHC.

7   The best analysis of the fight over Ward's will is found in Wargo, "A Case Without Parallel." An additional source is "Ward's Will," *Detroit Free Press*, October 3, 1875, 5.

8   The provisions of Ward's will of 1874 and codicils are available in multiple locations. The copy used in the text was found in "Will of Eber B. Ward," Wallet ZW2I:

Eber Brock Ward Estate, Wallet 3, Theodore Romeyn Papers, 1836–1886, BHC. An additional source is Wargo, "A Case Without Parallel," 84–85. The inflation-adjusted currency values are according to https://westegg.com/inflation/infl.cgi, accessed February 8, 2021.

9   The first two quotations are from YUSEF, "The Ward Will Case: Statements Presented by Both Sides," *Detroit Free Press*, April 3, 1875, 3. The others are from "Eber Ward's Will: A Determined Fight between the Heirs in Prospect," *New York Times*, April 19, 1875, 8. An additional source is Wargo, "A Case Without Parallel," 87.

10  YUSEF, "The Ward Will Case: Statements Presented by Both Sides," *Detroit Free Press*, April 3, 1875, 3; "Bill of Complaint," March 30, 1875, Wallet ZW2I: Eber Brock Ward Estate, Wallet 3, Theodore Romeyn Papers, 1836–1886, BHC; Wargo, "A Case Without Parallel," 88–89.

11  With the exception of the final quotation, the quotations are from "Bill of Complaint," March 30, 1875, Wallet ZW2I: Eber Brock Ward Estate, Wallet 3, Theodore Romeyn Papers, 1836–1886, BHC. The final quote is from Wargo, "A Case Without Parallel," 89.

12  "Ward's Will: At Last the Long-Threatened Trial Begun," *Detroit Free Press*, September 22, 1875, 1.

13  Ibid.

14  The quotation is from "Ward's Will," *Detroit Free Press*, September 25, 1875, 1. Additional information is from "Ward's Will," *Detroit Free Press*, September 26, 1875, 5.

15  The quotations are from "Dr. Slade's Testimony," Wallet ZW2I: Eber Brock Ward Estate, Wallet 3, Theodore Romeyn Papers, 1836–1886, BHC. Additional information is found in Wargo, "A Case Without Parallel," 91–93.

16  "Ward's Will," *Detroit Free Press*, September 26, 1875, 5.

17  The first quotation is from "Ward's Will," *Detroit Free Press*, October 1, 1875, 1. The second is from "Ward's Will," *Detroit Free Press*, October 2, 1875, 1.

18  The first series of quotations is from "Ward's Will," *Detroit Free Press*, October 3, 1875, 5. The final quotation is from Wargo, "A Case Without Parallel," 95.

19  "Ward's Will," *Detroit Free Press*, October 8, 1875, 1.

20  The first quotation is from "Ward's Will," *Detroit Free Press*, October 13, 1875, 3. The others are from "Ward's Will," *Detroit Free Press*, October 9, 1875, 1.

21  The first two quotations are from "Ward's Will," *Detroit Free Press*, October 10, 1875, 5. The last is from "Ward's Will," *Detroit Free Press*, October 12, 1875, 1.

22  "Ward's Will," *Detroit Free Press*, October 16, 1875, 1.

23  "Ward's Will," *Detroit Free Press*, October 17, 1875, 5.

24  The first quotation is from "Ward's Will," *Detroit Free Press*, October 26, 1875, 1. The second is from "Ward's Will," *Detroit Free Press*, November 11, 1875, 1.

25  "Ward's Will," *Detroit Free Press*, November 11, 1875, 1.

26  "Law and Justice," *Detroit Free Press*, November 13, 1875, 1.

27  Ibid.

28   The first quotation is from "Ward's Millions," *Detroit Free Press*, March 10, 1876, 1. Additional information is found in "Ward's Millions: The Great Suit Ended by Compromise," *Detroit Free Press*, March 18, 1876, 1. Different sources reported various figures as to the amount of Catherine's payout, but the range was generally between $100,000 and $125,000. But during another trial involving Ward's estate in the 1890s, Catherine's brother T. R. Lyon testified that she paid $105,000, so this is the figure used in the text. See *Owen vs. Potter*, 1:721, Records and Briefs, Michigan Supreme Court, 72, April Term, 1897, State Law Library at the Library of Michigan, Lansing, MI.

29   "The Ward Will," *Chicago Tribune*, March 19, 1876, 4.

30   *Owen vs. Potter*, 1:268.

31   The value of properties and lumber in Mason County totaled $691,220.89, information found in "Will of Eber B. Ward," Theodore Romeyn Papers, 1836–1886, BHC. The quotations are from Justus Stearns to William Stearns, March 27, 1930, Stearns box, Stearns, J. S.—84th Birthday 1929 folder, Mason County Historical Society Archive, Ludington, MI. Stearns speculates that Catherine Ward earned "profits over $6,000,000" but this probably refers to the overall value of her estate when she died. Catherine's brother T. R. Lyon confirms the struggle Catherine experienced concerning the price of lumber when he testified at another trial concerning Ward's will in the 1890s. See *Owen vs. Potter*, 1:758–60.

32   The quotations are from "A Celebrated Case," *Detroit Free Press*, July 1, 1892, 9. It is unclear why the creditors came after Catherine since the portions of the estate she inherited were to be specifically free from debt. But her correspondence from the 1870s, subsequent newspaper accounts, and trial testimony appear to confirm this. See *Owen vs. Potter*, 1:282, 776; exhibit 186, "E. B. Ward's Legacies," *Detroit Journal*, December 3, 1888, found in *Owen vs. Potter*, 3:2384–91; "A Celebrated Case," *Detroit Free Press*, July 1, 1892, 9.

33   "A Celebrated Case," *Detroit Free Press*, July 1, 1892, 9.

34   "E. B. Ward's Legacies," *Detroit Journal*, December 3, 1888.

35   The first two quotations are from ibid. The last is from "A Celebrated Case," *Detroit Free Press*, July 1, 1892, 9. An additional source is "Owen vs. Potter," 986.

36   The quotation is from "Eber Ward and Aunt Emily: How It Was She Who Started the Prosecution," *Detroit Journal*, n.d. An additional source is "Millions at Stake," *Detroit Free Press*, May 23, 1896, 5; both articles are found in Seitz Family Collection. A final source is "Owen vs. Potter," 977–88.

37   Patrick Brode, "Cameron, Alexander," in *Dictionary of Canadian Biography*, http://www.biographi.ca/en/bio/cameron_alexander_12F.html, accessed August 30, 2020.

38   The first quotation is from Goodenough, *Lumber, Lath and Shingles*, 55. All others are from "Lost Her Title and Her Fortune," *Sunday Vindicator*, February 14, 1897. Numerous additional sources chronicle the escapades of Clara Ward, princess of Chimay and Caraman. The most accurate appear to be those written during

her lifetime. However, several sources written more recently also include helpful information, although they contain minor inaccuracies. Unless direct quotations are taken from the following sources, they will not be cited again. Sources accessed include Grimm, "The Celebrated Princess Chimay"; "Clara Ward, Princesse de Caraman-Chimay: An American Dollar Princess," *Crowns, Tiaras and Coronets*, posted July 31, 2016, http://crownstiarasandcoronets.blogspot.com/2016/07/clara-ward-princesse-de-caraman-chimay.html, accessed August 29, 2020; "A Princess with Conneaut Connections," *Star Beacon*, April 1, 2012; Bill Loomis, "'Downton Abbey Theme' Played out in 1800s Michigan," *Detroit News*, April 22, 2017; Dee Tucker, "American Beauty Who Married a Prince 66 Years Ago Had Milwaukee Relatives," *Milwaukee Journal*, May 15, 1956; Passante, "Clara Ward, Paparazzi Princess"; "Princess of Chimay Dead, Passing of the American Heiress Who Wedded a Prince and Eloped with a Gypsy," *San Francisco Call*, July 16, 1898, 3; James Jensen, "The Captain and the Princess," presentation, 2018 (author's collection).

39  The first quotation is from "Lost Her Title and Her Fortune," *Sunday Vindicator*, February 14, 1897. The second is from Dee Tucker, "American Beauty Who Married a Prince 66 Years Ago Had Milwaukee Relatives," *Milwaukee Journal*, May 15, 1956. The inflation-adjusted currency values are according to https://westegg.com/inflation/infl.cgi, accessed February 8, 2021.

40  The first quotation is from "Lost Her Title and Her Fortune," *Sunday Vindicator*, February 14, 1897. The second is from Bill Loomis, "'Downton Abbey Theme' Played out in 1800s Michigan," *Detroit News*, April 22, 2017. The full name of Prince Joseph was provided by Alain Espourteille, the great-grandson of Prince Joseph. Alain Espourteille, email to author, December 12, 2021.

41  The quotations are from "Lost Her Title and Her Fortune," *Sunday Vindicator*, February 14, 1897. Additional information is included in "Princess of Chimay Dead," *San Francisco Call*, July 16, 1898, 3; *Ludington Record*, May 22, 1890. Different sources sometimes identify May 19, 20, or 30 as the date of their marriage, but according to the wedding invitation, the date was May 20, 1890. The invitation was found in Ward, Eber Brock 1868–1875, n.d., Eber Brock Ward Papers, 1848–1875, BHC. Just about all sources identify Clara as seventeen years old when she married Prince Joseph. However, the wedding took place in May and her birthday was not until June 17, so she was just sixteen at the time of her wedding.

42  The first quotation is from "Clara Ward, Princesse de Caraman-Chimay: An American Dollar Princess," *Crowns, Tiaras and Coronets*, posted July 31, 2016, http://crownstiarasandcoronets.blogspot.com/2016/07/clara-ward-princesse-de-caraman-chimay.html, accessed August 29, 2020. The second is from "A Princess with Conneaut Connections," *Star Beacon*, April 1, 2012. A contemporary article addressing the number of Americans who married into European royal families with a list of American girls who married princes is found in "Our American Princesses in the Courts of Europe," *Washington Times*, April 24, 1904, 7–8.

43 The quotation is from "Lost Her Title and Her Fortune," *Sunday Vindicator*, February 14, 1897.

44 The first two quotations are from Mabel Seitz to Charles Seitz, January 6, 1896, Seitz Family Collection. Mabel was the daughter of John Ward and a half cousin of Eber Jr. The last is from "Lost Her Title and Her Fortune," *Sunday Vindicator*, February 14, 1897. Another source is "Boni de Castellane," *Wikipedia*, https://en .wikipedia.org, accessed September 2, 2020.

45 The quotations are from "Clara Ward, Princesse de Caraman-Chimay: An American Dollar Princess," *Crowns, Tiaras and Coronets*, posted July 31, 2016, http://crownstiarasandcoronets.blogspot.com/2016/07/clara-ward-princesse-de -caraman-chimay.html, accessed August 29, 2020.

46 The first quotation is from "Princess of Chimay Dead," *San Francisco Call*, July 16, 1898, 3. The second is from "Lost Her Title and Her Fortune," *Sunday Vindicator*, February 14, 1897.

47 The first quotations are from "The Eloping Princess," *New York Times*, December 25, 1896, 5. The last is from "Lost Her Title and Her Fortune," *Sunday Vindicator*, February 14, 1897.

48 The quotation is from "Clara Ward, Princesse de Caraman-Chimay: An American Dollar Princess," *Crowns, Tiaras and Coronets*, posted July 31, 2016, http:// crownstiarasandcoronets.blogspot.com/2016/07/clara-ward-princesse-de -caraman-chimay.html, accessed August 29, 2020. Additional sources include "Divorces Granted in Europe," *New York Times*, February 3, 1897, 7; Passante, "Clara Ward, Paparazzi Princess." It is possible that an additional factor led Clara to divorce her husband. According to Clara's great-grandson, Alain Espourteille, Joseph was having an affair. He kept a mistress, with whom he had children, but they never married because he considered her to be below him in status. Espourteille explained that Clara became furious when she found out about Joseph's other family, prompting her to seek a divorce. Alain Espourteille, telephone conversation with author, November 28, 2021. After hearing this story, the author contacted Philippe de Caraman-Chimay, the current prince of Chimay, who declared, "I have no idea if my grandfather had a mistress and two children. What I know for sure is that Clara was not an angel. . . . For the rest of the story, you surely know about her and the scandals she provoked." Philippe de Chimay, email to author, February 13, 2022.

49 The first quotation is from "Gone with a Gypsy," *Ludington Record*, December 24, 1896, 3. The second is from *Wyandotte Herald*, February 24, 1899. The third is from "Latest Folly of the Misguided but Beautiful Princess de Chimay," *New York Journal and Advertiser*, November 13, 1898, 15. The last is from "Lost Her Title and Her Fortune," *Sunday Vindicator*, February 14, 1897.

50 The first quotation is from "The Eloping Princess," *New York Times*, December 25, 1896, 5. The second is from "Deserted Her Gypsy Lover," *New York Times*, January 28, 1897, 2.

51  The quotation is from "Mme. Rigo's Photographs Suppressed," *New York Times*, August 8, 1897, 15. Additional sources include "Latest Folly of the Misguided but Beautiful Princess de Chimay," *New York Journal and Advertiser*, November 13, 1898, 15; Bill Loomis, "'Downton Abbey Theme' Played out in 1800s Michigan," *Detroit News*, April 22, 2017.

52  The quotations are from Healy, *Confessions of a Journalist*, 340. Information concerning compensation for Clara's performances is found in "Princess de Chimay in Demand," *Topeka State Journal*, January 12, 1897, 6; *Bourbon News*, March 23, 1897, 4. Additional sources include "Princess Chimay on Stage," *New York Times*, March 22, 1897, 7; "The Former Princess of Chimay Was Not Allowed to Appear on the Paris Stage," *New York Times*, April 16, 1897; Bill Loomis, "'Downton Abbey Theme' Played out in 1800s Michigan," *Detroit News*, April 22, 2017; Passante, "Clara Ward, Paparazzi Princess."

53  At least one researcher, Maggie McNeil, argues that Clara and Rigo inspired the Toulouse-Lautrec painting *Idylle Princière*. See McNeil, "The Princess de Caraman-Chimay," *The Honest Courtesan* (blog), January 22, 2012, https://maggiemcneill .wordpress.com/2012/01/22/the-princess-de-caraman-chimay/, accessed September 7, 2020. The Europeana Collections website offers a note concerning the painting: "Allusion to the affair between the Princess of Chimay and the gypsy Rigo." See "Princely Idyll," *Europeana Collections*, https://classic.europeana.eu/, accessed September 7, 2020. The Rigójancsi cake is discussed in Nikolina Demark, "Rigo Jancsi: A Cake, a Legend, a Forbidden Love," *Total Croatia News*, April 18, 2018, https://www.total-croatia-news.com/, accessed September 7, 2020; "Rigójancsi," *Wikipedia*, https://en.wikipedia.org/, accessed September 7, 2020.

54  The quotation is from "Princess Chimay Is Declared a Spendthrift and Conservator Appointed," *Evening-Times Republican*, May 23, 1901, 2. An additional source is "Lost Her Title and Her Fortune," *Sunday Vindicator*, February 14, 1897. The number of articles discussing the exploits of Clara and Rigo are seemingly never ending. They appear in newspapers throughout the United States. In addition to those previously identified, here are just a few: "De Chimay's Gipsy Dead," *Daily Ardmoreite*, June 9, 1899, 4; "Rigo Goes to China," *Indianapolis Journal*, June 12, 1899, 2; "Princes Chimay: Will Reside in Egypt," *El Paso Daily Herald*, March 27, 1899, 1; "Princess de Chimay: She Denies She Will Give Public Performances," *Salt Lake Herald*, January 15, 1897, 7. An additional source is "Clara Ward, Princesse de Caraman-Chimay: An American Dollar Princess," *Crowns, Tiaras and Coronets*, posted July 31, 2016, http://crownstiarasandcoronets.blogspot .com/2016/07/clara-ward-princesse-de-caraman-chimay.html, accessed August 29, 2020. The inflation-adjusted currency values are according to https://westegg.com/ inflation/infl.cgi, accessed February 8, 2021.

55  The first quotation is from "The Princess Chimay Tires of Her Gipsy," *Spokane Press*, January 30, 1903, 2. The others are from "Princess Chimay Loves Again," *Evening Statesman*, July 12, 1904, 3. Additional sources include "Chimay Buys off Rigo and Marries Riccardo," *Washington Times*, August 18, 1904, 2.

56 Hughes, "The Erratic Erotic Princess Chimay." A profile of Dr. Hughes is found in "Dr. C. H. Hughes, 77, Noted as Alienist, Dies at Home Here," *St. Louis Star and Times*, July 13, 1916, 3. Dr. Geoff Kramer, author of a popular textbook in clinical psychology, read the analysis of C. H. Hughes. His comments help to offer context for the "diagnosis" offered by Hughes. "First, just in general, the field of clinical psychology was in its infancy in 1904 when Dr. Hughes wrote his article. Back then, most psychologists were laboratory empiricists concerned with measuring and understanding individual differences, reaction times, child development, intelligence, etc. Clinical psychologists—those concerned with mental illness and treatment—were in the minority. The perception of psychologists as professionals who diagnose and treat persons with disorders did not really become dominant until after WWII. That's not to say that there were no clinicians before that, but rather that clinicians back then were trained as doctors who took an interest in neurology or psychiatry. It took decades for doctors to cede turf to the invasive, non-MD psychologists. In the late 1800s and early 1900s, clinical practice was dominated by case study methods. The cases focused on often involved dissociative states and sexual deviance. Partly owing to the strong Victorian/European influence—consider Freud and his contemporaries—clinical psychology advanced by one after another write-ups of interesting cases, almost as if there was a competition to see who could document the weirdest case. In 1904, there was no agreed upon diagnostic classification system, no agreed upon nomenclature for judging what was normal versus abnormal. The criteria for deciding what was abnormal was often left up to whatever doctor was presenting the case. . . . The term nymphomania, used liberally in Dr. Hughes's article on Princess Chimay, made it into the first *Diagnostic and Statistical Manual of Mental Disorders*, published in 1952. For many psychiatrists, strong sexual desires experienced by women were indications of diseased minds. The term was finally removed in the 1980s. But there still exists debate about whether certain forms of 'sexual addiction' should be considered disorders that require treatment." Geoff Kramer, email to author, August 8, 2020.

57 Hughes, "The Erratic Erotic Princess Chimay," 360.

58 "Clara Ward Asks Divorce," *New York Times*, July 16, 1910, 4; "Detroit Princess Dies After Eventful Career," *Detroit Free Press*, December 19, 1916, 1; "Clara Ward, Princesse de Caraman-Chimay: An American Dollar Princess," *Crowns, Tiaras and Coronets*, posted July 31, 2016, http://crownstiarasandcoronets.blogspot .com/2016/07/clara-ward-princesse-de-caraman-chimay.html, accessed August 29, 2020.

59 The quotation is from "Mrs. Eber Brock Ward Will Not Get a Divorce," *The Times*, June 13, 1900, 4. Eber Jr.'s relationship with his wife's maid is also described in "Princess Followed in Her Mother's Footsteps," *Detroit Free Press*, December 21, 1916, 10.

60 The first quotation is from "Princess Followed in Her Mother's Footsteps," *Detroit Free Press*, December 21, 1916, 10. The second is from Mabel Seitz to Charles

Seitz, January 6, 1896, Seitz Family Collection. For Morrow, see "John M. Morrow," https://gw.geneanet.org/, accessed September 7, 2020. An additional source is "The Passing of a Remarkable Woman," *Ludington Daily News*, April 25, 1916, 3.

61 "Princess Followed in Her Mother's Footsteps," *Detroit Free Press*, December 21, 1916, 10; "Princess Disinherited," *New York Times*, May 29, 1915, 15; "Son Would Break Mother's Will," *Detroit Free Press*, October 1, 1916, 4. The newspaper article identifying the breakdown of Catherine's will identifies only three grandchildren (Princess Marie de Chimay, Prince Joseph de Chimay, and Eugenia Phyllis Ward); however, Eugenia had a twin, so presumably, her twin received an equal share.

62 The first quotations are from "Detroit Princess Dies After Eventful Career," *Detroit Free Press*, December 19, 1916, 1. The final quotation is from "Clara Ward Is Dead in Paris," *Sun*, December 19, 1916, 1. Additional information is taken from "Clara Ward Dies in Italy," *New York Times*, December 19, 1916, 3.

63 The quotations are from "Clara Ward Died Rich," *New York Times*, May 22, 1917, 11. Additional information is taken from "Clara Ward Left $1,124,935 Estate," *New York Times*, December 23, 1916, 11; "Clara Ward Is Dead in Paris," *Sun*, December 19, 1916, 1.

64 The quotation is from Mabel Seitz to Charles Seitz, January 6, 1896, Seitz Family Collection. See also "Clara Ward's Kin Wills $1,035,000," *Detroit Free Press*, November 14, 1918, 1. The inflation-adjusted currency values are according to https://westegg.com/inflation/infl.cgi, accessed February 8, 2021.

65 The quotation is from Bancroft, "Memoir of Capt. Samuel Ward," 343.

66 "Will of Eber B. Ward," Theodore Romeyn Papers, 1836–1886, BHC.

## Epilogue

1 "A Surprise," *Detroit Free Press*, December 27, 1871, 1.

2 The quotations are from ibid. Additional sources include "Death of the Artist Stanley," *Detroit Free Press*, April 11, 1872, 1; Hassrick and Besaw, *Painted Journeys*, 257–58.

3 The quotation is from Hassrick and Besaw, *Painted Journeys*, 257. An additional source is "A Surprise," *Detroit Free Press*, December 27, 1871, 1.

4 Justin Wargo effectively contends, "The diminution of Ward's remembrance was significantly affected by a messy yet thrilling court case over his will that was sensationalized in both the local and national press." See Wargo, "A Case Without Parallel," 82. Another source is Stiles, *The First Tycoon*, 549.

5 The quotation is from "The Last Reminder Gone," *Detroit Free Press*, April 11, 1879, 8. Additional sources include Downie, "Scrap book," Eber Brock Ward Collection, 1939, BHC; Rex G. White, "Gay Clara, Wild and Beautiful, Is Gone with the Wind," *Detroit News*, March 23, 1947.

6 The quotations are from "Capt. Ward's Faith in City Justified," *Detroit Free Press*, October 27, 1925.

7 Mark R. Wilson, "North Chicago Rolling Mill Company," *Encyclopedia of Chicago*, http://www.encyclopedia.chicagohistory.org/, accessed September 27, 2020.

8 The first quotation is from Downie, "Biography of Eber Brock Ward." The second is from Ward, *The Autobiography of David Ward*, 4.

9 Andreas, *History of Milwaukee*, 1617–18.

10 "Real Builders of America," 596.

# Bibliography

## Manuscript Collections

Bowling Green State University, Center for Archival Collections, Bowling Green, OH
   Great Lakes History Collection, GLMS 101-Kenneth R. Hall Collection
Burton Historical Collection of the Detroit Public Library, Detroit, MI
   Eber Brock Ward Collection, 1939
   Eber Brock Ward Papers, 1848–1875
   Fort Street Presbyterian Church Records, 1849–1962
   Samuel Ward Papers, 1844
   Theodore Romeyn Papers, 1836–1886
   Ward Family Papers, 1807–1945
Clarke Historical Library, Central Michigan University, Mount Pleasant, MI
   E. B. Ward Family Papers
Community Pride and Heritage Museum Archive, Marine City, MI
   Ward Family Collection
Leelanau Historical Society, Leland, MI
   Leelanau Historical Collection
Milwaukee County Historical Society Research Library, Milwaukee, WI
   Korn Papers
New York Historical Society, New York, NY
   Ludington Family Papers
Seitz Family Collection (personal collection)
State Law Library at the Library of Michigan, Lansing, MI
   *Owen vs. Potter*. Records and Briefs, Michigan Supreme Court, 72, April Term, 1897.

## Newspapers

*Bayview Compass*
*Bourbon News*
*Buchanan County Bulletin*
*Burlington Free Press*
*Chicago Tribune*
*Cleveland Morning Leader*
*Daily American Telegraph*
*Daily Ardmoreite*
*Daily Cleveland Herald*
*Daily News*
*Detroit Advertiser
   and Tribune*
*Detroit Daily Post*
*Detroit Free Press*
*Detroit Journal*
*Detroit News*
*Detroit Post*
*El Paso Daily Herald*

Evening Star
Evening Statesman
Evening-Times Republican
Fredonia Censor
Grand Haven News
Grand River Times
Indianapolis Journal
Islander
Lake County Star
Ludington Chronicle
Ludington Daily News
Ludington Record
Mason County Press
Mason County Record
Memphis Daily Appeal
Milwaukee Journal

Nashville Union and
    American
National Era
New York Daily Tribune
New York Herald
New York Journal
    and Advertiser
New York Times
Portage Sentinel
Port Huron Commercial
Port Huron Times-Herald
Salt Lake Herald
San Francisco Call
Spokane Press
Spokesman-Review
Star Beacon

Stark County Democrat
St. Louis Republican
St. Louis Star and Times
Sun
Sunday Vindicator
Times
Toledo Blade
Topeka State Journal
Vermont Watchman
    and State Journal
Washington Times
Watertown Republican
Western Reserve Chronicle
Wheeling Daily Intelligencer
Wilmington Journal
Wisconsin Tribune

## Government Documents

Chandler, William. *History of the St. Mary's Falls Ship Canal.* Lansing: W. S. George, 1878.

*Detroit City Directory, 1850.* Detroit: Dunklee, Wales, 1850.

Johnson, J. D. *Detroit City Directory, 1853–54.* Detroit: R. F. Johnstone, 1853.

Kappel, William M. *Salt Production in Syracuse, New York ("The Salt City") and the Hydrogeology of the Onondaga Creek Valley.* Washington, DC: U.S. Geologic Survey, 2000. Available online at https://pubs.usgs.gov/fs/2000/0139/report.pdf.

Langson, William J. *Thirteenth Annual Statement of the Trade and Commerce of Milwaukee.* Milwaukee: Evening Wisconsin Printing House, 1871.

——. *Fifteenth Annual Statement of the Trade and Commerce of Milwaukee.* Milwaukee: Daily Sentinel Book and Job Printing House, 1873.

——. *Sixteenth Annual Statement of the Trade and Commerce of Milwaukee.* Milwaukee: Cramer, Aikens & Cramer, 1874.

——. *Seventeenth Annual Statement of the Trade and Commerce of Milwaukee.* Milwaukee: Sentinel, 1875.

——. *Nineteenth Annual Statement of the Trade and Commerce of Milwaukee.* Milwaukee: Cramer, Aikens & Cramer, 1877.

Maccabe, Julius P. Bolivar. *Detroit City Directory, 1837.* Detroit: William Harsha, 1837.

*Shove's Detroit City Directory, 1852–53.* Detroit: Free Press Book, 1852.

U.S. Department of Commerce. *Statistical Abstract of the United States, 1922,* no. 45. Washington, DC: GPO, 1923.

U.S. Department of Labor, Bureau of Labor Statistics. *History of Wages in the United States from Colonial Times to 1928,* no. 604. Washington, DC: GPO, 1934.

Weeks, J. W. *Detroit City Directory, 1873–1874.* Detroit: Tribune, 1873.

——. *Detroit City Directory, 1874–1875.* Detroit: Tribune, 1874.

Weeks, Jos. D. *Report on the Manufacture of Glass*. Washington, DC: GPO, 1884.

Wellings, James H. *Detroit City Directory, 1846*. Detroit: A. S. Williams, 1846.

## Published Pamphlets

*Annual Report of the Silver Mining Company for Silver Islet for 1873*. New York: John W. Amerman, 1874.

*Lake Superior Iron, Wyandotte Rolling Mill, and Eureka Iron Company, Detroit, Michigan*. Detroit: Daily Advertiser Steam Power Press, 1860.

National Convention of Manufacturers. *Report of the Delegation Sent to Washington by the National Manufacturers Convention, Cleveland, Ohio, December 18, 1867*. American Broadsides and Ephemera series 1, no. 12568. Washington, DC, 1868.

Roop, Lewis W. *Pittsburgh Plate Glass Company*. Pittsburgh: Pittsburgh Plate Glass, 1940.

Ward, Eber B. *Address of E. B. Ward of Detroit Delivered Before the Manufacturers National Convention, Held at Cleveland, May 27, 1868*. American Broadsides and Ephemera series 1, no. 12628. Cleveland, 1868.

——. *The Farmer and the Manufacturer: Address to the Wisconsin State Agricultural Society*. Detroit, 1868.

——. *Protection vs. Free Trade, National Wealth vs. National Poverty*. Detroit, 1865. Available at Burton Historical Collection, Detroit Public Library.

——. *Reasons Why the Northwest Should Have a Protective Tariff and Why the Republican Party Is the Safest Party to Trust with the Government*. Detroit, 1860. Available at Burton Historical Collection, Detroit Public Library.

——. *Washington, January 16, 1868. To the Honorable [blank] Sir*. American Broadsides and Ephemera series 1, no. 12629. Washington, DC, 1868.

## Books, Journal and Magazine Articles, and Theses

Andreas, A. T. *History of Chicago: From the Earliest Period to the Present Time*. Vol. 2. Chicago: A. T. Andreas, 1885.

——. *History of Milwaukee, Wisconsin: From Pre-historic Times to the Present Date*. Vol. 2. Chicago: Western Historical, 1881.

——. *History of St. Clair County, Michigan*. Chicago: A. T. Andreas, 1883.

*Annual Report of the Flint & Pere Marquette Railway Company Made to the Stockholders for the Fiscal Year Ending December 1, 1868*. Detroit: Daily Post Book and Job Printing Establishment, 1869. Available at Bentley Historical Library, Ann Arbor, MI.

Babson, Steve. *Working Detroit: The Making of a Union Town*. Detroit: Wayne State University Press, 1986.

Bancroft, William L. "Aunt Emily Ward: Some Events in the Life of a Unique Woman." *Michigan Pioneer and Historical Collections* 21 (1894): 367–70.

——. "Memoir of Capt. Samuel Ward, with a Sketch of the Early Commerce of the Upper Lakes." *Michigan Pioneer and Historical Collections* 21 (1894): 336–67. A copy of this manuscript is also available in the Ward, Eber folder, Michigan Community Pride and Heritage Museum Archive, Marine City, MI.

BarnettLeRoy. "Making America's First Steel in Wyandotte." *Michigan History* 88, no. 4 (July–August 2004): 28–34.

Beasley, Norman. *Freighters of Fortune: The Story of the Great Lakes*. New York: Harper & Brothers, 1930.

Benedict, Michael Les. *The Impeachment and Trial of Andrew Johnson*. New York: Norton, 1973.

Boyer, Stephen. *The Enduring Vision*. Boston: Wadsworth, Cengage, 2013.

Brands, H. W. *American Colossus: The Triumph of Capitalism, 1865–1890*. New York: Doubleday, 2010.

Braude, Ann. *Radical Spirits: Spiritualism and Women's Rights in Nineteenth-Century America*. Boston: Beacon, 1989.

Brody, David. *Steelworkers in America: The Nonunion Era*. Cambridge, MA: Harvard University Press, 1960.

Buel, Gene, and Scott Buel. *Images of America: Marine City*. Charleston, SC: Arcadia, 2012.

Burr, E. D. "Navigation vs. Banking." *Michigan Pioneer and Historical Collections* 28 (1900): 652–53.

Burrows, Edwin G., and Mike Wallace. *Gotham: A History of New York City to 1898*. New York: Oxford University Press, 1999.

Burton, Clarence M. *The City of Detroit Michigan, 1701–1922*. Vol. 1. Detroit: S. J. Clarke, 1922.

Cabot, James L. *Images of America: Ludington, 1830–1900*. Chicago: Arcadia, 2005.

Canham, Hugh O. "Hemlock and Hide: The Tanbark Industry in Old New York." *Northern Woodlands* (Summer 2011): 36–41. Available online at http://northernwoodlands .org/articles/article/hemlock-and-hide-the-tanbark-industry-in-old-new-york.

"Captain Eber B. Ward's Fortress." *Detroit Monthly* 1, no. 3 (May 1901): 20–21.

Carlisle, Fred. *Chronography of Notable Events in the History of the Northwest Territory and Wayne County*. Detroit: O. S. Gulley, Bornman, 1890.

Carroll, Lyllian M. "The Lake Erie Netherlands." *Northwest Ohio Quarterly* 51, no. 4 (1979): 115–31.

Casson, Herbert N. *The Romance of Steel: the Story of a Thousand Millionaires*. New York: A. S. Barnes, 1907.

*Catalogue of 525,000 Acres of Pine Timber Lands belonging to the Saint Mary's Falls Ship Canal Company*. Detroit: Advertiser and Tribune, 1863.

Catlin, George B. "Oliver Newberry." *Michigan History Magazine* 18 (Winter 1934): 5–24.

———. *The Story of Detroit*. Detroit: Detroit News, 1923.

Chandler, William. *History of the St. Mary's Falls Ship Canal*. Lansing: W. S. George, 1878.

Christian, E. P. "Historical Associations Connected with Wyandotte and Vicinity." *Michigan Pioneer and Historical Collections* 13 (1889): 308–24.

Cox, Robert, S. *Body and Soul: A Sympathetic History of American Spiritualism*. Charlottesville: University of Virginia Press, 2003.

Crampton, Emeline Jenks. *History of the Saint Clair River*. St. Clair, MI: St. Clair Republican, 1921.

Curtis, W. M. "The Wyandotte Silver Smelting and Refining Works." *Transactions of the American Institute of Mining Engineers* 2 (May 1873–February 1874): 89–101.

Detroit & Milwaukee Railway Company. *Condition and Prospect of the Detroit and Milwaukee Railway, from Detroit to Grand Haven*. Detroit: Steam Power Presses of E. A. Wales, 1855.

DeWindt, Edwina M. *Proudly We Record . . . The Story of Wyandotte, Michigan*. Wyandotte: Rotary Club of Wyandotte, Michigan, 1985.

DeWindt, Edwina M., and Joseph C. DeWindt. *Our Fame and Fortune in Wyandotte*. Wyandotte: Rotary Club of Wyandotte, Michigan, 1985.

Dickinson, Frederick W. "A Short History of the Leland Iron Works." In *A Short History of the Leland Iron Works*, edited by Harley W. Rhodehamel, 6–12. Leland, MI: Leelanau Historical Society, 2007.

Dickinson, John N. *To Build a Canal: Sault Ste. Marie, 1853–1854 and After*. Columbus: OH: State University Press for Miami University, 1981.

Donahue, Raymond M. "Captain Samuel Ward, Pioneer of Great Lakes Transportation, 1784–1854." Master's thesis, Wayne State University, 1973.

Dunbar, Willis F., and George S. May. *Michigan: A History of the Wolverine State*. Grand Rapids, MI: William B. Eerdmans, 1995.

Duncan, Francis. "The Story of the D&C, Part I." *Inland Seas* 7, no. 2 (1951): 219–28.

———. "The Story of the D&C, Part II." *Inland Seas* 8, no. 1 (1952): 49–55.

———. "The Story of the D&C, Part IV." *Inland Seas* 8, no. 3 (1952): 167–76.

Durfee, W. F. "An Account of the Experimental Steel Works at Wyandotte, Michigan." *Transactions of the American Society of Mechanical Engineers* 6 (November 1884 and May 1885): 40–60.

———. "The Development of American Industries since Columbus. IX. The Manufacture of Steel (Concluded)." *Popular Science Monthly* 40 (November 1891–April 1892): 15–40.

Eaton, David W. "How Missouri Counties, Towns, and Streams Were Named." *Missouri Historical Review* 11, no. 2 (1917): 164–200.

Elliott, James L. *Red Stacks over the Horizon*. Grand Rapids, MI: William B. Eerdmans, 1967.

Ellis, David M., ed. *The Frontier in American Development: Essays in Honor of Paul Wallace Gates*. Ithaca, NY: Cornell University Press, 1969.

Engelhardt, Eliasz. "Apoplexy, Cerebrovascular Disease, and Stroke: Historical Definition of Terms and Definitions." *Dementia & Neuropsychologia* 11, no. 4 (2017): 449–53.

Farmer, Silas. *History of Detroit and Wayne County and Early Michigan*, vol. 1. Detroit: Silas Farmer, 1884.

———. *History of Detroit and Wayne County and Early Michigan*, vol 2. Detroit: Silas Farmer, 1890.

Farrand, Mrs. B. C. "St. Clair County: Reminiscences of Mrs. George Palmer." *Michigan Pioneer and Historical Collections* 7 (1886): 564–66.

Fassett, Josephine. *History of Oregon and Jerusalem Township: The Story of Two Communities.* Camden, AR: Hurley, 1961.

Felch, Alpheus. "Early Banks and Banking in Michigan." *Michigan Pioneer and Historical Collections* 2 (1880): 111–24.

Fergus, Robert. *Chicago River and Harbor Convention: An Account of Its Origins and Proceedings.* Chicago: Fergus, 1882.

Fitch, Catherine A., and Steven Ruggles. "Historical Trends in Marriage Formation: United States 1850–1990." In *The Ties That Bind: Perspectives on Marriage and Cohabitation*, edited by Linda J. Waite, 59–90. New York: de Gruyter, 2000.

*Flint and Pere Marquette Railway Company, Project for the Construction of 140 Miles of Its Road.* Detroit: O. S. Gulley Book and Job Printer, 1864. Available at Bentley Historical Library, Ann Arbor, MI.

Foner, Eric. *The Fiery Trial: Abraham Lincoln and American Slavery.* New York: Norton, 2010.

———. *Gateway to Freedom: The Hidden History of the Underground Railroad.* New York: Norton, 2016.

Formisano, Ronald P. *The Birth of Mass Political Parties: Michigan, 1827–1861.* Princeton, NJ: Princeton University Press, 1971.

Forster, John H. "The History of the Settlement of Silver Islet, on the North Shore of Lake Superior." *Michigan Pioneer and Historical Collections* 14 (1890): 197–205.

Fox, Cynthia G. "Income Tax Records of the Civil War Years." *Prologue* 18, no. 4 (Winter 1986): 250–59. Available online at https://www.archives.gov/publications/prologue/1986/winter/civil-war-tax-records.html.

Frost, Karolyn Smardz, and Veta Smith Tucker, eds. *A Fluid Frontier: Slavery, Resistance and the Underground Railroad in the Detroit River Borderland.* Detroit: Wayne State University Press, 2016.

Fuller, George Newman. "An Introduction to the Settlement of Southern Michigan from 1815 to 1835." *Michigan Pioneer and Historical Collections* 38 (1912): 539–79.

———. "Settlement of Michigan Territory." *Mississippi Valley Historical Review* 2, no. 1 (June 1915): 25–55.

Gamber, Wendy. *The Female Economy: The Millinery and Dressmaking Trades, 1860–1930.* Urbana: University of Illinois Press, 1997.

Gara, Larry. *Westernized Yankee: The Story of Cyrus Woodman.* Madison: State Historical Society of Wisconsin, 1956.

Goodenough, Luman W. *Lumber, Lath and Shingles.* Detroit: Daniel W. Goodenough, 1954.

Goodspeed, W. A. *History of Franklin, Jefferson, Washington, Crawford and Gasconade Counties, Missouri.* Chicago: Goodspeed, 1888.

Gordon, Robert B. "The Kelly Converter." *Technology and Culture* 33 (1992): 769–79.

Gordon-Reed, Annette. "The Fight over Andrew Johnson's Impeachment Was a Fight for the Future of the United States." *Smithsonian Magazine*, January 2018, 22–24.

Gottschalk, Stephen. *The Emergence of Christian Science in American Religious Life.* Berkeley: University of California Press, 1973.

Gray, Susan E. *The Yankee West: Community Life on the Michigan Frontier*. Chapel Hill: University of North Carolina Press, 1996.

Grimm, Joe. "The Celebrated Princess Chimay." *Michigan History*, January/February 2013, 14–19.

Hannah, Frances Caswell. *Sand, Sawdust, and Saw Logs: Lumber Days in Ludington*. Ludington, MI: Frances Caswell Hannah, 1955.

Harrington, Daniel B. "Daniel B. Harrington." *Michigan Pioneer and Historical Collections* 5 (1884): 138–43.

Hassrick, Peter H., and Mindy N. Besaw. *Painted Journeys: The Art of John Mix Stanley*. Norman: University of Oklahoma Press, 2015.

Hatcher, Harlon. *Lake Erie*. New York: Bobbs-Merrill, 1945.

Haviland, Laura S. *A Woman's Life Work: Labors and Experiences of Laura Smith Haviland*. Cincinnati: Walden & Stowe, 1882.

Hawley, Thomas A., ed. *Historic Mason County*. Ludington, MI: Mason County Historical Society, 1980.

Healy, Chris. *Confessions of a Journalist*. London: Chatto & Windus, 1904.

Hilton, George W. *Lake Michigan Passenger Steamers*. Stanford, CA: Stanford University Press, 2002.

*History of Mason County Michigan, with Illustrations and Biographical Sketches of Some of Its Prominent Men and Pioneers*. Chicago: H. R. Page, 1882.

Hoganson, Kristin L. *The Heartland: An American History*. New York: Penguin, 2019.

Hoogenboom, Ari. "Thomas A. Jenckes and Civil Service Reform." *Mississippi Valley Historical Review* 47, no. 4 (1961): 636–58.

Howe, Daniel Walker. *What Hath God Wrought: The Transformation of America, 1815–1848*. New York: Oxford University Press, 2007.

Hughes, C. H. "The Erratic Erotic Princess Chimay: A Psychological Analysis." *Alienist and Neurologist* 25 (1904): 359–66.

Hunt, Robert W. "A History of the Bessemer Manufacture in America." *Transactions of the American Institute of Mining Engineers* 5 (May 1876–February 1877): 201–16.

Hurlbut, Frances B. *Grandmother's Stories*. Cambridge: Riverside, 1889.

Hyde, Charles K. *The Northern Lights: Lighthouses of the Great Lakes*. Lansing: Two-Peninsula, 1986.

Ivey, Paul Wesley. *The Pere Marquette Railroad Company*. 1919; repr., Lansing: Michigan Historical Commission, 2012.

Jenks, William Lee. *St. Clair County Michigan: Its History and its People*. 2 vols. Chicago: Lewis, 1912.

Johnson, Rossiter. *The Twentieth Century Biographical Dictionary of Notable Americans*. Boston: Biographical Society, 1904.

Jones, Mrs. George N. "Miss Emily Ward, Commonly Known as 'Aunt Emily.'" *Michigan Pioneer and Historical Collections* 38 (1912): 581–89.

Joy, James F. "Railroad History of Michigan." *Michigan Pioneer and Historical Collections* 22 (1894): 292–304.

Klein, L. "Notes on the Steam Navigation upon the Great Northern Lakes." *American Railroad Journal, and Mechanics Magazine*, n.s., 6, no. 10 (May 15, 1841): 296–302.

Kopmeier, John H. *From Mayville to Milwaukee: A History of the Iron and Steel Industry in Southeastern Wisconsin, with Depictions of the Industry.* Milwaukee: Milwaukee School of Engineering, 2011.

Korn, Bernhard C. "Eber Brock Ward, Pathfinder of American Industry." PhD diss., Marquette University, 1942.

———. *The Story of Bay View.* Milwaukee: Milwaukee County Historical Society, 1980.

Kramer, G. P., D. A. Bernstein, and V. Phares, *Introduction to Clinical Psychology.* 8th ed. Upper Saddle River, NJ: Pearson Education, 2014.

Kursch, Daisy Estes. "Beulah Brinton of Bay View." *Milwaukee History* 10, no. 2 (1987): 38–46.

"Long Hours, Hard Work the Custom in Iron and Steel 80 Years Ago." *Steel Facts*, no. 84 (June 1947): 6–7.

Lorch, Emil. "The Detroit and Cleveland Navigation Company Warehouse at Detroit." *Michigan History* 36 (December 1952): 389–94.

Lyon, Sydney Elizabeth, ed. *Lyon Memorial.* Detroit: Press of William Graham, 1907.

Macfarlane, Thomas. *Silver Islet.* Montreal: Dawson Brothers, 1880.

Machiavelli, Niccolò. *The Prince.* Edited by Peter Bondanella. New York: Oxford University Press, 1984.

Mansfield, John Brandt, ed. *History of the Great Lakes.* Vol. 1. Chicago: J. H. Beers, 1899.

Maw, W. H., and J. Dredge, eds. "The Invention of the Bessemer Process." *Engineering* 61 (March 27, 1896): 413–14.

Maybee, Rolland H. *Michigan's White Pine Era, 1840–1900.* Lansing: Michigan Historical Commission, 1960.

McElroy, Frank. *A Short History of Marine City, Michigan.* Marine City, MI: Marine City Rotary Club, 1980.

McGarry, Molly. *Ghosts of Futures Past: Spiritualism and the Cultural Politics of Nineteenth-Century America.* Berkeley: University of California Press, 2008.

McGovern, George. *Abraham Lincoln.* New York: Henry Holt, 2009.

McHugh, Jeanne. *Alexander Holley and the Makers of Steel.* Baltimore: Johns Hopkins University Press, 1980.

McLaughlin, Doris B. *Michigan Labor: A Brief History from 1818 to the Present.* Ann Arbor: Institute of Labor and Industrial Relations, University of Michigan–Wayne State University, 1970.

McRae, Norman. "Camp Ward, Detroit." *Detroit Historical Society Bulletin* 24, no. 8 (1968): 4–11.

Meek, Forrest B. *Michigan's Timber Battleground, A History of Clare County, 1674–1900.* Clare, MI: Clare County Bicentennial Historical Committee, 1976.

Meints, Graydon M. *Pere Marquette: A Michigan Railroad System Before 1900.* East Lansing: Michigan State University Press, 2020.

Merk, Frederick. *Economic History of Wisconsin during the Civil War Decade*. Madison: Wisconsin Historical Society, 1916.

Metcalf, Allan. "Acknowledging the Corn." *Lingua Franca Blogs: The Chronicle of Higher Education*, November 24, 2014. https://www.chronicle.com/blogs/linguafranca.

Mills, James Cook. *History of Saginaw County, Michigan*. 3 vols. Saginaw: Seemann & Peters, 1918.

———. *Our Inland Seas: Their Shipping and Commerce for Three Centuries*. Chicago: A. C. McClurg, 1910.

"Minutes." *Michigan Pioneer and Historical Collections* 21 (1892): 15.

Misa, Thomas J. "Controversy and Closure in Technological Change: Constructing 'Steel.'" In *Shaping Technology/Building Society, Studies in Sociotechnical Change*, edited by Wiebe E. Bijker and John Law, 109–39. Cambridge, MA: MIT Press, 1992.

———. *A Nation of Steel: The Making of Modern America, 1865–1925*. Baltimore: Johns Hopkins University Press, 1999.

Montgomery, David. *Beyond Equality: Labor and the Radical Republicans, 1862–1872*. New York: Knopf, 1967.

Morris, Charles R. *The Tycoons; How Andrew Carnegie, John D. Rockefeller, Jay Gould and J. P. Morgan Invented the American Supereconomy*. New York: Henry Holt, 2005.

Mott, David C. "William Duane Wilson." *Annals of Iowa* 20 (1936): 360–74. Available online at http://dx.doi.org/10.17077/0003-4827.5861.

Mull, Carole E. "The McCoys: Charting Freedom from Both Sides of the River." In *A Fluid Frontier: Slavery, Resistance and the Underground Railroad in the Detroit River Borderland*, edited by Karolyn Smardz Frost and Veta Smith Tucker, 215–25. Detroit: Wayne State University Press, 2016.

———. *The Underground Railroad in Michigan*. Jefferson, NC: McFarland, 2010.

Nagle, Michael W. *Justus S. Stearns: Michigan Pine King, Kentucky Coal Baron, 1845–1933*. Detroit: Wayne State University Press, 2015.

Nartonis, David. "The Rise of 19th-Century American Spiritualism, 1854–1873." *Journal for the Scientific Study of Religion* 49, no. 2 (2010): 361–73.

Nasaw, David. *Andrew Carnegie*. New York: Penguin, 2006.

Natale, Simone. *Supernatural Entertainments: Victorian Spiritualism and the Rise of Modern Media Culture*. University Park: Pennsylvania State University Press, 2016.

Neu, Irene D. "The Building of the Sault Canal: 1852–1855." *Mississippi Valley Historical Review* 40, no. 1 (1953): 25–46.

———. *Erastus Corning: Merchant and Financier, 1794–1872*. Ithaca, NY: Cornell University Press, 1960.

———. "The Mineral Lands of the St. Mary's Falls Ship Canal Company." In *The Frontier in American Development: Essays in Honor of Paul Wallace Gates*, edited by David M. Ellis, 162–91. Ithaca, NY: Cornell University Press, 1969.

Nichols, David Andrew. *Peoples of the Inland Sea: Native Americans and Newcomers in the Great Lakes Region, 1600–1870*. Athens: University of Ohio Press, 2018.

Orear, George Washington. *Commercial and Architectural St. Louis*. St. Louis: Jones & Orear, 1888.

"Owen vs. Potter." In *Northwestern Reporter, Containing All the Decisions of the Supreme Courts of Minnesota, Wisconsin, Iowa, Michigan, Nebraska, North Dakota, South Dakota*, 73:977–88. St. Paul, MN: West, 1898.

Passante, Anna. "Clara Ward, Paparazzi Princess." *Bayview Compass*, August 1, 2010. Available online at https://bayviewcompass.com/clara-ward-paparazzi-princess.

———. "Milwaukee Iron Company." *Bay View Compass*, May 1, 2010. Available online at https://bayviewcompass.com/milwaukee-iron-company/.

Peterson, Paul. *The Story of Ludington*. Ludington, MI: Mason County Historical Society, 2011.

Potter, David. *The Impending Crisis, 1848–1861*. New York: Harper & Row, 1976.

Potter, Orrin W. "Early Rail Making in Chicago." *Bulletin of the American Iron and Steel Association* 30, no. 4 (February 1, 1896): 26.

*Proceedings of the Convention of Iron and Steel Manufacturers and Iron Ore Producers, at Pittsburgh*. Philadelphia: American Iron and Steel Association, 1879.

"Real Builders of America: Captain Eber Brock Ward." *Valve World* 7, no. 2 (1911): 595–96.

"The Remarkable Family of Ward." *Inland Seas* 17 (Spring 1961): 58–60. Originally published in *Marine View and Marine Record* 26 (September 11, 1902): 27.

Rogers, Daniel T. *The Work Ethic in Industrial America, 1850–1920*. Chicago: University of Chicago Press, 1978.

Rogers, Robert P. *An Economic History of the American Steel Industry*. New York: Routledge, 2009.

Roop, Lewis W. "Works No. Nine." *Pittsburgh People* 1, no. 3 (November 1940): 4–6.

Roosevelt, Theodore. *The Naval War of 1812; or, The History of the United States Navy during the Last War with Great Britain*. New York: G. P. Putnam's Sons, 1900.

Ross, Robert B., and George B. Catlin. *Landmarks of Detroit: A History of the City*. Detroit: Evening News Association, 1898.

Schoolcraft, Henry R. *Personal Memoirs of a Residence of Thirty Years with the Indian Tribes on the American Frontiers*. Philadelphia: Smithsonian Institution, 1851.

Seelye, John. "'Rational Exultation': The Erie Canal Celebration." *Proceedings of the American Antiquities Society*, January 1, 1985, 241–67.

Shaw, Ronald E. *Erie Water West: A History of the Erie Canal, 1792–1854*. Lexington: University Press of Kentucky, 1966.

Shinn, Charles William. "Captain Eber Brock Ward." Master's thesis, University of Wisconsin, 1952.

Sibley, Harry H. "A Dreamer's Vision That Became a Reality." *Michigan Manufacturer and Financial Record* 17, no. 6 (February 5, 1916): 6–7.

Smith, H. P., and W. S. Rann, eds. *History of Rutland County, Vermont*. Syracuse, NY: D. Mason, 1886.

Stark, George W. *City of Destiny: The Story of Detroit*. Detroit: Arnold-Powers, 1943.

Stebbins, Giles. *Upward Steps of Seventy Years*. New York: United States Book Company, 1890.

Stewart, Aura. "Recollections of Aura P. Stewart of St. Clair County of Things relating to the Early Settlement of Michigan." *Michigan Pioneer and Historical Collections* 4 (1883): 324–54.

Stewart, Mrs. E. M. S. "Incidents in the Life of Mr. Eber Ward, Father of Capt. E. B. Ward of Steamboat Fame." *Michigan Pioneer and Historical Collections* 6 (1884): 471–73.

Stiles, T. J. *The First Tycoon: The Epic Life of Cornelius Vanderbilt.* New York: Vintage, 2009.

Stone, Joel. *Floating Palaces of the Great Lakes: A History of Passenger Steamships on the Inland Seas.* Ann Arbor: University of Michigan Press, 2015.

Streeter, Floyd Benjamin. *Political Parties in Michigan, 1837–1860.* Lansing: Michigan Historical Commission, 1918.

Swank, James M., ed. "The Association and Its Work." *Bulletin of the American Iron and Steel Association* 38, no. 1 (January 10, 1904): 4.

———. "The Bessemer Process in the United States." *Bulletin of the American Iron and Steel Association* 40, no. 2 (January 20, 1906): 12.

———. *History of the Manufacture of Iron in All Ages.* 2nd ed. Philadelphia: American Iron and Steel Association, 1892.

Taylor, Paul. *Old Slow Town: Michigan during the Civil War.* Detroit: Wayne State University Press, 2013.

Temin, Peter. *Iron and Steel in Nineteenth-Century America: An Economic Inquiry.* Cambridge, MA: MIT Press, 1964.

Trefousse, H. L. *Benjamin Franklin Wade.* New York: Twayne, 1963.

———. *Impeachment of a President: Andrew Johnson, the Blacks, and Reconstruction.* New York: Fordham University Press, 1999.

Utley, H. M. "The Wild Cat Banking System in Michigan." *Michigan Pioneer and Historical Collections* 5 (1884): 209–22.

von Gerstner, Franz Anton Ritter. *Early American Railroads: Die innern Communicationen (1842–1843).* Translated by David J. Diephouse and John C. Decker. Stanford, CA: Stanford University Press, 1997.

Waite, Linda J., ed. *The Ties That Bind: Perspectives on Marriage and Cohabitation.* New York: de Gruyter, 2000.

Walton, Ivan H., and Joe Grimm. *Windjammers: Songs of the Great Lakes Sailors.* Detroit: Wayne State University Press, 2002.

Ward, David. *The Autobiography of David Ward.* New York: privately printed, 1912.

"Ward's Canal." *Historical Society of Northwestern Ohio* 10, no. 4 (1938): 7–9.

Wargo, Justin. "Awful Calamity! The Steamship Atlantic Disaster of 1852." *Wisconsin Magazine of History*, Winter 2014–2015, 16–27.

———. "'A Case Without Parallel': The Sensational Battle over Eber Brock Ward's Will and Subsequent Legacy of Detroit's First Great Industrialist." *Michigan Historical Review* 39, no. 2 (2013): 77–103.

Warnes, Kathy Covert. *Ecorse, Michigan: A Brief History.* Charleston, SC: History Press, 2009.

Waters, Thomas F. *The Superior North Shore: A Natural History of Lake Superior's Northern Lands and Waters,* Minneapolis: University of Minnesota Press, 1987.

Weisberg, Barbara. *Talking to the Dead: Kate and Maggie Fox and the Rise of Spiritualism.* New York: HarperOne, 2004.

Welter, Barbara. "The True Cult of Womanhood." *American Quarterly* 18, no. 2, part 1 (1966): 151–74.

White, Peter. "Sault Ste. Marie and the Canal Fifty Years Ago." *Michigan Pioneer and Historical Collections* 35 (1907): 345–58.

Whittlesey, Charles. *Ancient Mining on the Shores of Lake Superior.* Philadelphia: Collins, 1862.

Wilentz, Sean. *The Rise of American Democracy: Jefferson to Lincoln.* New York: Norton, 2005.

Williams, Mentor L. "The Chicago River and Harbor Convention, 1847." *Mississippi Valley Historical Review* 35, no. 4 (1949): 607–26.

Yearly, Clifton K. "Richard Trevellick: Labor Agitator." *Michigan History* 39 (December 1955): 423–44.

# Index

McQueen, Catherine (née Lamberson), 48

McQueen, Daniel, 48

McQueen, Maryell. *See* Ward, Polly (Maryell) (née McQueen)

McQueen, Susan, 101

Meddaugh, E. W., 232

*Mercury*, 196

Mexican-American War, 134

*Michigan*, 55

Michigan Central Railroad, 61, 69, 76–80, 92, 101, 102, 103, 105, 111, 173, 233

Michigan Fever, 37–38

Michigan's Lower Peninsula: map of, 39

Michigan Southern Railroad, 103, 111

milliner (profession), 24, 31, 267n38

Milwaukee Iron Company, xvii, 160–66, 185, 213, 214, 217–19, 257, 259, 294n10; photo of, 162

Mitchell, Alexander, 161, 163

Moffat, Hugh, 226

*Montgomery*, 106

Montreal Mining Company, 204

*Moonlight Adventure on the St. Clair River*: painting of, 22

Moore, Reuben, 65

Morrell, Daniel J., 181, 183–84

Morrow, Catherine. *See* Ward, Catherine (née Lyon)

Morrow, John, 249

*Morton. See J. D. Morton*

Mushet, Robert F., 180

*Music*, 196

National Convention of Manufacturers, 156

National Manufacturers Association, 156

Native Americans: aid Emily Ward, 22–23; Black Hawk War and, 36–37; frustration of, 23, 36; John Mix Stanley's paintings of, 254; removal from land of, 20, 36; return Eber Brock Ward to Newport and, 17; War of 1812 and, 7, 14, 23, 38–39

Navarre, Jerome, 195–96, 197

Newberry, Oliver, 32, 55

new Manifest Destiny, xix, 139, 156–60, 185, 257

Newport Academy, 116–18, 123, 162, 259, 287n32; photo of, 117

New York State Inebriate Asylum, 210

North Chicago Rolling Mill, 160, 163, 188, 237, 257; Bessemer steel and, 213–15, 217, 219; competition with Milwaukee Iron Company, 161, 217, 294n10; establishment of, 122–23; fire at, 125; lack of skilled workforce, 124; living conditions for employees, 125; Panic of 1857 and, 124; reorganized from Chicago Rolling Mill, 123. *See also* Chicago Rolling Mill

Northern Transportation Company, 90

North West Company, 91

*Ocean*, 74, 75, 77, 79, 85–86, 258

*Ogdensburg*, 87–90, 258

Ojibwa, 91

*Old Black Sam. See Sam Ward*

Owen, Abba (née Ward), 10, 14, 30–31; accident involving schooner *Savannah*, 45; birth of, 7; considers marriage, 31; death of, 118, 119; lives in Ohio, 15, 21, 24; marries Benjamin F. Owen, 41, 45, 118

Owen, Benjamin F., 41, 45, 118

Owen, John, 103

Owen, Orville, 118

Owen, Tubal C., 233

*Pacific*, 71, 75, 77, 79

*palace steamer*, 71–73

Palmer House, 163, 165

Panama Canal, 93

Panic of 1837, 43

Panic of 1857, 123–24, 174

Panic of 1873, 1, 179, 194, 198, 203, 209, 218–22, 225, 255

Patchin, Jared, 230, 231, 234–35

*Pearl*, 75, 79, 131, 167; photo of, 74

Pettey, J. Bryon, 87

*Philo Parsons*, 144

phrenology, 80–81, 121

Pierson, Rev. Arthur A., 225

*Planet*, 104, 106

Pleasanton, Stephen, 27

*Plymouth Rock*, 72

Polk, James K., 91, 134

Pond, Ashley, 230

popular sovereignty, 134, 137

Pottawatomi Creek Massacre, 137

Potter, Ellen (née Owen), 123

Potter, Joshua, 9

Potter, Orrin W., 123, 161, 214, 238

Potter, Sally. *See* Ward, Sally (née Potter)

Potter, William, 6, 7

"Powder Plot," 63–64

Pray, Abigail. *See* Ward, Abigail (née Pray)

Pray, Sylvester, 113

Presbyterian General Assembly Meeting (1818), 136–37

Ward, Eber Brock (*continued*): efficiencies at businesses, xvi, 194–95, 215–17; divorce of, xviii, 50, 156, 167, 169–71, 185; William Downie and, xviii, 258; E. B. Ward and Company and, 215–16; employs latest technologies, xvii, 114, 213–14; engages in fishing industry, 29–30; engages in land speculation, 41, 176; environmental impact of businesses, 191, 199, 259; estate of, 227–30; Eureka Iron Company and, 104–15, 180–83, 257; Eureka Mine Company and, 207–9; events on day of death, 1–3, 221; expands fleet of vessels, 54, 70–75, 79; experiences stress and anxiety, 220–21; expresses contentedness with life, 84; family life unsatisfactory, xvii–xviii, 167–69, 188, 259; fears insanity might run in family, 168; Flint & Pere Marquette Railway and, xvi, 173–77, 185, 195; Fort Street Presbyterian Church and, 135–36; funeral of, 224–27; *General Harrison* and, 35, 41, 42–44, 51, 54, 255; Girard College and, 118; William Gist and, 139–40, 152; Ulysses S. Grant and, 148–49; gravesite of, 226–27; gravesite photo of, 226; *Huron* and, 54–64, 67, 84–85, 96, 255; hypocrisy concerning lobbying and corruption, 83; inherits

bulk of Samuel Ward's estate, 95–96; Andrew Johnson and, 146; Kelly Process Company and, 180; labeled "iron king of the West," xv, 217; lack of mentorship to sons, xviii, 169, 188, 193, 198–99; lack of reference to wife and children in correspondence, 122, 170; Lake Steamboat Association and, 59–60; legacy of, xv, xix, 222, 255–60; Leland Lake Superior Iron Company and, 215–16; limited formal education of, 21, 39–40; Abraham Lincoln and, xix, 138–39, 140, 143, 151, 152–53, 260; lives in Rochester, New York, 25–26; lobbies in Washington, DC, xviii, 82–83, 90, 92, 156–60, 233, 258; James Ludington and, 155, 177–79, 185, 188, 208, 258; Ludington, Michigan, and, xvi, 1, 92, 94, 188–95; maintains control over business operations, xvii, 30, 112–13, 191–92, 194, 202, 251, 258; Michigan Central Railroad and, 61, 69, 76–80, 92, 101, 102, 103, 173, 233; Michigan land rush and, 38; Milwaukee Iron Company and, xvii, 160–66, 185, 213, 217–19, 257; moves to Detroit, 78–79; National Manufacturers Association and, 156; Native Americans and, 17; new Manifest Destiny and, xix, 139, 156–60,

257; Newport Academy and, 116–18, 259; North Chicago Rolling Mill and, 122–26, 188, 213–15, 217, 257, 294n10; Abba (Ward) Owen and, 45, 118–19; Panic of 1857 and, 123–24, 126; Panic of 1873 and, 1, 194, 198, 203, 209, 218–22, 252, 255; personality and quirks, xviii; philanthropy of, 116, 118, 135, 214, 259; philosophical outlook of, 126–27; photo of, 49, 145, 211; phrenology and, 80–81; physical appearance of, 2, 49; planned relocation to Kentucky and, 10–12; portrait of, 254; portrait of described, 254–55; "Powder Plot" and, 63–64; prohibits alcohol, 107, 111, 162–63, 194, 202–3, 205–6, 258; protective tariff and, 138, 148, 149, 151, 158–60; purchases property along Pere Marquette River, 93–94, 177; race between *Empire State* and *Ocean* and, 85–86; reinvests profits back into business empire, xvi, 70, 76, 209, 214; religious views of, 83–84, 135, 137, 225; reorganizes steamboat fleet, 101–4; Republican Party and, 54, 96, 103, 130, 135–39, 146–51, 152; ruthlessness of, xvii, 63–64, 102–3, 144, 178–79, 195, 258; safety record of vessels, 86–87, 89; scrip and, 124, 220, 259; seeks to corner the market on wood, 76; sense of humor and, 233;

Ward, Esther, 6

Ward, Frederick, 167, 171, 210–11, 213

Ward Furnace, 108 9, 115

Ward, Henry, 49, 167, 178, 210; fight at dinner table with Milton, 211 12; photo of, 49; Ward will trial and, 231; will of E. B. Ward and, 229

Ward, Jacob Harrison, 15, 21, 22; considered cognitively impaired, 40, 50, 95, 168–69

Ward, John, 167–69, 221; photo of, 168

Ward, Keziah. *See* Lewis, Keziah (née Ward)

Ward, Luna Kunz, 250

Ward, Mable. *See* Seitz, Mabel (née Ward)

Ward, Mary S., 167, 171, 210, 212, 229

Ward, Milton, 167, 210; death of, 238; fight at dinner table with Henry, 211–12; photo of, 192; Catherine Ward and, 227–29, 233; Eber Brock Ward and, 169, 189, 192–93, 233; Emily Ward and, 234; Ward will trial and, 234; will of Eber Brock Ward and, 227–30

Ward, Nathan, 95

Ward, Polly (Maryell) (née McQueen): adopted by Elizabeth and Samuel Ward, 49; death of, 170; photo of, 49; physical appearance of, 48, 49–50; suffers from anxiety, 122,

169–70; Eber Brock Ward and, 2, 48–50, 95, 169–71, 210, 213, 232, 259; Emily Ward and, 170, 210

Ward, Sally (née Potter) (mother of Eber Brock Ward), 6–7, 9, 11–12

Ward, Sally (sister of Eber Brock Ward). *See* Brindle, Sally (née Ward)

Ward, Samuel, 31, 83; adopts Polly (McQueen) Ward, 49; alcohol and, 163; brick home in Newport of, 15, 264–65n19; conservatism of, 75–76, 105, 115; death of, 94–95, 105, 120; early business activities of, 12–20; Erie Canal and, 17–19; expands fleet of vessels, 27, 41, 49, 54, 70–75, 79; gravesite of, 227; *Huron* and, 54–58, 64; Lake Steamboat Association and, 59–60; leader in Newport community, 15; *Michigan* and, 55; photo of, 13; physical appearance of, 8, 94; "Powder Plot" and, 63–64; safety record of vessels, 86–87, 89; *Salem Packet* and, 12–13; St. Mary's Falls Ship Canal Company and, 92, 93; value of assets owned jointly with Eber Brock Ward, 74–75, 80; Eber Brock Ward and, xv, 2, 5, 17, 19, 33, 39–42, 44, 50, 56–58, 74, 75, 80, 95–96, 171, 193, 209; Eber Ward Sr. and, 7–8, 15–16, 24, 26,

30; Elizabeth (Lamberson) Ward and, 12, 13, 15–17, 40, 48, 95; War of 1812 and, 8; Whig Party and, 50–52, 54; will of, 95–96; works in salt industry, 7

Ward, Samuel (son of Eber Brock Ward), 167

Ward, Zael, 55

Ward Cameron, Catherine. *See* Ward, Catherine (née Lyon)

Ward Lake Superior Line, 71

Ward's Canal, 196, 199, 259

Ward will trial, 230–36, 251

War of 1812, 7, 8, 12; Native Americans and, 7, 14, 23, 38–39

Wendell, Abraham, 46, 47

*Western Metropolis*, 103

*Western World*, 72

Whig Party, 50–54, 82–83, 91, 96, 103, 130, 134–36, 152

Whitney, John, 208

wildcat banks, 52

Wilson, William Duane, 83

Wisner, Moses, 174

Wolverton, Jacob, 50, 74

women's suffrage, 150–51

Woodman, Cyrus, 93

Woodruff, John S., 193–94

Woodward, Phebe, 7

Wyandotte Rolling Mill Company, 108, 109, 114, 163, 207; issues scrip, 124, 220

Wyandotte Savings Bank, 114; photo of, 114

Wyandotte Silver Smelting and Refining Works, 206–7, 209